THE CAMBRIDGE HISTORY OF SOUTHEAST ASIA

VOLUME THREE

From c. 1800 to the 1930s

D1569576

THE CAMBRIDGE HISTORY OF SOUTHEAST ASIA

THE CAMBRIDGE
HISTORY OF
SOUTHEAST ASIA

VOLUME THREE

From c. 1800 to the 1930s

edited by

NICHOLAS TARLING

CAMBRIDGE
UNIVERSITY PRESS

PUBLISHED BY THE PRESS SYNDICATE OF THE UNIVERSITY OF CAMBRIDGE
The Pitt Building, Trumpington Street, Cambridge, United Kingdom

CAMBRIDGE UNIVERSITY PRESS
The Edinburgh Building, Cambridge CB2 2RU, UK www.cup.cam.ac.uk
40 West 20th Street, New York, NY 10011–4211, USA www.cup.org
10 Stamford Road, Oakleigh, Melbourne 3166, Australia
Ruiz de Alarcón 13, 28014, Madrid, Spain

The Cambridge History of Southeast Asia was first published in hardback
in two volumes in 1992, reprinted 1994
Volume One ISBN 0 521 35505 2 (hardback)
Volume Two ISBN 0 521 35506 0 (hardback)

The Cambridge History of Southeast Asia is first published in paperback
in four volumes in 1999, reprinted 2005, 2007
Volume One Part One: From early times to c. 1500
ISBN 0 521 66369 5 (paperback)
Volume One Part Two: From c. 1500 to c. 1800
ISBN 0 521 66370 9 (paperback)
These two volumes contain the contents of 0 521 35505 2 (hardback),
with additional supplementary material
Volume Two Part One: From c. 1800 to the 1930s
ISBN 0 521 66371 7 (paperback)
Volume Two Part Two: From World War II to the present
ISBN 0 521 66372 5 (paperback)
These two volumes contain the contents of 0 521 35506 0 (hardback),
with additional supplementary material

The set of four paperbacks, containing the complete contents of *The Cambridge History
of Southeast Asia*, ISBN 0 521 77864 6 (paperback).

Printed by C.O.S. Printers Pte Ltd, Singapore

Typeface Palatino 10/11 pt. *System* Penta [MT]

A catalogue record for this book is available from the British Library

National Library of Australia Cataloguing in Publication data
The Cambridge History of Southeast Asia.
Bibliography.
Includes index.
ISBN 0 521 66369 5 (Volume One Part One).
ISBN 0 521 66370 9 (Volume One Part Two).
ISBN 0 521 66371 7 (Volume Two Part One).
ISBN 0 521 66372 5 (Volume Two Part Two).
ISBN 0 521 77864 6 (set).
1. Asia, Southeastern – History. I. Tarling, Nicholas.
959

ISBN 0 521 66371 7 paperback

CONTENTS

MAPS

NOTE ON SPELLING

The spelling of proper names and terms has caused editor and contributors considerable problems. Even a certain arbitrariness may have not produced consistency across a range of contributions, and that arbitrariness contained its own inconsistencies. In general we have aimed to spell place-names and terms in the way currently most accepted in the country, society or literature concerned. We have not used diacritics for modern Southeast Asian languages, but have used them for Sanskrit and Ancient Javanese. We have used pinyin transliterations except for some names which are well known in English in the Wade–Giles transliteration.

ABBREVIATIONS

AFPFL	Anti-Fascist People's Freedom League, Burma.
ASEAN	Association of South-East Asian Nations.
BKI	*Bijdragen van het Koninklijk Instituut voor de Taal-, Land- en Volkenkunde*, 's-Gravenhage.
BSPP	Burma Socialist Programme Party.
BWS	Burmese Way to Socialism.
DAP	Democratic Action Party, Malaysia.
DRV	Democratic Republic of Vietnam.
GCBA	General Council of Burmese Associations.
ICP	Indochina Communist Party.
ISDV	Indische Sociaal-Demokratische Vereeniging (Indies Social-Democratic Association).
ISEAS	Institute of Southeast Asian Studies, Singapore.
JAS	*Journal of Asian Studies*, Ann Arbor.
JMBRAS	*Journal of the Malay/Malaysian Branch of the Royal Asiatic Society*, Kuala Lumpur.
JSEAH	*Journal of Southeast Asian History*, Singapore.
JSEAS	*Journal of Southeast Asian Studies*, Singapore.
JSS	*Journal of the Siam Society*, Bangkok.
MAS	*Modern Asian Studies*, Cambridge, UK.
MCP	Malayan Communist Party.
MNLF	Moro National Liberation Front.
MPAJA	Malayan People's Anti-Japanese Army.
NLF	National Liberation Front, Vietnam.
NPA	New People's Army, The Philippines.
PAP	People's Action Party, Singapore.
PAS	Partai Islam se Tanah Malaya (Pan-Malayan Islamic Party).
PKI	Partai Komunis Indonesia (Indonesian Communist Party).

PNI	Perserikatan Nasional Indonesia (Indonesian National Association).
RVN	Republic of Vietnam.
SEAC	South-East Asia Command.
SEATO	South-East Asia Treaty Organization.
SRV	Socialist Republic of Vietnam.
UMNO	United Malays National Organization.

PREFACE TO THE PAPERBACK EDITION

Two ideas came together in the project for a Cambridge History of Southeast Asia. One was the concept of the Cambridge Histories themselves. The other was the possibility of a new approach to the history of Southeast Asia.

In the English-speaking and English-reading world the Cambridge Histories have, since the beginning of the century, set high standards in collaborative scholarship and provided a model for multi-volume works of history. The original *Cambridge Modern History* appeared in sixteen volumes between 1902 and 1912, and was followed by the *Cambridge Ancient History*, the *Cambridge Medieval History*, the *Cambridge History of India* and others.

A new generation of projects continues and builds on this foundation. Recently completed are the Cambridge Histories of Africa, Latin America and the Pacific Islanders. Cambridge Histories of China and of Japan are in progress, as well as the New Cambridge History of India. Though the pattern and the size have varied, the essential feature, multi-authorship, has remained.

The initial focus was European, but albeit in an approach that initially savoured rather of the old Cambridge Tripos course 'The Expansion of Europe', it moved more out of the European sphere than the often brilliant one-author Oxford histories. But it left a gap which that course did not leave, the history of Southeast Asia.

Southeast Asia has long been seen as a whole, though other terms have been used for it. The title Southeast Asia, becoming current during World War II, has been accepted as recognizing the unity of the region, while not prejudging the nature of that unity. Yet scholarly research and writing have shown that it is no mere geographical expression.

There have indeed been several previous histories of Southeast Asia. Most of them have been the work of one author. The great work of the late D. G. E. Hall dates back to 1955, but it has gone through several editions since. Others include B. Harrison, *South-east Asia, A Short History*, London, 1954; Nicholas Tarling, *A Concise History of Southeast Asia*, 1966; and D. J. Steinberg, et al., *In Search of Southeast Asia*, 1971. The authors of these works faced difficult tasks, as a result of the linguistic diversity of the area; the extent of the secondary material; and the lacunae within it.

Given its diversity, Southeast Asia seemed to lend itself to the Cambridge approach. A magisterial single-volume history existed; others had also made the attempt. A single volume by several authors working together had also been successful. But a more substantial history by a larger number of authors had not been attempted.

The past generation has seen a great expansion of writing, but Southeast Asia's historiography is still immature in the sense that some aspects have been relatively well cultivated, and others not. The historical literature on the area has become more substantial and more sophisticated, but much of it deals with particular countries or cultures, and many gaps remain. A range of experts might help to bring it all together and thus both lay the foundation and point the way for further research effort.

The Cambridge approach offered a warning as well as an invitation. There were practical obstacles in the way of histories on the scale of the original European histories. They got out of hand or were never finished. A summation that was also to lead other scholars forward must be published within a reasonable time-span. It must not be too voluminous; it must not involve too many people.

Practical indications of this nature, however, coincided with historio-graphical considerations. There were some good histories of Southeast Asia; there were also some good histories of particular countries; but there was, perhaps, no history that set out from a regional basis and took a regional approach. This seemed worthwhile in itself, as well as establishing a coherence and a format for the volumes.

In almost every case—even when chapters are the work of more than one person—authors have been taken out of their particular area of expertise. They were ready to take risks, knowing that, whatever care they took, they might be faulted by experts, but recognizing the value all the same in attempting to give an overview. Generally contributors felt that the challenge of the regional approach was worth the hazardous departure from research moorings.

Authors invited to contribute recognized that they would often find themselves extended beyond the span of the published work which has made them well known. The new history did, however, give them a chance—perhaps already enjoyed in many cases in their teaching—to extend into other parts of the region and to adopt a comparative, regional approach. The publishers sought a history that stimulated rather than presented the last word. Authors were the more ready to rely where necessary on published or secondary works, and readers will not expect equally authoritative treatment of the whole area, even if the sources permitted it.

At the same time, the editor and the contributors have had, like any historians, to cope with problems of periodization. That is, of course, always contentious, but particularly so if it seems to result from or to point to a particular emphasis. In the case of Southeast Asia the most likely temptation is to adopt a chronology that overdoes the impact of outside forces, in particular the Europeans. The structure of this history is not free from that criticism, but the contributors have sought, where appropriate, to challenge rather than meekly to accept its implications.

A similar risk is attached to the division of the material into chapters. The scope of a work such as this makes that all the more difficult but all the more necessary. Sometimes the divisions appear to cut across what ought to be seen as a whole, and sometimes repetition may result. That has been allowed when it seemed necessary. But it may still be possible to pursue certain themes through the book and not to read it merely in chronological sequence. Within the four major chronological divisions, chapters are in general organized in a similar order. The work may thus in a sense be read laterally as well as horizontally.

Some topics, including treatment of the arts, literature and music, have been virtually excluded. The focus of the work is on economic, social, religious and political history. But it will still be difficult to pursue the history of a particular people or country. The work does not indeed promise to offer this; though it offers guidance to those who wish to do this in its apparatus, the footnotes and bibliographic essay to each chapter, the historiographical survey, the list of bibliographies, and the index.

*   *   *

The work was originally published in 1992 in two hardbound volumes. The paperback edition is a reprint in four volumes with minor revisions. While the work in its two-volume format has been quite widely welcomed, it is hoped that the new format will make it more accessible, and in particular bring it more readily within the reach of those who teach and are taught about the region, as well as those who are simply curious about it. The four paperbacks may stand on their own, though it is also the case that the whole is more than the sum of the parts.

The first volume contains an essay on the historiography of Southeast Asia and Part 1 of the original Volume 1, 'From Prehistory to c. 1500 CE'. The second volume contains Part 2 of the original Volume 1, covering the years c. 1500 to c. 1800. The present volume covers the region from c. 1800 to the 1930s. The fourth deals with the period from World War II to the late 1980s, and also contains a bibliography of bibliographies on Southeast Asia.

Discussions about the work, both in the course of its preparation and since, have raised questions both about its regional approach and its periodization; questions that are indeed of enduring interest to historians and their readers but are not susceptible of enduring answers. The second volume entered a debate about 'early modern' Southeast Asia that has questioned the cohesion of the region as a unit of study and the appropriate periodization of that endeavour. The current feeling is that 'Southeast Asia' remains a useful concept, provided that we do not overplay its homogeneity, that we take the opportunity to contrast the history of the mainland states with those of the archipelago, and that we allow ourselves to compare the experience particularly of those states with that of states elsewhere in Asia and in Europe itself in the 'early modern' period. Delimiting that period, it is also agreed, should be determined not only by the impact of outside factors, including the commerce of China as well as of the Europeans, but also by the changes brought about by initiatives within the region, in particular the competition among the mainland states. These albeit tentative conclusions offer us the chance of a more appropriately differentiated history of the region and limit the risks that it remains a ghetto within historical studies as a whole. We also have the opportunity of reaching sound conclusions about the impact of the Europeans, accepting that it differs from place to place within the region and from time to time.

That problem also faces the study of the period encompassed by the present volume. In his famous article, 'On the possibility of an autonomous history of modern Southeast Asia' (*Journal of Southeast Asian Studies* 2, 2, July 1961, pp. 72–102), John Smail pointed out that, while the pioneering Dutch scholar J. C. van Leur had been able to envisage a new and better balance between the Dutch and the Indonesian factors in the history of the early modern period, he had said little about the nineteenth and twentieth centuries: the implication was, however, 'that the Indonesian world grows more and more insignificant', and we therefore 'have less and reason to want to look at things from an Indo-centric point of view' (p. 84).

Certainly most of Southeast Asia was in this period brought under some form of European rule, and all of it was affected by what Van Leur called 'the magic poison of modern capitalism' (*Indonesian Trade and Society* The Hague and Bandung: Van Hoeve, 1955, p. 285). Much of the writing on Southeast Asia tended, consciously or not, to reflect that, whether it was inspired by the triumphalism of the Europeans or the rallying of their opponents. But, while the winning of independence initially tempted historians unduly to diminish the role of the Europeans, it also stimulated them to study their opponents more fully. It then became possible to differentiate among the Europeans, and also to distinguish among their opponents the dynastic and the popular elements, those who wished at least temporarily to collaborate and those who wished to resist, those who relied more on outside support and those who drew more on their own resources.

Nor did the 'magic poison' affect all equally or simultaneously. Historians are inclined to accept c. 1870 as marking a shift in the process by which Southeast Asia became, without ceasing to supply jungle and marine produce for a range of markets particularly in Asia, much more a supplier of minerals, raw materials and commodities for world markets. But the date is only an approximation, and the changes were highly differentiated, both as a result of the distribution of resources and the policies of different governments. No colonial government, it is true, was likely to take the steps needed to spur industrialization, and that view was shared by the independent Thais, partly, as Ian Brown has shown in *The Elite and the Economy in Siam, c. 1890–1920* (Singapore: Oxford University Press, 1988), because they wanted to retain their independence. In the interwar period, however, and particularly in the depression, parts of Netherlands India and Indo-China were also differentiating themselves in this respect.

The nature of both political and economic change suggests the advantage for this period, as for the previous one, of admitting that our periodization must have jagged edges. The inclusion of the whole region in these changes must again not lead us to over-emphasize their similarity. Nor, though with that caution we can see the region as a satisfactory unit of study, should we be led to avoid comparisons with developments outside the region. Historians of empire have too often neglected Southeast Asia, though it offers a wide-ranging taxonomy of imperial rule. The closer study of its economic history—prompted in part by a reaction to a preoccupation with political issues during the struggle to set up independent states, and in part, too, no doubt, by witnessing the economic transformation of the area in a new 'age of commerce'—also suggests that the history of the region may contribute to a wider debate, that on the relationship between the two developments, the creation of colonial states and the spreading of the 'poison'. In an article on Dutch expansion in Indonesia, J. Thomas Lindblad has suggested that we look for the interaction at the local level as much as the central, if not more ('Economic Aspects of the Dutch Expansion in Indonesia, 1870–1914', *Modern Asia Studies* 23, 1, 1989, pp. 1–23). His new book, *Foreign Investment in Southeast Asia in the Twentieth Century* (Basingstoke: Macmillan, 1998)—one of the first monographs in a series on the modern economic history of Southeast Asia jointly published by Macmillan and the Australian National University—starts out with the same theme (p. 12).

A review of the first edition of the present work suggested that the opening chapter 'would have found more resonance in a compilation of essays on English imperial policy' (*Journal of the Economic and Social History of the Orient* 40, 1997, p. 113). My recognition of the power of the British in the nineteenth century, both political and economic, may have led to over-emphasis. An interesting debate has indeed been developing among Dutch historians, focusing on such works as Maarten Kuitenbrouwer's *The Netherlands and the Rise of Modern Imperialism* (Oxford: Berg, 1991), and summarized by Elsbeth Locher-Scholten in 'Dutch Expansion in the Indonesian Archipelago around 1900 and the Imperialism Debate' (*Journal of Southeast Asian Studies* 25, 1, March 1994, pp. 91–111). One issue at least, however, is the 'lack of the "foreign factor"' adduced in explanation of imperialism. 'As a European "dwarf" but a colonial "giant", the Dutch had always been dependent on the protection and cooperation of the British' (p. 100). The history of British imperialism certainly belongs elsewhere. That the experience of Southeast Asia is in some sense part of it, and that its discourse can also help in understanding the history of Southeast Asia, is the theme of my book, *The Fall of Imperial Britain in Southeast Asia* (Kuala Lumpur: Oxford University Press, 1993), and the completion of the *Oxford History of the British Empire* in which Southeast Asia in this phase is covered by Tony Stockwell, a contributor to the fourth volume of the present work, should offer additional perspectives.

Carl Trocki, author of the second chapter in the present volume, is one of several scholars who have drawn attention to the significance of the revenue farms in the states of the nineteenth century: they were at once an indication of the administrative weakness of those states, and contributed to the capital formation that promoted, for example, the opening of the Malayan tin mines; and in the latter sense were an example of the 'microlevel' interactions between the political and the economic, to which Lindblad has drawn attention. One of the most recent works in the field is *The Rise and Fall of Revenue Farming: Business Elites and the Emergence of the Modern State in Southeast Asia* edited by John Butcher and Howard Dick (New York: St Martin's Press, 1993).

Among the contributors to the Macmillan–Australian National University monograph series is the author of the third chapter in the present volume. In his new book, *The End of the Peasantry in Southeast Asia* (1997), Elson accepts once more 'the ever-present danger' in a regional study 'of over-reaching one's expertise' (p. xix). The compensation is a study that, generalizing without precluding particularising, expounds the role of the peasantry in our period, 'when peasant labour and production sustained, as never before, the economies of the region', and suggests its demise in more recent decades: '[t]he progeny of the late-nineteenth-century peasant still live in the countryside, but not with the permanence, rural focus and sense of local identity their forebears had' [p. xxii]. The project is also to include one-country works as well as those with a regional thrust. The first, Anne Booth's *The Indonesian Economy in the Nineteenth and Twentieth Centuries* (1998), adds to the considerable volume of recent work on the economic history of Indonesia, the largest state in the region.

Indonesia is also the country that has attracted the greatest attention from those who study nationalism and the nationalist movements in Southeast Asia. Among them are a number of Japanese scholars, putting in a new form, perhaps, a long-standing interest. Though our colleague, the late Ben Batson, is alas no longer able to contribute to it, a vigorous debate on Thai nationalism has also taken place, precipitated in part by the revival of a 'radical discourse' in the 1970s, and also more recently influenced by post-Marxist deconstructionism, as with Thongchai Winichakul's *Siam Mapped* (Honolulu: University of Hawaii Press, 1994). The debate among Philippines historians again takes place both in a public and a professional context, stimulated by centennial celebrations of the revolution.

Reynaldo Ileto took up in a regional context a topic he had tackled in a Filipino one, with his pathbreaking work *Pasyon and Revolution* (Quezon City: Ateneo de Manila Press, 1979). In that he sought to distinguish the nationalism of the élite and the millenarian aspirations of the 'masses'. The detail of that work has since been challenged by Glenn May in *Inventing a Hero. The Posthumous Re-Creation of Andres Bonifacio* (Madison: Center for Southeast Asian Studies, University of Wisconsin, 1996), but its general argument still stands. Work done on other countries, for example by Sartono on Indonesia and Hue-Tam-Ho Tai on Vietnam, underlines the significance of millenarianism in the region. It is also a topic that once more reminds us that while Southeast Asian history is a proper unit of study, its experience is shared with that of other parts of the world.

Nicholas Tarling 1999

FROM c. 1800 TO THE 1930s

INTRODUCTION

This volume of the work deals with Southeast Asia between the late eighteenth century of the Common Era and World War II. The opening chapter, which is in a sense complementary to the closing chapter of the previous volume, describes and endeavours to account for the incorporation of most of the region within the frontiers of European empires. Subsequent chapters describe the political structures, the economic and social life, and the religions and popular culture of the region. A final chapter includes a discussion of nationalism and nationalist movements.

In the previous phase, Spanish and Dutch realms had been established in maritime Southeast Asia. By the end of the nineteenth century, only Siam (Thailand) stood outside the formal empires of external powers. Those powers sought to avoid conflict among themselves by settling the frontiers of their territories. In so doing they took more or less notice of the previous history and present condition of the lands and peoples over which they claimed authority. Yet the frontiers had a degree of rigidity unusual in Southeast Asia.

Chapter 1 describes this outcome. It also endeavours to describe the process by which it was reached, and in particular to take account of the role within it of the rulers and peoples of Southeast Asia as well as the Europeans. Within the emerging framework, there was further interaction in many fields of human endeavour. This is in a sense the subject of the subsequent chapters in this volume, which also pursue lines of investigation that parallel chapters in the first volume. Chapter 5, too, deals with the emergence of nationalism within the colonial framework. The statecraft of the imperial period came under challenge.

Within the emerging framework of that period new political structures were established. This topic is the prime focus of Chapter 2. Though still necessarily relying on the collaboration of élite elements among the Southeast Asian populations, the structures set up by the outside powers were characteristically centralized and bureaucratized. By the early twentieth century the state was capable of reaching into the ordinary life of every inhabitant to a degree and with a persistence rarely known before in the region. This, indeed, applied in Siam, as well as in the territories the external powers acquired. But neither there, nor elsewhere, did centralization or bureaucratization necessarily produce uniformity: in some cases indeed what came to be seen as 'minority groups' within a realm containing a 'majority' gained a new degree of institutionalized cohesion.

None of the developments described in chapters 1 and 2 can be understood without placing them in the context of economic change. This is the subject of Chapter 3. Southeast Asia had long been affected by international commerce. In the period between 1800 and the Great Depression it had an unprecedented impact, particularly after 1850. This resulted from the development of the Industrial Revolution and the drive of Western capitalism. They contributed to the growth of state power, its centralization and bureaucratization. The relationship of governments and peoples were transformed. Migration to Southeast Asia reached new levels; so did migration within Southeast Asia. Cities expanded, often providing an extraordinarily unhealthy environment, but there was no call for substantial industry. The end in the 1930s of the long period of expansion in the world's economy exposed the narrow and dependent nature of the region's economy. The poor were hit hardest.

Intensified European penetration, political consolidation of the dominant states, and economic transformation especially mark the period from the mid-nineteenth century; it is marked also by a multitude of resistance movements, rebellions, and acts of insubordination. Those are the focus of Chapter 4. It seeks to present them in their own terms: not as the disturbances or dacoity of the apologists of colonial conquest; nor even as the precursors of more modern opposition movements. The movements are considered in terms of their thought, their perceptions of change, of community, of leadership. Religion, the other focus of the chapter, is seen as a crucial matrix for peasant interpretations of experience.

The popular movements of the later nineteenth and earlier twentieth centuries interleaved but did not coincide with more modern nationalist movements that emerged within the colonial framework. Nationalism and its alternatives are the subject of Chapter 5. There it is argued that there were alternatives to the nationalist movements that aimed to secure control of the colonial states and that were ultimately able to do so after World War II. There were those who favoured more gradual change. There were also nationalist movements among minority peoples, and there were movements, too, that sought to transcend the externally imposed frontiers of the imperial phase. Each of the colonial powers reacted in a different way. They were all to be swept aside by another external power.

THE ESTABLISHMENT OF THE
COLONIAL RÉGIMES

From the late eighteenth century, the involvement with Europeans, with things and ideas European, deepened and affected the whole of Southeast Asia; but it varied in intensity from people to people and from place to place; it increased through time but at no constant pace; and it took differing forms. Furthermore, it was always a matter, to a greater or lesser degree, of interaction, rather than simply of Western initiative or challenge and indigenous response. Nor were Western initiatives and challenges the only ones. Others came to Southeast Asia, too, though in some sense they themselves had already been stimulated by the Western ones. Islam, for example, had increased its hold on archipelagic Southeast Asia in the preceding period of European enterprise: linked more closely with its homeland by better communications in the nineteenth century, it was deeply involved in many of the social and political changes which that region now underwent.

The capacity of Europe to affect Southeast Asia increased in this period on a number of counts. First, the industrialization of Europe enhanced its economic power and political potential, though proceeding in different countries at varying rates with varying degress of completeness. Second, the world-wide improvement of communications—the introduction of steamships, the building of railways, the construction of the Suez Canal, the development of the electric telegraph—tied world and region more closely together. Third, European states became individually more integrated, more able to control their people and command their resources. Fourth, although (or because) they had so much in common, the states were at odds with each other, and the rivalry overseas that had long affected the fortunes of Southeast Asia continued to do so, though in new ways. At the same time as the Western states became more powerful, they also, though to differing degrees, became more democratized. A fifth factor, this did not necessarily work against an imperialist approach: it might intensify the rivalry among states, reducing their ability to manoeuvre; it might also commit them more irrevocably to expansionist policies, turning them into missions difficult for governments to abandon. The capacity of the Europeans to influence Southeast Asia was, sixth, enhanced by the growth of their power over the great neighbouring centres of population that had so long influenced it in a number of ways, India and China. But the changes in India and China did not eliminate their influence: they gave it new forms, and the modernization of Japan was both inspiration and threat. These factors were effective in Southeast Asia at different times, in different combinations, and in different ways.

The outcome was, however, not merely the result of all or any of these factors, singly or in combination. There were other actors on the scene— from Arabia, the heartland of Islam, now in closer touch, and from the United States, an independent commercial power from the late eighteenth century, rapidly industrializing in the later nineteenth century, developing imperial aspirations at the end of it. There were, too, the peoples of Southeast Asia themselves, who interacted with the Europeans and with others in a variety of ways, fighting, resisting, accommodating, adapting, turning and being turned to account, with greater or less vision, wisdom or acumen, at the popular and élite levels. Their aims are part of the story, though less clearly defined than those of the Europeans; and indeed they faced complex changes, difficult to appraise. In most cases, the existing state structures could not cope with the pressures put upon them and existing central authorities collapsed. Their replacements were endowed with territories out of a convenience more often European than Asian, designed, in particular, to avoid dispute among Europeans. And the new authority was, in substantial part at least, extraneous.

The political map of Southeast Asia was redrawn so that the region was almost entirely fragmented among the European powers. The process of drawing the frontiers was a long one; it was not complete—even on the map, let alone on the ground—till the early twentieth century. Most of the main lines of demarcation were, however, evident by 1870, before the full effects of industrialization were felt. Only more marginal territories remained for redistribution. They were marginal more in a geographical than a political sense. For their redistribution could still prompt disputes among the imperial powers that could become more than minor; and if those disputes did not escalate, or were readily resolved, the outcome was still important for the peoples concerned as well as for the imperial powers themselves, and, ultimately, for their successors.

In the drawing of the frontiers there was something of a paradox. In Europe the concept dealt with subjects and citizens in terms of their geographical locality rather than their personal allegiance; and the state laid claim to their taxes and imposed its obligations on an impersonal basis. That contrasted with much of previous Southeast Asian practice, especially in the archipelago where, insofar as geographical frontiers existed, they might be only vaguely defined. Often more important within states, even within some of the larger ones, were personal allegiances, client–patron relations, differential connexions between court and core, court and periphery; often more important among states were overlapping hierarchies, dual loyalties. Such structures better reflected the conditions of the Southeast Asian past. But the concept that the Europeans sought to apply in Southeast Asia also contrasted with the European present. In Europe frontiers had been created over a long period of time, often as a result of struggle, and within them new loyalties had been built up. Increasingly loyalty was to the state itself, as representing the nation in whose name, it had come to be accepted, its government ruled. No such

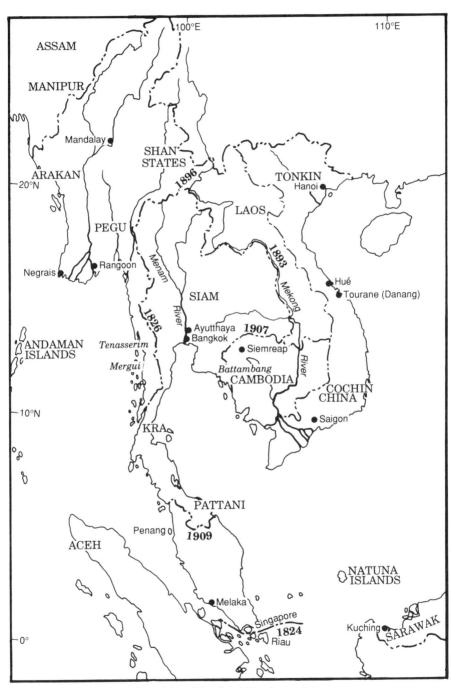

Map 1.1   Mainland Southeast Asia

ideology could apply to the colonial territories; nor was there a clear substitute for it. The colonial powers were utilizing a concept not only drawn from a system of international relations that differed but from one which they themselves were not in fact applying.

International relations in Southeast Asia came to be increasingly European. The frontiers were drawn so as to avoid disputes among the European powers. As a result, especially at the margins, they bore no firm relation to economic, social, cultural, ethnic or even geographical realities. The concept of a national frontier in Southeast Asia was applied in the general absence there of the relevant concept of nation. And it was applied with additional arbitrariness since it was designed to avoid conflict elsewhere.

The new governments, by necessity or design, often utilized or re-utilized old claims to suzerainty, old patterns of loyalty, old modes of administration, and at the same time they reshaped them. While their governments were relatively inactive, the discrepancy mattered less. And for a time they were to a greater or lesser degree 'law and order' states, 'arbitral' governments. The old central authorities might have been displaced, perhaps geographically as well as politically. But the new governments might still function in a limited way, adopting some Southeast Asian practices as well as European. Indeed they could give themselves—at least in their own eyes, and perhaps in the eyes of their subjects—a special role simply because of their limited function: they were there to reduce tensions among the 'opposite Interests and jarring Dispositions' to which, as Alexander Dalrymple said, colonies were so prone;[1] they were there to end tyranny, they sometimes rather more ambitiously claimed.

More tension would be felt when governments became more active— could old allegiances still be utilized?—and still more when they ceased to be arbitral—could the peoples then be held in the colonial framework? That question arose of course with twentieth-century moves—dictated by metropolitan politics but also by colonial change—towards indigenous participation in the central structures. Just because the pragmatic approach of the nineteenth century and the desire to avoid conflict among Europeans had made the territories often so heterogeneous, the tension was all the greater. A minority could live alongside an inactive government: it could accept alien arbitration. But could it accept majority rule?

The concept of the nation was developed in Europe to fill out the European concept of the state. It caused struggle enough there: it gave weapons to majorities and minorities, to those who would change frontiers and those who would insist on not changing them, to those who would challenge authorities and those who would uphold them. In Southeast Asia, the concept was again divisive as well as integrative. But, because the movements could initially challenge the Europeans, its divisiveness was at first often muted. Emerging nationalist movements could thus seek to play down tension, though their alien rulers might point it out

---

[1] 'Enquiry into the most advantageous Place for a Capital to the Oriental Polynesia', February 1764, Borneo Factory Records G/4/1, India Office Library.

or even play it up, so as to preserve their role. It could intensify when the Europeans withdrew and their succcessors sought to rule as nation-states these territories with frontiers which were so much the product of colonial convenience. Authority was again in question: the successor states had to be turned into nation-states.

The making of the frontiers thus assumes a primal position in an account of Southeast Asian history in the nineteenth century. Itself the product of interactions between European and Asian, it becomes, too, the framework for continuing interaction. It is also important as a factor in the history of the nationalist movements of the twentieth century and of the post-colonial states.

The nineteenth century was, more than any other, an age of migration: the economic transformations it witnessed set in motion or speeded up movements of people on an unprecedented scale. Europeans left Europe to help build up or to create new states elsewhere, in the Americas and Australasia, in Africa and, much less, in Asia. But other peoples also moved in increasing numbers as economic change picked up pace. Southeast Asia, always a recipient of Indians and Chinese, received them on a new scale, particularly in the territories which the British came to control. There was also migration, again not entirely novel, within Southeast Asia, within the frontiers that were being established and across them. For a colonial authority, again, these movements posed few problems and offered economic and political advantages. But in the twentieth century, those movements would make it more difficult to establish a participatory political system, or even an accepted central authority ruling on a national basis.

THE ROLE OF THE BRITISH

If there was varied interaction between Southeast Asia and Europe, the Europeans were also divided. Rivalry was a factor in their expansion, for the most part spurring them on. But the process of frontier-building and its outcome were also affected by the shifting distribution of power among the Europeans, the result in a sense of the differing impact on them of common factors. For much of the nineteenth century, Britain was the predominant state in Europe and thus in the world. The French presented a challenge in the eighteenth century, but they were defeated at sea in 1805 and on land in 1815. Politically secure in Europe, Britain also took the lead in the Industrial Revolution. That gave it yet greater strength, but also shaped the application of its power. Overseas its interests became substantially commercial and economic rather than territorial and political. It saw its dominion in India, begun in the earlier phase, as essential but exceptional. Elsewhere, a combination of strategic positions and economic and political influence should suffice to protect its interests. In Southeast Asia Britain sought security and stability; it did not necessarily seek to rule, though its power might be felt in other ways.

The nineteenth-century patterns of interaction in Southeast Asia were

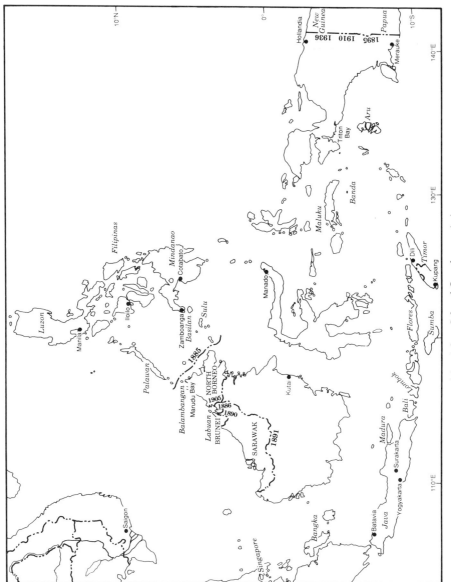

Map 1.2   Island Southeast Asia

naturally much affected by the influence and interests of the British, particularly during the period of their predominance. That predominance they did not use to eliminate their European rivals, but rather to constrain them. The Netherlands and Spain were now minor states in Europe; they were left with substantial holdings in Southeast Asia, with claims that the British were unlikely to challenge, with the option of implementing them in their own time provided they did not undermine Britain's interests. Even France, the eighteenth-century rival, was not obstructed in its Vietnam venture. In earlier centuries, European rivalry had rarely worked to the advantage of Asian states: it spurred the Europeans on, while the chance of playing the Europeans off against one another was often a chimera. But the new pattern of intra-European relations was perhaps still less advantageous. The fact that minor European powers could rely on Britain's restraint might indeed mean that they could refrain from enforcing their claims or establishing de facto occupation in other than immediately essential areas. But the autonomy which indigenous rulers might thus enjoy was somewhat illusory: they had no real chance of playing Britain off against the minor powers, and their status as independent actors on an international stage was diminished by this kind of semi-condominium. The British set the agenda for lesser European powers, and for the indigenous states also. Siam (Thailand) alone retained real independence at the end of the period: it had seen that it was no longer a matter of playing off one alien power against another, but of coming to terms with the British, and it was able to do so. Directly or indirectly, Britain's influence and interest were often decisive in determining the frontiers of the new Southeast Asian states, in locating the central authorities within those frontiers, even in shaping the policies those authorities pursued.

The challenges to the patterns thus established that emerged towards the end of the nineteenth century did not merely, nor even primarily, result from the changes and tensions within Southeast Asia. They reflected changes in Europe and the world at large, in particular the external challenges to Britain's power, as industrialization affected other parts of Europe and the world, and Britain and indeed Europe itself lost their extraordinary primacy. But by the late nineteenth century the major loci of authority in Southeast Asia had been settled, and the revived rivalry of the period affected only the rounding-out of frontiers. In this phase the British moved readily from tolerating others towards compromising with them. The conference on Africa and West Africa that met in Berlin in 1884–5, and included the European powers, Turkey and the United States, provided a principle: European states would accept the frontiers established by their rivals if their claims were backed by effective occupation. The recrudescence of rivalry was thus no more to the advantage of indigenous autonomy than its earlier diminution: indeed it clearly conduced to the establishment of outside control. Intensifying rivalry in Europe and the emergence of non-European powers, the United States and Japan, had the same effect. The former urged on compromise between Britain and France, helping to determine the frontiers of Burma, Malaya, Indochina and Siam. A combination of factors helped to ensure that Spain was replaced in the Philippines by the United States and that the authority of the Moro sultanates was finally destroyed. But in a sense these were adjustments of a system that had developed during the British primacy of the nineteenth century. The system was overthrown only by the Japanese incursion of 1941–2.

The making of the new frontiers in Southeast Asia in the nineteenth century had depended in some sense on British decisions. They in turn were affected by the essentially economic nature of Britain's world-wide interests; by its desire for European stability; by its acquisition of the raj in India; and by the importance attached to its trade with China. These concerns affected Britain's view of different parts of Southeast Asia in different ways. For this reason, though also for others, the outcomes differed. Much depended on the relationship of Britain with specific European powers. Where they were minor, it tended not to displace them, but to connive at their imperialism so as to avoid that of any powers that might be more threatening, and paradoxically that might reduce their immediate need to establish full control. Against major European powers, however, it might have to take more direct precautions, but that did not necessarily mean exclusion.

The attitudes and policies of other European powers have thus to be taken into account. The Dutch, whose dependence was underlined by British conquests and retrocessions, were prompted all the more to con-centrate on Java; on areas that could be made profitable; on development, peace and order. *Onthouding*, or abstention, was possible as well as desirable in the outer islands. The increased rivalry of the later nineteenth century, as well as new economic opportunities, spurred them on to round out their empire. Their concern over Islam was another factor. Generally they tried, as in earlier centuries, to avoid provoking it, and their war with Aceh was a challenge they found difficult to handle. Spain, whose weakness the British had also underlined by capturing Manila in 1762, recognized that it too was dependent on them and permitted them major economic opportunities in Luzon and the Visayas. The international rivalry of the late nineteenth century, and the challenge of Islam, led the Spanish into bloody but indeterminate efforts to make their claims over the Moro lands effective. In the late eighteenth century the French had seen a venture in Southeast Asia as a way of compensating themselves for British success in India and China. Their revival of interest in Vietnam in the 1850s, not opposed by the British, responded to a need to demonstrate the greatness of France overseas. That seemed all the more necessary under the Third Republic, when its position in Europe was under challenge.

The opportunities for these European states were determined not only by the British, but also by the Southeast Asians. Their states might attempt to adjust to new circumstances: they might not; if they did, they might fail; if they began the task, they might not realize that further adjustment would be needed. Even in the early nineteenth century, it seemed that Asian states would have to modernize to survive, and that they might need a greater or lesser degree of European influence to ensure that they did so. Such in itself might destroy ancient authority without replacing it, and make them weaker rather than stronger. The alternative might be piecemeal partition, itself weakening the core structure. If either or both of these outcomes determined their position by the late nineteenth century, the new pressures then exerted by international economic expansion and political rivalry might bring about a final dissolution.

THE DUTCH REALM IN THE INDONESIAN ARCHIPELAGO

While Britain occupied only Fort Marlborough in West Sumatra, two European powers were already established in Southeast Asia at the outset of the period, the Dutch and the Spaniards. Their empires differed in character. That of the Dutch did not involve widespread control. But the determination of the British, at once not to challenge their supremacy in the archipelago, nor to permit that to be done by others, assisted the Dutch to establish their power during the nineteenth century and reduced the possibility that Indonesian states could sustain their independence. An occasional rift with Britain urged the Dutch on, though they were usually careful to provide British merchants with commercial opportunities. More generally, the relationship enabled them to defer their empire-building till they were strong enough, or till they found it necessary or desirable because of the risks of the intervention of others or because of their own needs and urges. The Asian states might enjoy a practical, albeit misleading, freedom from Dutch intervention in the meantime.

In the closing decades of the eighteenth century, the Dutch still retained an Asia-wide empire, with Batavia (Jakarta) as its centre. But their hold even on the Malaysian-Indonesian area fell far short of territorial dominion. Its failure to compete in the Asian textile and opium trades, and the decline in its spice trade, had led the Verenigde Oost-Indische Compagnie (VOC, the Dutch East India Company) to concentrate on Java, and to see the peninsula and archipelago rather as an outwork for its empire there. In any case, the Dutch position rested for the most part on contracts and treaties with indigenous states, more concerned with questions of commerce than questions of government, more with deliveries of produce than transfers of sovereignty. What was critical for VOC, and as a result for the indigenous states, was the exclusion of European rivals. This the Dutch sought to ensure on paper all the more because they found it difficult to ensure in practice: 'they are afraid', said the British statesman Henry Dundas, 'that the communication we may have with the Natives would lay the foundation for their total shaking off of the miserable dependence in which they are held by the Dutch'.[2] The British had good commercial grounds for expanding such communication: their hold on trade with Asia and, through the country traders, within Asia, had improved; the East India Company needed archipelagic goods to amplify its trade to China. But there were other arguments against alienating the Dutch in the context of the European rivalries of the time. It was important not to drive the Dutch into the hands of the French, so expanding their threat to the new dominion in India, undermining the trade to China, and indeed damaging

[2] Quoted H. Furber, *Henry Dundas, First Viscount Melville, 1742–1811*, Oxford, 1931, 103.

the security of England itself. The Anglo-Dutch treaty of 1784 did not go beyond securing the right to navigate in the Eastern Seas. Remaining in West Sumatra, the British did not extend their political challenge except on the periphery of Dutch power, by acquiring Penang from the Sultan of Kedah in 1786.

A pro-French régime nevertheless survived in the Dutch Republic until the Anglo-Prussian intervention of 1787. Then the British attempted to put their interests in the Indies on a new footing while, as they thought, recognizing those of the Dutch, reaching an accord, they hoped, in the East and in Europe. Their concept involved a kind of delimitation—the first time, but not the last, that the notion was to emerge. The Dutch should remain in their settlements on the continent of India and the Malay peninsula; the British would secure the naval base of Trincomalee in Ceylon (Sri Lanka). But the VOC should transfer the right to Riau which it had lately secured from the Sultan of Johor-Lingga; this would afford protection for British ships en route for China and provide an entrepôt for British trade in the archipelago. In return the spice monopoly would be guaranteed: no British traders would operate, and no British settlements be made, east of the easternmost point of Sumatra. These ideas not even a friendly Dutch régime could accept, and the negotiations failed.

In the Napoleonic Wars that followed, the Dutch Republic again fell under French influence, and the British took over a number of Dutch possessions in India, Ceylon and the archipelago, and finally in 1811 Java itself. The defeat of France, and the establishment of the new Kingdom of the Netherlands, were the signal for the restoration of all the Dutch territories but those in Ceylon and at the Cape of Good Hope. But no provision was made in the convention of 1814 for the settlement of prewar disputes over the archipelago. By 1814, indeed, the British East India Company had no real interest in the spice trade; nor even in the archipelago trade in general, since Indian opium now substantially provided for its tea investment at Canton. But the interim administration of Java by Stamford Raffles and the opening of the trade to the East under the Company's Charter of 1813 had led to the establishment of British merchants on that island, interested in distributing British textiles and purchasing coffee. These viewed with concern the restoration of Dutch sovereignty and the prospect of a revived policy of commercial exclusion. The extensive renewal of treaties and contracts with the native states outside Java upon which the Dutch Commissioners-General embarked after the restoration of the colonies in 1816 likewise aroused the apprehension of country traders and of merchants and officials at Penang.

Raffles, like Dundas earlier, had pointed out the weakness of the Dutch position in the archipelago, but, with a wider sense of responsibility, he believed that the British should assure their trade and influence there by themselves establishing settlements and concluding treaties with Indonesian rulers. Indeed, by making the Company's Governor-General in India 'Batara', they should secure 'a general right of superintendence over, and interference with, all the Malay States', so as to support legitimate authority, suppress piracy, limit commercial monopoly and control arms

Map 1.3   The Malay Peninsula

traffic.[3] These views were not accepted in London. In 1815 the Secret Committee of the Court of Directors disapproved of the treaties Raffles made: 'such engagements are impolitic and injudicious; . . . calculated to involve the British Government in the internal concerns of those States, and the perpetual contests which they are carrying on with each other'.[4] Back in the archipelago at Fort Marlborough, Raffles modified rather than abandoned his plans. One argument he now used impressed his superiors in India: the importance of protecting the China route. Thus he gained the authority under which in 1819 he concluded a treaty of friendship with the yet independent Sultan of Aceh at one end of the Straits of Melaka (Malacca) and acquired rights from princes of Johor to a factory on Singapore island at the other.

The Secret Committee deplored 'the extension in any degree to the Eastern Islands of that system of subsidiary alliance which has prevailed perhaps too widely in India'.[5] But now decisions had to be taken on the archipelago, and the British government again moved towards a kind of conditioned delimitation. Raffles's schemes must be used, not to over-throw the Dutch empire, but again to press upon the Dutch a compromise by which its continuance could be reconciled with local British interests. In the view of the Foreign Secretary Lord Castlereagh, the government could not 'acquiesce in a practical exclusion' of British commerce from the archipelago, nor in complete Dutch control of the 'keys of the Straits of Malacca'. The prospects for a compromise would be affected by the preliminary question of 'the extent of the rights claimed by the Government of the Netherlands in the Eastern Seas'. The Dutch must

> distinguish how much of this claim rests upon strict possession, how much upon concession from the native princes, and by what limits in point of space, or by what rules of intercourse the Netherlands Government proposes to consider the rights and authority of that state to be restrained or modified towards the subjects of other powers frequenting those seas.[6]

The Dutch king, Castlereagh wrote, might 'hold Java and any other of his old possessions in direct colonial sovereignty in which of course he will establish the system he thinks the wisest, but which after all, my opinion is, ought not in prudence to be one of exclusive trade'. Beyond these limits he should have an understanding with Great Britain 'which may open the native commerce of the other islands to a fair and friendly competition, without the establishment of any other preponderating military or political

[3] Sophia Raffles, *Memoir of the Life and Public Services of Sir Thomas Stamford Raffles*, London, 1830, 59ff.
[4] Quoted John Bastin, 'Raffles and British Policy in the Indian Archipelago, 1811–1816', JMBRAS, 37, 1 (May 1954) 100–3.
[5] Secret Committee to Governor-General, 22 May 1819, Board's Drafts of Secret Letters to India, First Series, L/PS/5/543, 5, India Office Library, London.
[6] Castlereagh to Clancarty, 13 Aug. 1819, secret, FO 37/107, Public Record Office, London; H. T. Colenbrander, ed., *Gedenkstukken der Algemeene Geschiedenis van Nederland van 1795 tot 1840*, 's-Gravenhage, 1915–21, 8, 1. 130–2.

authority in those seas to counterbalance that which the Dutch now and long have exercised'.[7]

The exchanges were complicated by a concern about other powers. Raffles argued for an active policy. But if the British extended their challenge to the Dutch, their example might be followed by others, and that might damage British interests. It would be difficult to insist upon any British rights in respect of the commerce with Indonesian states in contractual relationship with the Dutch, a British negotiator argued,

> without admitting at the same time the equal right of other European nations, and of the Americans, to their share also. Perhaps as the policy of extending British establishments or connexions in the Eastern Islands has hitherto been considered by the British Government as at least extremely doubtful the utmost length to which our preliminary demand ought to go ... should be a stipulation that the Dutch will form no new engagements, especially on the Island of Borneo.[8]

In fact, the Dutch wished to avoid an inquisition into their 'title deeds'. While, therefore, the British accepted the spice monopolies in enumerated islands of Maluku (the Moluccas)—the fine spices they produced were now in any case also produced outside the Indonesian archipelago—the Dutch agreed that no treaty should be made thereafter by either power with any native power in the Eastern Seas 'tending either expressly or by the imposition of unequal duties to exclude the trade of the other party from the ports of such native power, and that, if in any treaty now existing on either part, any such article to that effect has been admitted, such article shall be abrogated upon the conclusion of the present treaty'. This became Article 3 of the treaty finally concluded on 17 March 1824. Article 2 of that treaty was designed to give Dutch trade 'the sort of protection which the British trade enjoys in the Indian ports' and under limitations allowed protective duties in Dutch possessions. The articles were less than clear. But it was in any case impossible to define the position too elaborately without arousing the jealousy of other powers. 'The situation in which we and the Dutch stand to each other is part only of our difficulties', wrote George Canning, one of the plenipotentiaries; 'that in which we both stand to the rest of the world as exclusive Lords of the East, is one more reason for terminating our relative difficulties as soon as we can'.[9] A challenge to the Dutch must be avoided, for it was felt that this might invite the intervention of other major powers in areas flanking the route to China. But too obvious and too close an agreement with the Dutch might provoke other powers to intervene. Before the war only one other power had been in question: France. Now France was defeated, though not eliminated, and others had penetrated to Asia, including the Americans, and both its victorious role in Europe and its interest in Japan even raised the question of Russia's involvement. At this juncture intervention was less actual than

---

[7] Castlereagh to Clancarty, 13 Aug. 1819, private, FO 37/107; *Gedenkstukken*, 8, 1. 132–3.
[8] Memorandum, n.d., Dutch Records, I/2/31, India Office Library.
[9] Note by Canning on Courtenay's memorandum of 15 Jan. 1824, Dutch Records, I/2/32.

potential: a blatant statement of overlordship might provoke a challenge otherwise avoidable.

The same consideration throws light on other important articles in the treaty of 1824. The Dutch had at first opposed and then finally accepted the British occupation of Singapore, and they also proposed to leave Melaka provided the British left Sumatra. As the Dutch plenipotentiary, A. R. Falck, put it, a line would be drawn between their respective possessions through the Straits of Melaka and passing north of Riau. In the treaty the proposed line was replaced by articles, effecting this same division in different words, less likely to arouse the jealousy of others. A difference arose over Aceh, which was important for its position at the head of the straits. It was now British policy to resign all Sumatra to the Dutch, and the more effective their control, the more effectively they would be able to exclude other major powers. The recency of Raffles's treaty of friendship with the sultan raised a difficulty, however, which could be overcome only by including, in notes attached to the treaty, stipulations binding the Dutch to establish security in Aceh without infringing its independence.

Falck's dividing line and the non-intervention articles substituted for it did not extend as far as Borneo, though he certainly believed that Borneo was to be left to the Dutch. This, however, was not stated in the treaty, partly because of fears that the British Parliament might object to the 'abandonment' of Borneo as well as of Sumatra, and, once more, partly because such an extended Anglo-Dutch agreement, if it were explicitly expressed, might arouse jealousy among other powers. Indeed the British plenipotentiaries probably felt that the arrangements made over treaty states removed the need, referred to earlier, for an 'opening' on the island of Borneo.

The treaty of 1824 was a form of delimitation: it excluded the Dutch from the peninsula, it admitted their predominance in the archipelago. It should not be seen as a stage in an advance towards a predetermined end, for much was left open and subject to argument, and there was no clear determination that two realms would be set up. Some options were, however, closed off. The precaution over other powers, though not expressed in the treaty, continued to be influential. Apprehension about them continued to restrain the British in handling Dutch relations with Indonesian states. And other powers were on the whole to respect the Anglo-Dutch relationship without always realizing the verbal weakness of the treaty of 1824. The arrangements affected the indigenous states all the more as a result. Britain was unlikely to take their part against the Dutch. The chances of their behaving as international actors, able to enter relations with third powers, was nullified by a combination of Dutch jealousy, British connivance, and European caution. Meanwhile, however, the weakened position of the Indonesian states might not be apparent. The Dutch, with a British guarantee, might often be able to avoid actual intervention.

The merchants of Penang and Singapore were opposed to Dutch extension on any terms, even if unaccompanied by protectionist measures, because they saw it as a threat to their entrepôt traffic, and a constriction of the scope of their operations. They differed not only from Raffles, who opposed Dutch authority but wanted to reform the Malay world and end its fragmentation, but from the government in London which preferred a regular European government administered by a minor power. For a while the Dutch in any case largely avoided expansion: they were deeply embroiled in the Java War of the 1820s, then in the Belgian breakaway struggle after 1830. These events, and the need for revenue, concentrated their attention on Java where they developed the forced-labour Cultivation System and also found a market, despite the treaty of 1824, for Dutch textiles. They were drawn into West Sumatra, however, by local initiative. Batavia had modest plans, Padang expansionist ones; and the authorities there could oblige their superiors to accept faits accomplis.

Returning to Padang after the British occupation, the Dutch committed themselves to helping the Minangkabau *penghulu* (chiefs) against the Padris, Wahhābi-style religious reformers, in 1824. A settlement was made with Bondjol, identified as the central Padri authority, while the Java War was on. On its conclusion, Governor-General Van den Bosch favoured securing the recognition of the Dutch régime throughout the archipelago. In Sumatra, he thought it would be sufficient for the Dutch to occupy ports, river-mouths, selected interior market towns: the aim should be to avoid direct intervention and concentrate on encouraging 'profitable activity'.[10] In West Sumatra, however, he agreed that order must be re-established. One bizarre notion was to use Sentot and some Javanese auxiliaries, but this proved counter-productive. From 1837 the war with the Padris was prosecuted with vigour and Minangkabau was incorporated in the Dutch realm.

Trade had been flowing from the interior to the east coast. There Jambi had acknowledged Dutch sovereignty in 1833–4. Inderagiri followed in 1838, then Panei and Bila, and Sultan Ismail of Siak sought Dutch protection. Merchants in the Straits Settlements protested. Rather surprisingly, the Foreign Office in London took their part. In the case of Siak, the British seemed to be faced with a threat of Dutch conquest. In the absence of any precise stipulation about conquest, as distinct from treaty-making, in the treaty of 1824, they attempted to counter this by reviving a treaty with the sultan made on behalf of the Penang government in 1818. In the case of neighbouring Jambi, they indeed faced the question of a Netherlands treaty with an indigenous power. But suppose, the Foreign Office wondered, the Dutch claimed sovereignty by treaty as they might by conquest? could conditions then be imposed on the exertion of their authority in respect of foreign trade? The Dutch indeed claimed that the stipulation of Article 3 of the 1824 treaty did not apply in such cases, though Van den Bosch's cautious successor, J. C. Baud, withdrew from the east coast pro tem. Palmerston, the British Foreign Secretary, was inclined to agree that Article 2 alone applied; and so the question of sovereignty, initially raised

---

[10] Elizabeth E. Graves, 'The Ever Victorious Buffalo: how the Minangkabau of Indonesia solved their "colonial question"', Ph.D. thesis, University of Wisconsin, 1971, 144.

by the problem of conquest, and then asked in relation to treaties, displaced the basis of the 1824 compromise. The distinction it had tried on Castlereagh's basis to draw between treaty states and possessions was now blurred.

Under the pressures of the Cultivation System and Dutch protectionism, Article 2 had, however, been found to afford little protection for British trade in Dutch possessions. The British Foreign Office endeavoured in the recession of the 1830s to uphold the cause of the merchants in Java, related as their interests were to those of important textile manufacturers at home. It was the failure to obtain any real satisfaction from the Dutch in this respect that was largely responsible for the Foreign Office's decision to take up the Straits Settlements complaints. By 1838 the official view had already shifted far from that of 1824: 'an extension of Dutch Influence, or Territorial Possession', it was remarked, 'would in all probability be attended with consequences injurious to British interest, and should be looked upon with jealousy by the Government of this country.'[11] In the 1840s, indeed, a more positive challenge to the delimitation of 1824 seemed possible. Adventurers were appearing as it were in the niches between actual and potential Dutch extension, in the no-man's-land which the Dutch had felt they could safely neglect. Now, despite the 1824 treaty, or because of the dispute over it, the Dutch feared that these adventurers might secure official backing. Baud ordered an archival survey of Dutch rights and contracts, and special commissioners were sent out to fill the gaps revealed. In general they were, however, only being papered over. Occupation rarely followed, and native rulers still tended to see the contracts more as treaties than as transfers of control. There was more forceful action in Bali, where the Dutch commissioner had secured treaties only by verbal promises of help against the Mataram kingdom in Lombok. The help not being forthcoming, the treaties were not ratified; the Dutch sent three expeditions to deal with the Bali rajas, though still no occupation followed. The renewal of Anglo-Dutch rivalry could indeed only diminish the independence of the Indonesian states, unless the British were prepared to abandon the 1824 settlement. Mere apprehension that they might do so drove the Dutch into affirming their claims over the Indonesian states and in some cases establishing a more formal control over them.

The British challenge to the Dutch in fact never went far. Nor did it last long. The improvement in overall economic conditions in mid-century meant that there was less domestic pressure on the British government, and the Dutch government, headed after 1848 by the liberal Thorbecke, began to liberalize its system. That did not remove the Straits Settlements objections to Dutch extension in Sumatra when it was renewed in the 1860s. In the 1850s Dutch policy had continued for the most part to be of a restrained nature. But after an English individual had responded to a request for help, the Dutch had made a treaty with Siak in 1858, and under it claimed dependencies to the north in the following years. Governor Orfeur Cavenagh supported the Straits Settlements protests, but the

---

[11] Strangways to Barrow, 9 Jan. 1838, FO 37/213.

Foreign Office, preferring regular European rule, used them to secure a new delimitation. This was the treaty of 1871, under which all objections to Dutch territorial control in Sumatra were withdrawn in return for a commercial open door. The appearance of other imperial powers on the scene, now less hypothetical than in the 1820s, only revalidated the pre-Palmerston approach. The extension of the Dutch was generally preferred to the intervention of other powers in the archipelago. As Under-Secretary at the Foreign Office, Lord Wodehouse had written in 1860:

> I believe the policy of Mr. Canning's treaty was much the wisest, viz., to leave to the Dutch the Eastern Archipelago. . . . The exclusive colonial policy of the Dutch is no doubt an evil, but it has been much relaxed of late. . . . It seems to me in many respects very advantageous that the Dutch should possess this Archipelago. If it were not in the hands of the Dutch, it would fall under the sway of some other maritime power, presumably the French, unless we took it ourselves. The French might, if they possessed such an eastern empire, be really dangerous to India and Australia, but the Dutch are and must remain too weak to cause us any alarm.[12]

The means by which the Dutch regained the sanction of the British they now applied to the other European powers penetrating the area, too: an open-door policy. Like Britain, the powers would be less likely to challenge the Dutch territorially if they found their policies acceptable commercially. The further internationalization of the area in the later 1870s and 1880s—especially the arrival of the Germans—again urged the Dutch to strengthen their claims, as did economic opportunity and local ambition. The indigenous states lost the autonomy they had possessed when, largely with British connivance, the Dutch had been content in many places with paper claims. For example, the year following the Berlin conference, J. A. Liefrinck, sent to investigate rumours of the wealth of Lombok, urged an end to the policy of 'benevolent indifference'.[13] In 1887, the raja refused, however, to make a supplementary treaty and accept a Dutch agent. Forceful action, the Council in Batavia urged, lest it should appear that Aceh had broken Dutch power; caution, decided Governor-General Pynacker, lest action resulted in another prolonged conflict, though the Sasaks revolted against the raja in the east of the island, and the local Dutch officials sought to provoke an incident. The next governor-general authorized an expedition. It succeeded only with difficulty.

For the most part Indonesian states had lost their independence by stages, involving treaties, Dutch pressure, British connivance, others' non-intervention or threats to intervene, their own incapacity; they were gradually subsumed into the Netherlands realm, the 'radical and internal weakness' of the Dutch turned to a semblance at least of strength. But Aceh had a tradition of independence, Islamic stiffening, and no real involvement in the treaty system, and the British inhibition in 1824 had made it extra difficult for the Dutch to incorporate it, as it were, from the

---

[12] Memorandum by Wodehouse, 18 Aug. 1860, FO 12/28.
[13] Alfons van der Kraan, *Lombok: Conquest, Colonization and Underdevelopment 1870–1940*, Singapore, 31–2.

top down. At the time of the 1871 treaty Aceh was still independent, and in the context of expanding colonial rivalry, this was worrying. 'The pretension of excluding others where one will not or cannot undertake matters oneself is in the long run, at least for a small power, untenable and . . . extremely dangerous.'[14] The Dutch took the kind of action they were to hesitate over in respect of Lombok. 'An end must come to the equivocal policy of Atjeh [Aceh] towards the Netherlands Government. That state remains our weak point as far as Sumatra is concerned. As long as it does not recognise our sovereignty foreign intervention will continue to threaten us like the sword of Damocles.'[15]

Earlier, under Governor-General Pahud, the Dutch had attempted to develop friendship without claiming sovereignty. But piecemeal advance on the west coast during the Padri struggle had made that difficult, and Dutch claims over the east coast under the Siak treaty of 1858 were a direct challenge to the Acehnese. The Acehnese war that ensued after 1873 showed the special qualities of the sultanate and of the role of Islam. But it also showed the general importance for the Dutch of the non-intervention of others and explained their normal preference for an essentially continuous political rather than military process of consolidation. The Dutch in fact did not secure total victory. The long struggle helped to reshape their policy towards Islam in general, and to promote their attempts to rationalize a realm pragmatically built up over several centuries. The British no longer opposed the infringement of Article 3 of the 1824 treaty that the process involved.

RAJ, COMPANY AND RESIDENCY IN BORNEO

In 1824 the British had probably intended that the Dutch should predominate in the archipelago, even in Borneo. But earlier they had been interested in the Brunei-Sulu region, and a combination of personal initiative and dissatisfaction with Dutch policy elsewhere led them back to Borneo in the 1840s. The government established the colony of Labuan and made a treaty with Brunei. It avoided taking over Sarawak, where the Brookes built a raj of their own. In the 1880s British protectorates were established over Sarawak, the territory of the newly-established British North Borneo Company and the remnant of Brunei, and a British Resident was established in the sultanate in 1905. Partly provoked by the Brooke venture and by the founding of the Company, the Dutch established their control more firmly over the rest of Borneo.

The apparent change in British policy towards the Dutch in Borneo derived in part from the partial break between the 'exclusive Lords' in the 1830s: Dutch policies had led Palmerston to declare that Dutch extension was in general not to British advantage. But something more positive was required to turn that shift of policy towards British intervention. Northern

---

[14] Gericke and Van Bosse to the King, 19 Apr. 1871, quoted A. J. S. Reid, *The Contest for North Sumatra*, Kuala Lumpur, 1969, 86.
[15] Loudon to Van de Putte, 25 Feb. 1873, quoted ibid., 95.

Borneo became of greater interest with the opening of trade to China and, since it possessed coal, with the development of steam communication. More important were the personal intervention of James Brooke, the most effective of the various adventurers in the no-man's-land left between the potential and the reality of Dutch imperialism, and the public support he was able for a time to secure. Even so, the change in official British policy was limited, and there was continual tension between Brooke and the government. With the Dutch excluded, the British needed to avert the intervention of other powers by other means. But they were not keen to take on additional responsibilities; unwilling or unable to displace or abandon Brooke, they became anxious not to be drawn on any further by him.

James Brooke's initial aim was to undo the policy of 1824. He wanted to revive Raffles's concept of a British empire in the archipelago by interven-ing where Dutch authority was weak or non-existent, and reforming and sustaining the indigenous states. Subjected to no formal relationship with the Dutch, the sultanate of Brunei became a field of activity as well as advocacy. Brooke planned at once to argue for and to demonstrate the validity of his policy by intervening in one of its dependencies, Sarawak, and restructuring its system of government so that law and order would be established and commerce flourish. British power could be involved, in particular because of the commitment to put down piracy, included in the treaty of 1824, and generally regarded as a duty for the British Navy. Support for his native allies in Brunei itself could be justified by arguing, too, that the Brunei region possessed coal which the British needed. With the assistance of others Brooke mounted a campaign at home, designed to influence the government by stressing the philanthropic and commercial objectives of the venture. The British government did not take over Sarawak, but it did give Brooke, raja there from 1841, some support, not only through naval activities, but by appointing him Agent with the Sultan of Brunei in 1844. The intervention produced a crisis with the Brunei élite in 1846. That led in turn to a further instalment of British intervention. Labuan was now made a colony and the treaty concluded with the sultan in 1847 secured a measure of extraterritorial jurisdiction and provided against cessions to other powers. There was still no British take-over, but Brunei was clearly, like states in the Dutch sphere, losing its room for manoeuvre.

There seemed some chance that Brooke might secure further backing for his Rafflesian plans: instructions given him as Commissioner and Consul-General to the Sultan and Independent Chiefs of Borneo in 1848 indicated that the position was designed 'to afford to British commerce that support and protection ... peculiarly required in the Indian seas in consequence of the prevalence of piracy ... and by reason of the encroachments of the Netherlands authorities in the Indian Archipelago'.[16] But questions about the possible abuse of British naval power at the raja's instigation reinforced doubts about a more expansive policy, which generally improving eco-nomic conditions in any case made less urgent. The extent to which public

[16] Palmerston to Brooke, 23 Feb. 1848, FO 12/6.

opinion was involved made the policy particularly subject to change if that opinion changed, and when a new government appointed a commission of inquiry in 1853, the policy, never fully adopted, was almost entirely abandoned.

Brooke was not, however, deprived of his raj, anomalous though it was for a British subject to be a ruler in his own right. Indeed, unable to exert influence over Brunei, he increasingly sought to extend the boundaries of his raj at its expense and to regard Sarawak as an independent state. His realm thus rested on displacing Brunei's, co-opting local Malayo-Muslim leaders, mobilizing, too, the energies of erstwhile Iban enemies, and, still more ambivalently, the energies of Chinese immigrants. It also still rested, despite all the tension and anomaly in the relationship, on British power. The British government would not push him out and so return to 1824— public opinion would not go that far—and indeed it was committed to protecting the lives and interests of British subjects, though not to support-ing an independent raj. Nor did it want any other power to step in, especially as the South China Sea became more vulnerable with the establishment of the French in Indochina. The raja at times threatened to look for support elsewhere. Rather paradoxically this—with the assiduous support of friends in high places—produced a kind of recognition of the Brooke régime with the appointment of a British consul in Kuching in 1863.

The raja's successor, his nephew Charles Brooke, had fewer inhibitions about pushing Sarawak's expansion: he had none of the romantic commit-ment to the old sultanate which the old raja had never quite lost. Brunei itself was, furthermore, open to expansion. It was a realm built in part on regional and ethnic checks and balances: depleted by the advance of Sarawak, they were the more difficult to operate. But the British govern-ment was anxious to avoid a further extension of an anomalous raj, and invoked the treaty of 1847 against the new raja's purported acquisition of the Baram in 1868. The weakness of Brunei, however, made this negative kind of intervention policy difficult to sustain. Other powers after all might intervene in defiance of the treaty of 1847. Indeed some United States adventurers secured concessions from the sultanate. That was, however, made to provide a way forward for the British. New concessions led to the founding of the British North Borneo Company, and the British govern-ment, seeking a more effectual way of excluding others without directly confronting them, and providing for law and order while limiting its own responsibility, gave the Company a charter in 1881. Brunei was thus smaller still. The British government envisaged its disappearance. The protectorate agreements made in 1888 with all three states, Sarawak, North Borneo (Sabah) and Brunei, were not designed to prevent this. They would prevent others intervening in the interim and damaging a safe and orderly partition.

Though further diminished, Brunei did not disappear from the map. That was partly a result of British decisions, partly of Brunei's. Resentful over the chartering of the Company, Raja Charles pressed ahead, but his acquisition of Limbang in 1890 helped Sultan Hashim of Brunei consolidate opposition to further cessions, and to some extent his policy of playing off raj and Company succeeded. But he would not have won the last respite for Brunei without a shift on the part of the British. From the late 1870s some officials in the Colonial Office had come to think that a more regular exertion of British authority was required in Borneo. At first they considered it could be achieved through the raj, and were critical of the creation of the Company, another anomalous régime. In the 1890s a new prospect seemed to open up: the creation in Borneo of a political system along the lines of that developed on the Malay peninsula. The appointment of a British Resident in Brunei was intended to be the first step. In a sense the British would be replacing one set of anomalies by another: a federation of indirectly-ruled territories. They did not succeed, but created a further anomaly. There were now three régimes in northern Borneo, all in different senses British, each differently constituted, and they were not pushed together like the Federated Malay States. It was thus possible for the bifurcated remnant of Brunei to pursue a political destiny that differed from that of Sarawak and Sabah: oil was to make it more different still.

Among the Dutch, *onthouding* had prevailed in the 1830s: in 1838 senior officials in Borneo were forbidden to set foot outside the immediate area of their Residencies. The activities of Brooke, and of another British adventurer, Erskine Murray, at Kutai, prompted a change of policy. 'Borneo has become the *point de mire* [focus] of all kinds of speculative enterprises', J. C. Baud lamented.[17] The Dutch not only protested but sought to affirm their position in Borneo as elsewhere. 'He who is sparing at seedtime cannot expect to reap a rich harvest.'[18] A number of treaties were made with states on the east coast, and a 'Government of Borneo' was set up in 1846 as a gesture against foreign intervention. The British North Borneo Company was also unwelcome to the Dutch, though they finally assented to an agreement in 1891 designed to settle the frontier between the territories they claimed and the three protectorates the British had now established. The Company venture had also precipitated a delimitation involving the Spaniards and the sultanate of Sulu.

SULU AND THE PHILIPPINES

Spain, with whom Sulu so often clashed, had by the late eighteenth century become a minor power, the presence of which generally caused the British no concern, and the friendship of which was desirable in Europe. The Spanish claim to empire in the Philippines was respected, all the more because like the Dutch—indeed perhaps more readily since their empire was based on different principles—they allowed the British real commercial opportunities. Only in Sulu were the British for a while mildly tempted to uphold indigenous independence from Spain. In the end, however, the choice the powers agreed upon was partition. The intervention of new powers prompted a delimitation and rounding-out of the older Spanish, British and Dutch empires in that region as elsewhere. The fate of

[17] Quoted G. Irwin, *Nineteenth-century Borneo*, The Hague, 1955, 155.
[18] Rochussen's words are quoted in ibid., 156.

Sulu was thus in part determined, not only by the policies of the British, but of those who ruled the Philippines, the Spaniards, and, from 1898, the Americans, who later shared power with nationalists mostly from Luzon and the Visayas.

Britain's relations with the Spaniards in the Philippines bore some comparison to its relations with the Dutch in Indonesia. By the late eighteenth century, Spain was no longer in itself a threat, but it could be a prey or an asset to Britain's rivals, the French. In the Seven Years' War (1756–63), the British took Manila. But it was not retained. It was important, if possible, to restore good relations with Spain in Europe, and Britain's policy overseas had to take that into account. The lesson was not lost on the Spaniards, however. It reinforced the dictates of Enlightened Despotism: if they were to retain their territories, they must rule them more efficiently. They must also develop them, and even open them up to foreign commerce. This would include the trade of the British and that of others, too, partly as a balance against the British, but one of which they could not complain.

Though with them there were no British treaties like that of 1824, the Spaniards, like the Dutch, both opened up commerce and consolidated their territorial control. Manila was formally opened in 1834, but had in effect been opened earlier; other ports followed in 1855, and without, for most of the century, effective Spanish competition, British merchants indeed did especially well, exporting rice from Luzon, then turning the Visayas to sugar. The development of the export trade indeed stimulated the development of a primarily mestizo monied élite. Some Spaniards saw the contradictions in their policy. The very steps taken to assure Spain's role were promoting new challenges to it. The colony, Sinibaldo de Mas predicted, would 'emancipate itself violently with the loss of considerable property and many lives'.[19]

The consolidation of Spanish control meanwhile proceeded with some effect. Military-political governments were extended in the mountainous interior of Luzon and by the introduction of steamers the Visayas were protected from the slave-raiding depredations to which they had been desperately exposed. But the southern islands, the source of many of the attackers, were not effectively brought under control. The footholds on Mindanao were indeed extended and the ancient sultanate of Magindanao virtually eliminated. In the Sulu archipelago, however, the position was different.

There, as in some parts of Indonesia, the position was a tripartite one: the British were involved, and they did not, as in the north, squarely back the Spaniards. Indeed, the Spaniards, apprehensive of them, were driven to a mixture of assertions of control over the inhabitants and diplomatic concessions to foreign powers. Their assertions of control failed to establish a firm position for them in the Sulu sultanate. There was a legacy of hostility between the missionary power and the Islamic sultanate, and the Spaniards had no Dutch-style success with an inveigling network of treaty

[19] Extract in E. H. Blair and J. A. Robertson, eds, *The Philippine Islands*, Cleveland, 1903–9, LII, 89.

relationships with what was in any case a segmented state. Treaties were made, but distrust on both sides reduced their effect. Convulsive military incursions were neither supportive nor in themselves decisive. Furthermore, the Sulus were able to engage in relations with other powers, including the British, uninhibited by the formality of a treaty like that of 1824. Even when the British, and indeed other powers, finally abandoned the Sulus to their fate, the Spaniards did not secure effective control.

At the outset of the period, some British authorities had been interested in limiting Spanish control in the Moro lands and in establishing themselves there. Before the conquest of Manila, Alexander Dalrymple, an emissary of the Madras government of the East India Company, obtained the cession of Balambangan, and after the return of Manila the Company determined, after much hesitation, to occupy the island as a base for trade in Southeast Asia. The settlement came to an early end in 1775, attacked by Sulus who were possibly encouraged by Spanish intrigues. It was reoccupied temporarily during the Napoleonic Wars, and Raffles was also interested in the area, in particular in Marudu Bay in northern Borneo. It was again this area that initially attracted James Brooke's attention and, even though he was to concentrate on Sarawak and Brunei, he did not forget the north. In 1849, as commissioner, he visited Sulu, and made a treaty with the sultan along the lines of that he had recently made with Brunei. Spain protested. The British government did not ratify the treaty. They were affected by criticism of Brooke, as elsewhere; they also wished to avoid offending Spain because of its European significance. Spain had indeed pointed out that France had desisted from a challenge in Basilan.

The Brooke venture precipitated a new Spanish expedition to Sulu, but no regular establishment of Spanish control. Piracy, the penetration of Islamic revivalism, the threat of other powers—in particular the evidence of German interest—all prompted the Spaniards to further and unprecedentedly violent action in Sulu in the 1870s. It was in this crisis for the sultanate that the North Borneo concessionaires secured a *pajak* or lease of the possessions the sultan claimed there, and the Chartered Company was seen as ruling initially in the names of the sultans of Brunei and Sulu. The partition was taken further in 1885 by agreement among the European powers. The Spaniards undertook not to support the Sultan of Sulu's claims over northern Borneo. Though critical of Spain's anti-Islamic violence, the British abandoned their half-hearted attempts to sustain the independence of the sultan, already partly compromised in a protocol of 1877. The Anglo-Spanish deal was the more readily made because of the interest of the Germans in the area. They had protested against Spain's violence, but insisted they wanted only guarantees of commercial access. The British went along with this so as to secure such guarantees, but also to prevent more extensive German action. The effect was, however, to spur Spain to greater, though still unsuccessful, efforts to establish effective control. Dalrymple, Brooke and others had talked of sustaining a neutral Sulu, but partition and partial absorption had ensued, substantially because the British had not been prepared to challenge the Spaniards, and had preferred them to the Germans.

The British were interested, too, in the outcome of the Spanish-

American War in the Philippines (1898). As the Spaniards had feared, internal opposition had coincided with foreign intervention, as it had to a degree at the time of the British occupation of Manila in the 1760s. It was not British intervention this time, but American. There was little chance of effectively resisting it. Nor indeed, their predominance damaged, could the British interpose. Their preferred solution was the continuation of Spanish control. If that were impossible, then in their view American control was preferable to German. In the event the Germans were left with the Carolines and Pellews, the Americans with the Philippines. But in Luzon they had to contend with the nationalist opposition, brought under control by a mixture of violence and co-option. In the Moro lands the Americans initially made a new treaty with the Sultan of Sulu, only later proceeding to assertion of direct control—in fact again applying a great deal of violence and leaving the sultan with a nominal religious authority. The nationalist government of Quezon refused to recognize a successor on Sultan Jamal-ul-Kiram's death in 1936, and the sultanate thus ceased to exist, except in respect of a claim to North Borneo. But its lands were not fully integrated into the Philippines. In the 1920s there had been talk of separating them and a Briton had dreamed of a Federated Sulu States Union, in some sense a new version of older neutrality proposals, but equally 'visionary'.[20]

The Germans had assented to the Sulu deal of the 1880s reluctantly. That was the period of Bismarck's colonial ventures and of the Berlin conference, contributing to Britain's establishment of the protectorates in Borneo, in turn leading to the settlement of the Borneo frontier with the Dutch in 1891. German activity also helped to define another frontier. Bismarck's colonial policy had launched Germany into New Guinea. Its demonstration of interest precipitated the Queensland annexation of the southeastern coast and the hoisting of the British flag at Port Moresby late in 1884; a settlement with the Germans followed in 1885. The Dutch had claimed the western side of the territory, in part as appanage of the sultanate of Tidore, and in 1828, apprehensive of British moves in northern Australia, had made a settlement at Triton Bay. In the late 1840s, again apprehensive of the British, they had arrogated rights over the interior. In 1895 they reached a boundary agreement with the British, and the Germans also accepted a boundary line at 141 degrees east. What became yet another post-colonial frontier was established by agreement among colonial powers. In 1902 the Dutch established a post at Merauke, designed to restrain the raids of the Tugeri tribes into their territory. The realm now extended, as the nationalists were to say, from Sabang to Merauke.

BRITISH MALAYA

Some suspicion of German intentions, more certainly a wish to take precautionary steps against foreign intervention, played a part in Britain's

---

[20] N. Tarling, *Sulu and Sabah*, Kuala Lumpur, 1978, 323–4.

policy towards the Malay peninsula. There the arrangement with the Dutch in 1824 contrived to exclude them from a territory with which they, like previous archipelagic powers, had long been concerned. But if the fortunes of archipelago and peninsula were thus unprecedentedly separated, that did not mean that British rule was necessarily to be established on the peninsula, nor did it prescribe the form such rule might take if it were. British interests could be sufficiently met for a time at least without it: with Penang, acquired in 1786, Melaka, finally transferred in 1824, and Singapore, occuped in 1819, Britain commanded the straits. It had no great economic interest in the interior until the development of a new demand for tin from the 1840s and for rubber at the turn of the century. Nor for some decades was there any risk of intervention by other European powers, which the presence of the British in the Straits Settlements tended to ward off anyway.

There was, however, a sense in which, as with the archipelago, the political situation was a tripartite one: it involved the British, the Malay states, and in this case not another European state, but an Asian one, Siam. Britain's intervention in the peninsula was partly defined by its perception of its relations with Siam and by the policies that Siam itself followed in the increasingly colonial world of the nineteenth century. The effect was initially to contribute further to the removal of the Malay states from the international ambit, but ultimately to produce a partition that, however inappropriate in terms of history or ethnicity, was to form the frontier of a post-colonial state. In a sense indeed the situation was more than tripartite. Siam was seen, and saw itself, in a larger international context: first that of the old Chinese-dominated system of international relations, second that of the new imperialist one. The outcome on the Malay peninsula is not fully explained, therefore, without an exploration of Siam's position.

Nor is it fully explained without recognizing that, though the British avoided formal intervention in the peninsula till the 1870s, and in the case of a majority of states till later still, they did intervene in a number of other less formal ways. Not only did their presence in the Straits Settlements help to insulate the peninsular states from contact with other European powers. Local merchants, local officials, local Chinese interests, Malay aristocrats and rulers themselves, tied the Straits Settlements and some of the states together, and helped to determine the form and scope of intervention and the pace of its arrival. The British-influenced Malay sultanates that provided the framework of twentieth-century Malaya were shaped in the nineteenth century.

In the French Wars, the settlement of the Dutch at Melaka had been taken over, and their prospective return under the convention of 1814 had stimulated the interest of the British East India Company's authorities at Penang in the fate of the neighbouring states: the Dutch might seek to re-establish a monopoly of the tin from Perak and Selangor. But the Thais were another factor. For them Kedah had a strategic importance, in view of their long struggles with Burma; and both the assertiveness of a new dynasty, and the ambitions of its southern viceroy at Nakhon Sithammarat (Ligor), encouraged them to extend their tributary relationship even beyond it. The rulers of Kedah had hoped to secure the support of the English, to whom Penang and later Province Wellesley, a strip of mainland territory, had been ceded, but in vain. In 1816 the Sultan of Kedah, as a Siamese vassal, had been instructed to invade Perak to secure tribute, and he refused to approve the cession to the Company of Pangkor, suggested by John Anderson, an official at Penang, as a depot for the tin trade of that settlement.

In 1821 the Thais themselves invaded Kedah. Some officials in Penang advocated intervention against them.

> We have become a preponderating power on this side of India and we ought to hold in our hands the scales of justice, to protect the weaker power against the usurpations of the stronger, to mediate between them all on every occasion when our interference can be effectual, and even at times to exhibit a tone of superiority to check the extravagant pretensions of the different states.[21]

Anderson himself suggested appointing a Resident in Kedah on the model of the Indian subsidiary alliances. But the government in India, then the immediate superior of the Straits authorities, refused to countenance on the peninsula the kind of policy it adopted on the subcontinent, or the kind of political structure it utilized, though Governor Robert Fullerton now argued that the removal of the Dutch from Melaka under the treaty of 1824 would simply open the way more fully to the Thais.

The war between the Company and Burma led, however, to negotiations between the British and the Thais at Bangkok. Before they began, Anderson was sent to Perak and Selangor, and the sultan of the former offered him Pangkor. At Bangkok, however, the negotiator, Henry Burney, secured less than the Penang authorities wanted. Pattani, which the Thais had overrun, was not brought into the discussions, though the Thais did agree not to obstruct the commerce of Kelantan and Terengganu, which they also claimed, and in effect a kind of frontier was thus delimited. The Sultan of Kedah, whom they had displaced, was not restored, but the Sultan of Perak was left himself to decide whether he would send tribute to Siam or not. A further emissary from Penang, James Low, persuaded him not to do so, and secured the cession of Pangkor. But this agreement was disapproved in Calcutta, as was a subsequent naval-military action, directed against pirates on the Perak coast but also designed to assist the ruler. The prime task, the Governor-General in Council insisted, was to sustain good relations with Siam, now based on the Burney treaty of 1826.

In subsequent years, nevertheless, the straits authorities managed still to intervene in the Malay states. They could do this only by indirect means, and their efforts tended in effect to preserve the states by working on and through them. In fact they enhanced the power of at least some of the rulers, who reacted positively to the changes that were taking place and the approaches that were made. In general the process made it more likely that the future association between the British and the peninsula

---

[21] Minute by Clubley, 16 Sept. 1823, Straits Settlements Factory Records G/34/91, India Office Library.

would centre on relationships with the Malay rulers. But these relationships, as they developed, differed from state to state.

In the Burney treaty, the British had not only failed to secure the restoration of the Sultan of Kedah, but had committed themselves to keeping him away from the vicinity of the sultanate. This they did not achieve, but the local authorities co-operated with the Thais in dealing with two 'piratical' descents on the Thai-ruled sultanate that his followers organized in 1831 and 1838. These attacks helped to persuade the Thais to change their policy, and the attitude of the British made it easier for them to accept Governor Bonham's mediation that led to the sultan's restoration as a Thai vassal. 'England is a great nation', Rama III (r. 1824–53) declared. 'We have made a treaty with her. She has shown herself to possess enough moral obligations, and is unlikely to undertake any uncalled-for measure.'[22] Kedah thus came to represent the tripartite sharing of authority in its own way: Thai supremacy, Malay rule, British influence. In Kelantan and Terengganu, Burney had avoided definitely recognizing Thai supremacy. The British tried to fend off its effective implementation by naval deployment ostensibly against pirates in the early 1830s, but they exerted less influence than in Kedah.

In Johor they exerted more. Ibrahim, the ruler, lived on Singapore island. He also saw the advantages in an association with British commerce and influence. He worked with the merchants in developing the state and with the authorities against piracy. Indeed he persuaded his neighbour, the ruler of Pahang, also to work against piracy and the slave trade. From this time, in fact, the rulers of peninsular Johor, though seen as parvenus by other Malay rulers, had a special association with the British. Indirectly, however, it provoked another clash with the Thais and a readjustment of the tripartite relationship.

The association between the British and Ibrahim of Johor was in some degree self-defeating as a means of extending peace and order on the peninsula. Other rulers were jealous of his special position. The heir to the old sultanate of Johor, recognized by Raffles in order to confirm the occupation of Singapore, had to be bought off in the treaty of 1855. More significant, the ruler of Terengganu, Omar (r. 1839–76), anxious to develop his own connexion with the British, resented their focus on Ibrahim. Governor E. A. Blundell wanted to respond. He solicited the Indian government's sanction for 'occasional visits to the independent Rajas around us, thereby establishing a more friendly intercourse and removing any misapprehension or obstacles that may exist. Such visits should be wholly devoid of any political aspect, and be merely paid as the marks of amity and friendship.'[23] He suggested also that Sultan Omar should send some of his sons to be educated at Singapore, where the Rev. B. P. Keasberry had established in his boarding school a separate school of noblemen, to which the rulers of Kedah and Johor were sending their scions.

---

[22] Quoted Kobkua Suwannathat-Pian, *Thai-Malay Relations*, Singapore, 1988, 90.
[23] Blundell to Secretary, 27 May 1856, Board's Collections 189619, p.67, F/4/2692, India Office Library.

Civil war in Pahang tested the policy, for Ibrahim and Omar intervened on opposing sides. Blundell's successor, Cavenagh, initially criticized Ibrahim, then backed him. Omar, previously apprehensive of the Thais, changed his attitude. Cavenagh authorized a naval bombardment of Terengganu in November 1862. It was this that helped to produce a new arrangement on the peninsula, though not the one that the governor had sought. Despite the bombardment, Ibrahim's opponents were victorious in Pahang, partly through invoking the support of the ex-sultan of Lingga, descendant of the rulers of the old Johor empire, and he finally accepted a revised frontier between that state and his own. Because of the bombardment, the British accepted the Thai claim to supremacy in Terengganu that they had earlier avoided explicitly acknowledging. The Thais had protested, and the British government listened. Moreover, the Colonial Office, responsible for the Straits Settlements after 1867, ignored the legacy of its predecessors, the Company and the India Office; its governor, Harry Ord, found it convenient to work through the Thais. Though Omar had tried to imitate Ibraham—who opened a direct contact with London in 1866—the northern states were now seen as part of the patrimony of Siam, where indeed by this time the British government had formal representation. The settled condition of Kedah, Terengganu and Kelantan was, Ord even inferred, largely the result of the Thai supremacy.

The violence of 1862, followed by the shift to Colonial Office authority, thus led to a break in the traditional attitude to the northeastern states over which Siam claimed supremacy, and indeed to a misinterpretation of the sequence of events that had created contemporary conditions in those states. This change of attitude did not, however, destroy what previous history had brought about. The northern states had been preserved from Siamese occupation and their rulers had a place in the pattern of Anglo-Thai relations. The ultimate transfer of Siamese rights to the British and the advisory position they assumed in the early twentieth century were thus prepared in the days of the Company and India Office governors. Though arrangements and attitudes changed in the 1860s, that did not obscure the long-term connexion of British and Malay rulers that ultimately prevailed south of the Pattani line that Burney had seen as the limit of negotiation.

Whatever the source of the orderliness of the northern states, it meant Ord was more concerned with Perak and Selangor. Those states had less effective structures and less effective rulers, and the instructions of the superior authorities had prevented intervention on the scale required for dealing with the issues raised by the expansion of tin-mining and Chinese immigration from the 1840s. Cavenagh had contrived to intervene in Perak in 1862 on the basis of the Anderson treaty of 1825, but, though he pressed for increased powers, he could not obtain them from his superiors. Nor could Ord. Only in 1873 did the Colonial Office authorize his successor, Sir Andrew Clarke, to consider intervention in the west-coast states.

The motives of the Colonial Office no doubt included its concern for order, the precondition for trade. Still more, it was concerned over the possibility of foreign intervention, which would undermine the strategic control of the straits that had been one of the main achievements of 1824.

Foreign intervention was perhaps unlikely, given the appearance of British predominance; private interests, benefiting from the very absence of foreign competition, may have exaggerated the risk. Evidence of actual interest in the region on the part of other Europeans is also lacking. There had been rumours back in 1870 that the North German Confederation was seeking a naval station in the Pangkor area; but they were apparently no more than rumours and were not taken seriously. Possibly no definite evidence is needed: the changes in Europe, in particular the creation of the Second Reich (1871), may have aroused apprehensions, or at least suggested a need to take precautions; and that may suffice for motivation in a world that was clearly changing and in which old certainties were being undermined. The concern expressed by Lord Kimberley (previously Lord Wodehouse) over the German presence in Sulu from the early 1870s may, however, have made him more conscious of a need for precaution on the peninsula.

That the Colonial Secretary saw a connexion between events in the Sulu region and events in the peninsula region is again suggested by his attitude to the chartering of the North Borneo Company. A principal aim was to keep North Borneo free of other powers. One possible occupant was Germany and one major objection was its newly-adopted tariff structure. The other issue was security. 'She is not a weak state like the Netherlands whom we can easily influence, and her presence near the Malay Peninsula might seriously weaken and embarrass our position by unsettling the minds of the natives.'[24] 'The Germans would be a too powerful neighbour, and their presence in Borneo would exercise a disturbing influence in the Malay Peninsula.'[25] The security of British interests in the two regions Kimberley saw as indivisible. If these were arguments about Borneo, they were also arguments about the peninsula. In a number of states, however, intervention did not seem to be required at least for the time being: Johor, for example, and the 'Siamese' states, too, though partly because of the concern to sustain Siam's own independence, which others might undermine if Britain showed the way.

Intervention thus was limited in geographical scope: the British went only as far as they needed. It was also limited in form. The Pangkor engagement of 1874 involved the appointment of Residents, who would give advice which the rulers had to take on all matters except religion and custom. The notion had been present with Anderson in the 1820s and had an Indian background. But what was surely in official minds was the example of Johor, the ruler of which seemed readily to accept more informal advice. In fact the experience and conditions of the west-coast states were different, and the assumption that it would be sufficient to give advice albeit on a more formal basis proved mistaken. The murder of the first Resident in Perak, J. W. W. Birch, prompted, however, a punitive expedition. Paradoxically this contributed to the maintenance of the tradition of advice and guidance. The Colonial Office, especially Lord

---

[24] Memorandum by Kimberley, 13 July 1880, FO 12/55; CO 144/54 [10768], Public Record Office, London.
[25] Memorandum, 22 Oct. 1880, PRO 30/29/143, Public Record Office, London.

Carnarvon, blamed the crisis not upon its own or Clarke's mistakes, but on his successor Jervois's advocacy of annexation, and refused to admit that its original conception of Residents was inadequate. The Perak War was in itself an education: it meant that advice would be accepted, and that the idea could be upheld since it was not the practice. So, again, a tradition built up before 1867 remained part of the pattern of twentieth-century Malaya. The installation of a Resident with long experience of Brunei perhaps also contributed to the success of the system, and it was applied to Pahang in 1888, against the background of increasing activity by European powers in Southeast Asia as a whole and by European concessionaires in Pahang in particular. There, however, it produced tension and disturbance. This helped to lead in 1895 to the creation of the Federated Malay States. Although some saw this as a model for Borneo, in fact it created a central government that made the concept of advice ever more myth than reality. When in 1909 Siam transferred its rights over the northern states, they accepted Advisers not Residents, indeed only with reluctance, and did not enter the so-called federation.

BRITAIN AND BURMA

Britain's policy towards Malaya had been affected by its interests in India and China. The former affected its attitude to Burma more deeply, but it was also shaped by the attitude of the Burman monarchs. There were issues relating to trade, and more serious issues relating to possible foreign intervention: but the respective attitudes to interstate relations perhaps presented a greater difficulty even than the latter. The British built a territorial raj in India, which had its own imperatives for foreign policy, differing indeed from those of Britain itself. Within India it could contemplate no challenge; on its frontiers it insisted on compliance. The attitude of the Burmans—particularly in view of the successes of the Alaungpaya dynasty—was too assertive to fit into such a pattern. These differences lay behind the conflicts that marked the course of Anglo-Burman relations. The result was the stage-by-stage annexation of the kingdom to the Indian empire. For a while it had seemed possible that the independence of the core of the old kingdom could have been preserved. But even Mindon Min (r. 1853–78) was reluctant to accept the degree of subordination paradoxically required, and his successor's government, less wise, coincided with a period of general international insecurity and a phase of particular French expansiveness that encouraged the British to take precautionary measures.

British contacts with Burma had been limited by the Dutch in the days of their predominance in seaward Asia. Then they were affected by the eighteenth-century rivalry with the French on the continent of India. The creation of a British dominion in India was greatly to affect British relations with the kingdom that Alaungpaya was recreating and that defeated the Mon revolt of the 1740s. The French threat again precipitated action. From bases in southern Burma they might affect the security of British India. Their settlement at Syriam prompted the British to settle at

Negrais. The opposition of Alaungpaya (r. 1752–60) to both, and the destruction of French power in India, virtually ended the British contacts; though the French were to use bases at Mergui and Rangoon in the next war, the British had few relations with Burma in the subsequent years. But while their power extended in India, the Burman kings, after sacking Ayutthaya, conquered Arakan, and this brought the two empires in contact again. The questions that now arose, difficult in themselves, were more intractable because of the political attitudes fostered in the interim.

One issue indeed arose from the conquest of Arakan itself. Refugees fled into British territory: the British were reluctant to return them, but unable to prevent their using British territory as a base for counter-attacks on the Burmans. A new war with the French led the governor-general to try to improve relations with the Burman court by sending Michael Symes on a mission to King Bodawpaya (r. 1782–1819). He was told that Burma could not deal with a subordinate government like Bengal, and warned the Company's authorities there of the 'characteristic pride and unbounded arrogance' of the Burmans, which might lead to further acts of aggression: they had 'an extravagant opinion of their own power', respecting British power less than the powers of the subcontinent itself. Symes thought that the British should make 'reasonable allowance for their mistaken principles', preserving a good understanding, but avoiding a close connexion: 'it is to our interest to maintain their independence, and to guard it from foreign encroachment.'[26] On the advice of William Francklin, Governor-General Wellesley subsequently considered making a 'subsidiary alliance' with Burma on the Indian model, and Symes was sent on a second mission. It was entirely vain. The Burmans were proud of their success, though also suspicious of British designs: they sought to evade a connection with the British, and with Bengal.

The British were anxious to check French influence. Continued Burman independence might be a sufficient guarantee against it, insulating their empire in India from direct contact with foreign powers. But they really wanted more. The British needed, as Symes had put it even on his first visit, to guard that independence. Further, they could not accept a challenge from the Burmans themselves that might by example undermine subsidiary relations on the subcontinent itself. The Burmans could retain their view of the world only in a kind of isolation that could no longer exist: even a distanced relationship of the kind Symes had at first envisaged was now outdated. Could a new balance be attained, given the very different concepts the two states had of their proper relationship? A subsequent British-Indian emissary, John Canning, reported that the king was not partial to the French: at most they were seen as a counterpoise to the English. In any case the French were soon to be defeated again. The other Burman perception remained. 'It seems that [the king] will treat with no power on earth as an equal . . . He will grant a boon but will not make a treaty.'[27] 'It might contribute to the future tranquillity of our eastern territory', the Governor-General in Council ominously commented in

[26] M. Symes, *An Account of an Embassy to the Kingdom of Ava*, London, 1800, 463–4.
[27] Quoted D. G. E. Hall, *Europe and Burma*, London, 1945, 96.

1812, if the Burman government were 'led to form a just estimate of the greatness of our power and the weakness of its own'.[28]

Though the issue of the Arakanese refugees died away, additional frontier issues emerged in Assam, Manipur, Cachar, and in March 1824 Governor-General Amherst pre-empted a talked-of Burman invasion by declaring war on Burma. He echoed the attitude earlier assumed in Calcutta: 'no permanent security from the aggression of the Burmese . . . can be safely calculated on, until that people shall have been made to feel the consequences of their provoking the British Government to depart from the pacific tone of policy it has hitherto pursued.'[29] The essential aim of the war was not to acquire territory, but 'to produce such an impression of the power and resources of the British Empire in India as will deter the Court of Ava from any attempt again to disturb the friendly relations which may be re-established by the result of the present contest'.[30] Amherst sought a balance: 'The Burmese had to be punished sufficiently so that they would not trouble British security again, and yet not so much as to turn them into a permanent and unreasoning foe who would be persistently troublesome in the future.'[31]

An initially ill-conducted campaign produced no immediate victory. The terms of peace were as a result stepped up to ensure tangible proofs of British success: otherwise 'the powers of India might have been tempted to believe the British Government had at last encountered an enemy which it had failed to humble'.[32] The First Anglo-Burman War ended with the treaty of Yandabo, finally secured in 1826, in which the Burmans ceded Arakan, Assam and Tenasserim, and agreed to cease interference in Manipur and Cachar. They also agreed to pay an indemnity, to receive a Resident at Ava, to send an ambassador to Calcutta. The British thus insulated their empire on the subcontinent from both foreign challenge and native insolence by acquiring much of the Burma coast. But this was hardly consistent with a friendly relationship with the rest of Burma unless, as Amherst had envisaged, the Burmans accepted the other implications of their defeat. In fact the old attitude remained.

Sent to follow up with a commercial treaty, John Crawfurd recommended against appointing a Resident: he would be an object of jealousy to a government 'indescribably ignorant and suspicious'.[33] Better, again, a stand-off, since the alternative was not compliance but conflict; better a distancing in which the Burmans could indulge their fancies. Disputes along the new frontiers led the Company, however, to revise Crawfurd's policy—perhaps conflict, arising anyway, could be thus avoided—and Burney was sent to Ava in 1830. The Manipur boundary was settled in

[28] Quoted G. P. Ramachandra, 'Anglo-Burmese Relations, 1795–1826', Ph.D. thesis, University of Hull, 1977, 279.
[29] Quoted G. P. Ramachandra, 'The Outbreak of the first Anglo-Burmese War', JMBRAS, 51, 2 (1978) 82.
[30] Quoted Ramachandra, 'Anglo-Burmese Relations', 391.
[31] L. Kitzan, 'Lord Amherst and Pegu: The Annexation Issue, 1824–1826', JSEAS, 8, 2 (1977) 182.
[32] Quoted Ramachandra, 'Anglo-Burmese Relations', 433.
[33] Quoted W. S. Desai, History of the British Residency in Burma 1826–1840, Rangoon, 1939, 50.

Burma's favour, though the indemnity remained. But, albeit Burney was able to establish good relations, King Bagyidaw remained 'full of the most ungovernable pride and arrogance ... most unwilling to admit the British Government as equal to his in pride and strength'. For him the presence of a Resident was 'a proof of our supremacy and a badge of his servility and vassalage'.[34] In a sense he was right: he did not wish to be reminded of it.

Unrealistic in a different way, the king's successor, Tharrawaddy (r. 1838–46), refused to bind himself to his predecessor's treaties. 'I am determined to place the relations between the two countries on precisely the same footing as they were previous to the reign of the late King who committed a blunder in going to war with you, and all of those acts I wish to have annulled and forgotten.'[35] Burney finally left the capital. He thought the king should be made to acknowledge the treaty and the authority of the governor-general, if need be by force, the British taking the opportunity 'of establishing a more extensive influence and control over the Court of Ava, and of placing our relations with this country on a more solid and secure footing'.[36] Burney's successor Benson also advocated force. Lord Auckland, the governor-general, opposed its use. The British had 'to make allowances for the prejudices and the headstrong pride of a new dynasty clinging in its intercourse with foreign nations to the distasteful usages of former times and vaunting its resolution to revert to them'.[37] Moreover, the British had greater problems on the northwest frontier. Auckland's concern with Afghanistan in fact led the Indian government to leave Anglo-Burman relations once more on a stand-off basis.

Complete isolation was not possible, however: there were trade as well as frontier contacts, and it was always possible that the escalation of a dispute would again open up the question of Anglo-Burman relations, laid to uneasy rest by the Afghan war. The Second Anglo-Burman War indeed emerged from a conflict between British traders and the Burman governor at Rangoon, over which the Bengal authorities acted firmly and a combustible commodore highhandedly. The war was the subject of Richard Cobden's critical pamphlet, 'How Wars are Got up in India'. But the governor-general, Lord Dalhousie, though annexationist in India, was perhaps less the aggressive empire-builder in Burma than the defender of British prestige on the subcontinent, which encouraged a concept of policy that differed from that of the commercial and manufacturing interests at home: 'the Government of India could never, consistently with its own safety, permit itself to stand for a single day in an attitude of inferiority towards a native power, and least of all towards the Court of Ava.' 'We can't afford to be shown to the door anywhere in the East.'[38] The second war was far more efficiently conducted than the first. But what was to represent the British victory this time? Dalhousie believed that the retention of Pegu, though ruled out at the end of the first war, was now 'the

---

[34] Quoted Desai, 71, 196.
[35] Quoted Desai, 296.
[36] Quoted Desai, 309.
[37] Quoted Desai, 390.
[38] Quoted D. G. E. Hall, ed., *The Dalhousie-Phayre Correspondence 1852–1856*, London, 1932, pp. xviii, xix.

only adequate measure for the punishment of the Burmese, for the reimbursement of expenses, and for ensuring future peace by crippling Burman power'.[39] The authorities in London wanted an Anglo-Burman treaty as well. That, however, Dalhousie thought would be superfluous: indeed it would invite further quarrels. The Burmans would, moreover, not readily sign it without a further advance to their capital, possibly involving the occupation of all Burma, which would be difficult and expensive.

Dalhousie's policy was in the event followed: the new king of Burma would in any case sign no treaty. The governor-general clearly implied that, while occupying the rest of Burma would be a burden for the British, it would not be necessary, since the reduced kingdom was likely to be compliant. Though signing no treaty, Mindon Min indeed sought to develop good relations with the British. Complimentary missions were exchanged in 1854–5 between the Burman capital and Calcutta, and new commercial treaties made in 1861 and 1867, so that steamers ran up the Irrawaddy and gained British trade back-door access to China. Mindon Min also engaged in measures of 'defensive westernisation'.[40] In themselves, those need not worry the British. More risky was his decision to develop relations with other powers. The mission to the United States of 1857 resulted in no treaty. The mission to Europe in 1872–3 led to a commercial treaty with France, though the French did not at first ratify it because of British concern over Mindon's desire for arms and for an offensive-defensive alliance. There were overtures to Russia in 1874. Mindon was asserting the status of Burma as an independent power. But he risked losing what remained of it: the British could contemplate only less than full independence for Burma and that the Burmans had to accept, if not formally recognize, if they were not to lose all.

Relations also deteriorated because of the 'shoe question'. Generally, British envoys had removed their shoes before a royal reception. Once an envoy made an issue of it in 1875, however, the British could not continue the practice. While from 1862 the British had a Resident at Mandalay, Mindon's capital, there was as a result less opportunity for him to resolve issues after 1875. In 1879 the Resident was withdrawn after the murder of Sir L. Cavagnari in Kabul. The way was more open than ever to court intriguers; open, too, to the increasing number of European adventurers and concessionaires that were penetrating into still independent parts of Southeast Asia.

The new king, Thibaw Min (r. 1878–85), missed perhaps the best opportunity of putting Anglo-Burman relations back on a satisfactory basis. Lord Ripon proposed a commercial treaty between India and Burma and a friendship treaty between Queen Victoria and Thibaw, which would at least meet the Burman desire for a connection with London, such as Mindon Min had pointed out Siam enjoyed. The opportunity was lost:

---

[39] Quoted ibid., p. xxv.
[40] Oliver B. Pollak, *Empires in Collision: Anglo-Burmese Relations in the mid-nineteenth century*, Westport, 1979, 113–14.

those at Mandalay opposed to improving Anglo-Burman relations, and so bringing back the Resident, pointed to the challenge that Britain was facing in Egypt as a reason for going no further. Adding rashness to unwisdom, the Burmans sent a mission to Europe, and its negotiations in France aroused British suspicions. The 1873 treaty with France was ratified. There was a supplementary commercial convention which Jules Ferry hoped Britain would interpret as a French 'desire to obtain something in independent upper Burma, where she was so jealous of her influence. This would make her more amenable to a trade-off which would enable us, should the occasion arise, to secure advantages in Siam, or at least a means of holding the British in check in the Malay peninsula.'[41]

Moreover, in January 1885 Ferry gave the Burman ambassadors a secret letter, offering to make arrangements for arms supplies when Tonkin had been pacified by the French. The letter was made public later in the year through the efforts of Andreino, the Italian consul in Mandalay who, as agent for the Bombay-Burmah Timber Company and the Irrawaddy Flotilla Company, had his own reasons for wishing to undermine a French connexion. The British determined on an ultimatum. Lord Randolph Churchill declared:

> It is French intrigue which has forced us to go to Burmah; but for that element we might have treated Theebaw with severe neglect . . . If you finally and fully add Burmah to your dominions before any European rights have had time even to be sown, much less grow up, you undoubtedly prevent forever the assertion of such rights, or attempts to prepare the way for such assertion.[42]

The occasion for the ultimatum was a commercial dispute involving leases by the Bombay-Burmah Timber Company, but the main concern of the British authorities was strategic. There were French and Italian speculators and concessionaires in Mandalay, but it was the political rather than the commercial implications of their activities that aroused concern. Despite the arguments presented by the late D. P. Singhal, the clue to British policy is, as Hugh Tinker pointed out, provided by a later remark of Lord Curzon's:

> India is like a fortress . . . with mountains for her walls . . . beyond these walls . . . extends a glacis of varying breadth and dimension. We do not want to occupy it, but we cannot afford to see it occupied by our foes. We are quite content to let it remain in the hands of our allies and friends, but if rivals and unfriendly influences creep up to it . . . we are compelled to intervene.[43]

The Third Anglo-Burman War relates to 'imperialism', inasmuch as one factor in precipitating it was the growth of European political rivalry and concession-hunting. But it related more clearly to a long-standing Indian

---

[41] Statement by Francois Deloncle, 1897, quoted P. J. N. Tuck, *French Catholic Missionaries and the Politics of Imperialism in Vietnam, 1857–1914*, Liverpool, 1987, 233.

[42] Quoted G. Keeton, *King Thebaw and the Ecological Rape of Burma*, Delhi, 1974, 243.

[43] Quoted H. Tinker, reviewing D. P. Singhal, *The Annexation of Upper Burma*, JSEAH 1, 2 (1960) 106.

political concern than to a movement in British public opinion. Burma must not challenge British prestige; still less must it be the scene of activity by another power.

In the days of British predominance, Burma's position had been insecure, since the rulers of India wanted it to assume a position of less than complete independence: its failure to do so led to partition. The advent of European rivals in the later nineteenth century gave Burma a temptation, not an opportunity: attempts to play off other foreigners against the rulers of India could bring only disaster. Ferry's scheme did nothing for France; it led to the end of Burma's independence.

In the two-week Third Anglo-Burman War, the British-Indian forces quickly occupied Mandalay, and King Thibaw was exiled. Lord Dufferin, Viceroy of India, now faced the problem which Dalhousie had avoided. His answer was annexation rather than protectorate. There was a vacuum in Mandalay and it was essential to provide against European intrigue. The Viceroy also thought annexation the best means of securing peace and prosperity. But he was mistaken: a long programme of pacification had to follow. Snodgrass, who fought in the First Anglo-Burman War, had criticized those who had thought that the conquest of the capital 'would have had a good effect upon the whole Eastern world'.[44] Dalhousie, governor-general during the second war, thought the entire subjugation of Burma would be 'most injurious to the interests of the British Government'.[45] The contrary view was that the Burmans awaited deliverance at the hands of the British. Brigadier-General George White, accompanying the expeditionary force in the third war, again recognized it was wrong. 'It is a mistake to suppose that these people were anxiously awaiting annexation. The more I see and hear, the more convinced I am that they are very loyal, in their easy-going way, to the house of Alompra.'[46] 'A considerable minority of the population to say the least, did not want us', as Sir Charles Crosthwaite put it.[47] Some resistance was led by real or pretended scions of the house of Alaungpaya, some by local leaders, and the British could not realistically see them as mere dacoits. There was reaction in lower Burma, too.

The establishment of British control in the frontier areas was also a prolonged process. The Shan rulers, for example, had paid tribute to the Burman court, though its influence had declined in the closing years of the dynasty. Their relationship with the new rulers had to be determined. From the outset the general British policy was to allow them autonomy, 'so long as they governed well, promoted trade, and paid a moderate tribute'.[48] Though there was some initial resistance, allegiance was secured on this basis by April 1888. 'The position of the Shan princes was . . . like that of a team of comparatively fine soccer players suddenly finding themselves in an American football game.' Mandalay was now in very different hands.

[44] J. J. Snodgrass, *The Burmese War*, London, 1827, 284.
[45] Quoted Muhammad Shamsher Ali, 'The Beginnings of British Rule in Upper Burma', Ph.D. thesis, London University, 1976, 139.
[46] Quoted ibid., 41.
[47] Quoted M. Aung-Thwin, 'The British "Pacification of Burma"', JSEAS, 16, 2 (1985) 250.
[48] Quoted Ali, 179.

The British set about drawing boundaries, claiming or rejecting areas 'according to the needs of the moment ... trotting out Burmese claims whenever it suited them, or ignoring such claims whenever necessary'.[49]

The frontier itself had to be settled with the Chinese and the French. China regarded Burma as a tributary state, but the British were concerned to avoid a quarrel, and in a convention of July 1886 agreed to send ten-year missions on a basis of equality. The Chinese had in any case been in no position to act, and saw Britain as an ally against France. The Burman kings had damaged their chance of survival by their failure to comply with British requirements, but their prospects had also been dimmed by the advance of French power in Vietnam. That involved the Chinese, too, and indeed they went to war with France.

BRITAIN, FRANCE AND VIETNAM

The French had shown interest in Vietnam as the British began to exclude them from India. The divisions and civil war in Vietnam in the late eighteenth century seemed to give them opportunity. But, once Gia-long (r. 1802–19) had reunited the empire, he sought to diminish foreign contacts, even with the French, and his successors went further still, in particular in their endeavours to exclude Catholic missionaries. The opening of China brought French warships to the area: with little commerce to protect, but concerned for French prestige, they were disposed to protect Christians. In the conflicts that ensued, the British did not intervene. They had sent a number of diplomatic and commercial missions to Vietnam, both before and after the opening of China, but the response was negative, even though they had endeavoured to play down their aggressive Indian image. The British decided that the French venture was acceptable, so long as it did not trench upon the independence of Siam and Laos, and thus upon the security of their interests in Burma, India and Malaya.

Anglo-French rivalry was the context for European intervention in Vietnam, as in Burma, in the mid-eighteenth century. In their contest with the British, the French looked not only to the Mon regions of lower Burma but to the Nguyen lands. A French mission of 1748–51 sought from Vo-Vuong, the southern ruler, a factory in Danang Bay and a repeal of the ban on Christian missionaries. British success in India and China continued to invite French attention to Vietnam. Vergennes argued that the French should pre-empt the English in Cochinchina, as southern Vietnam was called:

> If they decide on that place before us, we will be excluded for ever and we will have lost an important foothold on that part of Asia which would make us masters by intercepting in time of war the English trade with China, by protecting our own in the whole of India, and by keeping the English in a continual state of anxiety.[50]

[49] Chao Tzang Yawnghwe, *The Shan of Burma*, Singapore, 1987, 76–8.
[50] Quoted A. Lamb, *The Mandarin Road to Old Hué*, London, 1970, 64.

The British did indeed decide to send a mission to Cochinchina. But, though European rivalry thus again threatened to involve an independent Asian kingdom, in fact participation in the North American war distracted the French, while Vietnam, with the onset of the Tayson rebellion (1771–1802), seemed too chaotic to sustain Britain's commercial interest in new approaches to China from the south.

Vo-Vuong's grandson, Nguyen Anh, sought French aid in his contest with the Tayson. Even though the French had regained their Indian possessions, lost in the American war, the authorities there, more cautious than subordinates often were, proved reluctant to intervene. Under missionary pressure, however, Louis XVI's government made a treaty with a Nguyen mission in Paris in 1787, offering aid in return for the cession of Danang. Because of the reluctance of the Pondicherry authorities, no official aid eventuated, but Pigneau, head of the Société des Missions Étrangères, secured some volunteer help for the Nguyen cause.

Probably it was superfluous, and Gia-long, as Nguyen Anh became, would have triumphed in any case. But even in the minds of those it may have helped, it tended to associate division in Vietnam with foreign intervention, enhancing the tendency to associate unity with isolation. The Vietnamese, like the Burmans, were aware of British conquests in India; they were aware, too, that European rivalry might, as there, invite intervention. But the ideological preoccupations of Vietnamese rulers went beyond such tactical considerations and made it difficult to perceive, still more difficult to take advantage of, differences and changes of attitude among the Europeans. The British interest in Vietnam was limited: keeping the French out, perhaps opening up commercial opportunities. Unlike Burma, Vietnam was beyond the ambit of Indian considerations and the realm of Indian prestige. Adjusting to British needs could have been reconciled with, even provided for, Vietnam's independence. But meeting negative responses from Vietnam, and disappointed over its trade, the British were to drop their opposition to French settlement, provided it remained within limits.

Anxious to avert the establishment of French influence in newly-reunited Vietnam, Wellesley sent the Roberts mission to Gia-long. But neither then, nor after the French wars, were the Vietnamese open to the further development of French influence, and Gia-long's successor, Minh-mang (r. 1820–40), indeed tried to limit that of the missionaries. The British sent another envoy, Crawfurd, in 1822. He was unsuccessful, and indeed, going even further than the Burman kings, Minh-mang refused to receive him on the ground that he was emissary only of a governor-general. The British took no further action: their purposes in Vietnam differed from their purpose in Burma. The Vietnamese were, as Crawfurd put it, 'far removed from the sphere of our Indian politics'.[51] French influence was non-existent. Vietnam, too, was a feudatory of China, which it was desirable not to offend lest the Company's tea trade at Canton be disturbed as a result. In Burma Crawfurd was to recommend a stand-off. More

---

[51] John Crawfurd, *Journal of an Embassy from the Governor-General of India to the Courts of Siam and Cochin China*, London, 1830, I. 473.

realistically he recommended in respect of Vietnam merely an occasional complimentary mission from the king's government, which might help the indirect trade with China. But an additional commercial contact there was no longer really needed, since opium supplied the investment in China, and no move was made.

The change in Britain's relations with China suggested a change in its relations with those states seen and seeing themselves as its feudatories. The Company lost its monopoly in 1833, and under pressure from the free trade relations deteriorated into the first Anglo-China war. As a result the first of the nineteenth-century 'unequal treaties' was made, treaty ports opened, extraterritorial jurisdiction granted, customs duties limited, Hong Kong acquired. Now, the ex-missionary Charles Gutzlaff argued, was the time for a new mission to Vietnam, sent by the king's government. Sir John Davis, his superior, supported the idea: 'the recent example of China, to which the ultra-Gangetic nations of the Continent of Asia have been in the habit of looking with awe and respect, might influence the latter very favourably in the event of any overtures on our part towards a more extended intercourse'.[52] But his mission of 1847 was entirely vain. Heavy rains gave the Vietnamese a pretext to avoid Davis' visiting the Nguyen capital, Hué: 'we shall . . . part on civil terms at least, and if more progress has not been effected it may be attributed perhaps to the impression made on this timid and cautious people by the late conduct of the French'.[53]

Third parties were indeed involved. One reason was continued Catholic activity on the part of missionaries in defiance of the Nguyen régime. An American ship intervened violently in their favour in 1845. More significant were the French. They had no commerce in East Asia, but like the Americans they had, since the opening of China, ships. Moreover, with the British in occupation of Hong Kong, it seemed necessary for the French also to have a base in East Asian waters. One possibility, Basilan, an island in the southern Philippines, was ruled out by Spanish opposition. Another was to secure Danang, allegedly ceded in 1787. In any case the French navy acted in support of the missionaries, and Danang was the scene of the violence to which Davis referred. Earlier he had hoped that this would assist his mission. But both the Chinese war and the actions of the French and Americans had persuaded the Vietnamese rulers to adhere even more closely to an isolationist policy applied indifferently to all the powers. Not altogether surprisingly, they did not distinguish the different nuance in British policy: the British expanded elsewhere, and might well do so in Vietnam. But undoubtedly ideology and fear of subversion obscured the perception that the British were more powerful in general and more restrained towards Vietnam in particular, and diminished the possibility of improving relations with them and so reinforcing their interest in Vietnam's independence. Isolation was not a realistic policy, nor was playing off one European against another. The best option was to come to terms with the British. But for the Vietnamese, as for the Burmans, that proved impossible, though for different reasons.

[52] Davis to Aberdeen, 1 Aug. 1845, FO 17/100.
[53] Davis to Palmerston, 26 Oct. 1847, FO 17/130.

Similar factors affected the fortunes of John Bowring who, as Superintendent of Trade at Hong Kong, inherited instructions to open up the East Asian countries, and succeeded in Siam. He sent Thomas Wade to investigate the prospect of a favourable reception from the Vietnamese.

> The manner in which this announcement is received will enable me to judge whether it is best I should proceed alone, or wait the period when I can be accompanied by the Ministers of France and the United States. I am disposed to think their presence might be an embarrassment and not a facility in my proceedings.[54]

Wade landed with a single follower and took up residence, 'my hope being that when the authorities found me fairly planted on shore, they would either forward me to the capital, or bring me in contact with some one deputed by the Prime Minister to receive the [Bowring] letter. In this I was disappointed.'[55] Bowring observed that 'the same repulsive and exclusive spirit which characterizes all the Indo-Chinese populations East of the Ganges was displayed in every possible form'.[56]

Disappointed of a purely British approach, Bowring was now prepared to co-operate with the French. Their policy was, however, becoming more extreme. They resorted to violence to secure the reception of their envoy's letter. Later that year the Emperor Tu-duc (r. 1848–83) had a Spanish bishop decapitated to discourage the rest. Napoleon III had been considering missionary proposals for intervention in Vietnam, and this episode provided the occasion. The commission he appointed argued for expansion.

> Force of circumstances seems to have confined France to the European territories which she possesses today. Hence it would be unacceptable if, denied expansion in Europe, she were forced to restrict her capabilities for action to these narrow confines while other maritime nations try to strengthen their power and resources in regions which Providence seems to have held in reserve to receive the superabundant expansionary capacities of Europe.

Other maritime nations could share in the trade, their opposition, if it existed, being thus counteracted. French rule would be welcome to the Vietnamese, too: 'our domination would be a deliverance for them from a hateful yoke'.[57] Danang should be seized to guarantee the execution of a treaty providing for the protection of missionaries and for commercial concessions and an indemnity.

In August 1858 a joint Franco-Spanish expedition seized Danang, but it could not attack Hué overland. Instead it proceeded to Saigon, captured early in 1859. Despite the protests of the missionaries—who wanted action elsewhere and believed there would be a rising against the Nguyen in the north—the French began to concentrate on founding a colony in the south. Even so there was, as the commission had anticipated, no British

---

[54] Bowring to Clarendon, 7 May 1855, FO 17/229.
[55] Memorandum in Wade to Bowring, 17 Sept. 1855, FO 17/233.
[56] Bowring to Clarendon, 8 Oct. 1855, FO 17/233.
[57] Quoted Tuck, 49–52.

opposition. The tripartite relationship had become a dual one, to the disadvantage of Vietnam.

In Hong Kong the *Register* indeed proclaimed that the Anglo-French jealousies of Pigneau's days had died out.

> We may doubt the success of any commercial settlement at Tourane [Danang], but if it is to form a link in the chain of European intercourse with the East, if it is to aid in spreading western civilisation and a more liberal policy in this quarter of the globe, it is not France alone but the whole of commercial Europe that will profit by the step, and we of all others, should be the first to wish the expedition God speed, even though the motives in which it first originated were those of opposition to our own power.[58]

The official British attitude did not differ. The aim was to provide stable conditions for British trade: if the Vietnamese had failed to respond, the French were acceptable. 'They have long had a fancy for locating themselves there', Bowring wrote. 'It will tend to the extension of Trade and there is perhaps no locality where less mischief will be done as regards our interests.'[59] In Europe the British sought to discover the 'ulterior object', if any, of the French. The major concern the British ambassador expressed was over non-Catholic Christianity in Vietnam. Britain had no special interest in Vietnam's commerce, and Vietnam had failed to interest the British in its political independence. There was no good reason to upset good relations with France in Europe by taking up the cause of Vietnam. The French venture in Vietnam might have advantages: its disadvantages could be provided against.

A memorandum prepared for the Indian government after the capture of Danang suggested that French expansion would open Vietnam to commerce. That expansion must be kept within certain limits but could be tolerated so long as Siam and Laos remained independent of France. A French fleet at Danang might indeed check the Russian fleet in the north; an eastern Cherbourg was not 'cause for serious anxiety'.[60] The British Admiralty, however, was to find that the establishment of the French on one side of the seaway to China added to the importance of Labuan and northern Borneo on the other. Perhaps the major immediate impact of the French expedition on British policy was in fact to strengthen a wavering interest in north Borneo. In the longer term, however, the French seemed to be bursting the territorial limits the British favoured.

The French had secured the three eastern provinces of Cochinchina, and then, under local initiative, took over the western provinces, meeting no opposition from the dynasty, though a great deal from the partisans. The colonial authorities were disposed to move north in the 1870s, especially as they realized that the Red (Hong) River might provide the access to China which, as the French naval lieutenant, Doudart de Lagrée, had shown, the

[58] *Hong Kong Register*, 31 Aug., 7 Sept. 1858.
[59] Quoted N. Tarling, *Imperial Britain in South-East Asia*, Kuala Lumpur, 1975, 124–5.
[60] Quoted B. L. Evans, 'The attitudes and policies of Great Britain and China towards French expansion in Cochin-China, Cambodia, Annam and Tongking 1858–83', Ph.D. thesis, University of London, 1961, 41.

Mekong did not, and also because they were apprehensive of the Germans. Paris at first sought to restrain them, then removed its curb. In 1882 a small French expedition was sent to deal with disorder obstructing Red River traffic, and another the following year secured control over lower Tonkin. Defying the Chinese, to whom Hué had appealed, the French established an effective protectorate over the rest of Vietnam. Occupying Tonkin and taking up Vietnamese claims brought the French into Laos, and there they inherited a contest with Siam. By 1893 the crisis of Siam's independence itself seemed to be at hand. In that the British were interested.

THE INDEPENDENCE OF SIAM

Siam was unique in retaining its independence throughout the colonial period. That was a result of its interaction with the policies of the British. Siam was prepared to compromise; and the needs of the British were less urgent than in Burma, less dispensable than in Vietnam. Initially they were restrained by their concern to avoid extension of territory in the Indian style, and to avoid conflict that might endanger the trade to China, to which like Vietnam Siam sent tribute. Local British authorities wanted a more adventurous policy on the Malay peninsula, but were on the whole constrained by their superiors. At the same time the Burney treaty of 1826 showed that the Thais were not entirely negative. The change in the relationship with China suggested a revision of that treaty. But again the British were doubtful and though Sir James Brooke was sent there, they did not take up the intemperate suggestions he made. The result was the peaceful negotiation of a new treaty in 1855. As the Dutch and Spaniards paid a price for their continuance as rulers in Southeast Asia, Siam paid a price for its independence—an 'unequal treaty'. It sought to limit its dependence on the British, without destroying the guarantee offered by a relationship with the strongest of the Western powers, by developing relations with other powers also. In addition it paid a price territorially, in Cambodia, in Laos, in Malaya. But it also effectively sought defensive modernization, again relying primarily, but not merely, on advisers from Britain.

Siam was, to borrow Crawfurd's terms, 'within the pale of our Indian diplomacy' in view of British interest in the 'tributary' states of northern Malaya. But the installation of a British envoy at the Thai capital, Bangkok, would only be a source of irritation, Crawfurd had felt. 'The sea on one quarter, and impracticable mountains and forests on another, are barriers which, together with the fears and discretion of the Siamese Government, will in all likelihood preserve us long at peace with this people'.[61] The Supreme Government in Calcutta had indeed been doubtful about sending Burney to Bangkok:

---

[61] Crawfurd, I. 472.

all extension of our territorial possessions and political relations on the side of the Indo-Chinese nations is, with reference to the peculiar character of those states, to their decided jealousy of our power and ambition, and to their proximity to China, earnestly to be deprecated and declined as far as the course of events and the force of circumstances will permit.[62]

But, under the impulse of the Burma wars, very much part of Indian diplomacy, the governor-general sent the Burney mission. Though no envoy was placed in Bangkok, treaties were made that sought to regulate commerce there and to settle the position of the Malay states in the context of Anglo-Thai relations. Amherst—belligerent over Burma—instructed the Penang officials carefully to abide by the agreements with Siam. They must not exaggerate, he said, the menace involved in the proximity of the Siamese to their settlement.

> Our only national object of policy hereafter in relation to the Siamese should be to endeavour to allay their jealousy of our ultimate views ... and to derive from our connexion with them every attainable degree of commercial advantage, by practising in our intercourse with them the utmost forbearance, temper, and moderation both in language and action, by striving to cultivate a friendly understanding with the Court and its provincial Governors in our neighbourhood, and above all, by faithfully and scrupulously observing the conditions of the treaty which fixes our future relations.[63]

The feudatory status of Siam in relation to China argued, as with Vietnam, for restraint. But it now became in the case of Siam a matter of sustaining an agreement rather than, as in the Vietnamese case, of breaching isolation.

The change in the British relationship with China was an argument for a change in the relationship with Siam as with Vietnam and Japan. Trade had developed at Bangkok in the interim, though British merchants complained of high measurement duties and monopolies, and one of them, Robert Hunter, quarrelled with the government. Gutzlaff argued that a mission to Bangkok should seek to revise the commercial parts of the Burney treaty. The India Board was, however, unwilling to risk the relationship established by it: the Burney treaty was 'sufficient for the objects of trade and Friendship', and the Board doubted 'the policy of risking the advantages possessed under the present treaty in an attempt to obtain greater advantages under a new engagement'.[64] The Singapore merchants pressed the idea, however, and the India Board grudgingly gave in. Palmerston also accepted the notion that Sir James Brooke, currently commissioner and consul-general in Borneo, should undertake the task, and he was given instructions that covered Vietnam as well.

The instructions authorized Brooke to visit Siam if he thought that

---

[62] Governor-General in Council to Governor in Council, 19 Nov. 1824, Straits Settlements Factory Records, G/34/99.

[63] Governor-General in Council to Governor in Council, 23 July 1827, Straits Settlements Factory Records, G/34/142.

[64] Ripon to Aberdeen, 11 Mar. 1846, FO 17/117.

he 'might be able to make some arrangements that would effect an improvement in the British Commercial Relations with that Country'. The commercial stipulations, it was suggested, might bear some relation to those made with other 'imperfectly civilized States', such as China and Turkey. The other stipulations should provide for 'the unrestricted right' on the part of resident British subjects to exercise Christian worship, and for 'the exclusive jurisdiction of British authorities over British subjects', as provided for in Brooke's Brunei treaty of 1847. In conducting negotiations with the Siamese and Vietnamese, Brooke was to 'be very careful not to get involved in any dispute or hostile proceedings which would render our position in Siam or in Cochin-China worse than it now is, or which might compel Her Majesty's Government to have recourse to forcible measures in order to obtain redress'.[65]

Brooke himself appears at first to have contemplated establishing with the next king the kind of relationship he had sought to establish in Brunei.

> I consider that time should be given to the work of conciliation, that their prejudices should be gradually undermined, rather than violently upset, and that as we have delayed for thirty years doing anything, that in the course of this policy we may wait till the demise of the king brings about a new order of things. Above all, it would be well to prepare for the change, and to place *our own* king on the throne [namely Mongkut], ... a highly accomplished gentleman, for a semi-barbarian.[66]

But Rama III, still on the throne, was opposed to a new treaty: why, he ironically asked, was one necessary, since he had one with the Company? Brooke was encouraged to put in formal proposals, and these were rejected. The Siamese ministers had 'never encountered anyone else who came to conduct diplomatic negotiations like a professor giving instructions—instructions that pour forth like waters flooding forests and fields'.[67] Now the envoy advocated a different programme.

> The hope of preserving peace by an expedient Policy—by concession, submission, by indifference, or by any other course, than by rights firmly maintained by power justly exerted, is both a delusion and a cruelty; and after years of embarrassment and the sacrifice of a favourable prestige leads to a sanguinary war.
>
> An adherence to this principle has raised our Indian Empire, and established the reign of Opinion which maintains it; and the departure from this principle has caused the present deplorable condition of our relations with Siam ... there is no other course open to Her Majesty's Government, except to demand ... either a more equitable Treaty in accordance with the observance of civilized nations, or a total withdrawal of British subjects and their property from Siam.
>
> Should these just demands firmly urged be refused, a force should be present immediately to enforce them by a rapid destruction of the defences of

---

[65] Palmerston to Brooke, 18 Dec. 1849, FO 69/1.
[66] Brooke to Stuart, 17 June 1850, in John C. Templer, ed., *The Private Letters of Sir James Brooke*, London, 1853, II. 304.
[67] Quoted W. F. Vella, *Siam under Rama III*, New York, 1957, 139.

the river, which would place us in possession of the capital and by restoring us to our proper position of command, retrieve the past and ensure peace for the future, with all its advantages of a growing and most important commerce.[68]

Siam, Brooke was arguing, as Penang officials had in 1823, should not only be brought within the pale of Indian diplomacy, but treated, indeed, in subcontinental terms of opinion and prestige.

Abandoning any plan to go to Vietnam, Brooke argued for intervention in Cambodia: it was to be, as it were, the Brunei of mainland Southeast Asia.

> Cambodia . . . is the Keystone of our Policy in these countries—the King of that ancient Kingdom is ready to throw himself under the protection of any European nation, who will save him from his implacable enemies, the Siamese and Cochin Chinese. A Treaty with this monarch at the same time that we act against Siam might be made—his independence guaranteed—the remnants of his fine Kingdom preserved; and a profitable trade opened—The Cochin Chinese might then be properly approached by questioning their right to interrupt the ingress and egress of British trade into Cambodia . . .[69]

The British government did not follow Brooke's recommendations: it avoided the violence he advocated. In respect of Siam, it preferred to await the change of ruler rather than resort to warlike demonstration. This was consonant with the trend of British policy towards Siam as so far conducted by the Indian authorities and the India Board. Brooke had been told that, if he did not succeed, he should at least not make it necessary for the government to engage in a punitive operation. The India Board had opposed any negotiation that might risk relations with a marcher territory for a doubtful advantage. The Foreign Office had finally secured its grudging assent to the mission, but had inherited some of its unwillingness to engage in political adventure. Furthermore, it was widely held, as at first by Brooke himself, that the accession of a new king in Siam would in any case bring a more liberal policy. Anglo-Siamese relations would broaden down from the Burney precedent: their narrowing was only temporary, and was not a cause for violent interruption. The Thais benefited from the earlier decision of Rama III in avoiding the consequence of his later decision. But the prospect of Mongkut's accession was also important. As the Phraklang's son told Brooke, the new king 'fully understands the relations of Foreign Nations . . . any intercourse or consultation may hereafter be conducted in an easier manner than before'.[70] Though the attacks on Brooke in respect of his Borneo policy meant that he did not go, instructions were in fact again issued to the Hong Kong authorities; Bowring successfully carried out the mission and a treaty was signed in 1855.

The treaty, Bowring rather exaggeratedly told his son Edgar, brought

---

[68] Brooke to Palmerston, 5 Oct. 1850, FO 69/1.
[69] Brooke to Palmerston, 5 Oct. 1850, confidential, FO 69/1.
[70] Letter to Brooke, 23 Apr. 1851, FO 69/3.

Siam 'into the bright fields of hope and peaceful commerce'.[71] It displaced
the measurement duties and monopolies by a system of export and import
duties, opened the rice trade, and provided for the appointment of a
consul and for extraterritorial jurisdiction. But for Siam the 'bright fields of
hope' were political as well as commercial. The Thais had again come to
terms with the predominant power in Asia and so, by contrast to the
Vietnamese, given themselves a guarantee for the future. France and the
United States were expected to send missions to Siam also. The Kalahom
said he was glad Bowring had arrived first, for the Thais 'had trusted that
he would be the pioneer of the new relations to be opened between them
and the West, as they could then count upon such arrangements being
concluded as would both be satisfactory to Siam, and sufficient to meet the
demands that might hereafter be made by other of the Western Powers'.[72]
The Thais perceived the nature of European rivalry more accurately than
others: the powers could not now readily be played off, but one power
being stronger than the others, coming to terms with it would limit what
the others could demand. The British secured a strategic interest and
commercial opportunity in return for the recognition of Siam's independence. Though at this juncture involving no territorial changes, the
deal was not unlike those that they made formally or informally with
European authorities in island Southeast Asia. The treaty in this case was,
however, based on the 'unequal' model applied to 'imperfectly civilized'
states. It was amplified the following year by the Parkes negotiations.

Parkes brought a royal letter from Queen Victoria to King Mongkut
(r. 1851–68), however, which reduced Siam's 'inequality'. It 'touched his
heart and flattered his ambition'.[73] In fact the king's ambition, and the
object of the concessions he made, was to secure the recognition of Siam as
an independent state among the European nations. In this he had succeeded, and so given his state a better chance of survival than that of
Burma or Vietnam. In Vietnam the opportunity had not been taken; in
Burma there was no such opportunity before Ripon's neglected offer.

The 1855 treaty brought other changes in its wake. A British envoy was
placed in Bangkok and direct contact established with London. Though
Malaya was not covered in the Bowring treaty, the Anglo-Thai relationship
in respect of it necessarily altered. Dealing directly with the northern
Malay states became more difficult for the government of the Straits
Settlements, and the bombardment of Terengganu enforced a change of
view the more effectively because of Siam's connexion with the government in London. The strain in relations that the bombardment temporarily
created enhanced the French opportunity to step into Cambodia. Now
based in southern Vietnam, they challenged Siam's interest in Cambodia
by offering its king their protection, which he reluctantly accepted. This
outcome in fact the India Office was itself ready to accept, as the French
did not move into Siam itself nor into Laos. For the British, Siam now

[71] Bowring to E. Bowring, 13 Apr. 1855, English Mss. 1228/125, John Rylands Library,
    Manchester.
[72] Quoted Tarling, *Imperial Britain*, 180.
[73] Parkes to Clarendon, 22 May 1856, FO 69/5.

became a buffer not a marcher territory. In 1867 it gave up its claims over Cambodia in return for the provinces of Battambang and Angkor. Resented by the Cambodians, that too could be accepted by the British, and another part of the pattern of relations between Siam and the West was set till the turn of the century.

The advance of French power into central and northern Vietnam meanwhile modified the understandings over Malaya. If Siam were after all to fall under French influence, the security of northern Malaya would be threatened. The Thais, however, wished to retain their claims over the states there, and a British challenge to them might incur their hostility and turn them towards France, if not encourage the French to challenge the Thais elsewhere, rather as the Terengganu crisis had occasioned their move into Cambodia. To strengthen British influence without alienating the Thais, a new expression was given to the tripartite relationship in some of the northern Malay states: the Resident Councillor at Penang was appointed Consul to Kedah and Perlis.

The French moves in Laos produced a crisis for Siam but also for the British; they saw it as a buffer, not only now for their Malayan interests and for lower Burma, but also for upper Burma, which they had recently conquered. Pavie, French envoy in Bangkok, indicated in March 1893 that France intended to assert a claim to all territory east of the Mekong, and a naval demonstration at Bangkok in July was designed to secure Thai compliance. Britain urged Siam to accept French demands so as to avoid their being stepped up, and at the same time tried to restrain France. The French government agreed to establish a buffer in the north, where part of the Shan states, tributary to Burma, now British, extended east of the Mekong. The Thais had to renounce their claims over Laos east of the Mekong, but the French did not get Battambang and Siemreap: 'the disgorging is a noble operation', Lord Rosebery congratulated himself.[74] The British then sought the creation of the promised buffer, but in vain. Instead, in 1896 they, too, surrendered their claims east of the Mekong, making the river the frontier of Laos and Burma, and in return secured something of a French guarantee of the independence of Menam valley, inasmuch as each power agreed not to advance without the other's consent. The Thais might well, however, conclude that Britain had stopped short of affording them the support they expected. The agreement may indeed also have been a sign of Britain's diminished predominance: insurance with the major power was no longer sufficient. It had to compromise with other powers. That was no more a guarantee of Asian independence than European rivalry had been: perhaps it promised even less.

The British realized, however, that the agreement of 1896 did not cover their concern with the peninsula, particularly north of the Malay states, where, moreover, there was interest in a canal through the Isthmus of Kra. The French might not intervene there, but, as European rivalry intensified, another power might. German activity was now of renewed concern and

[74] Quoted Chandran Jeshurun, *The Contest for Siam 1889–1902*, Kuala Lumpur, 1977, 49.

greater actuality. In April 1897 the British made a secret agreement with Siam, in which the latter promised to cede no rights on the peninsula without British consent, in return securing a promise of British backing against third-power attempts to acquire dominion there. Siam also agreed to make exclusive commercial concessions in the area subject to British approval. In order to appease Thai sensitivities, the agreement was so secret that even Sir Frank Swettenham, as governor of the Straits Settlements, could not be told about it, albeit that the Colonial Office knew, 'though we pretend we do not know, that Sir Frank Swettenham knows of the Treaty'.[75]

The development of the peninsula, in particular the impact of the rubber boom, led to a further regulation of the Anglo-Thai relationship with northern Malay states. Swettenham planned to assist Siam to secure written agreements from the sultans, giving it de jure status, if it would employ British officers as Residents, and this resulted in the joint declaration of 1902, a reformulation of the tripartite sharing of political power in the states. The agreement did not, of course, cover Pattani, and the Sultan of Terengganu would not accept a Thai-appointed Resident, seeking, rather, something like the relationship between Johor and Britain.

In any case these arrangements all proved transitional. Pressed by developments in Europe, France and Britain moved closer together, and in 1904 the erstwhile rivals made an agreement resolving many of their overseas disputes. In the case of Siam, it reaffirmed the understanding of 1896. 'England says to France, "You strip him on one side, I will strip him on the other. As to the middle, we may leave that alone for the present."'[76] The editor of Blackwood's Magazine was perhaps even more cynical than he should have been, for the Menam basin continued to be left alone. But outlying parts of Siam were not. In the same year France had acquired sections of Luang Prabang on the west bank of the Mekong. Three years later it returned some of these acquisitions, while Siam ceded back the Cambodian provinces of Siemreap and Battambang. France also reduced its extraterritorial rights in Siam. A similar adjustment followed with Britain. The 1897 restrictions on commercial concessions had proved inconvenient to the Thais. They wanted funding for the railway system that would consolidate their kingdom. They again wanted to reduce extraterritorial rights. To secure these objectives they ceded to Britain their rights over the northern Malay states, though the British there had the task of negotiating with rulers whose independence they had done something to keep alive. Outlying territory could be bargained for greater equality, the Thais had decided; and they had retained their capacity to do so, while the lesser states, Laotian, Cambodian, Malayan, had to submit to partition and changes of allegiance. King Chulalongkorn (r. 1868–1910) had thought to include Siam's tributaries in his programme of centralization and modernization: now he abandoned that. The priority lay elsewhere.

With this agreement the Thais adjusted to a world in which British

---

[75] Quoted Suwannathat-Pian, 155n.
[76] Quoted in R. S. Stetson, 'Siam's Diplomacy of Independence, 1855–1909', Ph.D. thesis, New York University, 1969, 176n.

predominance had been further compromised. With it, too, tripartite power-sharing in the peninsular states ceased. Pattani remained part of Siam. To the south the Malay states became part of what was increasingly seen as British Malaya, though it was represented by no single formal political entity.

THE POLICIES OF THE WESTERN POWERS

Analysis of Western policy involves considering the impulses and the motivations behind it; the interest-groups involved, which in fact also affected the policy itself; the shifts over time; the options available to policy-makers; the means at hand; the information drawn on, the perceptions attained.

In a general sense the Europeans, the chief Western actors for much of the century, were impelled by their political and economic strength and strategic advantage, which had increased since their initial successes in Asia, and would increase further with their industrial and technological revolutions and enhanced capacity to mobilize their resources. On these advantages they wished to build. They were also impelled by other purposes, not necessarily mere rationales, nor mere products of the pursuit of wealth and power, though related to their success and to their wish to build upon it: to convert, to civilize, to spread European culture. They were impelled and motivated, too, by their own rivalry, always a compulsive element in the projection of Europe overseas.

For the central part of the period, that rivalry was muffled by the predominance of the British among them and in the world as a whole. It was not of course inconsistent that the British would pursue in such a phase relatively moderate policies. Their economic success, advantaged by their early industrial revolution, also conduced to political moderation. The result was a tendency to temporize with other European powers and to look to non-European powers outside their ambit to modernize themselves. They had a kind of imperium in Southeast Asia, determining or influencing the policies of others, but generally not themselves ruling, allowing those others to take their time over strengthening, modernizing or partitioning as the case might be. All the same, India affected British policy, and its political and strategic needs were quite different from those of a great industrial and commercial power, though it made its contribution to the success of that power. Britain had to provide there for the security of a territorial dominion and for its insulation from foreign menace. Its policy towards Burma was thus quite different from its policy elsewhere in Southeast Asia. Britain's interest in China also affected its view of Southeast Asia. That country should not, indeed, become another India, but its commerce, and the route to it, were important. That made for a strategic interest in the Straits of Melaka and the South China Sea, and also, at least for a while, encouraged a moderate policy in Siam and Vietnam.

The relative moderation of the British was not necessarily shared by other European powers established in Southeast Asia. They were constrained to treat British commerce fairly, but, a lesser power in the shadow of a greater, the Netherlands was tempted to follow compulsive economic practices like those of the Cultivation System. Politically the minor powers could generally rely on the overall guarantee of the British. But moments of uncertainty could lead to convulsive and even violent action, and this increased, in Sulu as in Aceh, when British predominance declined and other powers seemed likely to intervene. These were some of the effects of leaving the archipelagic world to minor European powers. The French were not a minor power, but their enterprise on the mainland was still driven by a wish to assert their greatness in Europe. They rightly recognized that the British would not oppose their venture on economic grounds.

With all the Western powers, policy was made not merely, sometimes not primarily, by central governments, though they often expected non-Western governments to respond with all the immediacy and coherence that they failed to display themselves. As a result, its main thrusts could be given different emphases; they could even be contradicted, particularly before trans-world communication began to inhibit local initiative and enhance the input of metropolitan governments. There were several levels of government, and with all the Western powers—with the British on the peninsula, the Dutch in the outer islands, the Spaniards in the Philippines, the French in Indochina—local officials tended to go beyond their instructions or even act in defiance of restraints by superiors. There were also tensions between official and mercantile interests, again at various levels. Government and commerce might have different views of the priorities and purpose of intervention. In the case of the relations of the Straits Settlements with Sumatra, for example, merchants developed an interest in the preservation of a status quo not officially seen as advantageous in the longer term. The expansion of European economies and their increasing penetration into Southeast Asia in the later nineteenth century expanded the role of private interests: concessionaires might or might not seek or receive the backing of governments, local or central. The differing interests in some sense represented frontiers that might be successive rather than coterminous. While Britain was predominant and other powers did not feel pressed to extend their control, there was scope for adventurers, pursuing their own interests—even, in the case of Raja Brooke, creating his own sub-colonial order. The effect in most cases was to induce the neighbouring colonial power to extend its effective frontier. The last decades of the nineteenth century offered a range of opportunities for private enterprise, for concessionaires, gun-runners, legal advisers, until a new series of compromises was reached between older and newer powers and new frontiers were established or old ones further consolidated.

A time-shift is reflected indeed in the changing balance of these interests and authorities within states and, as well, in the conduct of their relations with one another. Before about 1870, Britain's predominance was evident; after 1870 apprehended and actual challenges increased, partly as a result of political changes within Europe, partly as a result of shifts in the distribution of economic power. The Industrial Revolution was indeed another factor: by 1870 other countries not merely European were effectively following Britain's example or overtaking Britain, often pursuing protectionist policies in order to do so. On both counts increased competitiveness ensued overseas. The patronage of a predominant power was less available: it was moved to compromise with others. More formal demarcation and partition ensued under rules that themselves were formalized at Berlin. The political and economic changes were both affected by the development of communications, including the opening of the Suez Canal in 1869 and the linking of the telegraph in 1870–1. Economically the opening-up of Southeast Asia was expedited and its links with world markets tightened. Politically, the input of metropolitan governments were enhanced, themselves pressed by an increasing variety of interests and pressure-groups, and by an advance of democracy at home that often made for rigidity overseas. The Dutch government had been against the war with Aceh, but found it difficult to pursue peace once it had started. Events in Asia could also influence the metropolis. Ferry fell because of an incident in Vietnam, and the Third Anglo-Burman War was an election issue.

In part as a result of these processes, though also as a result of Southeast Asian policies and reactions, the Western powers adopted different options. There were, of course, a number of patterns. In earlier centuries—even in the eighteenth—Europeans had dealt with states in Southeast Asia in some sense on terms of equality, sometimes ruthless, rarely patronizing. This was so even in the archipelago where there was more involvement than on the mainland. With the increase of European power, and the failure of Asian states to cope with the economic and political pressures to which they were subject, other alternatives were opened up. One option might be to partition a state; another to protect or dominate it and reform it. Partition was not always the resort of the strong, rather, perhaps, the reverse: the Dutch nibbled at the periphery of Aceh, having failed to dominate at the centre, making the prospect of ultimately so doing more difficult. Nor did protection necessarily lead to Raffles-style reform: it might simply be a convenient means of acquiring control and indeed claiming additional territory as the French acquired Vietnamese claims over Laos and Cambodia.

The emphasis in British policy, at least outside areas more or less consigned to the Dutch or the Spaniards, was on the maintenance and reform of Asian states. Some reformed themselves: Siam, most successfully; others, less fully, less lastingly. But the attempt was not always welcome. It might threaten British interests particularly if it involved attempts to diversify international relationships in the context of European rivalry. But even in Burma the British sought a less than independent state rather than absorption of territory into the empire: only when they failed did they resort to partition and incorporation. In Malaya the British accepted the continued integrity of states with which local officials had developed relations that survived the changes of the 1870s, and indeed helped to shape them. Sarawak was in some sense a native state, as at times James Brooke angrily claimed. The British could not allow it to act with the ultimate degree of independence, namely to seek protection from another European state. But for the most part the unrealistic plans which the first raja developed along these lines were not supported by his friends and relatives, and were not carried out. The British finally adopted a form of protectorate, as over North Borneo, that allowed the authorities a very large, and ultimately embarrassing, degree of autonomy. In respect of other areas, especially in the archipelago, officials, and less often merchants, saw advantage in the regularization expected from the expansion of the colonial authorities, the presence of which the British had sanctioned. The same view applied to Vietnam, even on the part of private interests, after its failure to respond positively to British initiatives, and the French began to establish themselves.

More clearly than for the British, for other European powers the establishment of colonial authority was often in itself a desirable objective, and for metropolitan as well as for local officials, at least in the longer term. The Dutch were set on the rounding-out of the realm of Netherlands India and the Spaniards on the control of all of the Philippines. Dominion in French Indochina the Third Republic saw as compensation for disappointment in Europe and elsewhere. But, though their aims might differ from those of the British, they recognized that they could rarely be achieved by the mere application of force. The means they adopted were indeed not unlike those of the British, though the objective might differ.

There were phases of great violence on the part of all the Europeans, and indeed of the Americans, in Burma and Indochina, in the Philippines and Netherlands India. But force was adopted in association with other means, or where they had failed. The British dropped diplomacy in Burma and turned to war in 1824, and again in 1852, in the hope that they could prompt a change of attitude, their main aim throughout. By contrast the Dutch sought the progressive incorporation of native states into Netherlands India. But again force was only part of their method. Their greatest success indeed came over time with the combination of diplomacy, the possibility of force, and the severance of indigenous states from other international contacts: using force was a confession of failure; it was expensive and damaging, as the case of Aceh made dramatically evident. There the Dutch fell into a mode which the Spaniards had never escaped from in Sulu. European powers generally hoped that limited force or the threat of force might be sufficient to produce the political change they sought, making available the native instruments of authority and administration they needed to acquire.

The Europeans were strong at sea: steamers made them stronger. Where land force was used, it was generally not provided merely from the metropolis. The British had the superb resource of the Indian army. Other powers, more riskily, tended, like the British in India itself after the Mutiny, to rely on peripheral or minority elements, the equivalent of the martial races of British India. It was not surprising that two elements— old aristocracies or parvenus who became identified with colonial rule, and minorities who provided soldiers for colonial governments—might find it most difficult to accommodate to the rule of the successor states.

Finally it is clear that the impulses of the Europeans were shaped and their actions affected by the information available to them and the perceptions they brought to its selection and appreciation. In some cases information might be intentionally misinterpreted. Piracy is a case in point. One reason for the frequent use of the term in the nineteenth century was the British commitment to put it down. It was an impediment to trade, and its suppression would promote law and order on the seas. The Anglo-Dutch treaty of 1824 provided for co-operation against it, and other states and rulers were enjoined to work against it, like the Sultan of Brunei in the 1847 treaty. Naval forces could be involved and head money was payable. Since British power was considerable, but British policy relatively restrained, those who wished to use it could readily be tempted to apply the term rather widely, to attempts of the sultanate of Aceh to establish entrepôt trade, to the attacks of Iban upon the core rivers of Sarawak, to the marauding and slave-trading of the Ilanun and Balanini of the Sulu islands and northern Borneo, state-building enterprises though they might be.

European contemporaries themselves disputed the application of the term, for example at trials of captured Ilanun or in criticisms of James Brooke. Were those pirates properly so-called, who acted under authorization from the Sultan of Sulu? Was being an opponent of the extension of the raj of Sarawak sufficient qualification for being treated as a pirate? The issue, indeed, is not merely the intentional misuse of the term. The questions which contemporaries asked marked an extension to the archipelago of a European system of laws, and the response might invite further action. If the Sultan of Sulu had authorized piracy, should he not be held responsible? Or the Spaniards?

Piracy, as earlier in Europe, might indeed be a form of marine warfare, used either in enforcing the rule of an existing state, or establishing the power of a new state, or in displacing one political constellation by another. Indeed contemporaries recognized that, by seeking to put it down, they were interfering in a political process. At times, they had to deny the legitimacy not only of the states involved and their purposes, but of the dynamic of change involved. Putting down piracy involved displacing the states that existed or reforming them.

The outcome sought might again influence the analysis of the origins of the problem. Piracy, Raffles argued, originated in the decay of the native states as a result of Dutch incursions and monopolies, and Brooke and others followed this line, which supported a policy of order by restoration. The argument was more attractive than the notion that Malays were 'inveterate' pirates, and it has helped historians also to probe into the purpose and process of suppression. But again it is dangerous to generalize. The piracy of the Johor empire was clearly related to the 'breaking down of larger government',[77] though demonstratively abandoning it gave Temenggong Ibrahim an alternative source of power. But the analysis fits Sulu less well. Piracy became a source of power and wealth, since, as Warren has demonstrated,[78] it enabled the sultanate in its slave-raiding form to acquire the population that sustained its trade between Borneo and

[77] Owen to Ibbetson, 24 Oct. 1830, Board's Collections 52586, p.119, F/4/1331.
[78] J. F. Warren, *The Sulu Zone 1768–1898*, Singapore, 1981.

China for the better part of a century. That was still, of course, a decline in terms of the larger aims of the Moro sultanates of the sixteenth and seventeenth centuries. But it was in some sense a creative response to the conditions of the late eighteenth and early nineteenth centuries. For a time Sulu prospered. But its association with piracy and slave-raiding did not suggest that its further decline could be averted. For it added to the ambivalence over its relations with the British, and gave the Spaniards an argument against them and against Sulu itself.

In the case of piracy, indeed, the application of international law generally worked to the disadvantage of the independent Asian states involved, and generally, though not always, to the disadvantage of the pirates. For the most part, indeed, it was on the European side in this as in other cases. Moreover, it could be invoked or disregarded as seemed convenient. The Sultan of Aceh could not close ports, but Raffles could. The British could challenge or condone a Spanish blockade of Sulu as seemed expedient. It is possible to argue that the application of international law, in those positivist days, was in itself a piece of imperialism. Yet it could at times check the Europeans by acting on their own rivalries and on the tensions among their authorities—the Governor of Penang and the Recorder quarrelled over the treatment of Kedah—or between authorities and private interests, or among private interests themselves. It could also spur them on: pirates would be drowned rather than taken in for trial. Lawyers are found advising indigenous rulers—like J. C. Mitchell in the case of Lombok—though not always to happy effect. In that case it urged the Dutch on.

There was a kind of reverse misconception, that the Asian states were states in a European sense and that their central authorities were as effective as Europeans liked to think their own were. Moderates might thus expect too much of them, and be disappointed; reformers might have to go further than they wanted; extremists might demand too much and rejoice at the outcome. But perceptions of their weakness could also be exaggerated. If central authority was weak, it did not follow that the state was weak. Conquerors might bite off more than they could chew. There was a widespread, but often unfounded view that the masses were awaiting delivery from native tyrants, supported also by the European belief that order and good government would liberate economic enterprise and help to create wealth. There was, at least till the late nineteenth century, only a limited perception of the ideological and religious underpinnings of the Southeast Asian states. The contemporary reports convey no real understanding of the Confucian preconceptions and purposes of Minh-mang, nor of the Buddhist role of the Burman kings.

In the archipelago Islam was rightly seen as an antagonist, but the European powers each handled it differently. The Dutch had long sought to play down its influence by rather crude methods: towards the end of the century, its post-Suez revival and sophistication made them, under the influence of their frustration in Aceh, and of the Dutch Islamicist Snouck Hurgronje's research and advocacy, more subtle. The Spaniards, building their empire on conversion, were cruder still: there was little chance of the kind of accommodation with Sulu that the Dutch achieved with many of the states of the archipelago. Indeed, the Spaniards' attacks on Sulu in the 1870s helped to inspire Islamic resistance elsewhere: they found Sulu *panditas* travelling to Mindanao 'with the sinister goal of uniting among themselves the Moros, whose disunity had been up to then the greatest advantage the Spaniards had perceived'.[79] The United States, with no commitment to conversion and with the capacity to secure better information, yet behaved with even greater violence in the face of fanatic resistance. The British were more cautious, in part again because of an Indian factor: they had more Muslim subjects than any other state, and the Mutiny there added to their wish to avoid clashes between Europeans and Muslims in general. In Malaya they left Islam—as they hoped—to the sultans. One of their criticisms of Spain in Sulu was that the Spaniards would raise up general jihad against European rule in Asia.

The story is better understood if the other side of it is also borne in mind. The policies, purposes and perceptions of the Europeans have been summarized. What were those of the Southeast Asians?

SOUTHEAST ASIAN POLICIES

The Maritime Region

The indigenous authorities in the archipelago, for the most part long connected with the Dutch and with diminished international personality, had less scope to determine the outcome of the encounter with the nineteenth-century West than those on the mainland. Dundas had suggested that the Dutch might be overthrown, but only with the aid of foreign powers. In fact the British were generally cautious over disturbing the pattern of Dutch power: they might prefer to inherit it than destroy it. What they did in the interregnum and after would certainly not encourage indigenous rulers to think that they could either rely on rivalry among the Europeans or seek the support of the more powerful of them against the less.

Indigenous rulers were not, of course, consulted over the Anglo-Dutch treaty of 1824; they would apprehend its outcome, like that of the convention of 1814, only through the actions that followed it. Dipanagara's aim in the Java War of 1825–30 was, as Ali Basah Penjalasan put it, 'to restore the high state of the Islamic religion throughout the whole of Java'.[80] An appeal to the British would be unlikely. But it would certainly have met a negative response, though the merchant John Palmer might lament the outcome.[81] In western Sumatra, the replacement by the Dutch of the British authorities, who had been in some areas for 150 years, was apparent. 'Our Privilege of Trade at the Dutch Ports seems to supersede the necessity for retaining any Settlement on Sumatra', Palmer commented: 'but the contempt of the Feelings of the Natives and our Engagements

[79] Quoted R. C. Ileto, *Magindanao, 1860–1888: the career of Datu Uto of Buayan*, Ithaca, 1972, 43.
[80] Quoted P. B. R. Carey, 'Javanese Histories of Dipanegara', BKI, 130 (1974) 287.
[81] Quoted N. Tarling, 'The Palmer Loans', in D. P. Crook, ed., *Questioning the Past*, St Lucia, 1972, 116.

with them will deservedly load us with obloquy everywhere.'[82] The position of the states in the outer islands in contractual relationship with the Dutch was less clear. Obviously the renewal of their contracts was the least the Dutch could seek. For a while, however, the indigenous rulers might retain a good deal of autonomy, though they might not know why, and they might feel able to admit foreign merchants and even adventurers without fully realizing the danger of so doing.

Only in the case of Aceh had the British felt that the recency of the relationship with the sultan established by Raffles justified a special reservation in 1824. The Penang authorities did not, however, see fit to negotiate the end of his treaty: any arrangement with Aceh would only encourage its 'tendency to overawe and subjugate the numerous petty states with whom our trade is conducted'.[83] Perhaps as a result, the ruler of Aceh rather paradoxically continued to set some store by the Raffles treaty and was less inclined to turn to the Dutch. He certainly retained an effective independence that encouraged them to proceed by partition rather than by protection, leaving the Acehnese and foreign merchants beyond the frontiers to trade or clash as they might meanwhile. The piecemeal encroachment of the Dutch led Sultan Ibrahim to turn to other powers in the 1850s. But that was to go beyond what the Dutch could allow. When the independence of Aceh was made plain by the Anglo-Dutch treaty in 1871 and the publicity it received, they had to foreclose on the sultanate. The Dutch usually applied force only to back up a system of contractual relations: the latter lacking in Aceh, they needed the force all the more, and that was one reason why they could not bring the war to an early end, even though there was little chance of European help for their opponents, and the sultan's appeal to Turkey elicited only a gesture. In the course of the struggle, a reason for their normal policy became apparent: Islamic elements in society, always strong, secured leadership. The Dutch had precipitately abolished the sultanate and failed to compromise with the *adat*-chiefs or *ulëëbalang* (hereditary chiefs), though these saw that prolonged resistance eroded their position and enhanced that of Muslim extremists. With the latter the Dutch could not readily come to terms, and the struggle had its echoes in other parts of the archipelago. Snouck Hurgronje wrote:

> Had a sultan or scion of the royal house, endowed with exceptional strength of will and clearness of judgment, placed himself at the head of the struggle *à outrance* which took place when the Dutch came to Acheh, and inspired the Achehnese people by precept and example, such a prince would without doubt have been for the invaders anything but a negligible quantity . . . As it is, an ulama who preaches holy war is able to deprive an Achehnese ulëëbalang of the allegiance of a considerable portion of his subjects; how much more could have been accomplished by a raja who was the ulamas' equal in sacred authority, and over and above this was clothed with the legendary traditions of the past greatness of Acheh![84]

[82] Palmer to Prince, 10 May 1825, quoted Tarling, *Imperial Britain*, 52.
[83] Memorandum by Fullerton, 21 Mar. 1825, Straits Settlements Factory Records G/34/100.
[84] C. Snouck Hurgronje, trans. A. W. S. O'Sullivan, *The Achehnese*, Leyden, 1906, I. 145.

Previous to 1871 the British had offered some challenge to the Dutch advance from Siak over states on the east coast of Sumatra with a dubious allegiance to it. In the 1860s a number of rulers sought British help, but the support that eventuated was mainly local, and it did little but prompt the Dutch to act more firmly. Even in respect of states where contractual relationships were more continuous, the process of absorption into the Dutch domain was not always smooth. The period of *onthouding* perhaps again gave indigenous rulers a false confidence. The Dutch, however, intervened if economic interference seemed likely to become political, or private interference official, particularly after Brooke's adventure had shown the dangers. The ruler of Lombok, for example, still had a remarkable degree of autonomy in the 1850s, but he could not turn his international connexions to account, for doing so would only prompt the Dutch to act. The Dutch decided to eliminate that autonomy, however, only in a later phase when they resolved to round out their empire under the impact of increasing European penetration and of the impulse of their own imperialism. They could intervene among divided rajas and could undermine the loyalty of the Sasak peoples. But they could not break the bond of raja and followers at the very core of the kingdom, which was expressed in the final suicide attacks, *puputan*.

The sultanate of Brunei, by contrast, was a survivor, but at a price, or several prices. It was not involved in the Dutch network, though perhaps the Anglo-Dutch treaty of 1824 had intended that it should be. A deterioration in Anglo-Dutch relations and a personal initiative on the British side helped to avert that. But it was also the result of a Brunei response. Initially that was dictated in part by the rivalries of the Brunei rulers as much as or more than by their concern to prevent a Dutch take-over. Perhaps indeed they were slow to recognize the threat of European control, poorly informed as they were of the outside world, relatively isolated, kept in touch only by interested parties. It may as a result have been easier to think in terms of playing off outside elements one against another, an adaptation, perhaps, of a traditional diplomatic mode of holding the Brunei empire together. Raja Muda Hassim looked to Brooke; his rival, Pg Makhota, looked to the Dutch. With them Brunei had no contractual relations and less than others need fear provoking them. Hassim still had the wisdom to enquire which was the cat, which the rat. And would the cat act?[85]

The traditional diplomatic view seemed still to prevail among Bruneis when their range of international contacts was narrowed. The Dutch were excluded under the treaty of 1847, the Americans and the Spaniards by their own incompetence and by the demi-official British venture that led to the founding of the British North Borneo Company. Brunei could survive between raj and Company, Briton and Briton. But it was a costly diplomacy: what came to face Brunei was partition between them. Brunei determination to call a halt, though not unanimous, helped to bring about the establishment of the Residency, as it were, for want of something better: Britain against Britons. Sultan Hashim, who achieved this, was one of the party that had destroyed Brooke's allies in 1846, even though

[85] N. Tarling, *The Burthen, the Risk and the Glory*, Kuala Lumpur, 1982, 30.

Brooke's aim had been to restore the sultanate Raffles-style, and one of those who had subsequently sought support by accepting piecemeal partition. But, with the aid of a change in British policy, he managed to avert the total disappearance of the sultanate.

If James Brooke had sought to prod Brunei into reform, he and his successor in the event built up the separate state of Sarawak. But that rested not only on the partition of Brunei, but on a series of accommodations on the part of the chiefs and peoples of the raj as it expanded. The old focus of loyalty was displaced, but the chiefs had other options open to them, since the raj, lacking in external strength especially after the first raja's break with the British government, needed collaborators all the more. The Malayo-Muslims at the river-mouths became in a sense joint rulers with the white raja, while the original Iban opponents of Brooke rule became its doughty warrior class and assisted in its expansion. In some degree the raj became an autonomous actor on the Southeast Asian stage, even an independent state, a Malay state, as Raja James claimed. An alternative is to see it as a pseudo-colonial state, ultimately relying on British power. Perhaps the truth is somewhere in between.[86] The rajas themselves were clear that their system was superior to colonial rule or rule in the style of the Federated Malay States. But neither before nor after the 1888 protectorate agreement was it truly an independent state, and if it was a Malay state, it was one that accommodated to Britain in special ways.

The state of North Borneo was different again. With its creation its peoples were cut off from political contact with other Europeans, though an obligation to the Sultan of Sulu remained: they were faced with an alien government with no traditional basis and no obvious collaborators. It was resisted by Mat Salleh on a largely traditionalist, only partly Islamic, basis: it secured little help from the British government, but the opposition got none from other governments. A kind of compromise was proposed in 1898, by which Mat Salleh would be accepted as a chief in the interior; but this the Company officials ruled out, though the managing director, W. C. Cowie, a man with a local trading background, favoured it. A laborious series of expeditions was required to eliminate the opposition. A more regular system was gradually established, but it took time to build a chiefly infrastructure.

The establishment of North Borneo represented a partition of Sulu as well as of Brunei. For the Sulus the British connexion, though of limited duration, was a decisive factor in their long relationship with Spain. Their aim was to preserve independence in face of Spanish military action, diplomatic blandishment, religious crusade. The Spaniards established a claim, but no effective control, and indeed, following the Balambangan episode, the Sulus were able to build a new prosperity on arms, slaves and the China trade. A relationship with the British developed which could, however, afford little reassurance, given the piracy issue, and the uncertainty of their commitment to Sulu's independence despite the treaties made by Dalrymple and Brooke and their advocacy of its neutrality. The

[86] cf. Sanid Said, *Malay Politics in Sarawak 1946–1966*, Singapore, 1985, 11, 16–17.

Sulus had seized an opportunity to sustain their state and its special balances between co-operation and rivalry, patronage and dependence, centrality and segmentation. But it was no guarantee of a safe future: the sultan's appeals to the British would meet a qualified reception; and sympathy for him and his people was evoked more by the violence and irregularity of Spain's proceedings and the fear that they might provoke an Islamic reaction. The sultan yet retained sufficient independence at the end of the Spanish régime to make a treaty with the United States, and some of those associated with the Company hoped that the British would yet be able to follow in Sulu the kind of policy they followed on the peninsula. Any such hope was destroyed by the Americans. For them the Bates treaty was mere temporizing, while they dealt with the insurrection in the north. Dislodging the sultan's power, however, faced them with bitter Islamic-inspired resistance.

'We have been struck with amazement at the dispensation of the Lord, the Creator of all the worlds, who has accomplished his divine will and decree in a way which is not comprehensible to us, parting brother from brother, father from son and friend from friend.'[87] That was the reaction of the Bendahara of Pahang to the treaty of 1824, which destroyed the unity of the Malay world. Subsequently new patterns emerged on the peninsula, the result not only of British policy or of the different positions and structures of the Malay states, but also of their different levels of perception and statesmanship. No British Resident was ever appointed to Johor, though its example perhaps helped to introduce the system elsewhere. A fragment of the old empire of Johor, its future was deeply influenced by its rulers, the erstwhile Temenggongs. They recognized that no foreign intervention could be sought: the problem was to maximize independence from the colonial neighbour even so, if not turn him to account. They associated themselves with the Straits Settlements government, demonstratively breaking with the pirates of the old régime, but also received advice from British merchants and lawyers, conveniently or otherwise nearby, and even made a connexion with London. Riskily they sought to expand their political influence; realistically they developed Johor's economy by facilitating Chinese immigration and enterprise. In some ways they were a model, and at times, in a sense because of that, a vexation to those governors who sought more formal colonial control: they were, in a sense, native Raja Brookes. They also knew when to give in: finally accepting an adviser, but still carving out autonomy. Perhaps it was the parvenu character of these rulers that led them temporarily to try aggrandizement; it also made them pragmatic.

Other rulers had to cope with the pre-eminence which the ruler of Johor had secured for himself and, disposed to work with the British, eliminate his monopoly of the British connexion. Sultan Omar of Terengganu was one. He, too, broke with the pirates and sought relations with Singapore, and Governor Blundell responded. But Johor's ambition and the Pahang civil war led him, too, into risky policies that, perhaps unexpectedly, paid off. Terengganu was bombarded, but the policies of Blundell's successor,

---

[87] Quoted B. W. Andaya, *Perak: The Abode of Grace*, Kuala Lumpur, 1979, 2.

Cavenagh, were disapproved. The price was recognition of Thai supremacy, but it did not destroy Terengganu's autonomy.

In Kedah that supremacy was already accepted. The sultan had secured no promises of help against the Thais when he ceded Penang, and indeed the followers of his dethroned successor were officially treated as pirates in the 1830s. But there was private help, and legal obstacles could be turned to account. In any case, whatever their superiors said, the Straits Settlements authorities were anxious to limit effective Thai supremacy on the peninsula. If it could be done by avoiding its theoretical recognition, so much the better. But if it could be done only by avoiding or limiting its practical implementation, even though it was theoretically accepted, that was an acceptable alternative. The Kedah ruler accepted the deal which Bonham promoted. Malay rulers in the northern states swung among the options left open to them as a result of the lack of formal Thai control and the local British unwillingness to second it: side with the Thais, oppose them; side with the British, oppose them; even play off one with the other. Overall they did extraordinarily well. Incorporation in Siam, Pattani-style, was avoided; so was incorporation in the Federated Malay States.

The Burney treaty left the Perak chiefs to decide the question of their allegiance to Siam, and Governor Fullerton sent Low over to make sure that they chose to reject it. That action the superior authorities disapproved, but their disapproval of the Low treaty was never notified to the Perak authorities. The Thai option ceased to be available, but Perak was divided in other ways. The Malay chiefs were alive to the benefits of the tin trade and encouraged Chinese immigration via the Straits Settlements. But it was not done centrally, as in Johor's case, and its impact upset the distribution of power in the sultanate. The governors tried everything: invoking old treaties; dealing direct with local chiefs; using the ruler of Johor; finally installing a Resident. But what that meant for the élite became apparent only with the work of Birch; and what had to be accepted became apparent only with the expedition to avenge his assassination. Better perhaps to accept and work to limit rather than resist. Educated in Malay, Sultan Idris (r. 1887–1916) learned English when he came to the throne of Perak so as to keep open his lines of communication.[88] The fact that the British did not annex but appeared still to advise gave the rulers some scope, though its limits were a warning to Johor and the northern states to avoid a Resident if they could. Pahang accepted one only reluctantly, and some resistance followed. The northern states accepted only advisers. 'The Malays, like other races, hate foreign interference', King Chulalongkorn commented in 1903. 'It is a big misconception when the British say the Malays respect and support them . . . If Malay leaders have sought British assistance, it is because Great Britain is a great power.'[89]

The Mainland

Mainland Southeast Asia, more independent than the archipelago at the

---

[88] J. M. Gullick, *Malay Society in the late Nineteenth Century*, Singapore, 1987, 60.
[89] Quoted Suwannathat-Pian, 157n.

outset of the period, operated with different political dynamics. The great kingdoms were those of the Burmans, the Thais, and the Vietnamese. Each had its own problems of integration, even in regard to the core of the realm: the endemic weakness of patrimonial systems, like those of the Burmans and the Thais; the intractable problem for the Vietnamese of holding a kingdom together through applying a version of the Confucian system of the Chinese. Each kingdom also had an expansive urge, which thrust the Thais, for example, not only into the Malay states, but into Laos and Cambodia; it thrust the Vietnamese also into those luckless states; and brought the Thais and the Burmans into competition over the Shan states. Each state in any case contained minorities: the Burmans loosely integrated or failed to integrate Karens, Arakanese, Mons, Kachins, Chins, Shans; the Thais, Malays and Shans; the Vietnamese, Chams, Khmers, hill peoples. The states were also at times at odds with each other. The Thais and the Vietnamese avoided direct conflict: the conflict was at the expense of the intermediate states of Laos and Cambodia. The Thais and the Burmans had, by contrast, a legacy of direct conflict, and indeed the foundation of the most recent Thai kingdom followed the Burman destruction of Ayutthaya in 1767. Intra-regional dynamics, a more effective and a more comprehensive influence on political life on the mainland than in the archipelago in the late eighteenth century, were all to be altered by the subsequent imposition of the imperial régimes, though to some extent they facilitated it.

Perceiving the advent of the imperial powers clearly and assessing their nature were indeed made more difficult, not only by the traditional preoccupations and relationships of the mainland states—Vietnamese rulers could not believe that trade was an aim in itself[90]—but by the fact that so far the Europeans had had little impact on the mainland. In the archipelago, their presence was of long standing; they could not be dislodged, unless they dislodged each other, and it seems to have been widely, though not universally, recognized that at best it was necessary to compromise with them, to work within the framework they established. The mainland states had no such background. They had more experience of a suzerain power that worked in a different way. China intervened on the mainland with spasmodic violence and with dramatic effect. But for the most part it was content with a confession of vassalage and indeed made that profitable to its tributaries.

The relationship was not nurtured on the Chinese side by mere desire for flattery or mere domestic need: it was also China's means of providing security. It was natural, indeed, for a continental state to seek to insulate itself from outside threat and establish a surrounding zone of what might be called submissive neutrality and diminished independence. The most striking feature of the late eighteenth century was perhaps not so much the increased activity of European traders and empire-builders as the re-emergence (at their initial instance) of a large state on the subcontinent of India, which had the security imperatives possessed by other such states. Of this the mainland states were indeed aware. If Burma fell more outside

---

[90] A. B. Woodside, *Vietnam and the Chinese Model*, Cambridge, Mass., 1971, 263.

the Chinese sphere than Siam or Vietnam, it fell more inside the pale of an Indian diplomacy. Siam and Vietnam were also aware of the conquests of the British Company and apprehensive of them, but they responded differently. Characteristically too, they changed their relationship with China in different ways as the international position changed.

Burma was the least fortunately placed geographically, so far as India was concerned, and its approach to international relations made it unlikely to accept the diminished independence which essentially was the objective of the new rulers of India. Independence could be retained on the mainland as it could not in the archipelago, but only on conditions. The problems that arose between the states were, as a result, additionally difficult to solve, and helped to lead to two wars that stage by stage partitioned the Burman kingdom. The parties in Burma that favoured compromise could readily be undermined. The British rulers of India found it difficult to avoid taking up otherwise unsatisfactory causes. Even the modernization of this kingdom, otherwise not unwelcome, must have limits. Should it arm itself? should it grant concessions to foreigners? A third war, involving a foreign threat, led to a final incorporation. By this time, partly thanks to a legacy of distrust and the presence of disorder, incorporation seemed preferable to continuing the dynasty in a subsidiary relationship in what may be seen as a more normal pattern for the British in Asia. Resistance continued even so; perhaps indeed it was enhanced. The dynasty had failed to turn it to account.

The Nguyen rulers in Vietnam also failed to turn resistance to account. Their unification of a kingdom difficult to hold together and long divided de facto made them the more anxious over subversion and the more unwilling to modify their version of Confucianism. The approaches of the West offered them nothing that they wanted: commerce was not a general boon but a limited monarchical perquisite. Missionary endeavour recalled civil war and foreign intervention, and undermined assimilation of the great tradition. The conquests of the British in India added to the distrust, since it was far from clear to the Vietnamese that the British in Southeast Asia would behave differently; nor did they in Burma. For the Vietnamese, the best chance was to come to terms with the major power so as better to resist any other, and this option was available in the sense that it was not in the archipelago. But the Vietnamese, poorly informed in any case, were unable to take advantage of the option, and had no ally against the French save their ineffective Chinese suzerains.

Though Minh-mang was curious about the West, neither he nor his bureaucracy could abandon a Confucianist consensus. When the conflict came, there was élite and mass resistance. A French officer recognized 'the existence of a national spirit among the Annamese, whom we have always thought ready to accept and indeed worship any master who would allow them to plant and harvest their rice'.[91] The dynasty, facing a challenge in the north, compromised, vainly hoping to regain Cochinchina by negotiation. The partisans were disavowed: 'the Emperor does not recognise us,

[91] Mark W. McLeod, 'The Treaty of Sai-gon and the Vietnamese response to French intervention', Ph.D. thesis, University of California, Los Angeles, 1988, 145.

but it is indeed our duty to carry on our struggle for the safeguarding of our fatherland'.[92] On moving north, the French were able to choose a figurehead Nguyen ruler, and this option they selected, by contrast to the British approach in Burma. They still faced resistance, and it was belatedly invoked by Emperor Ham Nghi. Righteous uprisings or *khoi nghia* were led by scholars and gentry, but at least in Bac Giang Province there was a more lower-class movement led by Hoang Hoa Tham.[93]

The Thai reaction was more positive than the Burman and the Vietnamese. Their position was in their favour: more remote from India than the Burmans, more remote from China than the Vietnamese, less ideologically committed than they were, but more integrated than either. There was a legacy of flexibility, indeed, but perhaps the Ayutthaya conquest was in one sense a piece of good fortune. The new régime, based in Bangkok, was outward-looking and encouraged immigration and commerce. Rama II was unwilling at first to receive Crawfurd, but was persuaded to do so. More aware of British power as a result of the First Anglo-Burman War, Rama III accepted the Burney treaty. He was unwilling to accept one from Brooke, but his successor accepted one from Bowring. Even though it inhibited the full independence of his kingdom, the Bowring treaty preserved it in essence. The dynasty rightly perceived the need in this period not so much to play off the outside powers, as to accept the predominance of the greatest and seek to diminish that predominance without alienating it. King Norodom (r. 1860–1904) of Cambodia rightly envied Chulalongkorn: he had a 'a court of consuls'; in the Cambodian court there was only one representative.[94] The Thai kingdom had also to accept a measure of partition. But it surrendered territory not as the price of non-cooperation or as an alternative to co-operation, but as a complement to a pattern of co-operation which involved successive accommodations, and that sufficed to preserve the essential independence of the core of the Thai realm. 'It is sufficient for us to keep ourselves within our house and home; it may be necessary to forego some of our former power and influence',[95] as Mongkut had realistically put it. A Catholic mandarin, Nguyen Truong To, estimated that Siam was no stronger than Vietnam. 'However, when it engaged in contact with Westerners, that country knew how to wake up to reality immediately.'[96]

An Overview

The European states displayed division and diversity; but they possessed arms, assumptions and technology in common, and rivalry urged them on. Southeast Asian states were also divided among and within themselves, and they displayed no unity in meeting the challenge from outside. Their divisions in fact had long helped the Europeans. By this time,

[92] Quoted Truong Buu Lam, *Patterns of Vietnamese Response to Foreign Intervention*, New Haven, 1967, 11.
[93] Woodside, *Community*, 29.
[94] Quoted Milton E. Osborne, *The French Presence in Cochinchina and Cambodia*, Ithaca and London, 1969, 177.
[95] Quoted A. L. Moffat, *Mongkut, the King of Siam*, Ithaca, 1961, 124.
[96] Quoted Woodside, *Vietnam*, 261.

indeed, states in the archipelago had little scope for opposing the Europeans and little chance of acting in common: their internal divisions left them additionally exposed. Islam was to inspire opposition to the West, and be inspired by it; but despite their apprehensions, it did not stop the advance of the Europeans. The mainland states were initially able still to pursue traditional objectives, but that may have distracted them from meeting the new challenge. Traditional divisions among and within them were still strong. Even as his relations with the British deteriorated in 1823, the king of Burma, with his Thai enemy in mind, sent an embassy to Vietnam, headed by a Eurasian 'addicted to intoxication'.[97]

Survival may have been the main task. Some did not even see that, though growing conscious of British dominion in India, and later of Chinese decline; none except perhaps Siam were ready, like the Japanese, to undertake the changes that might be required in society, policy, economy. The impulse may have been to maintain the status quo: and the failure of such a policy, and resultant loss of territory, as in the case of Arakan or Cochinchina, only made adaptation at once more urgent and more difficult. Even those states that went beyond that, like Sulu, pursued a traditional dynamic. That there were answers was shown in Southeast Asia by Siam, elsewhere in Asia by Japan. But they were fortunate in circumstance as well as well-led, though differently led: one by a centralizing monarchy, the other by a post-revolutionary oligarchy. Both were able to see a priority, to formulate a response; both were strong enough to carry through a compromise.

Diverse elements indeed contributed to the making of policy in the various Southeast Asian states. Being a ruler did not mean being an autocrat: generally the ruler's power was strongest at the centre, often even there depending on patron–client allegiances. Where control of the periphery was weak, depending again on patron–client connexions, a unified response to European pressures was unlikely: changes of allegiance were part of the traditional dynamic. At the centre, ministers and court officials would be jockeying for power, often seeing the contacts with the Europeans in terms of factional politics, if not offering advice on the contacts that differed for less interested reasons. In many states there was tension between the religious and the secular. In the mainland Theravāda countries, the king was seen as the protector of Buddhism, an aspiring *cakkavatti*; in the archipelago, Islam at once supported the sultan's rule and sought to shape state and society; in Vietnam the Confucian ethnic was sustained by the Nguyen dynasty as a means of upholding its fragile unity, in effect challenging and channelling village loyalties. The hold of the state on the masses was uncertain: religious leaders might have more hold than the state; secret societies more than the Confucianist élite. The peasants indeed might not be reliable, though there is little evidence that, as Europeans tended to say, they longed for deliverance from native oppressors, and that could not necessarily be said even of minorities. Rather the masses, like the minorities, were an uncertain quantity. Involving the

---

[97] Burney to Ibbetson, 5 June 1824, Straits Settlements Factory Records G/34/95.

masses in politics, even in a resistance struggle, might be socially risky for the rulers and the élite. Mass opposition remained unused till too late in Burma and Vietnam. The minority peoples were less reliable still, though few hastened to shift their allegiance to the Europeans.

The year 1870 appears to offer, on a number of counts, a significant chronological division in terms of the making of European policies. It also affords, in part as a result, a division in terms of their impact. For that reason the date must also be of significance in Asian policy, whether or not it was so perceived. From then on, indeed, there was even less room for manoeuvre. Now on the mainland, as already in the archipelago, the European challenge was unavoidable. Indeed for the most part there could be little hope of sustaining independence, or even autonomy: the interaction would have to continue within the European framework. Within this periodization, other dates were also of significance: outside the archipelago, the establishment of paramountcy in India, the initial British defeat of China, later the victory of Japan over China and Russia. Inside, the crucial historical moments differed from state to state, recognized as such at the time or not: 1873, say, for Aceh, 1824 (or 1885) for Burma, 1826 or 1855 for Siam, 1859 for Vietnam.

Various policy options could be conceived, even attempted, taking more or less account of the Europeans. One conceivable option was to pursue traditional objectives in isolation from them; but that was impossible even for Minh-mang to achieve, though it was the course that, despite his curiosity about the West, he had to favour. Another was to contain or resist them, if need be by force, though after a phase of isolation that was likely to be even more risky than before. In any case long-term resistance might undermine the state, producing peasant rebellion or populist Islamic challenge. The third option was to compromise, 'to adjust our position to circumstances', as Nguyen Truong To put it in the 1860s.[98] But what would represent compromise? Retaining as much of the old customs and culture as possible and as much of the territory as possible? Or proceeding to a greater degree of modernization and avoiding a direct challenge to the interests of the Europeans, but perhaps attempting to operate on their ground, using their expertise, invoking their international law? The latter the Thais managed. Others found it difficult to compromise, perhaps even more so after partition had begun, because of opposition within. It was also difficult to modernize without appearing to threaten European interests, or getting caught among them, like the rulers of Kelantan, making concessions to private interests disapproved by the government of the Straits Settlements.

The methods at the disposal of the Asians for pursuing their options were various. Diplomacy was, of course, one, though it is usually more effective when power is explicitly or implicitly behind it. An isolationist could try politely asking visitors to leave, and later resort to executing those who persistently returned. Diplomacy might also be used to attempt containment: working with a predominant power, perhaps at a cost;

---

[98] Quoted Truong Buu Lam, 90.

playing off the foreigners, though that was a risky policy and could in fact prove provocative. Diplomacy was also a means to compromise, and it was a means, too, of turning the desire to modernize to account and of realizing that objective. Diplomacy was one option, force was another: but still less effective if not backed by power. Prompt submission might avoid catastrophe and include an element of compromise; fuller submision might facilitate modernization, and make possible an eventual come-back. But that was an argument used more by collaborationists after conquest than by negotiators before.

Asian policies were, like European, affected by information available and perceptions applied. Information might be hard to come by, biased, filtered. Monarchs rarely ventured beyond courts—Thibaw had never been more than five miles from Mandalay—and were often apprehensive over invoking popular resistance. Some were illiterate, like Sultan Hashim of Brunei or Bendahara Ahmad of Pahang. Their sources were frequently low-level: adventurers, missionaries, self-seeking consuls, lawyers. What information was available might be recast or obscured by the framework of its presentation: a monarch might not be able to bear receipt of some news or the mode of some approach. Tradition might stand in the way. And yet information was vital. What indeed was Europe? was it one or many? how could you appraise the powers? which indeed was the cat and which the rat? Could you ignore the unbelievable defeat of China sufficiently to avoid less easy options? Did you perceive the difference between the British and British India? Could you distinguish between a European government and subordinate officials or merchants, who often had no reason to emphasize the distinction themselves? Did faction struggles obscure reality? Even the experienced Kinwun got it wrong in Mandalay in 1885. Judgement was vital, too. 'The British and the French can entertain no other feelings for each other than mutual esteem as fellow human beings, whereas the likes of us, who are wild and savages, can only be regarded by them as animals', wrote King Mongkut in 1864. 'The only weapons that will be of real use to us in the future will be our mouths and our hearts constituted so as to be full of sense and wisdom for the better protection of ourselves.'[99]

INTERACTION AND ACCOMMODATION

The European approach to Southeast Asia varied from area to area and time to time. But that was not the sole reason for diversity of response. There was a range of possible 'solutions' or 'accommodations', the availability of which did not depend only on the Western powers. The most pre-emptive of them, conquest, was indeed rarely the first to which the Western powers resorted. Others might serve for longer or shorter periods. But, if there was an opportunity for those others, it had to be perceived and seized.

[99] Quoted Likhit Dhiravegin, *Siam and Colonialism*, Bangkok, 1974, 22.

Certainly the availability of solutions did in part depend on the needs of the Western powers. Those needs, quite often the more vigorously expressed because of the lack of a coherent or overall policy, were diverse. The Europeans might seek to protect merchants or missionaries; they might seek only a measure of law and order; they might seek political dominance. They would be influenced by their own cultural, religious and political traditions and a wish to demonstrate success to constituencies in Europe. They might be driven by rivalries in Europe or be rivals of other colonial powers in Southeast Asia, which they might come to terms with or seek to pre-empt.

For much of the period, particularly before the 1870s, the impact of the Europeans was indeed mediated by the predominant interests of the British. Those were not concentrated in Southeast Asia itself, and they had no interest in conquering it or making further Indias of Further India. The policies of other powers might be made in the shadow of British power, even shaped by it, but Britain left room for a diversity of approach and timing.

There were indeed shifts over time. Britain's predominance was marked up to 1870. Thereafter Southeast Asia was more fully open to the impact of the Industrial Revolution, and other Western powers showed increasing interest in Southeast Asia as in Africa. At Berlin new rules were accepted by the rivals in the absence of an overbearing empire. Rival Europeans would accept as valid only certain minimum forms of control. It was an impulse either to intensification of control, or to partition, or to both. Rivalry among the Europeans now gave Asians fewer options rather than more. De facto autonomy might be curtailed, lest a claim were effectively challenged.

If there were differences in the Western approaches, there were a range of accommodations to them. If those approaches changed over time, there might be phases also in the accommodations to them. One form of accommodation could succeed another, not necessarily in regular steps: resistance sometimes followed a series of adjustments that had turned out to be insufficient. Even resistance, however, did not quite rule out accommodation. The parties came to terms in some sense: the colonial régimes could not rule without collaborators, and collaborators they could find from the old or from new social elements, again with a range of motives, patriotic or personal in ambition. Accommodation continued within the new frontiers. A colonial régime might admire and wish to utilize the native leaders that had fought it, as the Brookes used the Iban, and the Company contemplated using Mat Salleh. It might fear the social disruption that could follow the displacement of traditional leaders. Alternatively, like the French in Cochinchina, it might actively seek an alternative élite.

The kind of accommodation depended in part on the character of the régimes involved at any particular time, as well as on the current position and objectives of the relevant Western power and its relationship with the other powers. The attitude of those régimes varied, of course, with their geographical position. That might mean that they were more exposed to the Western powers, though they might also be better informed about them and have a longer tradition of adaptation. It might give them greater means or hopes of resistance, through mobilizing their own resources in manpower or matériel, or through calling on great neighbours.

The régimes also varied in their nature. Some were more loosely integrated, some more centrally controlled. Neither condition of itself predicted the outcome of relations with the West, though the former perhaps made break-up more likely. Central control was significant for success, provided those with control made the right judgements and continued to make them as conditions changed. But aspiration to central control without its actuality was no substitute: it might indeed make for an unhelpful rigidity of response. There were also different kinds of central control. In monarchical states, central authority might be accepted in theory only, on the understanding of its practical limitations. The coherence of the state, again, might depend less on administrative effectiveness or adequacy than on the projection of modes of behaviour sustained by ritual and observance. Possessors of this kind of authority would find it especially difficult to come to terms with a Western power that went beyond the most minimal demands, for contacts might undermine ideological unity, and indicate insufficiency. If that unity was already insecure, the régime might be among the less adaptable, fearing to lose what control it had. Alternatively, or successively, it might fear actively to resist, lest such authority as it had were lost in the process and an alternative leadership emerged.

There were indeed questions of and opportunities for judgment for the leadership: it was not only a matter of geographical conditions and ideologies on the one hand and of Western interests on the other. The questions related in part to those Western interests. Handling the West depended on knowledge of them. How good was information at hand? Even if information were adequate and adequately interpreted, the problem itself remained. Was it best to resist the West, or to make concessions and preserve what you could, or to submit promptly and resist from within? Could you risk playing one power against another, if that option were open, or would you thereby precipitate a pre-emptive strike?

Decisions about such questions related not only to information and judgment about information. They also related to the domestic situation. Did the relations between the ruler and the ruled permit a choice? Was it constrained by an ideological or religious prescription, breach of which would deprive the régime of sanction or support? Did connections with non-Western suzerains prevent accommodation to the West, or offer a way of avoiding it? Tributaries might take advantage of demonstrated weakness, or they might themselves come to terms with the Western powers, making it difficult to fit them into the traditional pattern. For the tributaries, there were also problems. Coming to terms with the West might on the one hand be obstructed by a suzerain. That suzerain might on the other hand come to terms with the West and so reduce tributary status still further. More generally a state—like Johor—might see advantage in associating with the West so as to increase its influence over a neighbour. The alternative to submission was to resist or—as with Terengganu—to seek direct relationship with the Western power. Rarely, too, was an élite united in its reponse: indeed, the very intractability of the problems faced tended to add to division.

Asian policies, options, methods, have been analysed largely in terms of states, though to adopt that definition of political activity was in some sense itself a piece of Europeanization. To describe the result of the interaction of European and Asian in terms of the loss of independence may also not be entirely apt. It may even be anachronistic, for the sense of identification with a state was often limited, and the state was not necessarily seen as one among others. Even if the establishment of a colonial framework was clearly the outcome, consciousness of the implications might penetrate to the mass of the people only slowly. Not every change was so dramatically signalled as that in Burma.

> The city people had not been fully aware that the king was to be taken away until they saw our troops marching with Theebaw and the royal family in their midst. Then they awoke to the fact and a great cry went up from men, women and children alike. They bowed down to the ground doing shikko ... an enormous crowd ... assembled, ... and at intervals their lament rose up on the night air. A few stones and clods of earth were thrown.[1]

The people of Mandalay felt that their religion was in danger as well as their identity. Colonial powers in Southeast Asia generally avoided such drama. The interaction of Asian and European was a continuum, within a changed framework.

The framework was indeed just that: it allowed for a diversity of relationships, though all testifying to the increased political influence, if not hegemony, of European peoples and ideas. The hegemony of the Europeans, but not their ideas, was to be displaced only by changes outside Southeast Asia, just as it had been brought about so largely by them, though in both cases the outcome was also to a greater or lesser extent the work of Southeast Asian peoples. In the meantime the patterns of the colonial period were various. Some countries came under direct rule, some indirect; minorities and peripheral peoples often had new opportunities; one state indeed avoided the complete loss of political independence.

The reasons for the more or less general imposition of the colonial framework deserve reconsideration if only perhaps because of their apparent obviousness. Clearly it is primarily a question of power. The Europeans had more power at their disposal than before: more indeed, than any other single world centre had ever possessed. It was bound to be felt in Southeast Asia as elsewhere, given that region's locus and its intrinsic interest, its existing conditions and links; given, too, the Europeans' superiority at sea, their hold on India and later China, their traditional determination, their industrial prowess, their advanced technology. In these general terms the Asian states were at a disadvantage. In addition, the impact of the Europeans was not diminished, but if anything increased, by their rivalry; but the divisions among the Asian powers

---

[1] *The Pioneer Mail*, 16 Dec. 1883, quoted Ali, 44.

impeded any opposition they presented, and their individual modernization was spasmodic.

Only one substantial state survived with real independence; and considering features of Siam's history may help to explain why others failed.
Japan, too, may be compared with Southeast Asian states, and perhaps
most obviously to Confucianist Vietnam. At once its greater capacity for
adaptation is revealed in its combination of a deep sense of unity with
divisions, its insistence on tradition with a readiness to learn. Even so
Japan came nearer to a colonial solution than is sometimes realized, and it
benefited from a prevalent moderation among outside powers and a useful
connection with the most important of them.

Few Southeast Asian political entities were in so fortunate a position.
In the archipelago, many were already too entangled with the Europeans
to take political decisions save within that framework, and the British had
less interest in their fate than in that of the Dutch and the Spaniards. On
the mainland, isolationism was clearly not a viable option, though the
Vietnamese sought it. They had something of the sense of the unity of the
Japanese, but without the sophisticated diversity of views with which it
was combined. The Burmans' view of the world was in a sense like the
views some Japanese treasured, an expansionist one informed by a Buddhist ethic, that could only bring them greater humiliation the more
adjustment was deferred. Burma was also less well placed than Siam. The
latter was beyond the influence of Indian diplomacy, and later a buffer
between two empires. But it also acted positively towards the Europeans:
partly because it had an unusual degree of central control, thanks to
Bangkok's position; partly because it had a new and outgoing dynasty;
partly because it had the wit to recognize that the Europeans were at once
one and divisible and that among them the British were for the most part
the most powerful. It was fortunately placed in time, too: it was expanding
after a disaster; it had territory which it could spare, and which it was not
too obstinate to abandon if necessary. It could compromise.

Southeast Asia after all was unlikely to be a centre of world power; it was
likely to be deeply affected by changes in the distribution of power
elsewhere, and placed in a position of responding to them. The Europeans
were indeed to be displaced initially by the Japanese who had adopted
much that was European. In turn they were displaced by the Allies led by
the United States, and the Southeast Asian peoples had to try to determine
their future in yet another international context, that of a world dominated
by the US and the Soviet Union.

Even in such a context there was scope for judgment and decision. So
there had been in the making of the framework the Southeast Asian
peoples so largely inherited. And in turn they had partly depended on the
quality of information available to them, and their ability to interpret it.
The sources available in the nineteenth century were certainly defective.
Another way of appraising the contacts of European and Asian is by
considering them on a personal basis. Michael Symes and Henry Burney
gave lively accounts of their meetings with Burman leaders, and so did the

latter.[2] Those Vietnamese officials who met Thomas Wade, however, found it difficult to convey his message. The influence of the consular writer at Brunei, Enche Mohamed, was the greater because of the illiteracy of the sultan and the absence of British officials. The intermediaries between Europe and Asia were a diverse band, indeed a motley one.

THE COLONIAL RÉGIMES

The colonial framework outlined one of a succession of state systems in Southeast Asia. The statecraft of each had, within the limits of opportunity and judgment, involved a range of devices in endeavours to fulfil the purposes of the state: alliance, allegiance, violence, patriarchal and bureaucratic relationships, the backing of ideology, religion, law. The colonial system, like earlier systems, used elements of the old, combined with new elements, in an attempt to realize its objectives. Its combinations differed in different areas because its purposes differed and because those areas differed. It had some of the features of the contemporary European state system—in particular the emphasis on territory and frontier—and these often distinguished it from a Southeast Asian system that tended to deal in terms of people rather than land. But colonialism stopped short of the ideological association of state and citizens that the Europeans had worked towards. There were elements of modernity in the colonial approach, some indeed pointing that way, but that was not a conclusion the régimes could readily draw. Nationalisms clashed, that in Europe with that in Asia. At the same time the colonial régimes could not utilize fully the kinds of loyalty that earlier régimes had evoked, those based, for example, on Islam or Buddhism, and their attempts to co-opt rulers or aristocracies tended to change, even erode, the position of those leaders. They claimed, with greater or less justification, to offer good government. Even if their claim were justified, its ambit was limited. 'Thakin, you may say she was not a good queen, he was not a good king, but they were our own', Queen Supayalat's maid of honour said to Fielding Hall after Thibaw's removal. 'Do you think we can love a foreign master as we loved our king, who was, as it were, part of ourselves?'[3] In the face of this attitude, we must ask why were the colonial régimes successfully established and why did they endure so long?

An answer to the first question has been attempted in the preceding pages. In the archipelago, even more than on the mainland, the old kingdoms were weak in themselves, and often their hold could be readily undermined, sometimes with aid from within. On the mainland, even more than in the archipelago, the states were at odds with each other, and there were errors of information and judgment among the rulers. These

[2] cf. Thaung Blackmore, *Catalogue of the Burman Parabaiks in the India Office Library*, London, 1985.
[3] Quoted Ali, 44.

factors limited the need for European force, though that force was available, particularly at sea, and could, as in India, be enhanced with Asian allies and recruits. It was not realistic, Emperor Tu-duc argued, to fight the French. 'Do you really wish to confront such a power with a pack of cowardly soldiers? It would be like mounting an elephant's head or caressing a tiger's tail. ... With what you presently have, do you really expect to dissolve the enemies' rifles into air or chase his battleships into hell?'[4]

European force was perhaps more effective as a threat than as an actuality: it could get bogged down, sometimes literally, like the *Sphinx* on the bar of the Menam during Brooke's mission, sometimes figuratively, like the Dutch in Aceh. It was certainly more effective unused but available in combination with diplomacy. A further reason for the successful establishment of the colonial framework was its readiness within limits to compromise and turn to account those whose allegiance it needed. Initially at least it often had only limited purposes: to establish and maintain order, to ensure stability. That made it more acceptable, though it is doubtful that its message for the masses was so well received as it hoped. The masses were entitled to ask whether it would really relieve them from 'oppression'. If it did, was it only to install a different sort of oppression, perhaps less mediated by cultural factors and bonds of patron–client reciprocity?

What in any case was to replace it? Those it perforce bred up had their answer: to borrow the nationalism that identified people and state in Europe, and to build support on its basis within the frontiers the Europeans had established. But they could not defeat the colonial régimes on their own: the destruction of those régimes required the intervention of the Japanese and later the United States. Then the nationalists had their opportunity. Their success in gaining independence meant that they faced new problems: they had to consolidate régimes from which more was now expected amid divisions that had been only partially concealed during the fight against the colonialists. And, for good or evil, they had to accept the framework created in the colonial period. It was within that framework that their nationalism had largely emerged, and the Japanese had not effectively broken it down. The new world order was even less likely to welcome changes in it than the colonial powers that had earlier divided most of Southeast Asia among themselves. This was the challenge for a new statecraft.

BIBLIOGRAPHIC ESSAY

The historiography on this subject, perhaps even more than most, is affected both by attitude and by availability. The European sources are exceptionally copious; the stances writers take particularly controversial. In the light of the former, it is difficult to represent the views and policies of Asians. In the light of the latter, particularly in combination with the former, it is difficult to maintain a balance.

---

[4] Quoted Tuck, 175.

Sophisticated historical writing in the field was relatively sparse until the early twentieth century. Even then, it tended to be cast in a heroic or imperialist mould, like the writings of D. C. Boulger (*The Life of Sir Stamford Raffles*, London, 1897) or Henri Cordier (a series of articles in *T'oung Pao* on French colonial policy), or like those of P. H. van der Kemp (a series of articles on Anglo-Dutch relations mainly in *De Indische Gids* and *Bijdragen tot de Taal-, Land-, en Volkenkunde*). It tended to be nationalistic in tone, not merely over against Asians, but other Europeans also.

The application of professional historical values is more obvious in the inter-war period with the writings of D. G. E. Hall (e.g. *The Dalhousie-Phayre Correspondence*, London, 1932), W. S. Desai (*History of the British Residency in Burma 1826–1840*, Rangoon, 1939), and L. A. Mills ('British Malaya, 1824–1867', JMBRAS, 1925, reprinted 1960), and it intensified after World War II, when, moreover, primary sources became more freely available. Writers of the 1950s and early 1960s established a new framework, though still perhaps concerned more with policy than with impact, with one side of the story. They included C. D. Cowan, *Nineteenth-century Malaya The Origins of British Political Control*, London, 1961; G. Irwin, 'Nineteenth-century Borneo, A Study in Diplomatic Rivalry', VKI, XV (1955); Emily Sadka, *The Protected Malay States, 1874–1895*, Kuala Lumpur, 1968; Neon Snidvongs, 'The development of Siamese Relations with Britain and France in the reign of Maha Mongkut, 1851–1868', Ph.D. thesis, University of London, 1961; Walter Vella, *Siam under Rama III*, New York, 1957; Damodar Singhal, *The Annexation of Upper Burma*, Singapore, 1960; and the present author in his earlier books: 'British Policy in the Malay Peninsula and Archipelago 1824–1876', JMBRAS (1957) reprinted Kuala Lumpur, 1969; *Anglo-Dutch Rivalry in the Malay World, 1780–1824*, St Lucia, London, and New York, 1962; and *Piracy and Politics in the Malay World*, Melbourne and Singapore, 1963.

Shifts in attitude began to correct this approach from the early 1960s. At times, however, they could be so severe as almost to dislodge the whole endeavour, and to put the validity of what was seen as purely political or merely diplomatic history in question. The challenge was sometimes associated less with a new research thrust than with a reversal of viewpoint.

Greater balance and nicer nuance quickly followed. The later 1960s saw in this field, as in others, the appearance of work that reached a new level of sophistication, and it continued in the following decade, in, for example, A. J. S. Reid, *The Contest for North Sumatra*, Kuala Lumpur, 1969; John Ingleson, 'Britain's Annexation of Labuan in 1846', *University Studies in History*, V, 4, Perth, 1970; Milton Osborne, *The French Presence in Cochinchina and Cambodia*, Ithaca, 1969; and Peter Burns, *The Journals of J. W. W. Birch*, Kuala Lumpur, 1976. Other examples were Oliver Pollak, *Empires in Collision: Anglo-Burmese Relations in the mid-nineteenth century*, Westport, 1979; Charles Keeton, *King Thebaw and the Ecological Rape of Burma*, Delhi, 1974; Robert Pringle, *Rajahs and Rebels*, London, 1970; Carl Trocki, *Prince of Pirates*, Singapore, 1979; and J. F. Warren, *The Sulu Zone, 1768–1898*, Singapore, 1981. Books by Rollins Bonney, *Kedah, 1771–1821*, Kuala Lumpur, 1971; Eunice Thio, *British Policy in the Malay Peninsula, 1880–1910*, Kuala Lumpur, 1969; and Khoo Kay Kim, *The Western Malay States, 1850–*

1873, Kuala Lumpur, 1972 added to our knowledge of Malaya. Chandran Jeshurun, *The Contest for Siam 1889–1902*, Kuala Lumpur, 1977; Pensri Duke, *Les relations entre la France et la Thailande (Siam) an XIXe Siècle*, Bangkok, 1962; and Thamsook Numnonda, 'Negotiations regarding the cession of the Siamese Malay States, 1907–9', JSS LV (1967) added to our knowledge of Siam. The present author produced his books on the Borneo and Sulu region (*Britain, the Brookes and Brunei*, Kuala Lumpur, 1971, and *Sulu and Sabah*, Kuala Lumpur, 1978), while new light was thrown on the creation of British Burma by Ernest Chew, 'The Fall of the Burmese Kingdom in 1885', JSEAS, X, 2 (1979); G. P. Ramachandra, 'The outbreak of the first Anglo-Burman War', JMBRAS, LI, 2, 1978; and Muhammad Shamsheer Ali, 'The Beginnings of British Rule in Upper Burma', Ph.D. thesis, University of London, 1976.

The 1980s have seen attempts to examine or re-examine Asian sources, in particular by scholars from Australia, Malaysia and Thailand, like A. C. Milner (*Kerajaan*, Tucson, 1982), Alfons van der Kraan (*Lombok: Conquest, Colonization and Underdevelopment, 1870–1940*, Singapore, 1980), Ian Black (*A Gambling Style of Government*, Kuala Lumpur, 1983), Shaharil Talib (*After its own Image: The Trengganu Experience 1881–1941*, Singapore, 1984) and Kobkua Suwannathat-Pian (*Thai–Malay Relations*, Singapore, 1988).

The potential of the subject is far from exhausted: in a way, indeed, it is central to the contacts of Europe and Asia. But that, as the present chapter again suggests, does not make it easier to deal with.

CHAPTER

2

POLITICAL STRUCTURES IN THE NINETEENTH AND EARLY TWENTIETH CENTURIES

In the nineteenth and early twentieth centuries profound changes took place in the political order in all Southeast Asian countries. A main feature of these changes was the foundation of European-style state administrations within territories formally defined by European imperialism. Colonial rulers created centrally controlled and functionally organized bureaucracies to govern regions which were delineated with little or no regard for indigenous conceptions of political or cultural boundaries. The personalistic and quasi-feudal complex of arrangements which had been the hallmark of earlier political systems was overridden and often eliminated.

The change was one that began slowly and then began accelerating with almost blinding rapidity as European industrialism and nationalism remade the entire world. At the beginning of the nineteenth century much of the region remained outside the control of any European power. Only Penang, Melaka (Malacca), Java, some of Maluku (the Moluccas), and part of the Philippines could really be said to be under European control. By 1850, the European advance was limited to a few British footholds in Malaya, the beginnings of a French presence in Indochina, a few Dutch treaties and the British occupation of Arakan and Tenasserim. During the next three decades, much of the region was divided into spheres of influence among the various European powers, and the political boundaries which characterize the region today had been fixed. Actual control of population, however, was limited to a few metropolitan centres: elsewhere it was exercised through treaties with otherwise autonomous chiefs or through loosely governed intermediaries. European rule was little more than claims of sovereignty and the rights to certain revenues and economic privileges.

By the 1920s, the whole of Southeast Asia had undergone a radical change. The clear linear borders shown on the map now divided the region into discrete political and administrative units. Networks of roads, railroads, telegraph wires and postal systems connected the economic centres of the various European empires with their hinterlands. The

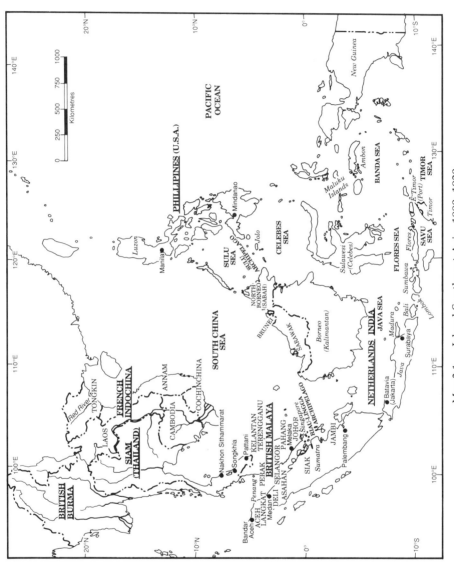

Map 2.1   Island Southeast Asia, 1880–1930

bureaucratic grids of central control had sprung out into respective 'national' hinterlands standardizing laws, languages, currencies, and even weights and measures according to their respective European usages.

The nature of the new political order was a radical departure from what had preceded it. In most areas, for the very first time, the arm of the state was capable of reaching into the daily lives of ordinary villagers on a sustained and intensive basis. Salaried government officials began to undertake the tasks of tax collection, law enforcement, land management, the judiciary, and public works, according to uniform, centrally determined, and very often alien standards. In addition to these accepted functions of government, the newly created administrations came to engage in an ever-increasing range of new activities, including education, public health and sanitation, and social and economic policy. These changes ushered in the era of the modern state in Southeast Asia.

The elimination of the traditional order was often a violent process. Age-old political forms were swept away in a matter of a few short years by fiat, or else were crushed by ruthless suppression. Those who resisted the imperialist advance invariably found it a hopeless, if not suicidal enterprise. Several entire political entities, such as Bali, Aceh and Sulu, perished in paroxysms of frenzied violence. More than once poorly armed but dedicated and often religiously motivated warriors threw themselves against Gatling guns, heavy artillery, repeating rifles and the disciplined infantry forces of industrialized states.

Officially, the new colonial order made no compromise with the Southeast Asian world. Confident to the point of arrogance, European administrators and military leaders in the region possessed both the will and the capability to destroy the old order and thus believed they had the power to create a new one. Unofficially, all was not as it seemed, and the realities of exercising effective administration were far beyond the actual capability of the imperial powers. They could destroy and thwart indigenous political and social initiatives, but they could not create what they imagined. The high tide of European colonialism continued to be characterized by compromise, qualification, half-measures, and inevitably frustrating results. The gap between aims and achievements was usually blamed on the 'laziness', the 'incompetence' and presumed racial, cultural and moral inferiority of the indigenous peoples. Despite the failure of stated European objectives, however, fundamental change was effected although it was often entirely unintended and sometimes contrary to the initial purpose.

The powerlessness of the indigenous peoples was more apparent than real. If active resistance was hopeless in the long run, it could be a very long run indeed as the Dutch discovered in Aceh. More difficult to control was passive resistance, indifference, and even self-interested co-operation which could subvert the best-laid plans. The weight of superior numbers and pure inertia worked to impede European efforts. Nor is it accurate to see Southeast Asians as merely reacting to European initiatives. Individuals, classes and entire ethnic groups took advantage of the opportunities that presented themselves. Many indigenous peoples actively moved, often with surprising alacrity, to align themselves with whatever new

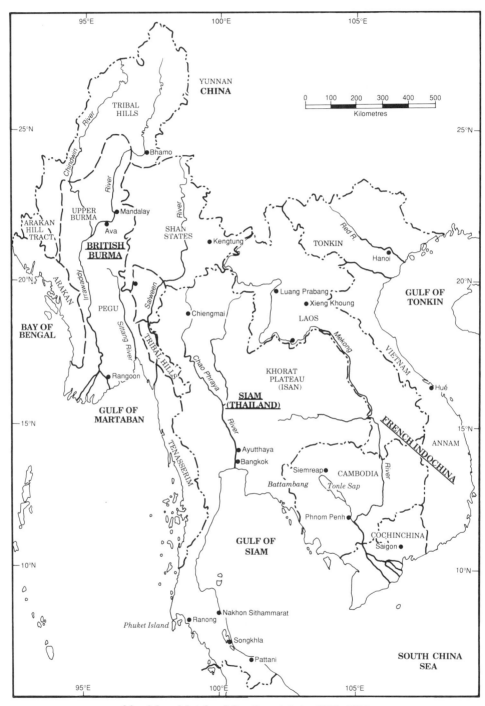

Map 2.2   Mainland Southeast Asia, 1880–1930

centres of power appeared. Nothing was more deceptive than the illusion of total European control, for, in learning from the West, the most ardent collaborators prepared themselves to throw off foreign rule. By the 1930s, indigenous political and administrative élites or subélites in every European colony were beginning the quest for autonomy and independence. Even in Siam, where royal absolutism had created a centralized bureaucracy and military, modern education and the administrative competence of well-trained commoners had created a challenge to the monarchy.

The first section of this chapter is devoted to the role played in these newly created states by the 'collaborating' classes. In each case, it was necessary for the colonial rulers to rely on the co-operation of one or more groups of Asians in order to exercise effective control. A key variable was in the nature and status of the indigenous collaborator class. In some instances, these were the traditional ruling classes who had accepted the reality of Western domination. In other instances, marginal or minority populations came to fill these functions. Whatever the case, the changes directed and organized by Western colonial rulers deeply altered the nature and composition of the indigenous ruling classes. There was a fundamental alteration of the traditional relationship between rulers and ruled, in addition to a redefinition of both the rules and the realm.

In the early part of the nineteenth century, as in the past, colonial governments depended on almost feudal relationships with local collaborating classes. Thus traditional élites were often given some official recognition, and day-to-day government was conducted through them. The slowness of transport and the general isolation of Europeans in the tropics led to the creation of Eurasian or mestizo classes which assumed a life and culture of their own in places like the Dutch and Spanish territories. Even in the British-controlled Straits Settlements, control of the Chinese was accomplished through adaptations of the Dutch system of the *Kapitan China* or through revenue farmers and secret society headmen.

In the years after 1880, most of these arrangements were terminated as they were seen to place too much power in the hands of non-Europeans. Nevertheless, it continued to be necessary to maintain some sort of collaborating class if colonies were to be run effectively. Clerks, runners and minor office functionaries had to be Asians and had to be hired locally. If nothing else, there was the cost factor. European personnel were prohibitively expensive. In some cases the new Asian clerks were simply a new generation that accepted demotion and made the best of it. In other cases, particularly in the many new territories that were annexed or simply taken over after 1880, it was a case either of domesticating the former ruling class or else of creating entirely new classes to perform the mundane functions of colonial government. In Burma, the British came to rely on Indian immigrants to staff the lower levels of the bureaucracy, while in Laos and Cambodia the French used Vietnamese, and in Borneo and Sumatra the Dutch employed Javanese.

Although it was intended that power over policy formulation would be kept in European hands and the functions of primary decision-making were located more firmly in the metropole, considerable influence came to rest in the hands of these local classes, if only on an informal basis.

Moreover, they generally obtained a Western education and were exposed to radically different social and political ideas. In the years after World War I, these people sparked off movements for independence and self-government.

The second section of this chapter approaches the question of direct and indirect rule. Generally speaking, the depth and nature of the changes wrought by colonial rule depended on the degree to which indigenous political and social institutions were retained. In those places where colonial rule occurred as a result of treaties or some form of accommodation with local leaders and institutions, European control was exercised, at least nominally, through the indigenous structures, and was known as 'indirect rule'. This was the case in the Malay states, much of the Netherlands East Indies, and in Cambodia and Laos. 'Direct rule' was said to characterize situations in which the colonial takeover was accomplished by conquest or cession and the former political institutions (if, indeed, any had existed) were abrogated and new ones were created. British Burma, French Cochinchina, the Straits Settlements, and parts of the Spanish Philippines and the Netherlands East Indies represented examples of this variation.

While the legal status of the prior political institutions could be taken as a formal guide to the presence of a system of direct or indirect rule, in practice there was often little to distinguish the systems. During this period, legal niceties were respected only at the convenience of the colonial power, though such technical points once again became of importance when questions arose regarding the structure of the post-colonial state. In the late nineteenth and early twentieth centuries, indirect rule often signified no more than a transitory stage between the inception of a colonial presence and the development of a more comprehensive administrative machine. In most places, by the end of the 1920s, the state had been radically transformed through functionalization, rationalization and the extension of the European presence. On the other hand, in some respects, rule was always conducted through non-European intermediaries.

The third topic of this chapter is the imposition of 'law and order', certainly an ambiguous undertaking by any standard and even more so in colonial Southeast Asia. Initially, Europeans had been content to allow local law and custom to serve as their guide in daily administration. The only exception was the Philippines, where the Spanish friars saw it as their duty to combat paganism and to resist the advances of Islam. Generally speaking, however, the situation in British and Dutch colonies, where business came first, was marked by compromise. By the middle of the nineteenth century Europeans felt themselves drawn into local politics because of 'instability'. Colonial rule thus advanced on the justification of 'restoring order', suppressing piracy and 'protecting' peaceful trade.

These attitudes were gradually transformed by the bourgeois reformist movements of the metropoles in the 1890s. By the end of the nineteenth century all European states had come to see their role in Southeast Asia as one of bringing 'civilization'. Whether they conceived of it as the 'White Man's burden' or as a *mission civilisatrice*, all colonial régimes came to justify themselves as organized to secure the welfare of the native peoples. Such pretensions may seem hypocritical at a time when the most strenuous efforts were simultaneously being made to exploit local economic resources for the benefit of the European metropole and while draconian measures to control labour and restrict indigenous political life were taken with little compunction. Nevertheless, debt slavery, in fact most forms of slavery, were eliminated, as were piracy, head-hunting, cannibalism, trial by ordeal, the arbitrary rule of native chiefs and the power of secret societies. Uniform systems of law and justice were instituted. Taxation was regularized and the administrative norms of the West were established within the various territories controlled by each power. The final stage in the imposition of law and order came as nationalist consciousness and the desire for political autonomy stirred the indigenous peoples. At the same time the new Asian working classes of the region began to organize for economic justice. Each colonial power came to create security forces, secret police organizations and spy networks to suppress political movements and labour unions. These too, became a part of the colonial heritage of the post-imperial order.

In almost every new state of the region, the new colonial rulers created what J. S. Furnivall has styled 'plural societies'. These social formations, which are the topic of the fourth section, came about as a result of a variety of conditions. Sometimes they were caused by the accidental nature of the process of colonial takeovers. At other times, ethnic groups would be separated or thrown together because of the manner in which the border-lines were drawn or redrawn, an exercise often conducted in conference rooms in European capitals, and done in the interest of perceived econom-ic or administrative efficiency, or to satisfy the strategic concerns of the various European powers.

As a result, the political units which emerged from this period fre-quently included a multiplicity of racial and ethnic groups. Just as often, the new lines split territories which had formerly been the possession of a single ethnic community, or traditional state, between two new political entities. In addition, these years were also marked by significant popula-tion shifts. Economic specialization developed along ethnic lines with the 'new' or capitalist sectors being taken over by newcomers. Likewise, social stratification often rearranged and reinforced ethnic barriers.

In addition to social shifts, the colonial régimes sought to impose linguistic uniformity in areas where none had ever existed. This happened in two ways, sometimes both together. European languages became the lingua franca of the new administrative territory as happened in Burma, Indochina, Malaya and the Philippines. In other areas, one of the local languages that already enjoyed widespread use was pressed into service as an administrative language, as was the case with *bahasa melayu* in Indo-nesia. Even in countries where indigenous languages had official status, European languages became the language of higher education of the élites. As a result, those Asians who sought positions in the colonial bureaucra-cies studied the European languages and imbibed the cultural peculiarities of the Western metropole. Regardless of the benefits or disadvantages of this change, those who became educated found themselves even further removed from the concerns and everyday lives of their own rural compatriots.

Whatever the cause, however, the results tended to be surprisingly similar. Different racial and ethnic groups found themselves thrown together within the same political units but paradoxically often under separate administrative and even legal structures. Relations between minority populations and groups that would become 'national majorities' after World War II were often 'suspended'. In Burma, British administrators in the minority areas institutionalized the customs and political structures of the Shans, Karens and others, while Christian missionaries put their languages into written forms based on the Roman alphabet, just as Malay, Indonesian, Tagalog and Vietnamese were converted to Roman letters. In other areas of Southeast Asia, Chinese immigrants flocked into the newly created economic sectors while the colonial legal and administrative structure effectively insulated most of the indigenous peoples from the affairs of its Chinese residents. The colonial heritage has left these new 'national' territories with the ambiguous heritage of clearly-drawn national borders enclosing collections of heterogeneous and antagonistic ethnic communities.

The final section offers a study of two contrasting cases. The nineteenth century saw the traditional Burmese state and finally the Burmese monarchy collapse as it sought to resist increasing British pressure. By contrast, the kings of Siam (Thailand) yielded and accommodated themselves to British and other Western demands for open borders, unrestricted trade and extraterritorial privileges. At the beginning of the twentieth century Burma and Siam seemed to represent opposite poles of the 'colonial' experience. In 1886 and 1887, with the conquest of upper Burma and the abolition of the monarchy, the British began the process of totally restructuring the country's administration according to the model of British India. Placed under the most rigorous form of direct rule, Burma became the most thoroughly colonized state in the region. Siam, by contrast, remained technically independent. Its monarch moved beyond compromise with the West and embarked upon a process of administrative reform, centralization and modernization. Although usually treated as an exception in Southeast Asia, since it was not formally taken under European control, Siam may be seen as an extreme example of indirect rule. It can be argued that the combination of unequal treaties, foreign economic predominance and the presence of foreign advisers made the position of Siam quite similar to the situation of one of the unfederated Malay states, such as Johor. In the final analysis, in both countries, regardless of who directed the process, the results were quite similar in certain respects. Like all the other states of Southeast Asia, they found their territories delineated by Europeans and were subjected to the processes of administrative centralization and rationalization according to European models. They found their social and political structures rearranged and transformed by migrants, new economic forces and shifts in the class structures. Nevertheless, by 1930, Burma appeared to have moved further down the road of political modernization and economic development than Siam. The latter was still run by an absolute monarchy, and a traditional élite clung to power through the persistence of quasi-feudal institutions.

The years immediately preceding World War II saw the European order in Southeast Asia under a variety of challenges. The trauma of World War I and the economic stress of the world-wide depression had seriously undermined Western power. At the same time, the social and political order which had been created to serve European interests had taken on a life of its own, and everywhere nationalist movements sought either to overthrow or to succeed to the political order which had come into being. Political liberation of Southeast Asia, however, would occur within the structures created by European colonialism.

INDIGENOUS COLLABORATION

European domination was based on superior military technology, economic strength and the possession of national and mercenary armies. Despite this power, successful European administration needed co-operation from strategic indigenous groups. In the first instance, Europeans themselves were simply too thin on the ground to undertake the tasks of day-to-day administration on any but a fairly high level. In pre-modern times, it was necessary to take Asians into partnership and to allow them a share of power within the colonial apparatus. These groups lost status with the rationalization of the state.

Nevertheless, Asian collaborators were still necessary. As the role of government became both more extensive and more intensive, the demands upon colonial administrative structures increased immeasurably. Language and cultural barriers alone necessitated a class of subordinates whose role it was to convey an increasing number of directives to broader sectors of the local populations. These intermediaries were drawn from a variety of sources, depending on the local situation and historical development of each colony. Sometimes they were members of traditional ruling groups, sometimes they were newly risen classes, in other instances they were immigrants. Whatever its origin, a class of indigenous, or at least local, collaborators was necessary for successful colonial rule.

The Dutch and Spanish empires in Java and the northern two-thirds of the Philippines were pre-modern creations and had come into being in the sixteenth and seventeenth centuries. The conditions of the age necessitated the development of local ruling classes dependent upon European patronage and support. In both areas local élites were brought into the colonial régime and often exercised considerable powers. These included village headmen in the Philippines who became *gobernadorcillos*, or regional chiefs such as the *bupati* in Java whose traditional duties to their former overlords were subsumed by the Verenigde Oost-Indische Compagnie (VOC, the Dutch East India Company) and converted into the delivery of trade produce.

In the Netherlands East Indies, a close association had grown up between the Javanese *priyayi* class and the Dutch. Although each performed specific functions in civil administration, the political partnership between the *pangreh pradja* and Binnenlandse Bestuur was an unequal one but, because of its long-standing nature, it was quite complex. Nor was it the sort of thing that could be diagrammed on an organizational chart.

Throughout the nineteenth century the *pangreh pradja* continued to function both as the successors of the pre-colonial chiefs and as agents of the Netherlands government.[1]

Heather Sutherland suggests that the relationship between the European civil service and the *pangreh pradja* was characterized by continued bargaining 'between elites of two races and of two cultures'. The cultural foundations were important. The *priyayi* did not see themselves as traitors to the traditional order or as betrayers of their peoples. Rather they were merely respecting what they understood as 'power'. According to Sutherland, the intellectual base of the *pangreh pradja* was in their perpetuation of the traditional ideas of status and aristocratic values. These included 'continuing beliefs in supra-human aspects of life and government', the importance of local family cults, and belief in the importance of graves. 'Belief in the possibility of working with transcendental forces was virtually universal among the Javanese, and the cultivation of power by mystical exercises was very common, a hallmark of priyayi culture.' The Javanese thus stressed moral and religious aspects of government. They perceived a need for an essential harmony between spiritual and physical environments. The persistence of these beliefs was a reminder that the *priyayi* had evolved from feudal chiefs to government administrators during the nineteenth century.[2]

The relationships that grew up between the European colonial régimes and these traditional collaborator classes are difficult to typify. They were ambiguous and complex to say the least, and were marked by compromises and contradictions. It was difficult to tell where the European left off and the Asian began. In fact, it could be argued that these early colonial states were more Asian than European. The earlier colonial governments, such as those in the Philippines and the Netherlands East Indies, were much like traditional Southeast Asian states. They depended on patron and client links between several layers of local chiefs whose segmented polities ultimately gave them a certain standing that was recognized by the local populations. Tax collections, law and order, public works and religious affairs were seen as the responsibility of the regional chiefs or even village authorities whose relations with the centre had been essentially personal.

The rationalization of the state brought a move to revise these relationships. Positive steps were taken to demote those groups who had, in earlier years, actually exercised power, including those who had facilitated the imperial advance. Most régimes took steps to deprive these groups of the spheres of private power they had come to possess within the colonial political and social order. The new administrative arrangements were also aimed at removing the traditional social and political cement that had bound traditional leaders to their peoples. By the beginning of the twentieth century, Southeast Asians were finding themselves declining in status and power.

---

[1] H. Sutherland, *The Making of a Bureaucratic Elite*, Singapore, 1979, 2.
[2] ibid., 4–6.

Whole classes of the colonial populations that might have been counted as allies in earlier years were likewise demoted or abolished as Europe drew closer to its possessions in Southeast Asia. The Eurasians of the Netherlands East Indies, especially Java, whose decline had begun in the beginning of the nineteenth century, were close to becoming outcasts by the 1880s. Jean Gelman Taylor[3] has traced the process of their displacement in the colonial society and state of the late nineteenth century. For such groups, the imposition of racial and cultural barriers between Asians and Europeans was particularly degrading.

In other countries, however, these classes were not displaced. In fact, they managed to position themselves so as to inherit power when the colonialists ultimately departed. Their success or lack of success in so doing depended largely on their ability to maintain a power base in the local society. This was particularly true in the Philippines where the mestizo classes as well as some of the creoles were already raising the nationalist banner by 1870. The efforts by the Spanish during this time to modernize their administration in Philippine and concurrently to avoid sharing power with the *ilustrados*, led to the Philippine revolution and the takeover by the United States. Not all of these groups went peacefully into oblivion.

In the case of the Straits Settlements, British rule during most of the nineteenth century had rested on the collaboration of the Straits Chinese, especially the *kapitans*, the secret society headmen, the revenue farmers and *baba* merchants who had come to occupy semi-official positions. Similar groups of Chinese also existed in Batavia and other Javanese towns, in Saigon, Bangkok and Manila. Very often, their power within the Chinese communities, or in local society in general, was rooted in secret societies and groups of revenue farm police.

In particular, the opium revenue farms, which were invariably controlled by Chinese, came to be perceived as the most glaring examples of enclaves of the state in private hands. The revenue farmers exercised power over the local population through their own networks of spies, thugs and informers. As a first step in the rationalization process, economic and political power were separated. Between 1885 and 1910, the revenue-farming systems were increasingly restricted and ultimately abolished and converted into government monopolies. This happened first in the French possessions and later in the Dutch and American colonies and finally in the British territories and Siam.

Even where efforts to decrease the influence of these classes in the colonized areas were largely successful, many managed to maintain some footing on the socio-political mountain. In British Malaya the Straits Chinese were well-enough established and often wealthy enough to move into the middle ranks of the expanding bureaucracy as clerks and sometimes even as professionals. Individuals such as Song Ong Siang, Dr Lim Boon Keng and Tan Cheng Lock occupied places of prominence in local society during the first half of the twentieth century. It can even be argued that their cultural descendants did in fact inherit at least Singapore. These

[3] *The Social World of Batavia: European and Eurasian in Dutch Asia*, Madison, 1983.

were the graduates of Raffles Institute and the other English-language schools. The class of 'Queen's Chinese' that formed the Straits Chinese British Association were the predecessors of the English-'stream' Chinese, who, in the case of Singapore, have taken charge of the post-colonial society.

Despite these efforts at rationalization and decreasing traditional power bases, collaborators continued to be particularly important to colonial governments in the years after 1890, when increasing numbers of specialists were recruited from European civil services to perform technical tasks in fields such as medicine, public sanitation, and engineering in mines, railroads and construction. Unlike earlier colonial officials, who came to Southeast Asia prepared to serve for periods ranging from a decade to life before returning home, the servants of the modern administrations could often expect to return to the metropole after two to three years. Sometimes they could be reposted from a colony in Southeast Asia to one in Africa or Southern Asia or even in the Americas. Their commitment was not to a particular Southeast Asian area or state but to a career in a global imperial bureaucracy.

European officials were expensive. They came with their wives, their children and as much European cultural baggage as they could manage. They expected medical and retirement benefits, paid 'home leaves' for themselves and their families, and of course high-quality education, in European schools, for their children. They needed housing and amenities of a European level as well as staffs of servants to undertake the tasks which were considered unfit for white people in the colonies. The sheer numbers of people needed for efficient administration meant that most of the lower ranks had to be recruited locally. Such a rank of semi-skilled clerks, runners and village-level personnel also served to place a status barrier between the power élite and the menial public employees. It also prevented the appearance of a class of poor, or even average, whites who might dispel the illusion that the Europeans were racially superior to all Asians.

The push for bureaucratic standardization in the Netherlands Indies, which reached a peak between 1910 and 1915, brought a real shift in relations between the Dutch government and the *priyayi*. During these years the formerly independent feudal chiefs were forced to accept their new status as merely a part of a centralized bureaucracy.[4] Although some *priyayi* families gained financially as the government began to promote large-scale economic enterprise, most tended to slip in economic status. They were integrated under centrally directed control and thus became less dependent on popular support than on Dutch approval.[5]

The elimination of Spanish authority in the Philippines by the United States brought the US up against the resistance of the *ilustrado* class which had begun the revolt against Spain in the first place. During the early years of the twentieth century, the American relationship with the *ilustrados* was probably unique in Southeast Asia. Unlike other colonial powers, the

---

[4] Sutherland, 2.
[5] ibid., 11–14.

Americans saw their possession of the Philippines as only temporary. Americans wished to build a benevolent colonial government which would gain the co-operation of the people and at the same time educate them for self-government. The new colonialists were convinced that the *ilustrados* were as yet unprepared for self-government. As William Howard Taft wrote:

> While they [the *ilustrados*] deal in high sounding phrases concerning liberty and free government they have very little conception of what that means. They cannot resist the temptation to venality, and every office is likely to be used for the personal aggrandizement of the holder thereof in disregard of public interest.[6]

Taft would have preferred to place power in the hands of the 'people'. However, it was necessary to solicit the support and co-operation of the élite in order to end the war which frustrated Filipino nationalists and armies of peasants were waging against the United States. American administrators found it expedient to allow the co-operative elements of the Filipino élite an increasingly larger role in government and to look the other way as they enriched themselves at the expense of the peasants and increased their traditional power within the local communities. Norman Owen points out that the contradictory goals of cheap and expedient administration coupled with republican ideals led to a 'perpetual compromise' which ultimately allowed the *ilustrado* class to take power. Taft had warned against the tendency 'merely to await the organization of a Philippine oligarchy or aristocracy competent to administer government and then turn the islands over to it'.[7]

Although the Americans were newcomers to the colonial game in 1899 and 1900, their decision to seek the co-operation of a group within the native society and then to attempt to remould it to their purpose was one that was taken by all colonial régimes throughout the region. Even though not all did so with the intention of training a ruling class to succeed them, most colonial administrative policies achieved the same end. A class of indigenous functionaries was trained to fill the lower ranks of the civil and military services. Groups that had begun as élite classes in pre-colonial or 'early' colonial society, such as the Malay aristocrats, the Filipino *ilustrados* or the Javanese *priyayi*, were converted into civil servants or, as they preferred to be called, government officials.

In other cases, new, non-élite groups were identified by the colonial powers as preferred allies. Traditional leaders were eliminated altogether in Burma. The old circle headmen were abolished and new 'village' headmen were appointed as civil servants. Likewise in Cochinchina, the elimination of the traditional mandarins necessitated the employment of ordinary Vietnamese as government servants. In some instances where,

---

[6] Michael Cullinane, 'Implementing the New Order: The Structure and Supervision of Local Government during the Taft Era', in Norman G. Owen, ed., *Compadre Colonialism: Studies on the Philippines under American Rule*, Ann Arbor: Michigan Papers on Southeast Asia no. 3, University of Michigan, 1971, 15.

[7] Norman Owen, 'Introduction: Philippine Society and American Colonialism', in ibid., 5–7.

for a variety of reasons, local leaders were unavailable, 'foreign' Asians came to serve in these roles. In Annam and Tonkin, where the traditional hierarchy of mandarins was left in place, a new civil service, made up largely of Frenchmen, was organized alongside it. On the other hand, the lack of suitable personnel in the Cambodian and Laotian protectorates led the French to employ Vietnamese. In Burma and Malaya, the British often found it convenient to use Indians, and in the case of the latter, Chinese.

In the military services the use of alien or minority populations as soldiers seemed even more prevalent. Following policies that had been developed in India, the British specialized in cultivating certain populations as military allies. Two-thirds of the British military in Burma were made up of Karens, and the other third were mostly Kachins and Shans. In the Netherlands East Indies, the Dutch had long made it a policy to employ Ambonese in the colonial military. In Malaya, the British frequently employed sepoys from India.

A side-effect of the recruitment of local personnel for government service was the establishment, in virtually all colonies, of school systems. These were often followed by the appearance of private schools, generally run by Christian missionaries. The language of instruction was usually the European tongue of the colony. Schools using the vernacular as a medium of instruction were also founded, but these tended to be seen as less prestigious. The impact of the schools was, of course, far-reaching, since it had the effect of creating cultural allies for the colonial powers. This class of individuals began to separate themselves from their native cultures and to adopt not only Western languages, but values, prejudices, life-styles and, most ironically, expectations. Advancement according to merit, an essential element of Western education, was a dangerous precedent in colonial systems founded on the erection of racial barriers. Personal humiliation and the frustration of expectations created by the Western educational experience fuelled the first generation of anti-colonial revolutionaries in the 1930s. The protégés of the European rulers became their competitors.

The increasingly racist aspect of European administrations began after a time to create a backlash, and this profoundly altered relations between European and Asian members of the colonial élites. Theories about the nature of Southeast Asian political thought and political practice developed by scholars such as Benedict Anderson and Anthony C. Milner[8] indicate that indigenous rulers and chiefs might have initially seen it as their duty to collaborate with colonial rule. Because of the rather gradual process of the colonial takeover as well as the fact that groups like the priyayi saw themselves as servants of power, they did not see their activity in co-operating with the Dutch government as an act of treason. In other cases, such as in British Malaya, Malay chiefs who collaborated with the colonial advance also saw themselves as continuing to serve the kerajaan, the government. The idea that a colonial government was necessarily an

---

8 Anderson, 'The Idea of Power in Javanese Culture' in Claire Holt et al., eds, *Culture and Politics in Indonesia*, Ithaca, 1972; A. C. Milner, *Keraja'an: Malay Political Culture on the Eve of Colonial Rule*, Tucson, 1982.

alien entity had not actualy forced itself into the consciousness of local ruling classes. It was really only with the development of nationalism that Southeast Asians came to perceive a fundamental difference between the interests of the state and their own societies. Certainly a part of this awareness of difference came as a reaction to European racism.

In a country such as Siam, where there was no formal colonial government, the monarchy itself can be seen as both the collaborator and the colonialist. So far as foreign powers were concerned, the two Thai monarchs who ruled during the years of European advance, Mongkut (r. 1851–68) and Chulalongkorn (r. 1868–1910), carefully accommodated themselves to European demands. They gave up territories; they signed treaties that compromised their control of customs, foreign nationals and trade; they accepted the advice of foreigners on reforming their own political, economic and social systems; and they went so far as to hire European experts to carry out such changes. The reforms in Siam resulted in the centralization and the enhancement of the monarch's power within the realm.

Internally, Chulalongkorn used the modernization programme to eliminate the hereditary court officials and the *chao muang*, the provincial élites who had made the local governorships their family preserves. They were replaced with the representatives of the Bangkok-based bureaucracy which was under the control of the Western-educated brothers of the king. New officials were recruited from the Bangkok élite and from among the children of provincial families which were willing to accept education in exchange for their loss of hereditary privilege. These provincial élites lost their former military status, and European advisers were hired to train a professional military armed with modern weapons.

The two early twentieth-century Chakri monarchs (Rama VI and Rama VII) were much less adept at managing the apparatus of the central state that Chulalongkorn had created. They may be seen as the first of the colonial rulers to be toppled by their own class of collaborators. The participants in the 1932 coup d'état had a great deal more power vis-à-vis the monarchy, and thus did not need to wait until the imperial military was neutralized by outside forces. They in fact led the military force.

By forming alliances with sectors of the local population, colonial rulers were acting out of expediency. The results of these policies proved to be profoundly dangerous to the colonial governments. The indigenous allies gained an intimate familiarity with the colonial system that ultimately turned them into the most dangerous of enemies, possible replacements for the European rulers. In addition to this peril, Europeans had created a class who excelled at collaboration, who understood instinctively the nature of colonial power, and who were prepared to collaborate with whomever held the balance of military strength. European colonial officials were often stunned by the alacrity with which 'their natives' responded to the Japanese promise of 'Asia for Asians' in 1942.

In the case of the Philippines, as in Malaya, Cambodia and Laos, the traditional élites were fortunate enough to succeed. They followed the path from traditional leadership to colonial ally to post-independence élite, staying on top while the world changed beneath them. In the Netherlands East Indies, the transition was not so smooth. The extent to which these classes found themselves associated with anti-nationalist interests in the midst of revolutionary turmoil was usually a function of how far they had allowed themselves to become separated from their own societies. The new administrative class in Vietnam, often Catholics, strove to become 'French'. In the post-colonial era, the situation would be particularly difficult for those ethnic or social minorities that had served the European state and then found themselves isolated in the years of nationalist revolution.

DIRECT AND INDIRECT RULE

J. S. Furnivall, in his classic work on colonial rule in British Burma and the Netherlands East Indies, noted that the two countries shared many similarities.

> But in respect of colonial practice they show a striking contrast. In Burma the British have from the first relied on western principles of rule, on the principles of law and economic freedom; in Netherlands India the Dutch have tried to conserve and adapt to modern use the tropical principles of custom and authority.[9]

This statement points up the key distinctions Furnivall discerned between systems of direct and indirect rule in Southeast Asia. The rationale for direct rule flowed from the impulse to reform which was an important element in classical eighteenth-century European political thought. It was first attempted in Asia by the English liberals Warren Hastings and Lord Cornwallis in India.[10] The impulse came to Southeast Asia with Thomas Stamford Raffles, who experimented with classical liberal principles in Java and implemented what he called a 'system of purity and enterprise' in Singapore. Western imperialism in Southeast Asia thus created these systems of direct rule as a part of the idealistic effort to reconstruct the world according to a rational design.

The early systems of indirect rule such as that of the Dutch in the Indies and of the Spanish in the Philippines were born of no distinct plan but, according to Furnivall, simply emerged as expeditious methods of extracting economically valuable commodities from unwilling Asian producers. At the beginning of the nineteenth century, individuals like Raffles saw these systems as corrupt and exploitative. By the end of the nineteenth century, the ideological ground had shifted and the difficulties of various sytems of direct rule conduced to the proposition that indirect rule was more humane since it softened the harsh impact of economic freedom and avoided adverse indigenous reactions to unfamiliar codes of law. As a result, indirect rule came to be seen as a method of helping natives to gain independence on their own through slow but genuine development.

These criteria may cover the general distinctions between the two

---

[9] J. S. Furnivall, *Colonial Policy and Practice*, Cambridge, UK, 1938, reprinted New York, 1956, 10.
[10] ibid., 28.

systems, but there is much more to it. Labels conceal both differences and similarities. Furnivall appears correct in his judgment that there was no sharp line between systems of direct and indirect rule in practice. British rule in the Malay states was called indirect, but was really quite intrusive and bore little resemblance to the administration of the Dutch East Indies. In the Philippines, where the United States instituted a completely new system, they ended up by preserving much of the informal power structure and in ruling through the *ilustrado* and *cacique* classes. On the other hand, French indirect rule in Annam and Tonkin was every bit as intense and intrusive as was the direct rule system of Cochinchina. Thus the labels covered a wide variety of actual practice. Moreover, whatever label was used, the system changed over time as it was adapted to local conditions and revised as a result of pressures from home governments and colonial economic interests. Nevertheless, the distinction is a useful one, if for no other reason that the fact that indirect rule often maintained the legal status of the traditional political system in the post-colonial era.

In its broadest sense indirect rule signified a co-operative relationship between elements of the local ruling or élite classes and the colonial power. European sovereignty, whatever it entailed, was carried on within the context of the traditional political institutions. The old system, as well as its ruling class, retained its legitimacy. In the case of Java, Dutch control had been first grafted on to the top of the old 'feudalistic' system and over time the *bupatis* and regents had been transformed into bureaucrats, but their functions continued to be largely of a police and economic nature. Their charge was to preserve *rust en orde* (peace and order). Until the early years of the twentieth century the Dutch continued to rely on customary law for the arbitration of disputes and on the personal, 'inherited' authority of the *bupati* or regent (the major Javanese officials) to ensure that the functions of government were carried out.

In other situations, such as the Federated Malay States, the British Residential system had come into existence as a result of treaties with the sultans. British officials were installed at the courts of the rulers to give 'advice'. By the 1880s, these 'Residents' had taken over the functions of law enforcement, legislation, tax collection, and had created the foundations of the modern administrations. Regardless of the level to which they were involved in the direction of affairs, however, the de jure sovereignty of the Malay rulers was maintained. This was a contrast to Java, where the alien system was placed above the traditional system, and colonial rule was exerted through the indigenous ruling class. In Malaya, the colonial system came into being as a layer of government between the traditional rulers and the people. French government in the protectorates of Laos and Cambodia was similar in structure to the British system in Malaya.

In the case of direct rule, Furnivall suggested that in practice it involved the attempt by Europeans to impose Western-style administrations and systems of law upon Southeast Asians and simply to abrogate whatever had been before. Legalistically this meant the abolition of pre-existing monarchies and their supporting hierarchies of chiefs and officials. At the same time, provincial, district and village boundaries and other administrative categories were redefined. It meant the introduction of new definitions of property, court systems and procedures and a redefinition of the individual's relationship to the state.

In practice, perfectly executed direct rule never really existed, simply because it would have taken an administration entirely staffed by Europeans to make such a system possible. The rule of the United States in the Philippines was instituted with what appeared to be the most ambitious aims of all Southeast Asian colonial régimes. After seizing the islands from the Spanish in 1899, President William McKinley prayed over the problem and decided that the United States had a duty to 'civilize' the Filipinos. Under the administration of William Howard Taft, Americans set out to remake the Filipino society along American lines. Michael Cullinane has noted that Taft's administration saw the introduction of 'all the basic American democratic institutions'. These included an electoral process, a civil service based on merit, an American-style judiciary, a constitution with a bill of rights, a three-tiered system of local, provincial and national government, and an elected Filipino legislature with a political party system.

The American system began with an emphasis upon local self-government with the aim of building democracy 'from the bottom up'. Very quickly, however, American administrators discovered that the Filipino élites who came to fill posts in municipal government were regularly 'mishandling public funds' by voting all available revenues to pay their own salaries. American administrators began tinkering with the system they had superimposed on the islands. On the one hand they moved towards greater centralization in order to prevent the 'crying evils' of unrestricted Filipino rule, and at the same time they were forced by rising costs and the need to encourage Filipino co-operation to permit an increased Filipinization of local government. In the end, the *ilustrado* class succeeded not only in taking control of the government from the bottom up, but also managed, through the electoral process, to organize themselves to protect their class interests on a national basis. Thus, what began as a system of direct rule aimed at total reform of society ended as one that confirmed the dominant position of the traditional oligarchy. In effect, American rule operated very much like the system of indirect rule in the Netherlands East Indies, where local and regional élites mediated the impact of foreign influence. But unlike the Dutch colony, the American administration became a part of the local system rather than vice-versa. The Javanese *priyayi* lost their traditional constituency, whereas the *ilustrados*, the *caciques* and large landowners actually strengthened their position in the Filipino political and economic order.

Even within specific colonial entities, systems of direct and indirect rule came into existence alongside one another as a result of a variety of circumstances. Prior to this period, there had been little cohesion within traditional Southeast Asian political units. With the possible exception of Vietnam, the major states of the mainland were what Stanley J. Tambiah has termed 'galactic polities'. Within the island world the pattern of the 'segmented state', which James Warren has applied to the Sulu sultanate, best describes the relatively loose pattern of political association among autonomous Malay *negri*. Throughout the region, there was little distinction between domestic and foreign relations, so far as the central authorities of the major political units were concerned. The model format for these relations continued to be the 'mandala', whereby the central authority attempted to manipulate the circles of states and principalities around it. And, in fact, initially, the European colonial establishments behaved according to these patterns as well.

The European 'forward movement' in the mid-nineteenth century was the first step in the rationalization of the state apparatus, because it drew a clear distinction between domestic and foreign. The borders which were created in this process, however, did not automatically create domestic uniformity. Despite all of the steps toward rationalization and moderniza-tion, the colonial empires were still not much more than haphazard collections of historical 'accidents'. For instance, British-controlled Malaya, as late as 1942, while all of it might have been coloured pink in most maps, was really an ill-assorted administrative patchwork. There were the three Straits Settlements which were a Crown Colony, under direct rule; and the four Federated Malay States under indirect rule, each with its own sultan but actually run by Residents under the authority of a central administra-tion in Kuala Lumpur. The five unfederated states were under even more indirect rule, with each sultan maintaining his own administrative élite with varying degrees of sophistication and efficiency, and the newly-installed British Advisers having far fewer powers than the Residents in the Federated States. In northern Borneo, Sarawak was under the auto-cratic rule of the Brooke family; North Borneo (modern Sabah) was under a chartered company; and the sultanate of Brunei was a protectorate.

The innovative and truly alien presence in the midst of this hodge-podge was the federation which would, in time, become the core of the successor nation-state. This was a totally new political creation for which there was no historical precedent. As Rupert Emerson was at pains to point out,

> the Federation is in almost every aspect the creation not of Malays, but of the other people who have come into Malaya. It is the latter—the British in the political sphere and the Chinese, British, and Indians in the economic sphere—who found the bounds of the States too small to encompass their activities and reared above them the larger federal structure.[11]

It was this creation of larger political superstructures by all of the colonial powers that remade the map of Southeast Asia and thereby created the vessels for the new states. In almost every case, the administrative appa-ratus of these new amalgamations was wholly European in inspiration and organization. On this level, rule was always direct, and as time passed, more and more of the political and administrative power was exercised by these central structures. In 1909, within the Federated States a federal council was created under the presidency of a High Commissioner with what Emerson styled 'an invisible grant' giving it unlimited power to legislate.

In the Netherlands East Indies, the Dutch had succeeded in establishing their influence within a vast sweep of islands from Sumatra to New

[11] R. Emerson, *Malaysia*, New York, 1937, reprinted Kuala Lumpur, 1964, 175–6.

Guinea. By the 1940s, their territory was a crazy-quilt of individual arrangements, treaties, conquests, protectorates and concessions. Generally speaking, some form of indirect rule characterized most of the colony. The introduction of the 'Short Declaration' made the rapid expansion of the Dutch holdings possible in the early years of the twentieth century. Any chief who recognized the authority of Batavia (Jakarta) was confirmed as the legitimate ruler of his territory. Between 1898 and 1911, some 300 'self-governing' states came under Dutch control.[12] In some of these, a form of the Javanese system was attempted, but on the whole it was quite inappropriate for the relatively lower populations in the outer islands.

The Dutch had moved forward so quickly to affirm their claim to these places, particularly in Sumatra, Sulawesi and Borneo, that they bit off more than they could possibly chew, let alone digest. They lacked the resources to man and finance administrations for these new states. This was especially true in the period after about 1900 under the Ethical Policy which demanded a certain show of interest in the welfare of the people. European economic interests further required the construction of public works and services to support their penetration. As a result, Emerson notes that 'the Dutch were forced into a more or less makeshift acceptance of the widely divergent native institutions which they found at hand, functioning at first under the somewhat casual and unco-ordinated supervision of this improvised corps of Dutch and native officials'.[13] In some cases the Dutch government found it necessary to post Javanese members of the *pangreh pradja* to administrative posts in Borneo and Sumatra.

Furnivall noted that systems of indirect rule usually had a separate system of direct rule which applied to European residents of the colony who lived under some approximation of the metropolitian system. This dichotomy between systems was quite striking in the areas that were subject to large-scale European economic penetration. The Sumatran Cultivation District, the region around Deli and Medan, stands as a case in point. This area, which ultimately grew to constitute a region some 320 kilometres long and about 80 kilometres wide, had been 'purchased' or 'rented' from the sultans of Deli, Langkat and Asahan by European 'planters', actually corporations, and was literally governed by its own system of law standing entirely outside the governments of the traditional Malay sultanates. The area came to be populated by immigrants who made up the labour force, first Chinese and later Javanese. The mixed bag of European estate managers were also outsiders. The sultans grew to be exceedingly wealthy, and the Malay, Minangkabau and Batak subjects continued to live much as they had always lived.

On taking over the Philippines, the United States seems to have assumed that the Spanish claim to the Muslim areas of the south, particularly Mindanao and Sulu, was as strong as the claim to the other portions of the islands. The Americans thus occupied the Moro areas as a part of their entire conquest. In addition to the 'insurrection', as the Yankees called the Filipino Revolution in the north, they also found themselves faced with

[12] D. G. E. Hall, *A History of Southeast Asia*, New York, 1981, 622.
[13] Emerson, 426.

resistance from the peoples of Sulu and Mindanao. The Muslim peoples of this region had never considered themselves under Spanish rule in the first place, and thus saw little basis for the American presumption. In the end, American rule in the south was far less direct than it was even in the north, and local administration tended to continue in the hands of the local élites. The introduction of Western concepts of property, however, did lead to the economic development of the region, largely by Christian settlers from the north and by foreigners. These settlers stood outside the jurisdiction of the traditional Moro *datu* or headmen.

French Indochina came to be composed of five major administrative divisions, each ruled with different degrees of intensity. The Laotian principalities and Cambodia, which the French claimed on the basis of their misinterpretation of the concept of Vietnamese 'suzerainty', emerged as indirectly ruled territories. Laos involved the creation of an entirely new state within borders formed by the amalgamation of lands which had never before been under a single administration.

Initially, the only part of Indochina which was directly ruled was Cochinchina. Between 1897 and 1902, under Paul Doumer, the administration was unified and the 'protectorate' of Tonkin became for all practical purposes a directly ruled territory. In Annam, Laos and Cambodia, royal courts continued to exist along with their ministers, officials and 'mandarins', together with a French administration under a *Résident Superieur*, a Privy Council and a Protectorate Council. The states were divided into provinces, each placed under the charge of a Resident and a native official who continued to rule under his guidance. Hall points out that the system came to resemble that of the Netherlands East Indies, particularly in Java. In both cases the distinction between direct and indirect rule was legal rather than practical.

The real distinction often lay in national styles and definitions of what constituted government. It is thus important to examine the impact of the various systems as they affected the indigenous societies, rather than the stated intentions and theories of European rulers. Furnivall contends that in the English system of colonial government the officials, both European and native, became magistrates and tax collectors. They administered judgements under the rule of English law. Even in Malaya where Malay custom and religion were left to traditional authorities, the sphere of *adat* and religious law was greatly circumscribed and redefined. Officials found themselves responsible for large numbers of people and thus encountered them only through the impersonal medium of the court system.

> Thus British colonial administration on the system of indirect rule emphasises the judicial aspect of native authority, encourages greater formality in native courts and insists on close supervision over native judicial procedure by British officials. On the Dutch system even the European officials are policemen, agents of policy; on the British system even native officials tend to become magistrates and judges, servants of the law.[14]

[14] Furnivall, 285.

Furnivall's judgment on the British system of direct rule was far from flattering. With the increase in courts came a massive increase in crime in Burma. In comparison to the Dutch system he noted: 'It is a common complaint that under indirect rule, in Java or Malaya, officials coddle the people, treat them as children; but under direct rule, they are apt to treat them as naughty children.' So far as economic development was concerned:

> The Malay, . . . left aside by the main current of economic development, remains stagnating in a backwater, and the progress of the last sixty years has merely changed him 'from a poor man in a poor country to a poor man in a rich country'; relatively at least he is poorer than before.
>   Burma provides another type of economic development—by native enterprise under direct rule . . . yet the cultivators have been transformed into a landless rural proletariat and the country as a whole is conspicuous for the growth of crime.[15]

Direct or indirect, the general trends of all systems by the end of the first decade of the twentieth century were contradictory. On the one hand there was the movement toward greater centralization, rationalization and efficiency; on the other, there was a contrary movement, both intentional and unintended, leading to the development of indigenous anti-colonial political movements. At the end of the nineteenth century, the Dutch had come to be concerned for the welfare of their colonial subjects. They thus instituted the Ethical Policy, which was to foster both economic development and village self-government. The Americans had taken Kipling's unsolicited advice and picked up the 'white man's burden' and were preparing their 'little brown Brothers' for American-style democracy, while the French developed their *association* with the Vietnamese, Lao, Cambodian and assorted populations of Indochina in pursuit of the *mission civilisatrice*. In Burma, the British were moving toward the creation of a certain level of self-government, and in Malaya they were beginning to train an élite that would replace their own rule.

Paradoxically, the actual movement was toward more direct rule. Indirect rule was, in a sense, a transition. Between 1880 and 1940, Europe grew even closer and communications within the colonies became faster with the construction of railroads, telegraphs and metalled roads. From the metropoles came demands for a growing variety of reforms: on the one hand, toward greater welfare, and on the other toward improved access to local resources on the part of European capitalist interests. Together with these came equally insistent demands from metropolitan legislative bodies to reduce costs and to find local revenues for colonial improvements.

This movement, however, was not necessarily uniform. The patchworks remained. Inaccessible areas, although included within the borders of some state, often remained unchanged by colonial rule. Regions that seemed to offer no immediate financial benefits, or which lacked economic resources, were bypassed by the roads and telegraphs. Rule in these areas

---

[15] ibid., 414, 424.

continued to be indirect. This was particularly true of the highland areas of the mainland states and the interiors of the islands, where a multiplicity of tribal and other peoples continued life in traditional ways. If their lives were changed by the colonial experience it was only because of the arrival of Christian missionaries, and prohibitions against head-hunting, slavery and other such practices.

The debate over what constituted direct or indirect rule may seem irrelevant in the context of the radical nature of the changes that were actually inflicted upon the indigenous social, political, economic and cultural landscapes. In the years after the Pacific War, however, the legalities once again came into play. Where colonial advances had taken place on the basis of treaties and formal agreements with indigenous authorities, then their postwar successors were often able to gain recognition as legitimate and sovereign—as happened in Malaya, Cambodia and Laos. In other areas, such as Vietnam and Indonesia, colonial rule was seen by nationalist forces to have destroyed the integrity of these agencies and they, together with their claims, were swept away by the tides of revolution and civil war.

LAW AND ORDER

Take up the White Man's burden—
Send forth the best ye breed—
Go bind your sons to exile
To serve your captives' need.

Rudyard Kipling

Damn, damn, damn the Filipino
Pock-marked khakiac ladrone;
Underneath the starry flag
Civilize him with a Krag
And return us to our own beloved home.

American marching song, c. 1900.[16]

During the nineteenth century the mission of bringing 'law and order' formed a major part of the European agenda. This impulse may be illustrated by the British, who began their first real penetration of the region at the beginning of the century with their occupation of Dutch territories during the Napoleonic wars. It seemed to individuals such as Raffles that a kind of endemic chaos existed throughout the island world. Raffles considered the phenomenon of Malay piracy to be the result either of a flaw in the Malay character or else of the 'decay' of earlier Malay empires. This second possible cause was thought to have been brought on by repressive Dutch and Spanish policies of monopoly that restricted

---

[16] Quoted in R. Roth, *Muddy Glory*, Hanover, 1981, 85.

trade. As a result, impoverished Malay rulers were unable to control their unruly followers who took to the seas and preyed upon peaceful native trade.

While it is probably true that Dutch activities, such as the sack of Riau in 1784, had prevented the formation of powerful maritime states in the islands, it seems that piracy and slave-raiding were an integral part of the maritime Malay political process. It is also possible that the influence of British trade, which initially focused on the sale of guns and opium to places like Sulu, Riau, Makassar and Aceh, might have unleashed opportunistic forces within maritime society. James Warren has suggested[17] that the upsurge of British country trade in the late eighteenth century was a major incentive for Sulu raiders, who increasingly sought slaves to aid them in procuring more trade goods so they could buy more guns and opium.

As a classical liberal, Raffles recommended the promotion of free trade and (after his indifferent success as lieutenant-governor of Java) the establishment of a port, where goods of all nations might be traded under the security of the British flag. This ideal was realized in his foundation of Singapore. While he eschewed the formation of a territorial empire and entanglement in Malay politics, he felt it incumbent on Europeans to enjoin native chiefs to suppress priacy in their domains. They also aimed to end slave-raiding and slave-trading that seemed an integral part of Malay piracy. The subsequent campaign to suppress piracy became a major rationale for the expansion of European power in the island world. As resources became available to the colonial powers, naval expeditions from the 1840s onward swept Southeast Asian waters; where treaties and blandishments were ineffective, search-and-destroy missions followed. British and Dutch gunboats moved from the Straits of Melaka to the Riau archipelago and the coasts of Borneo. Later in the century, Spanish squadrons finally succeeded in reducing the Sulu strongholds to ruins. While the results of these pacification programmes did not lead immediately to intensive colonial control, they did prepare the ground for European and Chinese economic penetration which often set off a new wave of conflict, necessitating further intervention.

Disorder on the borders was almost a constant theme in the history of British take-overs in Burma, as it had been in India. Each step was taken with the stated intention of securing 'law and order' in the neighbouring region, and each annexation was followed by another. As British and Indian economic interests chafed at the continuing recalcitrance of the rump Burmese state, they laid the groundwork for the final step in the absorption of Burma. It resulted in the abrogation of the traditional monarchy.

Cooler heads in the Indian administration and the India Office had counselled against the elimination of the Burmese monarchy. They wished to overthrow King Thibaw (r. 1878–85), but favoured an arrangement which would have permitted indirect control, and maintained traditional structures under a pliable monarch and British protection. They were

---

[17] *The Sulu Zone*, Singapore, 1979.

fearful of increased costs, a labour shortage, and the endemic rice deficit in upper Burma. British commercial interests in lower Burma, however, favoured total take-over. The protectorate scheme failed when the Burmese officials with whom the British had hoped to collaborate fled with Thibaw. As a result, the Viceroy of India, Lord Dufferin, announced on 1 January 1886 that Thibaw's domains had been annexed to Her Majesty's dominions. When he visited Mandalay in February, he abolished the *hlutdaw*, the royal council, put upper Burma under direct administrative control, and made Burma a province of British India.

This led to the total collapse of the old order and set the stage for outright rebellion. The British had decapitated the 'beast', only to discover that it immediately regrew a thousand more heads. In the past, they had fought only the rulers; now they found it necessary to fight the society. With the collapse of civil administration, villagers organized foraging parties to seek rice, money, fuel and provisions for their own communities. Those who gave up their arms at the order of the British-directed *Hlutdaw* became targets for the wandering bands of dacoits, most of them ex-soldiers of the disbanded Burmese army. Foraging bands organized themselves as guerrillas, and the British faced an entire countryside in armed uprising against the colonial forces. What was expected to be a quick and surgical coup had mushroomed out into a big, messy pacification. Quickly, the rebellion spread to lower Burma and then to the Shan who supported a *sawbwa* (a Shan chief) as candidate for the Burmese throne. This was not an organized effort, but a widespread and spontaneous collection of localized uprisings. The major work of pacification took about three years. By the beginning of 1889, there were 233 police and military posts in Burma, and the British forces in upper Burma numbered 18,000.[18]

Ultimately, the entire region from the Shan plateau to Dien Bien Phu was torn by disorder. It was exacerbated by the activities of armed Chinese bands known by the colours of their flags. They had fled from China following the defeat of the Taiping Rebellion. Earlier, Francis Garnier had led a campaign against them in Tonkin. Following his death, French forces were withdrawn, only to return in 1884 when France annexed Tonkin. This move brought France into a costly war with China, while at the same time a rebellion broke out in Cambodia, there was a revolt in Saigon, and Vietnamese troops from Annam crossed the border into Cochinchina. Following the suppression of these revolts, the pacification of Tonkin continued until 1895.

The earlier Dutch campaigns against pirates set the stage for one of the most extended and violent confrontations in the island world. The Dutch had always considered the north Sumatran state of Aceh an irritation. The Dutch official and ethnologist, C. Snouck Hurgronje, put them among 'the least well mannered of the inhabitants of the Archipelago'.[19] By the 1870s Dutch economic interests in the Straits of Melaka had begun a propaganda campaign to undercut Aceh's flourishing pepper trade with

[18] C. Crosthwaite, *The Pacification of Burma*, London, 1912, 128.
[19] C. Snouck Hurgronje, *The Achehnese*, Leiden and London, 1906, I. 119.

Penang. Aceh was styled a 'pirate nest' and was said to be threatening commerce in the western part of the archipelago. Having already brought Siak and the neighbouring states of Deli, Langkat and Asahan under their control, the Dutch began to develop what would become the Cultivation District of East Sumatra. An attack on the seat of the Acehnese sultan in 1873 was driven into the sea. The Dutch returned and took the town at great cost to both sides. In the battle the sultan was forced to flee and the Acehnese sultanate was effectively destroyed.

This was a signal for the Acehnese *uleebelang*, or regional chiefs, to rise up and defend their own districts against the invaders. When the Dutch finally succeeded in suppressing these chiefs, they found themselves confronted with a religiously inspired guerrilla war led by the village *ulamā* or clergy. In the end, the war between the Dutch and Aceh lasted nearly four decades, and at times it tied up most of the army of the Netherlands East Indies and nearly bankrupted Batavia. The war transformed Aceh-nese society as well. Prior to the Dutch invasion, James Siegel has noted, there was little connection between the various institutions of Acehnese society: the sultanate, the chiefs, the villagers and the religious leaders. The *ulamā* succeeded in mobilizing the people. 'They appealed to men to act not as villagers but as Muslims; to the *ulamā*, this meant forgetting traditional social identities.'[20] Although the religious war likewise failed, it did create in Acehnese society a readiness to respond to nationalist appeals in later years.

This conflict taught the Dutch to reshape their own tools of suppression. In 1906, the mobile, lightly-armed strike forces which had proved effective against the Acehnese were sent to Bali, where the island's kings had stubbornly resisted Batavia's attempts to dominate them. Faced with final defeat, many aristocrats despaired and committed ritual suicide rather than submit to Dutch rule. Armed only with spears and lances, they threw themselves, together with their women and children, at the Dutch guns, and perished. Lombok had already been annexed and other chiefs of island and coastal *negri* in the archipelago signed the Short Declaration that accepted Dutch rule.[21]

Thus, between the mid-nineteenth century and the 1930s, from Aceh to Sulu, European governments found themselves engaged in 'pacification' campaigns against traditional states and popular rebellions. In many cases the traditional rulers capitulated quite readily while the ordinary people decided to stand and fight. Colonialists came to realize that Southeast Asian societies were far tougher and far more resilient than their rulers. The rebellions mobilized the military and security forces of the colonial apparatus in almost every territory, whether or not it was a war zone. Colonial powers stood ready to enforce their rule with the sword, or more appropriately, the Maxim gun, the Gatling and the Krag. Because of the lopsided advantage in weaponry, money, communications, discipline, and technology, these contests were invariably won by the colonial forces.

---

[20] J. Siegel, *The Rope of God*, Berkeley, 1969, 74.
[21] M. C. Ricklefs, *A History of Modern Indonesia: c. 1300 to the Present*, Bloomington, 1981, chs 3–4.

They turned out to be brutal, guerrilla-type struggles which gave full play to European racist sentiments, and generally brought home-town American and European conscripts face-to-face with angry Southeast Asian peasants.

Usually these conflicts took place in the fringe areas and in regions which had not yet felt the force of colonial rule. As such, they were the result of the consolidations of empire that took place as the European powers moved to secure their control over regions which had formerly been only within their spheres of influence. The Dutch war in Aceh began as an attempt to remove the final obstacle to full colonial control over the island of Sumatra. In the early 1880s the four-cornered struggle in the highlands of mainland Southeast Asia began in earnest with the British pacification of upper Burma, the French expansion into the Lao states, and moves to secure their own borders by the Siamese and the Chinese. Finally, the Philippines erupted, with the first nationalist war of liberation beginning in 1896 against Spain and continuing to almost 1910 as the United States came in 1899 and moved against the revolutionaries. Later on, as economic conditions worsened in the years of the Great Depression, new peasant uprisings occurred in the central areas of Vietnam, Burma and the east-coast Malay states.

The American experience in the Philippines was marked by the extremes of the turn-of-the-century European colonial impulses. Framed with the noblest of intentions of 'leading the Filipinos to democracy', it was marked by one of the bloodiest wars in the region. The Americans had, in fact, blundered into the earliest nationalist movement in Southeast Asia when they joined forces with Emilio Aguinaldo in overthrowing the Spanish in 1898. Nevertheless, the enemies they faced were not all *ilustrados*, but a force that was only semi-nationalist and semi-traditionalist. The peasant forces actually constituted a radical popular uprising which was controlled by neither the old élite nor the new nationalists. Russell Roth has with some accuracy styled it one of America's 'Indian Wars'.

In the southern Philippines, where Americans faced the wrath of the Muslim *juramentado* or the *parrang sabbil*, the issue had nothing to do with nationalism. The Moros carried on a religious war against an army largely motivated by racism. From 1902 to 1913, United States forces fought a series of bloody battles with bands of Moro warriors who locked themselves up in coral stone *cotas* and fought to the death. The last major engagement was the battle of Bud Bagsak, fought in a volcano crater on Mindanao. It ended only when all 500 Moros defending the fortress had been killed, but campaigns against the Moros continued until 1935.

Hugh Clifford, who was sent to Pahang as the Resident at the sultan's court in 1888, has described life in the Malay states when Britain began 'moulding their history'. Rule by traditional chiefs was arbitrary, cruel, capricious and unlimited. The peasants were without rights and totally subject to the whim of the raja. The British saw themselves as bringers of law and order.[22] To Clifford, the most pernicious group at the courts of

---

[22] P. Kratoska, ed., *Honourable Intentions*, Singapore, 1983, 227.

Malay chiefs was the *budak raja*, the sultan's bodyguard, made up of young aristocrats.

> They dress magnificently in brilliant coloured silks, with the delightful blend-
> ings of bright blues which Malays love by instinct; they are armed with dagger
> and sword and spear, all beautifully kept and very handsome in appearance,
> and they pass most of their time in making love and in playing games of
> chance. Their duties are numerous but by no means heavy. They follow at the
> heels of the Sultan when he takes his walks abroad to guard him from harm,
> and to give a finishing touch to his magnificence; they row his boat, hunt
> game, and snare turtle doves in his company . . . murder those who have
> offended their master, seize property which he covets, abduct women, spy
> upon chiefs . . . Men such as these, who from their youth are taught to be
> unscrupulous, and to live expensively upon no settled income, quickly dis-
> cover means whereby money may be obtained . . . You must remember that
> this rabble is the only force by which the country is policed.[23]

With the arrival of Europeans, not only Malaya, but all of the other parts of Southeast Asia, shared in the benefits of 'civilization'. Hardworking and incorruptible administrators, such as the indefatigable district officers, travelled the countryside giving patient adjudication for no material reward. For the British in Malaya and the Dutch in the Indies the period was marked by a professionalization of the colonial civil services.

In Malaya the key to the new administrative structure was the Residen-tial system. Hugh Low created the model for it in Perak after J. W. W. Birch was killed. He succeeded by forming a council made up of the Malay chiefs, the Chinese leaders, the ruler and himself. They discussed his proposal for reforms; thus the Malays had a 'sense of influencing policy'. Governor Weld was impressed by Low's accomplishment and he made it the model for administration in all of the Protected States, as they were then called. Within a decade, however, the rather limited advisory role of the Residents was rapidly expanded to include most of the major functions of administration.

Weld also instituted reforms in the personnel selection process. Until 1883, Malayan civil service officers were a mixed bag of European adven-turers and Eurasians who had usually been recruited locally. Weld sacked half of the officials in Selangor during his first two years in office. Thereafter, the civil service officers were recruited in Britain by the Colonial Office and sent out as junior officers. In 1896 the Colonial Office instituted an examination which had to be taken by all potential recruits for official positions, and which really selected for public-school and univer-sity backgrounds.[24]

Similar moves toward professionalization of the colonial civil services were instituted in all the other European possessions of the region. Ultimately, the same impulse to develop a trained corps of administrators came to include indigenous officials as well. In Java, between 1900 and

---

[23] ibid., 233–5.
[24] John Butcher, *The British in Malaya 1880–1941: The Social History of a European Community in Colonial Southeast Asia*, Kuala Lumpur, 1979, 40–2.

1910, Colonial Minister Simon de Graaff introduced a series of reforms aimed at providing training for the *pangreh pradja*. These reforms were attempts to eliminate the old *magang* system, whereby experienced officials would accept the unpaid services of younger *priyayi* who worked with them as apprentices. De Graaff's reforms included an education requirement and the institution of rank lists. He also called for a distinction between functionaries and professional officials. These reforms went slowly because of a desire not to antagonize the *priyayi*, particularly in an era when nationalist political sentiments were beginning to raise their heads.[25] The Javanese *priyayi* ceased, however, to be the lords of individual states and became an élite class of officials operating throughout Java.

The Thai rulers were likewise moved to implement many of the same innovations in the realm of administrative centralization and rationalization as colonial governments undertook. A similar wave of reforms was begun in French Indochina under Governor Paul Doumer (1897–1902). He followed a Napoleonic pattern and unified civil administration throughout the French territories. He also abolished the last vestiges of indirect rule in Tonkin by eliminating the imperial viceroys. At the same time, he organized a unified government for the Laotian territories, creating the basis for the new state.

The French in Vietnam did not enjoy much of a respite between the suppression of traditional resistance and the upsurge of nationalist rebellions. As early as 1912, Vietnamese students and intellectuals had organized a nationalist group at the University of Hanoi: the Association for the Restoration of Vietnam. They were inspired by the successful overthrow of the Qing dynasty in China and the establishment of a republic. Under Phan Boi Chau's leadership they staged a number of demonstrations in Tonkin. These efforts were brutally suppressed, and the rebels were rooted out; many were beheaded and the rest imprisoned on Pulau Condore. At the same time, similar movements were beginning in the Dutch East Indies. Some began as religiously-inspired movements, such as the Sarekat Islam, and others, like the Budi Utomo, were inspired by ambitious bureaucrats; but they all clearly had overtones of nationalism. By the 1920s, the British were facing similar movements in Burma among both the educated élite and the pauperized peasantry.

European dominance was established in the region with military force, and finally reinforced with more rigorous measures to police the societies under their control. As a result, the security forces of the bureaucracy increased as threats to the state were perceived in the local population. Increasingly these came from the areas where administrative innovations had caused the greatest disruption to the majority peasant populations. If the wars succeeded in bringing into place the final elements of the modern authoritarian state, they also sowed the seeds of what would become wars of national liberation in the era after World War II.

In all the areas under European powers the same spectrum of policies, alternating between welfare and warfare, characterized the imperial advance. The attention given to efficiency and profit was generally more

---

[25] Sutherland, 67–85.

pronounced than that given to the welfare of the peoples. The policies reflected a variety of Western agendas: conservative, liberal, democratic, and sometimes socialist. The impulse for humanitarian reform was always tempered by demands for efficiency and functional rationality from home governments and metropolitan economic interests. Programmes which sought order, welfare and profit often led to conflicting measures, the resolution of which was generally decided by 'home' interests rather than those of the indigenous peoples. Colonial business and economic interests wanted ease of access to the resources and markets of the colonies. They wanted barriers against their competitors in the colonies. They wanted land and labour legislation that gave them security of property and an unlimited supply of cheap, well-disciplined workers. These interests had a deep influence on the development of administrative policies and legal frameworks, particularly in terms of labour and contract law and property codes. At the same time the cultural discipline of clocks, railroads, time-tables, and of the civil engineer, swept out from colonial urban centres across the paddy fields, hill farms, forests and seas of the region.

Throughout the region military pacification first destroyed or at least intimidated what remained of the traditional political order, and adminis-trative reform followed. In the end, Western-style law and a kind of order was imposed on the region. Whether individuals were better off, or 'happier' at the end of the process, and whether the costs were worth the benefits achieved are still matters of controversy. If the Europeans did not always do good, at least some of them did well. It is clear that Southeast Asians had little control over what happened to them during these years. Their world was destroyed and rebuilt around them; they had only the choice to accept or resist, and those who resisted usually died. On the other hand, those who accepted often gained control of the very tools which had first destroyed their predecessors.

The wars and the reforms did not put an end to protests. Before 1920, colonial régimes in Burma, Vietnam, Indonesia and the Philippines found themselves confronted with far more dangerous foes than poorly armed peasants led by visionaries promising paradise and invulnerability. The new enemies were of two kinds. On the one hand there were educated anti-colonialists seeking to establish nations inside the very administrative frameworks set up by the imperial rulers. They had in fact been created by the régimes they sought to displace. They were students, bureaucrats and urban workers. On the other hand, there continued to be peasant upris-ings as modern taxes were imposed and the impact of private property struck the villages. These movements, though traditionalist in their incep-tion, were quickly pre-empted by newly organized socialist and communist parties. The modern state had fathered modern peoples.

PLURAL SOCIETIES

Probably the first thing that strikes the visitor is the medley of peoples— Europeans, Chinese, Indian and native. It is in the strictest sense a medley, for they mix but do not combine. Each group holds by its own religion, its own culture and language, its own ideas and ways. As individuals they meet, but only in the market-place, in buying and selling. There is a plural society, with different sections of the community living side by side, but separately, within the same political unit . . .[26]

Furnivall's classic definition of the plural society applies to all Southeast Asian colonies. Together with ethnic, linguistic, cultural and religious differences, he noted that groups were also distinguished by occupational specializations. It was a sort of caste system without the religious sanction it had in India. He saw the plural society as the 'obvious and outstanding result of contact between East and West'.

He presented this type of social formation as one of the typical aberrations of the colonial situation in the tropics. Social and personal relationships had been atomized and commercialized. This rule applied within as well as among racial and religious groups. The force of custom had been eroded by the individual will for economic gain. As a result, the community, the village, the cohesive social and political units, had been transformed into 'crowds'. The play of economic forces, he argued, had been exempt from control by social will.

This analysis, constructed in the 1930s and informed by Marxist views, may place excessive responsibility at the feet of the colonial powers. Certainly custom was crippled by the intrusion of global economic forces. It is also clear that the social will of traditional communities was dispersed and abrogated with the introduction of European law and rational administration. Furnivall, one feels, did not deal adequately with the heritage of ethnic diversity in Southeast Asia in the years prior to European rule. Likewise, his overwhelmingly economic approach really does not touch on the sexual and psychological dimensions of plural societies.

In the traditional Southeast Asian countryside as well as the cities, diversity was the rule rather than the exception. Differences in language were common. Even within populations who spoke the same language, dialects proliferated if for no other reason than the low frequency of contact. The variety of ecological niches necessitated a high degree of regional occupational specialization. Thus, speakers of the same language might have widely diverse subsistence styles and whole categories of dissimilar customs. Contrasts between urban and rural cultures were extreme. Even in the mid-nineteenth century the Malays of the Riau and Johor courts considered groups such as the *orang laut* as barbaric and did not even see them as Muslims, a primary criterion for being a 'Malay'. Lifestyles practised by the various social classes were also widely different. In fact, it might be said that status was a far more significant criterion in the minds of Southeast Asians than was race or ethnicity.

If an argument can be made for the existence of ethnic diversity in pre-colonial Southeast Asia, so too can one be made for the presence of foreign communities. The port cities of the region, whether under indigenous or European control, were always polyglot collections of traders, travellers and adventurers from all over the world. Descriptions of cities such as

[26] Furnivall, 304–5.

Melaka, Ayutthaya, Bangkok, and Surabaya as they existed outside or prior to European domination suggest that foreign communities were not only welcomed but were usually permitted to govern themselves under the control of their own 'headmen'. It is clear that such arrangements were perpetuated in the British and Dutch port cities in the nineteenth century.

The traditionally low levels of population in Southeast Asia had made labour one of the scarcest of resources. Anthony Reid observes that the chronic labour shortage and the prevalence of slavery and kidnapping meant that not much security was expected from the state. As a result, patrons and clients relied on each other for support and protection. These conditions had long since given rise to 'systems of bonding based largely on debt, where loyalties were strong and intimate, yet at the same time transferable and even saleable'.[27] Such arrangements also further diversified the ethnic composition of Southeast Asian populations.

One means of off-setting the labour shortage was to encourage the immigration of groups of Chinese labourers, a process that began in earnest as early as the eighteenth century. The histories of G. William Skinner and Jennifer Cushman of the Chinese in Siam, and my own work on Singapore and Johor, have shown these newcomers were encouraged by local rulers. They pioneered the growth of tin and gold mining, and the cultivation of pepper, gambier, sugar and a number of other commercial crops which brought increased revenues to Southeast Asian political leaders. Studies of China have shown that the initial waves of Chinese migration were driven not by European influences but rather by internal economic and social conditions. It may be more correct to view the wave of Chinese migration as an independent movement which met the Europeans halfway in Southeast Asia.

The conditions of social diversity, as well as the tendency to commercialize labour, agriculture and mining, suggest that the foundations for what Furnivall called plural societies were already in place before the nineteenth century and before the intensification of European control. Were these relations substantially altered in the administrative changes that took place during the high tide of European colonial rule? The answer must be affirmative. Despite pre-existing conditions, the colonial experience can be seen as the primary causal factor in the creation of plural societies. Certainly, the levels of social stress and communal tensions which appeared in the twentieth century are evidence that some qualitative change had taken place in the societies of the region.

Two of the differences singled out by Furnivall seem most important. One is in the abrogation of indigenous 'social will' by the imposition of a European administration. The second was in the increase, both quantitative as well as qualitative, in immigration from other parts of Asia, particularly China and India. Not only did more of these groups migrate to the region than ever before, but they came to perform a greater variety of social and economic roles. This migration grew and was transformed within a social context controlled by Europeans. The rulers separated themselves from the indigenous society at large and at the same time

---

[27] A. Reid, *Southeast Asia in the Age of Commerce*, New Haven, 1988, I. 129.

required that immigrants and newcomers likewise maintain identities distinct from 'natives', thus setting new precedents.

Unlike earlier outside conquerors, the European ruling strata in this period ceased to acknowledge any social or legitimate sexual connection with the remainder of the peoples in their colonies. They were, in fact, responsible not to their subjects but to the legislatures, bureaucracies and citizenries of distant nation-states. This disconnection seems to have been a crucial element in the new situation. Colonial régimes were not responsive to the local social will, nor did they need to be. Administration was from the top down and with such a rigour that there is little to compare with it in world history. The relative power imbalance that existed between the colonial régimes and their Asian subjects at the beginning of the twentieth century was a truly extraordinary historical aberration, and one that could not and did not persist. Nevertheless, the imbalance made it possible for Europeans radically to affect the bases of Southeast Asian societies.

An important aspect of the power imbalance was that Europeans imposed their own perceptions of race and ethnicity upon Southeast Asian society. Recent social and anthropological studies of colonial society, particularly those by John Butcher and Jean Gelman Taylor,[28] indicate that Europeans began placing greater distances between themselves and Asian society in the nineteenth century. With the arrival of large numbers of European women and the establishment of European family life in the colonies, sharper lines were drawn against association with other races. Sexual liaisons between Asian women and European men, once accepted as a part of the normal order of things, became objects of scorn, and Eurasian and mestizo classes generally declined in status. This trend was buttressed by pseudo-scientific social Darwinist concepts about racial superiority and inferiority, and about the effect of the climate on culture, history and the quality of 'civilizations' which coloured the views of the societies under colonial rule.

There were also subtler elements, particularly the psychological outlook of the increasingly defensive European community, that increased racist tensions in the ethnic medley. John Butcher has detailed the intensification of anti-Asian prejudices amongst Europeans, both civil servants and individuals in the private sector, at the beginning of the twentieth century. A number of measures created legalized and formal racial segregation in the region for the first time, mostly to bar Asians from European enclaves. This included segregation on the railways, in the civil service, in housing (where possible) and especially in the 'clubs' and even in football teams.[29] Butcher suggests that this development of European racism was a paradoxical result of the 'success' of colonial administration in transforming its Asian subjects:

> at the very time that Europeans were most asserting their superiority the actual cultural differences between them and Asians were diminishing. . . . Far from

---

[28] Butcher, *The British in Malaya*; Taylor, *The Social World of Batavia*.
[29] Butcher, ch. 5.

promoting harmony, however, the narrowing of the cultural gap aggravated relations between Europeans and Asians. On the one hand Europeans wished to inculcate Asians with their values and to introduce them to their institutions and pastimes, but on the other as the gap narrowed they could not feel as certain of their distinctiveness, and by implication, their superiority . . . As the cultural and educational gap between Europeans and Asians closed, the colour bar, however it was justified, was the only remaining means Europeans had of maintaining their superiority over Asians.[30]

The English came to see themselves as a distinctive kind of 'community' and thus set a pattern for others to emulate. Certainly, there is little evidence that any Asians saw themselves as constituting this sort of discrete and racially 'pure' community until much later.

Ethnicity became confounded with social and political roles. A key example is the project in social engineering undertaken by the Brooke régime in Sarawak. Chinese were looked upon as 'economic' subjects and were encouraged to become active in the various subsidiary commercial activities in both retail and wholesale trade, in mining, and in agricultural pursuits such as pepper, gambier, tapioca, rubber and coconut cultivation. Malays were recruited into the lower ranks of the civil service, Europeans into the upper ranks. Iban were brought into the military and police services, also under European leadership. The Brookes, once having established their rule in the region, took steps to 'protect their native peoples' from disturbing outside influences. The same programme of assigned social roles implied also a programme of active discouragement. Thus, Malays, Iban and other indigenous peoples were discouraged from careers in economically profitable pursuits. Their lands were protected from commercial exploitation by Chinese, Indians and other 'greedy' foreigners. Chinese, by the same token, were not welcomed in government service, except as revenue farmers.

While the impulse toward social engineering was less pronounced in the remainder of British Malaya, the virtual paradigm of a plural society came into being with a similar stress on assigned social and economic roles. Whether in the Straits Settlements under direct rule, or in the Malay states under indirect rule, ethnic groups began to separate in economically distinct communities. As Europeans defined themselves as the ruling class, other groups were similarly defined. Chinese were economic, and went to the mines, the plantations and the cities. Malays were protected, and encouraged to remain peasants or fishermen. A variety of legal structures, some quite deliberate, some unintended, led to the same end: a plural society. Land policies, labour laws, natural resource regulations, language policy, educational programmes as well as police and social welfare programmes all moved to separate the various ethnic communities.

The administrative machinery constructed by the British literally built separate structures for the various ethnic and economic groups. Since the British continued to proclaim that these were Malay states under Malay rulers, actual government was always conducted in their names, and even

[30] ibid., 122.

though Rupert Emerson styled this a 'comforting and useful fraud', the official political structure remained a part of the sovereign right of the Malay rulers. This built a barrier against the Chinese and other newly arrived Asian immigrants.[31]

Chinese immigration, which had steadily increased throughout the nineteenth century, became a veritable flood by the beginning of the twentieth century. Immigrants funnelled through Singapore into the western Malay states as well as to the Dutch possessions in Sumatra and Bangka where they supplied a labour force for the expanding tin mines and rubber plantations. Their numbers also swelled the growing urban centres of the British territories both in Malaya and Burma, as well as in the Dutch, French and American colonies.

In Malaya a separate administrative agency was set up, first to deal with particular problems arising out of the presence of secret societies and Chinese women. This was the Chinese Protectorate. It became an entire sub-government, staffed with Chinese-speaking officers and charged with overseeing the 'Societies Ordinance', which in fact regulated all association within the Chinese population. The Protectorate ultimately claimed responsibility for immigration and labour welfare and organization, for Chinese schools, for control of Chinese prostitution, Chinese newspapers and the entire range of Chinese affairs. Not only were the Chinese separated from the other races, but linguistic and regional distinctions between the various Chinese 'tribes' were institutionalized. The only associations that gained government approval were the regional *hui-guan* which stressed differences of language and place of origin.

Indians had been coming to the Straits Settlements since their foundation, primarily as cloth merchants and moneylenders. In the last decade of the nineteenth century and the early years of the twentieth, the subcontinent came to be seen as a source of labour by the European owners of rubber plantations. Despite continuing attempts to control Chinese labour, European estate managers found themselves unable to cross the cultural barriers and were frustrated by the continuing influence of informal organizations among Chinese labourers. They wanted a cheap, abundant and tractable labour force, and they came to see it in India. In the 1880s Hugh Low and Frederick Weld asked the British government to permit the migration of Indian labourers to the Malay states. Most of the new generation of potential planters in the Malay states were British who had already had experience in India and Ceylon (Sri Lanka). The Indian authorities demanded that the Malay states establish 'protectors' of Indian immigrants, and implement a significant body of legislation to regulate the conditions of the new arrivals. These acts, while providing for some measure of welfare for the immigrants, also placed Indians, like Chinese, within a discrete administrative framework. Like the Chinese, the Indians were treated as 'sojourners' in a Malay land.

As rubber cultivation became established, thousands of Tamils came from southern India and Ceylon. In the Malay states they often found themselves isolated on plantations with their families and existing in

---

[31] Emerson, 140–1.

communities with virtually no connection whatsoever with Malaya at large. The expansion and success of European rubber planting led Chinese entrepreneurs to set up plantations as well, with their own labour resources. In some cases, pepper, gambier, sago and tapioca were interplanted with rubber. Thus, wealthy Chinese became plantation owners and less affluent planters became small holders. In any case, between 1890 and 1920 large areas of the Malayan countryside (most of it formerly under rainforest) were cleared and populated with isolated proletarian communities of foreign Asians who were more dependent upon the global market than they were upon the weekly market. The same sort of thing also happened in the Dutch possessions in Sumatra and Borneo, as well as in Cochinchina and parts of Cambodia. The Dutch used Chinese and later Javanese in Sumatra and the French began to recruit peasants from the Tonkin area to work on the plantations of Cambodia and Cochinchina.

Within this context, the entire export economy of the region came to be dominated by non-indigenous peoples. Depending on the particular colony, Chinese, Javanese, Vietnamese and Indians formed the migrant labour force and most of the thinly-staffed middle ranks of the new enterprises, while wealthy Chinese and European corporate interests controlled the commanding heights of the colonial economies. Most indigenous peoples found themselves, like the Malays who were left, as Furnivall has pointed out, becoming poor men in a rich land.

The social, administrative or economic role assigned to a specific community by the colonial power ultimately determined a discrete ethnic identity. In traditional Southeast Asian societies it is certain that individuals, families and villages were aware of differences between themselves and others, but rarely did their consciousness of kind become broad enough to include individuals and groups beyond their own village or immediate kin, and rarely did this sense of identity give rise to ethnic, religious or racial violence. In the Malay states, for instance, there was little sense of common identity between a Malay of Selangor and one of Kelantan, nor was there a discernible level of ethnic tension between Malays and Chinese, or Malays and Indians in either of those states. Few Malays showed concern with the fact that no Chinese and few Indians were Muslims.

Likewise, Vietnamese of Tonkin found little in common with inhabitants of the Mekong delta. The people of one island in the Netherlands East Indies certainly felt no particular bond to the people of another island controlled by the Dutch. The rigorous division of races, ethnic and linguistic groups was often a European colonial innovation. Long-standing colonial practices, such as those in Batavia and Manila, were marked by legislated distinctions between the various social, economic and ethnic groups. Although many of the medieval 'dress codes' that characterized early Dutch rule had disappeared by the twentieth century, the impulse to divide by race was everywhere an important aspect of the colonial order, and it was in colonial circumstances that racial violence began to raise its head.

In Burma, ethnic animosity developed much more rapidly than elsewhere. There, primarily because of the connection between Burma and British India, Indian migration into southern Burma was unrestricted. Indians came as agricultural labourers in the newly opened commercial rice production of the delta. More affluent migrants became landowners and moneylenders. Educated Indians and Anglo-Indians moved effortlessly into the civil service. In the towns the migrants came into competition with the Burmese middle class in trading and the professions. The rapid economic progress of the Indian immigrants created an explosive situation by the 1930s. Robert Taylor observes that British colonial rule in Burma had created a situation where there 'was almost an inverse relationship between the size of the various ethnic groups and their hold on political and economic power during the late colonial period'. Government was controlled by the British, Indians and Anglo-Indians. The economy, including banking, landownership, investment, internal and external trade, was dominated by the British, Indians and Chinese.[32]

The combination of pre-colonial conditions together with the particular policies of different colonial powers led to new realignments of the social order. In the case of French Vietnam, religion provided an area of diversity. In Cochinchina several Buddhist and Taoist sects had coexisted with officially sanctioned Confucianism. With the spread of French rule and the growing power of Vietnamese Catholics—if only because some of them knew French—reactions against colonial rule were often led by religious movements. This led to the creation of the peculiarly Vietnamese form of a 'sect' which began to emerge in the 1920s. These groups, the most well-known of which are the Cao Dai and the Hoa Hao, combined Christian, Buddhist, Taoist, Confucian elements as well as secret society ideology and ritual to form separate communities. Ultimately these sought to form their own military and political structures and to control their own territories.

Religion ultimately became a rallying point for Burmese anti-colonialist as well as anti-foreign movements. The influence of Christian missionaries seeking converts among minority peoples such as the Karen and the Shan, together with general British contempt for Buddhism, had a politicizing effect on Burmese Buddhism. Both the *pongyi* and the young people of the new Burmese middle classes responded to issues such as the 'shoe controversy'. As the Buddhist revival took place in the various mainland states, indigenous peoples who had become converts to Christian ideologies found themselves more sharply separated from majority communities.

While Islam as a source of anti-colonialism was only negligible in British Malaya, Muslim peoples in both the Philippines and Sumatra responded to the inroads of colonialism by militant resistance. The peoples of Sulu and Mindanao had a long tradition of defying Spanish Catholicism. Spanish pressure had reinforced the identification of Islam and their political identities. Americans did little to alter a heritage of armed separation.

Educational and language policies were yet another source of division in all colonies. Usually, the language of the ruling class became the language

[32] Robert H. Taylor, *The State in Burma*, London, 1987, 128–9.

of government and business. In Burma, the Philippines and Malaya, areas with complex ethnic landscapes, English became the lingua franca. Those indigenous peoples or Asian immigrants who had some command of the language were in privileged positions when it came to professional advancement. In all these countries there was no incentive for the immigrants and minority peoples to learn the majority tongues, since the language of advancement was the European language. The intrusion of European languages brought other cultural influences as well. The new states themselves were isolated from their neighbours in other colonial states and reoriented toward the European metropoles. Thus by the 1920s, one could visit classrooms in Cambodia and hear students at the *lycée* reciting lessons from books that referred to 'our ancestors the Gauls'.

In the Dutch East Indies language policy took a different track. Education in Dutch itself was pursued by the higher ranks of the Javanese civil service who saw it as a path to advancement within the Dutch system. At the same time, as the Dutch possessions grew in number, the use of Malay as a lingua franca became widespread throughout the Indies, thus providing a basis for unity where in fact virtually none had existed before. What would become *bahasa Indonesia* was a 'modernized' language with a Roman alphabet that spread throughout the Dutch domains. The numerous states which had come under indirect Dutch control by means of the Short Declaration remained 'watertight compartments', each an entity apart, though at the same time open to a wide range of exceptions. The use of a language like Indonesian brought these individual states into a broader community and put their peoples into touch with others who had previously been entirely alien to them.

On the other hand, the terms of the Short Declaration treaties created new kinds of pluralism within these states. The treaties applied only to the relationship between the rulers and their subject people, whomever they were understood to be, and the Dutch government. Virtually all others were not subject to the *adat* of the particular state, but under a different set of regulations. This included Europeans, 'foreign orientals', native civil servants, persons residing on land ceded to the central government, other natives from other states, and natives under labour contract. Each one of these categories was in fact governed under a separate rulebook: more watertight compartments.

The creation of colonial educational systems reinforced the divisions created by the influence of European languages. In Malaya British policies strengthened the barriers between the ethnic communities. The children of Malay aristocratic families received the Malayan version of an English public-school education at the Kuala Kangsar Malay School. For the average Malay, the educational horizon was the Muslim *pesantren* or *pondok* school run by a local teacher, which offered some instruction in memorizing the Koran. As early as 1872, the British realized that even peasants needed some education, and they embarked on the creation of a Malay-language educational system, to provide Malay villagers with at least three years of schooling. Frank Swettenham was of the opinion that instruction should be provided only on a need-to-know basis.

Whilst we teach children to read and write and count in their own languages, or in Malay ... we are *safe*. Beyond that, I should like to see the boys taught useful industries and the girls weaving, embroidery and mat-making, all profitable and all practised with a high degree of excellence in different states of the Peninsula.[33]

The British lack of enthusiasm for native education was matched by the Malays, who were unwilling to send their children to government schools. Finding qualified teachers was always a problem. In 1920, Richard Winstedt made provision for a teacher-training school. Ultimately the schools were staffed by the graduates of the Sultan Idris Training College for Malay teachers at Tanjong Malim.

For the more ambitious inhabitants of British Malaya, especially the children of Indians, Chinese and Eurasians, there were the private English-language schools set up by various missionary groups, primarily the Catholics. The religious orientation provided a disincentive for Malay attendance, thus creating yet another institutional barrier between the races. Chinese also saw merit in organizing schools to teach their own language, and wealthy Chinese merchants gained status within their communities by supporting Chinese education. Thus yet another separate 'stream' was added to the educational offerings in Malaya. By the 1920s, enlightened estate owners were beginning to provide schooling for the children of their Indian labourers, and thus Tamil-medium schools began to cater to yet another ethnic constituency.

The creation of plural societies seems, in the final analysis, to have resulted from a combination of factors. Ethnic diversity was a fact of life in the region long before Europeans arrived, but with administrative rationality and European racism things changed. The new territorial frameworks of the colonies within which relatively unified administrative structures came into being were in fact the foundations of the new nation-states. The new administration, however, identified and isolated these diverse elements, compartmentalizing some, protecting others and allowing still others greater freedom of action. The impact of market forces and the global economy continued the process by commercializing the ethnic occupational specializations. Language and educational policies drove home the final barriers.

In the example of Siam, a distinction between European and indigenous rule is apparent. The economic role of immigrant Chinese was similar to that in other regions, but the government's policy toward them was not hindered by the erection of exclusionist legal barriers to assimilation as was the case in the European colonies. Although anti-Chinese sentiment was given voice by King Vajiravudh in the years before 1920, it never fully separated the indigenous peoples from the immigrants.

The root of the problem was the creation of 'communities'. It seems that this was the real European innovation. The works of Butcher and Jean

---

[33] Quoted in P. Loh, *The Malay States 1877–1895*, Singapore and Kuala Lumpur, 1969, 169.

Taylor suggest that the Europeans created that notion by making themselves the model for all the other restricted communities. The final stage in the development of these plural societies came in the 1920s and 1930s, as nationalist movements began to stir among the various peoples of the region. In virtually every case the emerging national communities found themselves facing social constructions riddled with contradictions and discrepancies. The administrative territories which had been centralized under the various European powers included a multiplicity of ethnic groups, both indigenous and of foreign origin, many of which enjoyed privileged situations, or at least separate systems of control. In some cases, nationalist sentiments arose among foreign immigrants before they did among the indigenous peoples.

Thus, in Malaya and Singapore, Chinese nationalism had established itself before Malay nationalist groups began seeking autonomy. In fact, it might be said that the spectacle of Chinese political activity actually had the effect of galvanizing Malay nationalism. In most places, the Chinese came to be seen as a challenge to indigenous nationalist groups. This was the case in Indonesia, the Philippines and Vietnam. In Burma, the Indians bore the brunt of discrimination from nationalist militants. The very militancy of modern nationalism, arising as it did within the plural societies created by colonialism, came to see the 'non-national' communities as reminders of foreign domination. These minorities would suffer as a result of this heritage.

SIAM AND BURMA

These two neighbouring states on the Southeast Asian mainland are a study in contrasts. The period of state modernization shows these contrasts at their most extreme. Burma was invaded from India, annexed, and reconstructed according to British will. The entire territory was subjected to direct rule; no systematic effort was made to work within the traditional order. Siam, by contrast, escaped invasion and foreign rule. The state was ushered through its process of administrative and political modernization by its own traditional rulers. King Rama IV, Mongkut, accepted the unequal Bowring treaty in 1855 and opened the country to Western economic and cultural influences, making himself a leader in this process. His son, Rama V, Chulalongkorn, whose rule (1868–1910) spanned the period of European colonial expansion, is credited with preserving the state's independence.

Oddly enough, the goals and models of administrative centralization and political reform in both states were in many ways similar. The Siamese were strongly influenced by British methods of government, in both Malaya and Burma as well as at home. Much of the Thai modernization was accomplished with the advice of European specialists, and it was certainly spurred by pressures from British and French diplomats, merchants and missionaries who, in a sense, looked over the shoulders of the Thai throughout the period.

Nor was Siam free from foreign military threats and intervention.

During the last two decades of the nineteenth century, David Wyatt states, the country lost control of 456,000 square kilometres of territory to Britain and France. It is also true that throughout this period Siam was forced to carry out its programmes while bound by unequal treaties which allowed economic and legal privileges to foreign subjects, and placed restrictions on the type and level of taxes which the government could impose. The Thai were also severely restricted in their freedom of action in their own foreign affairs, particularly in regard to their neighbouring states. In many respects, the international status of Siam was quite similar to that of one of the indirectly ruled Malay states or to many of the outlying island states of the Netherlands East Indies. Moreover, the administrative reforms sponsored by the Thai king merely strengthened the state and really did nothing at all to promote the development of political freedom among the people. Socially, Thai society was very heterogeneous, including Malay, Mon, Lao, and indigenous hill peoples such as the Hmong and the Yao, as well as a significant number of Chinese immigrants. The Siamese social order was likewise divided by traditional distinctions of class and status that remain embedded in the language.

Clearly a major difference lay in the means by which reforms were introduced. The fact that the Thai modernization was 'self-inflicted' meant that the trauma was certainly reduced. Perhaps the Siamese experience is as good an argument as any against colonial rule, no matter how noble the intentions, but it is also clear that Siam's experience in many respects depended on what happened to its neighbours. The fact that an indigenous élite carried through the reforms seems to have allowed the Thai social order to retain a degree of cultural integrity that was stripped from the Burmese and other Southeast Asian peoples. A comparison of the two cases and consideration of some of the social, economic and cultural consequences will help in understanding the processes.

In Burma, where British rule was introduced from India, and was intended to displace the government of the Burmese monarchy, new classes arose to fill the ranks of the administration. After the annexation of upper Burma, British administrators in charge of the pacification moved radically to restructure the civil administration along the lines of the Indian system without regard to prior patterns of village and local government. The British invasion and pacification, accompanied by the immigration of large numbers of Indians and Chinese and the erection of separate administrations for minority populations, were a traumatic experience for Burmese society in general. The collapse of the Burmese social and political order in 1885 was a crisis of enormous magnitude for the culture as a whole.

John Cady has used terms like 'social deterioration' and 'cultural disintegration' to describe the impact of British rule. Virtually every other major historian of Burma in recent times has been in agreement in pointing to the generally detrimental impact of British rule on Burmese society and on its long-term political and social development. Furnivall's critique of the Indian model of direct rule and economic liberalism has been decisive in setting the tone of scholarly debate regarding Burmese development. Hall has criticized Crosthwaite 'who came with firmly fixed ideas of Indian

administration, [and] brought with him a ready-drafted scheme for making the village, as in India, the basic social and political unit'.[34] This was an
innovation that cut the traditional rural socio-political order to the heart.

Furnivall and more recent students make it clear that Crosthwaite really
did not understand the function of the circle headmen, whose positions
were abolished, and village headmen, who were created from virtually
nothing. The latter were given powers and functions that they had never
before enjoyed. The new class of village and local functionaries tended to
be Indian as often as Burman, because of the British view that there was an
insufficient number of trained Burman personnel.

The real problem was not so much the fact that the model for administrative and institutional reform was Indian, but that the officials who
implemented it neither knew nor cared very much about Burma. Their
knowledge and experience were based on what they had learned in India.
Crosthwaite's comments suggest that he really did not understand the
nature of property under Burmese customary law and that he did not have
a clear concept of the manner in which the traditional government had
been able to maintain political communication with its people. Perhaps
Furnivall was incorrect in styling the *myothugyi* as a popularly chosen
representative of the village, but neither was he a centrally appointed
bureaucrat who was periodically reposted. The township officer who more
or less took on his function as a sub-district officer had responsibility for
about a hundred villages. Under the British system his duties were
primarily to hear cases and collect revenue. Other functions of the state
were separated under specialist departments, so that education, sanitation, irrigation and other responsibilities were outside the ken of the
township officer and district officer.

The prolonged pacification programme was a response to the disorder
precipitated by the abolition of traditional rule; Robert Taylor argues that it
had the effect of requiring the colonial state to develop stronger instruments of suppression and social control. In a sense, it can be said that from
1885 until 1942, Burma was always under a form of martial law. Taylor
remarks on the irony that the British who came with the pledge to free the
Burmese from arbitrary government had replaced the 'shackles of custom'
with the 'fetters of regulation'.[35] Their policies resulted in the paradoxical
legacy of the colonial state in Burma:

> the great strength of the colonial state was its external sources of military
> power and administrative organization gained from Britain and India. The
> great weakness of the colonial state was its inability to sustain support, either
> active or passive, from the indigenous population.[36]

Another result of the British pacification of Burma was that there was
little room for mutual trust between Burmans and the English. As a result,
British policy generally favoured minority peoples. Most of the soldiers

[34] Hall, p. 771.
[35] Taylor, *The State in Burma*, 98–9.
[36] ibid., 115.

and police were Indians. Crosthwaite remarked that the failure to train Burmans as soldiers was 'a blot on our escutcheon'.[37] Nevertheless, the British trained Karen and Kachin regiments who, along with Indians, garrisoned the Burman, Shan and Chin districts.

In Siam, the reform of the traditional government on an internal basis presented a wide range of unique problems. In many ways the Thai ruler had to tear down and rebuild the house while he continued to live in it. Ministries in the capital and the palace had become the hereditary holdings of powerful families who controlled their own revenues, provinces, and economic resources through large patronage networks, and sometimes even had their own private armies. Provincial administration was chaotic, with many provinces under the hereditary rule of local dynasties. Other provinces were directly under specific ministries, such as the western provinces bordering Burma which were under the Kalahom and controlled by the ex-regent, Sri Suriyawong, the head of the powerful Bunnag family. Other groups dominated the government and revenues of the south, which was locally in the hands of Chinese *kapitans* and revenue farmers; and still other arrangements held true for the northeast where Lao chieftains enjoyed relative autonomy within their territories. It was necessary for a reformer first to pierce through this entrenched system. Such a government was the kind that the British had swept away in Burma.

The pace of reform in Siam was far slower than in that country. Initially Chulalongkorn's reforms were hindered partly by conservative factions who generally remained in power until 1885. Even though most of the older officials, particularly the leaders of the powerful Bunnag family, had disappeared by 1890, change was impeded by the lack of qualified, educated leadership. Chulalongkorn generally relied upon his own brothers and half-brothers to staff his remodelled administration. They were the only individuals who had received a modern education.

Gradually one ministry after another was reformed or consolidated as the old head died. New ministries and departments were initiated and given operative independence on a piecemeal basis, often functioning as temporary offices within the palace until such time as a ministry was capable of assuming its tasks in a responsible manner. The king first appointed his own choice to the Ministry of the Capital. This was followed by appointments to the Treasury and Foreign Affairs where he placed his own brothers. Most of the transfer of power from the old guard took place between 1882 and 1888, a period which saw the death of Prince Wichaichan, Chulalongkorn's archrival, and the ex-regent Prince Suriyawong. His brother, Prince Damrong, took charge of the Interior Ministry only in 1892, which was also the first year in which the heads of all of the ministries first met as a cabinet. At the same time, it was also necessary to introduce systems of auditing, bookkeeping, filing, registering correspondence and the practice of filing quarterly and annual reports.[38]

The reform of provincial and local government and the centralization of the state apparatus in Siam proceeded along British Indian lines. Local

[37] Crosthwaite, 131.
[38] D. K. Wyatt, *Thailand: A Short History*, New Haven, 1984, 193–201.

government was organized under a Ministry of Interior with provincial governors appointed by the ministry and with provinces broken up into districts or *amphur*, under the control of a centrally appointed *nai amphur* or district officer. Below that level, officers such as the village headmen and *kamnan* were chosen from the local communities. However, while the system certainly resembled a British Indian model, there were significant differences.

Reform of the courts and the legal system was an important step in breaking free of the unequal treaties and the consular jurisdiction. In this case, rather than following the British model, the Thai employed French and Belgian jurists as advisers and implemented a version of the Napoleonic code to carry through the changes. This reflected the general policy that governed the use of foreign advisers. Each ministry had several, and they were deliberately chosen from different nationalities (British, French, Belgian, American, Danish, German, etc.) to avoid the impression that one particular European country was unduly influencing the reforms. In many cases they had little experience of local conditions.[39]

The fact that Thai officials controlled the process meant that they were generally free to choose advisers as well as accept or reject their advice. While the reform of the legal system was guided and eventually approved by European advisers, the system was adapted to Thai realities. On the other hand, the introduction of a British legal system in Burma was a disaster. It bewildered the Burmese. British law courts and their judgements had little relevance to Burmese ideas of justice. Cady styled it 'a game of technicalities and rules which only the not-too-scrupulous legal profession seemed to understand and profit from'. Burmans, he said, were more concerned about personal dignity and affronts to status than about infringements against property, which is what concerned the British and Indian magistrates.[40]

Like the British, the Thai monarchs faced problems of resistance as the state was expanded and centralized. This was particularly true in the minority areas. In 1902, when Damrong's reforms were sweeping away the old order, three revolts arose in different parts of the country. In the south, Muslims led by the Raja of Pattani revolted as local governors resisted the transfer of their revenue to the central authorities. The area around Ubon in northeast Thailand erupted into the 'Holy Man's Rebellion'. Although it was led by a messianic monk who claimed that the end of the world was near and that many miracles would occur, the uprising was also supported by members of the old ruling families of the area. In the north, near Phrae, several hundred Shan who had come from Burma to work in logging and gem mining rebelled. They too had the support of local ruling families who resented the loss of their traditional privileges. In each case, the central government was able to suppress the rebellions with relative ease.

One of the major innovations of Chulalongkorn's reforms was the establishment of a professional military. This was a real contrast between

---

[39] ibid., 211.
[40] J. F. Cady, *A History of Modern Burma*, Ithaca, 1958, 146.

Siam and the colonized states. The Thai were the only Southeast Asians who were in a position to develop their own army before World War II. This, too, was done by royal princes and pioneered first in the Corps of Royal Pages in the palace. A Department of the Army was created in 1888 when the military was separated from the old Kalahom. In 1902, universal military conscription was introduced. Siamese forces had acquitted themselves well when fighting against the French in Laos in 1893. While they were unable to defeat European armies and navies, Thai forces were sufficient to crush domestic revolts. In a sense, Bangkok had become the imperial force, ready to civilize its own unruly 'natives' with modern weapons.

In Burma, the relations between Europeans and non-Burman minorities were one of the forces that helped to create a plural society. The heritage of these policies continues to stand as a block to national unification in Burma today. In the Shan, Karen and Kachin areas, local élites and aristocrats were usually maintained and much of the traditional social structure was left intact. In the hill areas, unlike lower Burma, the British often were quite willing to rely on systems of indirect rule. By contrast, in Siam such peoples were treated as feudal remnants who were reorganized into compartments of the central bureaucracy. By 1905, most of the hereditary chiefs, both Thai, Shan, Lao and Malay, had been relieved of their traditional revenues and administrative powers.

In Burma, while the lowlands were being ruthlessly modernized under direct rule and flooded with aggressive new immigrants, hill peoples were in a sense being put into a museum. But some of these groups were converted to Christianity and taught English. Their own languages were, for the first time, written down, codified and brought into print—usually in the Roman alphabet. This creation of print communities had an important role in strengthening ethnic and 'national' consciousness. While the same missionaries were also active in the hill areas of Siam, their presence did not have the same divisive effect as in Burma.

The numbers of Chinese migrants into Siam grew considerably during this period. By 1910 Chinese amounted to nearly 10 per cent of the total population, numbering about 792,000, most located in the provinces around Bangkok. In Siam, as elsewhere in Southeast Asia, the Chinese moved into the labour market, particularly into the plantations, mines, market-gardening and the urban workforce. They almost totally dominated the retail trade and the domestic and international rice trade. Many Chinese prospered, some gained government positions, and many were assimilated over the course of the nineteenth century. In southern Siam the proportion of Chinese was much higher in relation to the general population, particularly in the tin-mining areas around Phuket, Ranong and Nakhon Sithammarat. Here the Thai rulers had appointed Chinese headmen to become provincial governors. Although many of them were replaced in the administrative reforms of the period, the southern border provinces continued to be dominated by wealthy Chinese families who in many cases were branches of Penang families, such as the Khaw.[41]

---

[41] J. W. Cushman, 'The Khaw Group: Chinese Business in Early Twentieth-century Penang', JSEAS, 17, 1 (March 1986), 58ff.

The Thai situation closely approximated the plural societies of other Southeast Asian states. There was a similar ethnic division of labour. Ethnic Thai, even peasants, were often unwilling to accept low-paying, hard-labour jobs so long as rice agriculture remained a profitable occupation. Those who were more ambitious among the Thai sought advancement in the Buddhist monkhood or government service. The Chinese came to dominate the modern sector of the Thai economy, and as the numbers increased they became more of an identifiable community. The communal differences solidified as bureaucratic realities took effect and the old patronage networks that had formerly served as paths of assimilation disappeared. At the same time, more Chinese women came to Siam, and Chinese families gave greater permanence to the distinction between the Thai and the Chinese. In 1915, King Vajiravudh began to raise the banner of Thai nationalism and in a vitriolic essay singled out the Chinese as 'Jews of the East'.[42]

The growth of Siam's plural society suggests that, despite control by its own monarchs, the country was still subject to many of the same economic and social forces that affected other areas. The vast increase in migration, the arrival of Chinese women, and the pattern of Siam's economic growth depended on the processes of technological change, such as the development of regular steam travel and the growing ease of communications. There were also more liberal migration policies in China. It is also true that many Chinese enjoyed privileged status as the subjects of colonial governments and thus were able to operate under the protection of the unequal treaties. As a result, cities like Bangkok grew, very much like colonial port cities of Singapore, Saigon and Batavia, as Chinese centres.

Although Bangkok did have most of the marks of a colonial port city, it was also the centre of the Thai royal government and it functioned as the cult centre and religious focus of the country. The national shrines such as the Wat Po and the Temple of the Emerald Buddha as well as the royal palaces made the city the spiritual centre of the state. This was in stark contrast to Burma where the economic and political life of the colonial state now focused on Rangoon, while the former capital of Mandalay had been demoted and the former royal palace had become a British club. Perhaps the major difference in this respect was in the status of the Buddhist religion.

In Siam, Buddhism continued as the official religion of the country under royal protection. It thus functioned as a force for national unity and historical continuity. The reformed Thammayutika sect, which had been founded in the nineteenth century by Mongkut while he was in the monkhood, had a major influence. The sect was more rigorously intellectual than customary and less ritualistic. It put a heavy stress on education and took a leading role in promoting village-level education for the layman. Its own intellectual centre was the Buddhist university at Wat Bowonniwet. The sect had strong links to the royal family, and at the turn of the century it came under the leadership of Prince Wachiranan, another

[42] W. F. Vella, *Chaiyo! King Vajiravudh and the Development of Thai Nationalism*, Honolulu, 1978, 193–4.

of Chulalongkorn's brothers. When he became the Supreme Patriarch, he led a thorough-going reform of Siamese Buddhism including its religious practices, texts, and rituals, and the status of the *sangha* or monkhood. This created a channel of communication from the king to the village that did not rely on political or administrative channels. The traditional educational role of the village monasteries was vital in spreading the standardized script and literature of 'Bangkok Thai' as well as Western-style mathematics and science.

The contrast between Siam and Burma could not have been greater in this respect. The Burmese monks, who had performed a similar role in traditional education, vigorously resisted the colonial government's attempts to promote a modern syllabus through the monastery schools. The Siamese attempts went forward on the prestige of the monarchy, while in Burma the colonial government's relationship with the *sangha* ranged from outright opposition by the Buddhist monks to contempt on the part of the British. In the uprisings of 1885 and 1886, monks actually joined the fighting against British forces; where Karens were concerned, this had the effect of turning the pacification into religious and ethnic warfare. Vinton, the American Baptist missionary, wrote to Crosthwaite in 1886:

> The strangest of all is the presence of poongyees [Buddhist monks] on the battlefield. This is unheard of in history.
>
> The Karens universally interpret this as God's sign that Buddhism is to be destroyed forever. They say the challenge of Thebaw could be answered by the British government, but the challenge of the fighting poongyees can only be taken up fitly by Karens under their own missionaries . . . I have never seen the Karens so anxious for a fight. This is . . . welding the Karens into a nation . . . The heathen Karens to a man are brigading themselves under the Christians. This whole thing is doing good for the Karen. This will put virility into our Christianity.[43]

Thus, while in Siam Buddhism acted to unify the country and to strengthen the hand of the central government, in Burma religion served as a real source of division within society while at the same time dividing the Burmans from the government. Because of the abolition of the Burmese monarchy, there was no institution left in Burma with the prestige to regulate the *sangha*. Burmese Buddhist institutions thus fragmented, and it was Western-educated Burmese laymen who used the religion as a rallying point for resistance to colonialism. Significantly, the Burmese *sangha* had little to do with the growth of the Young Men's Buddhist Association.

In regard to language and educational policy, the Thai élite responded to the challenges of modernization with major attempts to reform the educational system and to turn it into an agency of centralization. Even though missionaries were permitted to operate within the country and they often stressed the teaching of English, no dual-language society developed in Siam as happened in Burma and every other colonized

---

[43] Cady, 139.

territory. Since modern literature, science and other general subjects were mediated through the Thai language, the language itself continuously moved forward and did not stagnate. The fact that individual Burmese advanced quickly in Western fields on the basis of English education obscured for a time the retrograde influence that the system had on Burmese in general. In the 1920s and 1930s, it often seemed that Siam was the laggard.

By the 1920s, Burma seemed to be advancing rapidly in terms of political and economic development. The British had created a modern commercial economy, and much of the population had been brought, one way or another, into the modern sector. Burmese exports, particularly of rice, were among the highest in the region, while in Siam economic growth was slower. This was due to a lower level of investment as well as to a less developed infrastructure. Also, despite the modernizing efforts of the monarchy, European-run administrations were much more efficient at protecting property, particularly European property, and at advancing European economic interests.

In terms of the growth of representative institutions and modern-style constitutional government, it also seemed that Burma was moving more rapidly than Siam. By 1921, Burma had, because of its connection with India, begun the process of developing instruments of self-government. Ironically, one of the rallying points for Burmese student activists was separation from India, and it continued to be a focus of protests until the mid-1930s when London decided to break the connection. Burmese pressures on British administrators were apparently quite successful. By 1923, a dyarchy constitution gave Burma a measure of self-rule. Elections were held in 1922, 1925 and 1928, though they seemed to have little relevance to the average Burmese, particularly the rural peoples. In 1937, a reformed constitution gave Burma an increased level of self-rule, but it continued to be too little too late for Burmese student activists.

In Siam as early as 1885 the monarch had resisted calls for a similar move toward constitutional government and parliamentary institutions. Chulalongkorn had been petitioned by a group of returned students to move toward democracy and to prevent the growing concentration of power in the hands of the executive. He refused on the grounds that the country was not yet educated and that the older men were incompetent while the younger ones were not prepared to govern. His successor, Vajiravudh, was able to govern as an absolute monarch, although generally limited by the presence of his father's brothers who continued to dominate the administrative structure. An attempted coup, shortly after he took the throne in 1912, confirmed his inherent reactionary tendencies and turned him firmly against constitutional government. Instead he is recognized as the founder of Thai nationalism and credited with the establishment of the state ideology, which stressed the identification of 'Nation, Religion, King', and left the country with a heritage of official, conservative nationalism. While not a popular force at this time, it later provided the basis for a more militant mobilization of Thai society.

Vajiravudh's successor was less fortunate in dealing with popular demands. Rama VII, Prajadiphok, faced rising demands for constitutional reform and greater responsibility from the non-royal members of the new military and civilian bureaucracy. He found himself confronted with a coup in 1932 led by civil and military 'promoters' such as Nai Pridi Panomyong and Phibun Songkhram. He abdicated, and when the dust had settled Phibun had ousted his erstwhile partners and created a military dictatorship. He embarked upon his own programme of modernization and nationalist reform, which owed much to his appreciation of Japanese and German models.

As war clouds gathered around Southeast Asia, both Siam and Burma, like some of the other countries of the region, had well-established nationalist movements. Most of them were organized largely by Western-educated élites who had first tasted power within the new bureaucracies of the colonial and semi-colonial states of the region. By the late 1930s, all had reason to move toward an anti-European stance, a position which left them well-prepared to welcome the Japanese in 1942.

BIBLIOGRAPHIC ESSAY

The most comprehensive treatment of the region's history remains D. G. E. Hall's *A History of Southeast Asia*, 4th edn, New York, 1981, despite its dated format. The nineteenth and twentieth centuries are covered in a more accessible fashion in David Joel Steinberg, et al., *In Search of Southeast Asia: A Modern History*, Sydney, 1987. In recent years a large number of histories and political studies have appeared focusing on specific countries or regions and based in large part on indigenous sources as well as colonial and other Western-language sources. These include Barbara Watson Andaya and Leonard Y. Andaya, *A History of Malaysia*, New York, 1982; Robert H. Taylor, *The State in Burma*, London, 1987; M. C. Ricklefs, *A History of Modern Indonesia: c. 1300 to the Present*, London, 1981; David K. Wyatt, *Thailand: A Short History*, New Haven, 1984; David Chandler, *A History of Cambodia*, Boulder, 1983. Older, but still useful surveys include Le Thanh Khoi, *Le Vietnam*, Paris, 1955; Milton Osborne, *The French Presence in Cochinchina and Cambodia: Rule and Response 1859–1905*, Ithaca, 1969; John F. Cady, *A History of Modern Burma*, Ithaca, 1958; and J. D. Legge, *Indonesia*, Englewood Cliffs, 1964.

Collaborator Classes

Literature on indigenous collaborator classes is quite recent as a separate topic: nevertheless the rise of local ruling groups since independence, many of which had clear connections to the colonial régimes, has spurred interest in this topic. Much of the literature has focused on the nineteenth and twentieth centuries. Heather Sutherland's *The Making of a Bureaucratic Elite, The Colonial Transformation of the Javanese Priyayi*, Singapore, 1979, and her 'The Taming of the Trengganu Elite', and Onghokham's 'The Inscrutable and the Paranoid: An Investigation into the sources of the Brotodiningrat Affair', both in Ruth McVey, ed., *Southeast Asian Transitions: Approaches through Social History*, New Haven, 1978, are some of the more outstanding works in this genre, the first two focusing on Java and the other on Malaya. Also useful are J. M. Gullick's *Indigenous Political Systems of Western Malaya*, London, 1958, and his more recent *Malay Society in the Late Nineteenth Century*, Singapore, 1989; M. C. Ricklefs, *Jogjakarta Under Sultan Mangkubumi, 1749–1792, A History of the Division of Java*, London, 1974; Anthony Reid, *The Contest for North Sumatra: Atjeh, the Netherlands and Britain 1858–1898*, Kuala Lumpur, 1969. Carl Trocki has examined the relationship of the Johor chiefs and the Singapore Chinese leadership with the British colonial state in the nineteenth century in *Prince of Pirates, The Temenggongs and the Development of Singapore and Johor 1784–1885*, Singapore, 1979; and *Opium and Empire: Chinese Society in Colonial Singapore, 1800–1910*, Ithaca, 1990. Studies of institutions such as revenue farms related to the overseas Chinese also provide important insights into the role of Chinese allies of colonial régimes. James R. Rush, *Opium to Java*, Ithaca, 1989, is an important contribution, as are the studies of the various Chinese communities by Maurice Freedman, G. William Skinner, Wang Gungwu, Wong Lin Ken, Edgar Wickberg, Lea Williams, and Leo Suryadynata. Works such as Anthony Reid, 'Habib Abdur-Rahman Az-Zahir (1833–1896)', *Indonesia*, 13 (1972), approach the question from the biographical point of view. Also of interest is some of the autobiographical work, best represented by Abdullah bin Abdulkadir's *Hikayat Abdullah*. Some work has been done on earlier periods such as the innovative study by Jean Gelman Taylor, *The Social World of Batavia: European and Eurasian in Dutch Asia*, Madison, 1983. The growth of indigenous élite classes in Indochina has been covered in David Marr, *Vietnamese Anticolonialism, 1885–1925*, Berkeley, 1971, and *Vietnamese Tradition on Trial 1920–1945*, Berkeley, 1981, and in Osborne, *The French Presence*.

Direct and Indirect Rule

Analyses of direct and indirect rule have a substantial historiographical tradition. One of the earliest studies, still durable, is Rupert Emerson's of British and Dutch colonial rule in Malaya and the Indies, *Malaysia: A Study in Direct and Indirect Rule*, New York, 1937. Another important and influential early study of this sort is J. S. Furnivall, *Colonial Policy and Practice: A Comparative Study of Burma and Netherlands India*, Cambridge, UK, 1948. Related questions are also raised in the works of Gullick, as well as those of Sutherland, Trocki and Robert Taylor. For the Philippines there is the collection of articles in Norman G. Owen, ed., *Compadre Colonialism: Studies on the Philippines under American Rule*, Ann Arbor, 1971, particularly Michael Cullinane's 'Implementing the "New Order": The Structure and Supervision of Local Government During the Taft Era'. Important studies of other countries in the region are found in McVey, ed., *Southeast Asian Transitions*. There is also a wealth of important material in the biographical works and memoirs of colonial officials in Southeast Asia. Important insights on the systems of rule in the Malay world are found in Anthony C. Milner, *Keraja'an: Malay Political Culture on the Eve of Colonial Rule*, Tucson, 1982, and Shaharil Talib, *After Its Own Image*, Singapore, 1986.

Law and Order

The literature on law and order in Southeast Asia is perhaps the best developed genre of colonial writing on the region. Such works as Sir Charles Crosthwaite, *The Pacification of Burma*, London, 1912; C. Snouck Hurgronje, *The Achehnese*, Leiden and London, 1906; Auguste Pavie, *Mission Pavie*, Paris, 1898–1904; Sydney Cloman, *Myself and a Few Moros*, Garden City, 1923; Victor Hurley, *Swish of the Kris: The Story of the Moros*, New York, 1936; and Henry Keppel, *The Expedition of H.M.S. 'Dido' for the Suppression of Piracy, with extracts from the Journal of James Brooke Esq., of Sarawak*, London, 1846, are representative examples of the memoirs of individuals involved in the colonial takeover of the region and major apologists for the establishment of European-style rule in most of the region. This has been added to by publication of earlier materials such as Paul Kratoska's collection, *Honourable Intentions: Talks on the British Empire in Southeast Asia Delivered at the Royal Colonial Institute*, Singapore, 1983, and Amin Sweeney, *Reputations Live On: An Early Malay Autobiography*, Berkeley, 1980. Studies written in the aftermath of colonial rule have been built upon examinations of the colonial archives: Nicholas Tarling, *Piracy and Politics in the Malay World*, Melbourne, 1963; Jagjit Singh Sidhu, *Administration in the Federated Malay States 1896–1920*, Kuala Lumpur, 1980; Milton Osborne, *The French Presence*; Emily Sadka, *The Protected Malay States, 1874–1895*, Kuala Lumpur, 1968; Anthony Reid, *The Contest for North Sumatra*; Eliodoro G. Robles, *The Philippines in the Nineteenth Century*, Quezon City, 1969; Russel Roth, *Muddy Glory: America's 'Indian Wars' in the Philippines 1899–1935*, Hanover, 1981. More recent studies, written from the perspective of indigenous successor régimes, often present a more critical version of events. Works in the latter category examine the often conflicting mix of indigenous political cultures with the rationalized structures of European colonialism. Examples include Benedict R. O'G. Anderson, 'The Idea of Power in Javanese Culture', in Claire Holt, ed., *Culture and Politics in Indonesia*, Ithaca, 1972; James Siegel, *The Rope of God*, Berkeley, 1968; James Warren, *The Sulu Zone*, Singapore, 1979; Heather Sutherland, *The Making of a Bureaucratic Elite*; and Robert Taylor, *The State in Burma*. Another important analysis of 'pacification' programmes conducted by colonial powers is James C. Scott's *The Moral Economy of the Peasant*, New Haven, 1976.

Plural Societies

J. S. Furnivall coined the term plural society and his works remain the starting point for serious study of the phenomenon, particularly *Colonial Policy and Practice*. This study not only defines the phenomenon, but also remains the only truly comparative study. Most of the literature is country-specific, or limited to a specific ethnic community. Numerous studies focus on groups such as the Chinese, especially where their presence poses serious economic and political questions such as in Malaysia. These include the somewhat dated but still useful work of Victor Purcell, *The Chinese in Southeast Asia*, London, 1965, and C. P. Fitzgerald, *The Southern*

Expansion of the Chinese People, London, 1972. Important views of Malaysia are presented in Philip Loh Fook Seng, *The Malay States 1877–1895, Political Change and Social Policy*, Kuala Lumpur, 1969; his *Seeds of Separatism: Educational Policies and Social Change 1819–1972*, Kuala Lumpur, 1975; K. J. Ratnam, *Communalism and the Political Process in Malaya*, Singapore, 1965; Michael Stenson's study of the Indian community, *Class, Race and Colonialism in West Malaysia*, St Lucia, 1980; and L. A. P. Gosling, 'Migration and Assimilation of Rural Chinese in Trengganu', in John Bastin and R. Roolvink, eds, *Malayan and Indonesian Studies: Essays Presented to Sir Richard Winstedt on his Eighty-fifth Birthday*, Oxford, 1964. For Singapore, there is James Warren, *Rickshaw Coolie: A People's History of Singapore*, Singapore, 1987. A unique approach to communal studies is John Butcher, *The British in Malaya 1880–1941, The Social History of a European Community in Colonial South-East Asia*, Kuala Lumpur, 1979. The classic study of Thailand is by G. William Skinner, *Chinese Society in Thailand: An Analytical History*, Ithaca, 1957; also important is Dorothy Hess Guyot, 'Communal Conflict in the Burma Delta', in McVey, *Southeast Asian Transitions*. The classic work on tribal minorities is E. R. Leach, *Political Systems of Highland Burma*, 1954. A recent addition is Ann Laura Stoler, *Capitalism and Confrontation in Sumatra's Plantation Belt 1870–1979*, New Haven, 1985.

Siam and Burma

The standard studies of Siam include David Wyatt, *Thailand: A Short History*, New Haven, 1984, as well as his *The Politics of Reform in Thailand*, New Haven, 1969; also valuable are the documents collected by Chatthip Nartsupha and Suthy Prasartset, *The Political Economy of Siam 1851–1910*, 1981. David M. Engel, *Law and Kingship in Thailand during the Reign of King Chulalongkorn*, Ann Arbor, 1975, is an important discussion of the reforms of Rama V. Another important view of Thai modernization is Stanley J. Tambiah, *World Conqueror and World Renouncer: A Study of Buddhism and Polity in Thailand Against a Historical Background*, Cambridge, UK, 1976. Recent Thai scholarship has taken a more critical view of the monarchy's role in modernization with the revival of works by the Thai Marxist, Jit Phumisak, translated by Craig Reynolds in *Thai Radical Discourse: The Real Face of Thai Feudalism Today*, Ithaca, 1987.

For Burma see Taylor, *The State in Burma*, and Cady, *A History of Modern Burma*. Other important studies of Burma include Josef Silverstein, *Burma, Military Rule and the Politics of Stagnation*, Cornell, 1977; Frank N. Trager, *Burma, From Kingdom to Republic: a Historical and Political Analysis*, 1966; and the more recent David I. Steinberg, *Burma, A Socialist Nation of Southeast Asia*, Boulder, 1982.

CHAPTER

3

INTERNATIONAL COMMERCE, THE STATE AND SOCIETY: ECONOMIC AND SOCIAL CHANGE

Economic and social change in Southeast Asia in the period from around 1800 to the outbreak of World War II flowed essentially from the unprecedented impact of international commerce on the economic and political structures of the region. Such commerce had long exerted a major role in shaping the nature of Southeast Asian politics and society but, driven by the imperatives of developing Western capitalism and the Industrial Revolution, particularly after about 1850, its global reach and irresistible dominance in this century-and-a-half transformed Southeast Asia with an astonishing thoroughness, rapidity and finality. In a sense, it created the modern state system in Southeast Asia, and in so doing gave rise to the attendant panoply of social change.

STATES AND SOCIETIES IN THE EARLY NINETEENTH CENTURY

Around 1800, the transformative role of this new form of global commerce was still in its infancy; Southeast Asia, accordingly, retained much of its political, economic and social integrity and dynamism. Through most of lowland riverine Southeast Asia, Indic-inspired élites of varying sizes and power, centred on a ruler of prestigious person and impeccable lineage, presided over patterns of social and economic organization that valued control and augmentation of manpower rather than territory or capital. Organized in bonded relationships, formal and informal, with their patrons, most of the subjects of these élites lived in thickly settled clumps which contrasted sharply with the sparsely populated and heavily forested landscape of most of Southeast Asia. 'State', indeed, is a rather grandiose title for what was essentially a knotting together of the leading ends of strands of vertically-shaped personal relationships. The institutions of state and governance were informal, impermanent, personal,

This essay has benefited from the comments of Ian Black, David Chandler and Norman Owen. Most of all I am indebted to John Butcher for his constant encouragement and challenging ideas.

malleable and negotiable, and always prey to contestation from courtly aristocrats or local potentates. Accordingly, administrative control was characteristically weak, diffuse, irregular and decentralized; effective power outside the core of the state was usually the preserve of territorial chiefs or quasi-autonomous tributaries. The varieties of authority were represented at one extreme by the starched and nervous version of Confucian organization employed by the Sino-Vietnamese state, from 1802 centred at Hué. This involved a clearer conception of a state as an impersonal entity and a mandarinal mode of administration, but even though it governed its subjects more formally, busily and efficiently than its Southeast Asian neighbours, the majority of eligible taxpayers still eluded the mandarin's head-tax list. At the other extreme stood locally fragmented chiefly settlements in sparsely populated uplands, lowland interiors and out-of-the-way coasts, free of any pretensions to statehood.

The 'stranded' nature of political and social organization was buttressed by ritual and ideology, but it was substantiated by a leader's ability to acquire wealth and distribute it among his followers. The exchange and redistributive networks upon which this structure depended reached from the remotest upland tribes of Southeast Asia to the busy commercial centres of southern China and west Asia; they provided Southeast Asian leaders with the revenue and reverence they needed to sustain their polities. A state's ruler was typically its greatest trader; to allow others an unrestricted right to trade was to risk the emergence of alternative centres of power. State-sponsored trade was usually organized on a tributary basis, focused on the China market and conducted by Chinese agents. It brought locally produced or collected rice, fish, pepper and exotic forest and marine products (ivory, feathers, sea cucumbers, gemstones, beeswax and resins, for example) into circulation to be exchanged for strategic goods such as weapons, gunpowder and building materials and especially luxury goods—silks, ceramics, fumigants, drugs, precious metals—for the use of domestic élites. State trading monopolies, however, were always difficult to maintain and likely to unravel in the face of competition from rival commercial networks, sometimes foreign, sometimes under the sway of aristocratic or regional élites. Thus the need, both financial and political, for the allied institution of revenue farming, whereby royal monopoly rights to demand produce or impose levies on consumption and other forms of activity such as local trade or gambling were sold off to local power figures (often foreigners who controlled local commerce) in return for a fixed sum and political co-operation.

The focus of this economic activity was the city. Wealthier and more imposing élites projected their power from grand (but sometimes, nonetheless, transferable) urban centres such as Ava, Bangkok, Hué and Yogyakarta. They peopled their capitals with slaves and bondsmen (a status usually acquired by falling into debt) who provided them with prestige, service, income, artifacts, manufactures, entertainment and culture; under the prevailing conditions of low population and physical insecurity there existed no urban free wage-labour market. Foreign merchants, quartered in discrete ethnic areas, provided a cosmopolitan flavour. Such cities aimed to encapsulate the essence of the wider polity and, indeed, larger cosmological forces, so as to represent and endorse the state's greatness and that of its king. The rulers of less prosperous states lacked this grandeur, but shared similar ideological pretensions.

It was the periphery, however, which provided the focal point with its context, significance and the means of its sustenance. The great majority of Southeast Asians lived not in cities but in subsistence-oriented lowland rural communities or fishing villages or, in much smaller numbers and at a further remove from the state's power, as upland or inland swidden peoples or sea nomads. The village was not the placid unit, self-sufficient economically and politically, portrayed in later romantic writings. The peasant economy was built around the production of irrigated rice. Much of the rice was consumed by the growers in combination with vegetables, fish and occasionally meat, but it was also needed to purchase items from outside the village—salt, for example, and porcelain and copper utensils, iron for weapons and for tipping ploughs, musical instruments, draught animals and even opium which, Raffles noted of Java in 1817, 'has struck deep into the habits, and extended its malignant influence to the morals of the people'.[1] To obtain these things, peasants relied on traders, usually Chinese, who ferried in goods from the major towns and exchanged them for rice and other agricultural surpluses or produce which villagers collected from the nearby forests (wood, rattan, gutta percha). Goods were generally moved along rivers, since roads were crude, dangerous, and unreliable, vehicles uncommon, and beasts of burden and porters expensive. Distinct from supra-local trade circuits, there were well-established and busy networks of periodical local markets where peasants exchanged the handicrafts they had manufactured or the tobacco they had grown for rice or dried fish or betel. Most exchange was in the form of barter, but at the same time money, usually in the form of copper or zinc pieces, was well known and used; there was a wide variety of coins scattered throughout rural Southeast Asia, most of them of very small value to suit the peddling nature of rural commerce.

A state's prosperity, as well as the longevity of a particular ruler, depended upon success in milking this hive of production, industry and commerce. Directly or indirectly, the ruler claimed a portion of its produce and levied taxes on its commercial activity, feeding the receipts into the higher circuits of national and international trade for his profit. He also made demands upon the labour power of his subjects to build the infrastructure—waterworks, bridges, roads—needed to enhance production. All this was achieved through the vertical ties of loyalty which aggregated personal followings. A strong, centralizing king necessarily commanded the loyalty and subservience of the bulk of the population; times of weakness and strife inevitably coincided with periods when central control of manpower had dissipated, with followers drifting off to local or courtly competitors. The structural instability inherent in the contest for followings circumscribed the state's demands on its subjects, because it simply did not have the means in these potentially volatile circumstances to enforce unreasonable demands on a regular basis. Thus

---

[1] T. S. Raffles, *The History of Java*, Kuala Lumpur, 1978 [first published 1817], I. 102.

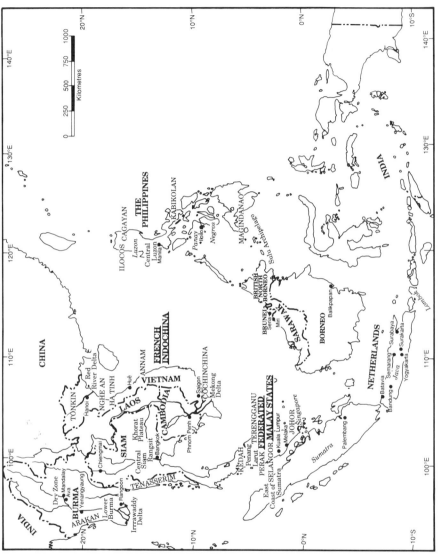

Map 3.1   Some sites of change in Southeast Asia, 1800–1942

its calls upon the village were characteristically light and irregular, and made with a good measure of consideration given to villagers' welfare. Remote settlements often provided little more than an occasional remittance of tribute in the form of a portion of the jungle and sea products they had collected. For their part, in return for their produce and labour services, followers enjoyed the prosperity, security, status and administrative and technological expertise channelled to them by the state, as well as the spiritual privileges of obtaining merit and sharing the glory of the ruler.

With the exception of northern and central Vietnam, peasant communities were not the clearly defined, spatially symmetrical and socially cohesive institutions so common today and, because of instability and the continuing need to forge relationships with new patrons, frequently they were not territorially based or sentimentally attached to specific sites. Peasant villages were somewhat random collections of plaited bamboo and thatch dwellings, most commonly built on stilts, strung along roads or river banks and often separated from each other by forest and fields. Their populations were very small: around 1815, for example, a typical Javanese village numbered between 200 and 300 people. Like the larger society of which it was the largest component, peasant society was hierarchical and stratified. There were relatively wealthy and powerful men in the village (subject to restraints on the exercise of their power like those on that of the state), and economically weak and dependent people; between these two poles were the mass of small landholders. Gender, like economics and politics, was an enduring line of division. The basic unit of peasant society was the male-headed family. While women could, in some peasant societies, hold land, it was generally the case that the male household head was the landholder, and thus formal village politics was the preserve of males. Perhaps reflecting this, most labour fell to women. A relatively strict sexual division of labour left men with the task of preparing fields and guarding the crop. Females, however, were usually responsible for transplanting, harvesting and hulling the crop, on top of their background duties of child-bearing and rearing, domestic labour, and a variety of other tasks such as weaving mats or baskets, or spinning cotton and weaving cloth for their family's use, or taking produce to the market to bargain over its sale. Peasant life was not a continually busy one; there were hectic periods at the beginning of the wet season (planting) and the start of the dry season (harvesting), and at times when corvée duty or military service was required, but a relatively large reservoir of time remained which could be spent in leisure or religious and social activities.

WESTERN MERCHANT CAPITALISTS

In this setting, Western mercantile activity, like that of the indigenous state traders of Southeast Asia themselves, was essentially directed at transporting goods produced by others in order to realize the highest possible profit on their sale in international markets, while protecting that activity from others' competition. It was exemplified most dramatically by the Spanish grasp on the Manila environs as a half-way house for the Acapulco–China trade, by the long and frequently successful efforts of the Verenigde Oost-Indische Compagnie (VOC, Dutch East India Company) to achieve a monopoly of the spices of eastern Indonesia, and by British country traders who, in their own way, linked Southeast Asian to Indian and Chinese trade. A deliberately self-limiting exercise, mercantile capitalism eschewed interference with indigenous polities except to make necessary arrangements for the delivery of desired trade goods; apart from strategically placed forts and 'factories', it avoided territorial conquest and the overheads which administration and defence of such territories involved unless these were deemed necessary to protect its more important commercial interests. While sometimes it superimposed itself upon the indigenous setting through its activities as tribute gatherer and trade director—even to the point, as the VOC did in the archipelago, of destroying previously vibrant indigenous trading networks—mostly it meshed its activities into the practices and routines already well established in Southeast Asia.

Before 1800, the two major exceptions to this pattern were in west Java and central Luzon, where colonial authorities had acceded to extensive territorial control. Both exceptions, however, had resulted from a warping by local circumstance of the logic of European mercantilist practice rather than from the adoption of new policies by the colonial powers involved, for in both cases monopoly, the blunt instrument of mercantilism, was predominant. In west Java, the encumbrance of territory had been as an indirect result of the need felt by the VOC to deal with indigenous potentates who were amenable to its commercial aims. From the 1670s onwards, the VOC had found itself caught up in Javanese dynastic disputes; by siding with winners it was endowed with slices of territory which had to be administered, defended and made profitable. This meant in turn a move from simply collecting produce grown by others to actively directing production, which in this case was achieved by co-opting local Javanese leaders, under limited European supervision, so as to have their peasantries cultivate and deliver large quantities of coffee, and lesser amounts of such items as indigo, cotton yarn and rice.

In the Philippines, the declining importance of the galleon trade, interchanging in Manila vast quantities of Mexican silver for Chinese silks, ceramics and other luxury products and to a lesser extent Indian piece goods, pressed the Spanish colonial government in the late eighteenth century to capitalize upon advances into provincial Luzon made by Catholic missionary friars and attempt to extract revenue by means of a production and marketing monopoly on tobacco. Under the tobacco monopoly specific areas, notably in northeastern Luzon, were set aside for forced peasant production of tobacco under the supervision of local chiefs who had been transformed into colonial agents; the tobacco was delivered at low prices to the government and resold at profit, mostly in monopoly marketing areas within Luzon where the production of tobacco was forbidden.

THE DEVELOPMENT OF INTERNATIONAL COMMERCE FROM ABOUT 1820

The well-worn patterns of Southeast Asian social and commercial organization began to change rapidly from around 1820, as international demand, fed directly and indirectly by the early phases of the Industrial Revolution in Europe and the end of the Napoleonic Wars, brought a quickening of trade and commercial activity in the region. In Java, Holland's desperation to halt its dismal slide into financial and political obscurity saw it intensify its efforts to squeeze profit from its loosely held territorial control. During the British interregnum in Java (1811–16), Raffles had already sought to do this by abolishing the role of local aristocracies as production and labour brokers and introducing a land tax to draw Javanese peasants into direct contact with the (British) international economy. His efforts failed, but important aspects of them, notably the land rent system, were retained by the Dutch. Under the umbrella of mercantile methods revived from the practice of the now defunct VOC, they became components of the Cultivation System (1830), a virtual state monopoly of production and sale. This scheme, the brainchild of a fierce and complicated character, Governor-General Johannes van den Bosch, forced peasants, under the leadership of their own chiefs, to grow specific export crops (coffee, sugar and indigo were the main ones) to be auctioned in Europe by the Nederlandsche Handel Maatschappij (Dutch Trading Company), to which they were consigned by the Indies government. Force was exercised, especially in the early years, by recourse to the moral authority of indigenous leaders, but with the passage of years the Cultivation System came to be practised as much through a combination of economic coercion (taxation) and incentive (for example, the rapidly increasing popularity of Dutch manufactured cottons amongst Javanese) as through the exercise of traditional authority. The overall success of this compound strategy is manifest in the staggering amount of peasant labour employed in the Cultivation System, around 70 per cent of all peasant households in the areas of Java under direct Dutch rule in the 1830s and 1840s, gradually reducing as the system began to be wound back from about 1850 (and all on a relatively small amount of peasant land, a Java-wide average of about 5 per cent at its peak in the early 1840s). While the Cultivation System enjoyed extraordinary commercial success—providing one-third of Holland's state revenue in the 1850s—it was essentially at odds with the new tides of commerce sweeping through Southeast Asia; its characteristic features of monopoly in production and sale, coercion, and the carefully protective modulation of the domestic economy were increasingly discordant with the emerging economic liberalist theme of the new era.

In the Philippines, by contrast, state monopoly was on the wane as Spain's imperial might crumbled; the tobacco monopoly endured, albeit in declining form, until laid to rest in 1882. Side by side with it, however, came erratic efforts by the colonizers to bring firmer control to the hinterland by tying local élites into the colonial governing apparatus and using their influence to expand, mostly ineffectively, the range of revenue-gathering devices. Unlike the Dutch, however, the Spanish were too weak and irresolute to stand in the face of changing international circumstances and attempt, by monopoly alone, to withstand more commercially advanced competitors. From late in the eighteenth century, patterns of trade and consequently production began to change significantly. Increasing penetration of the Manila market, first by British country traders and, at the end of the century and thereafter, by British and American merchants, together with the gradual development of a Chinese mestizo entrepreneurial group which moved out of the core towns and into the provincial countryside, opened up the Philippines to the world market (made official by the Spanish for Manila in 1834, and extended to other regional ports in 1855). Accordingly, the focus of Philippine trade swung away from Mexico and towards Asia and the West; its content changed from Mexican silver first to exotic tropical goods like birds' nests, tortoiseshell, sea cucumbers, ebony, and woods, and then to locally produced agricultural commodities, the quantities of which multiplied in response to commercial opportunity. Merchant houses, mainly British and American, were established in Manila from the 1820s; they provided the capital and merchandising facilities which allowed Chinese mestizo groups, now rapidly overcoming or merging with indigenous provincial landholding élites, to establish or expand the production of such cash crops as sugar (in central Luzon), tobacco (in Cagayan) and abaca (in Kabikolan). In time, the Chinese, whose numbers had grown rapidly with the removal of restrictions on Chinese immigration in the 1840s, began to usurp mestizo dominance of regional commerce, acting as retailing intermediaries for Western (especially British) products, of which the most important were textiles, and siphoning out the growing volume of Philippine produce. As far as the Spanish colonial government was concerned, its major contribution to these processes was 'to get out of the way'.[2] This pattern of commercializing agriculture was to remain virtually unchanged in the Philippines throughout the remainder of the colonial period. Its rapid growth, even in these formative years, was manifest in a tripling of the value of exports between 1825 and 1850, and the change in their composition from forest and sea products to sugar, abaca, coffee and tobacco.

The same pressures and opportunities for change were being felt in the wider reaches of Southeast Asia. In Siam, where the royal élite combined significant profits from trade with China with a wariness towards Westerners, the probings of Western traders eager for produce to feed on to the world market were having an effect. Rama III allowed individual Western merchants to operate, and in 1826 conceded some limited liberalization of trade in response to Henry Burney's mission on behalf of the East India Company. The preponderant response of the Siamese élite, however, was not capitulation but a determined effort to increase its economic strength and political control by expanding production and commerce for its own

---

[2] Norman G. Owen, 'Abaca in Kabikolan: prosperity without progress', in Alfred W. McCoy and Ed. C. de Jesus, eds, *Philippine Social History: Global Trade and Local Transformations*, Quezon City, 1982, 194.

benefit. As in the Philippines, immigrant Chinese were made welcome, especially from the reign of Rama III. Free of corvée obligations, they provided manpower to enhance production (in sugar and pepper plantations, in tin mines and on public works such as canal construction) and technical and commercial skills, so as better to service Siam's role in international commerce. On the western Malay Peninsula, tin mining had been long if sporadically carried on by Malay chiefs and, more often through the early nineteenth century, scattered Chinese entrepreneurs, using primitive labour-intensive techniques and financed by wealthy Straits Chinese merchants; now it began to grow in importance. It climaxed with the discovery of a rich detritus of ore at Larut in Perak in 1848 and subsequent important discoveries in the western valleys of the peninsula, which coincided with a rapid rise in world demand for tin which Cornwall's mines could no longer satisfy. To cater for this demand in a sustained way, mine operators could no longer rely on erratic and inefficient production by Malay peasants and small numbers of Chinese workers; increasingly they introduced technological advances such as the chain pump and, most important of all, attracted increasingly large numbers of southern Chinese immigrant labourers to work the mines. In the early 1860s, indeed, it was estimated that there were around 25,000 Chinese labouring in the tinfields of Larut alone.

The changing spirit of the times was most closely captured by Britain's establishment of trading centres at Penang (1786), Melaka (1824) and especially Singapore (1819), occasioning the Dutch to establish similar ports within their sphere of influence. This was the beginning of the age of 'free-trade imperialism', founded on the belief that 'free trade', commerce unhindered by protection and undiverted by the demands of territorial administration, inevitably meant Britain's economic success as well as greater prosperity for those peoples with which it traded.

Paradoxically, however, 'non-intervention' frequently provoked substantial change. The rapid development of the free-trade entrepôt of Singapore was itself a case in point. Its presence as an outlet for international commerce encouraged the growth of Chinese pepper and gambier plantations in Singapore and especially neighbouring Johor. Organized according to the *kangchu* system[3] with Chinese labourers and under a shifting cultivation régime, the plantations required little capital, supervision or skill, and promised rapid returns to the *kangchu* and his investors, not only from produce but from the income generated from the sale of opium to workers. The British in Singapore farmed out the monopoly rights to the sale of opium to Chinese syndicates; the *kangchus* acted as their local agents, a situation which helped them defray wage costs on their plantations. The revenue generated by this monopoly in turn financed Singapore's free-trade status. Thus sustained by reciprocity, Singapore quickly gained prominence as a collection and distribution

---

[3] The *kangchu* ('lord of the river') was a Chinese headman granted lease rights by the local Malay ruler to a stretch of river valley land for shifting plantation agriculture. He organized and controlled the immigrant Chinese who worked the plantation lands (James C. Jackson, *Planters and Speculators: Chinese and European Agricultural Enterprise in Malaya, 1786–1921*, Kuala Lumpur, 1968, 15–22).

centre for regional and international commerce. Trade included European piece goods (slow at first but later increasing to a flood), China tea, Indian opium, Malayan tin, Sumatran pepper, local plantation products such as gambier, pepper, and tapioca, and local forest produce, notably gutta percha. Singapore took over from Siam as the major entrepôt for archipelago produce en route to China and provided (with the industrious assistance of Bugis traders) a focus to reintegrate Asian regional trade in a manner not witnessed since the demise of old Melaka in the sixteenth century. Further afield in the Sulu archipelago, the demand by British country traders for 'Straits produce' like birds' nests, sea cucumbers and tortoiseshell to trade for China's tea provided the necessary conditions which galvanized local rulers to embark on a century of extensive slave raiding throughout the archipelago, procuring the labour power (a total of around a quarter of a million people) which they needed to collect items from the jungle and the sea to service the trade. The fact that at this time the West itself produced relatively little which Asians desired was the key to this style of obtrusive non-intervention. For the most part, Westerners had to acquire in Asia what they needed to trade in Asia; thus they had to attract Southeast Asian produce to nodal points for use in the China trade.

Elsewhere, the impact of developing commerce and closer international contacts was more restrained. In Vietnam, French missionaries and merchantmen nibbled away—sometimes with considerable success in the case of the missionaries (140,000 Catholics in west Tonkin alone by 1855)—for souls and profit without making a significant impact on the empire of the vigorous Minh-mang (r. 1820–41). The Vietnamese court, while evincing an interest in acquiring Western technology (notably steamships), satisfied itself with a small and closely controlled trade focused on China and mostly limited to luxury items (including Chinese books). Vietnam did not remain unaffected, however, suffering an inflation-causing outflow of silver to China, used by the Chinese to pay for their imports of British opium. The Lao and especially the Cambodian kingdoms did, by contrast, remain unaffected by the accelerating pace of international commerce. They were too poor, distant, difficult of access, unimportant, and preoccupied with failing battles to preserve their identities against cultural and political encroachment from Siam to the west and Vietnam to the east. Burma, like Siam, suffered the effects of Britain's importunity, partly in the name of free trade. The First Anglo-Burman War of 1824–6 resulted in the British annexation of Arakan and Tenasserim and some limited privileges for British commerce.

In retrospect, this period of accelerating international commercial contact may be seen as a transitional stage from the older, limited equilibrium of state-sponsored trade, monopolies and privileges to a new and highly complex mode of capitalism. As commercial activity gathered momentum, fuelled by the increasing rapacity of global trade, indigenous and foreign leaders and traders responded in a variety of ways, ranging through indifference, stolid opposition to its new demands, and cautious adaptation, to enthusiastic co-operation. The logic of commercial development, however, would soon limit those options to two: co-operation or ignominy.

THE CREATION OF A NEW ORDER FROM ABOUT 1850

Around the beginning of the second half of the nineteenth century under the powerful example of Britain, the West moved into the phase of high capitalism. Increasingly, the key to wealth and power was to be found in industrial production and not just mercantile commerce. The transformation in the dominant 'mode of production' in the West brought with it an inner dynamism and a consequent international competitiveness which led the West, more particularly Europe, to impose itself in new and dominating ways on much of the rest of the world. The Industrial Revolution placed extraordinary economic and social power at the disposal of the Western powers, and with that came the realization that such power demanded more elaborate and more intensive exploitation of less developed areas. It provoked different and radically heightened demands and patterns of consumption and it provided incentives, opportunities and even the means for that exploitation—developments in manufacturing and processing technology such as tin cans and pneumatic tyres, advanced weaponry, telegraphic communications between Europe and Southeast Asia, and rapid and cheap bulk transport of commodities and labourers by steamship.

The high age of the Industrial Revolution expressed itself in increasing competition among the colonial powers for the territorial annexation of most of Southeast Asia, a process that properly began in a halting and piecemeal fashion around 1850 and climaxed in the rush for empire in the concluding years of the century as Britain's industrial pre-eminence waned. In Indochina, from the pinpoints of influence established in the Mekong delta in 1859, French control expanded westwards to grasp Cambodia in a protective embrace, and north and northwest to the ancient core of the Red (Hong) River delta and the principalities of Laos. The British annexed lower Burma in 1852 and imposed 'free trade' commercial treaties on the Burmese kingdom in 1862 and 1867 which removed (on paper but not in fact) most royal monopolies and allowed free movement of people and goods. The simultaneous response of the increasingly harassed and desperate King Mindon was a programme of reforming centralization. This aimed at expanding the production of rice and manufactured and processed goods, developing foreign trade—much of which still passed through his hands—and amplifying royal revenues (through, for example, granting timber concessions to foreign firms, notably the Bombay-Burmah Trading Corporation), all to strengthen his state. It was too late; in 1886 the British swallowed the old Burman heartland. In Malaya, British 'intervention' in 1874 led to a pattern of action and reaction which saw the creation of the Federated Malay States in 1896 and gradually brought the remaining Malay states under formal colonial control through the second decade of the twentieth century. In the Indies, the Dutch, by dint of war and unilateral 'diplomacy', sewed together the people and lands of the 'Indonesian' archipelago to form a 'Netherlands East Indies'. In the Philippines, Spain and then (after 1898) the United States increasingly brought the disparate communities of those islands under a single state authority. The only exception to this pattern, the Siamese state, was forced to accommodate to British demands for free trade under the conditions of the Bowring treaty of 1855, which set import and export duties at fixed, low levels, and abolished most trading monopolies and internal taxes on goods and trade. Bangkok's response was a rapid elaboration of its already existing 'state strengthening' strategy, in this context involving the formal consolidation of its peripheral territories under centralized state control. By the beginning of the twentieth century, Southeast Asia's complicated and variegated political setting had been reduced to six states working on principles of political organization and political legitimacy quite different from those in force a generation or two before. Five of the states were run by Western colonial powers—the British in Rangoon and Singapore, the French in Hanoi, the Dutch in Batavia and the Americans in Manila. The other state, Siam, was run by a modernizing indigenous élite which shared many of the administrative and legal characteristics of the newly emergent colonial states.

PHASE ONE: LIBERALISM

From our perspective, the construction of a new Southeast Asian economic and political order may seem inevitable and perhaps even necessary. This masks, however, the complex interactions of policy, practice, effect and reaction which led to its creation, and which may best be understood by tracing the phased evolution of Southeast Asia's states from the situation of bewildering and apparently endemic political pluralism in the first half of the nineteenth century to one of centralized dominance at its end. The first phase, liberal capitalism, characteristic of practice in lower Burma, Cochinchina, central Siam, Malaya, Sumatra, and Luzon, was simply to create the conditions which allowed the adjustment, elaboration and incorporation of existing styles of production into global marketing systems. At the same time it spoiled and harassed arrangements obstructive to growth. It began around 1850, reached its apogee around the turn of the twentieth century and, overlapped by its successor phase, endured rather than prospered thereafter, for reasons which will become clear. The key feature of this first phase was its laissez-faire character, a reflection not just of popular ideas about the universal applicability of liberalism but more concretely of the limitations of state power and the lack of private Western investment capital. Its success was achieved with small amounts of capital and depended almost solely upon huge inputs of human labour; its development, unlike Java's under the Cultivation System, was not a last gasp of jealous mercantilism but a result of removing restraints on the penetration of international market forces. The concomitant values propelling growth were the newer ones of individualism and acquisitiveness rather than old customary obligation. These values were increasingly relevant and powerful in circumstances where international commerce could provide a diverse range of consumer goods for peasant producers. The result was change of a more rapid, free-wheeling, uncontrolled and fundamental sort than had previously been encountered. Some Southeast Asians caught up in these developments prospered, at least temporarily; many others suffered grievously. For all of them it was the beginning of a pervasively transformative era. The following are some examples of this stimulating but structurally limited phase in operation.

Rice Smallholding in Lower Burma, Cochinchina and Central Siam

While the region of the Irrawaddy delta was by no means unoccupied or uncultivated in 1852 when it was annexed by the British, it was relatively empty in terms of what was to come later.[4] Contemporary accounts put the population of the delta area at around one million, with about three hundred thousand hectares under cultivation. Then, as later, the production of rice was the central economic activity, with much of the surplus used to feed the population of upper Burma. Before 1852, however, development of the rice industry had been inhibited by the Burmese government's ban on exports; this held prices very low and, coupled with an undeveloped economy, provided little incentive for producers to cultivate surpluses above levels required for subsistence and tribute or to bring more land under cultivation. The British annexation of lower Burma transformed this self-contained, self-sufficient and relatively static peasant society. Almost immediately, the British removed the ban on rice exports and lifted trading restrictions, a decision that happened to coincide with a time when Europe was looking for new sources of rice because of the Sepoy Mutiny in India and the Civil War in the United States. Reflecting the influence of prevailing liberal ideas, the British also decided that the most efficient and reliable way of organizing rice production was to encourage Burmese smallholder rice producers rather than employ a system of large landholdings. This was accomplished by means of a system of land taxation based on small village cultivation, and land tenure laws which sought to maximize the possibility of smallholder ownership. Peasants, for example, came to own land on which they had originally squatted if they occupied it and paid revenue upon it for twelve years. In addition, the British provided stability, milling and exporting facilities, flood control and irrigation works and transport infrastructure (especially riverine), all invigorating the production and marketing of rice and the development by Burmese themselves of retailing networks and capital provision. The response of the Burmese smallholder was a massive development of agriculture in the last decades of the nineteenth century. Population increased fourfold in the last half of the century, predominantly through a high rate of natural fertility but also as a result of a remarkable immigration of poor, young, male peasants (sometimes seasonal labourers) from upper Burma's dry zone, where agricultural conditions and prospects were uncertain and, later, of impoverished peasants and

---

[4] This discussion draws heavily on Michael Adas, *The Burma Delta: Economic Development and Social Change on an Asian Rice Frontier, 1852–1941*, Madison, 1974, and to a lesser extent Cheng Siok-Hwa, *The Rice Industry of Burma 1852–1940*, Kuala Lumpur, 1968.

labourers from south-east India who, recruited and financed by labour-gang foremen (*maistry*), came to toil in Burma for a few years before returning home. The area under cultivation grew by a factor of eight and rice exports by a factor of twelve between 1885 and 1906, transforming lower Burma 'from an undeveloped and sparsely populated backwater of the Konbaung Empire into the world's leading rice-exporting area'.[5] So dominant did rice production and export become in the Burmese economy that rice accounted for up to three-quarters of Burma's exports by value before 1930.

Apart from the normal environmental problems of frontier develop-ment—the toil of land reclamation, dangers from malaria and wild ani-mals, attacks of crop-eating insects, and diseases of plough animals—the major difficulty facing peasant agriculturalists was credit. As the pace of development accelerated toward the end of the century, the provision of credit, previously made available by friends, shopkeepers and a small number of indigenous moneylenders, came to be dominated by Indian Chettiars; establishing facilities in rural areas and greatly increasing the amount of credit available, they acted directly as moneylenders for peasants and also provided finances for the host of indigenous money-lenders. As economic activity increased and finance became more readily available, the large-scale use of credit among peasants became the norm in delta society, a process fuelled by an improving standard of living and rising costs.

This first phase of development before the turn of the century was one of great expansion, growth and social mobility for peasant smallholders. Under prevailing conditions, even the poorest immigrant could aspire to own his own land, build a substantial dwelling, purchase large quantities of imported consumer goods (the quantity of cotton goods imported into Burma grew sixfold between 1873 and 1914) and generally enjoy a stand-ard of living hitherto unknown for a person of his rank. Even tenants shared in the burst of prosperity, because the large amount of available reclaimable land and the general shortage of labour gave them a strong bargaining position against their landlords; in some places, indeed, ten-ants were allowed to work holdings rent free.

Such prosperity, fluidity and development could last only as long as the frontier of opportunity remained open. By the early years of the twentieth century, land began to run out as population continued to expand. Moreover, ecological problems began to make their presence felt: for example, flood control embankments prevented the widespread deposi-tion of silt on farmland, and yields began to drop. Smallholders found the price of land rising steadily, hindering their ability to extend their hold-ings. Declining yields cut into their surpluses and placed them closer to the danger margin; credit became more expensive; inflation raised the costs of goods and services; market conditions became less predictable, especially after World War I. Most important of all, smallholders were firmly enmeshed in relations of credit dependency that limited their ability to respond to market forces—most of them, for example, had to sell their rice immedi-

[5] Adas, 4.

ately upon harvest to pay off accumulated debts, rather than stockpiling it until prices improved. Larger landholders and middlemen of various kinds—rice sellers, brokers, merchants—capitalized on these problems to increase their leverage over small producers. The result was that an increasing number of owner-cultivators fell into such extremes of debt that they had to part with their land. This, together with the fact that rising costs made land reclamation the preserve of wealthier producers, meant that a greatly increased proportion of land fell into the hands of larger landholders, many of them absentee non-agriculturist owners. The proportion of cultivated land owned by non-agriculturalists in lower Burma rose from 18 per cent in 1907 to 31 per cent in 1930 (although only a small proportion of them were Chettiars, who generally preferred control of money to control of land), and rates of tenancy increased accordingly. Petty smallholders who managed to retain their land did so only at the cost of dangerously increasing their levels of indebtedness: in one district in 1922, for example, nearly half the cultivators were indebted beyond their surpluses.

The increasing pressure felt by owner-cultivators was also felt by less fortunate classes. Tenants found their profits declining, and thus their ability to strike out on their own as owner-cultivators; moreover, as land began to run out and population thicken, the balance of power swung decisively in favour of landlords. Competition between would-be tenants forced up the rents: at the turn of the century, tenants had not paid much more than 10 per cent of their revenue to landlords; twenty-five years later, 50 per cent was common. At the end of the 1930s, nearly 60 per cent of lower Burma's agricultural land was under full fixed-rent tenancy. Landlords' dominance allowed them to exploit their tenants in new ways as well—by refusing to grant revisions of rent in bad seasons or forcing them to bear more of the costs of rice production. This in turn led to a highly mobile tenant population with a great increase in shorter-term tenancies. Landless labourers were probably in the most precarious position of all, with tough competition between a growing number of workers for a more or less static supply of jobs. Their number grew steadily, not so much from immigration from upper Burma—which dropped off steadily after the turn of the century as conditions there improved through enhanced irrigation facilities and the development of cash cropping—but from the growing number of Indian migrant labourers escaping from poor conditions at home and fanning out into the countryside from the cities where they had first settled, seeking seasonal or permanent work in agriculture, and also from former owner-cultivators dispossessed of their land. As employment possibilities shrank, so did wages, in both absolute and relative terms, and the cost of living kept rising inexorably.

The pattern of change in the Mekong delta of Cochinchina bore some remarkable similarities to that in lower Burma: an empty and unexploited frontier, a free-wheeling response to the quickening demand for rice on international markets following French annexation, a rapid growth of population fuelled by migration from the heavily populated and impoverished north. The French transformed the landscape to the west and south of Saigon by undertaking monumental earthworks and canal construction, using corvée labour until the 1890s but thereafter employing private French firms which used mechanized dredging and suction equipment to perform the task. More than 1300 kilometres of canals were dug, providing not just irrigation water but an excellent means of transportation. Land under rice cultivation in Cochinchina expanded from 274,000 hectares in 1873 to 1,174,000 in 1900 and 2,214,000 in 1930. Between 1860 and 1900, rice exports grew by a factor of ten, and then doubled again over the succeeding three decades. Vietnam became the world's third-largest producer of rice; up to 1931 the staple accounted for two-thirds of Vietnam's exports.

French policy and practice were manifest as early as 1862 when the lands of Vietnamese who had rebelled against or fled from the imposition of French rule were confiscated and sold off to speculators; they served severely to accelerate a pre-colonial trend towards the social polarization of landlordism and landlessness. The French granted ownership to settlers who squatted on virgin land to the east and north of Saigon, cleared it, made it productive, put a claim to it and paid taxes on it; nonetheless, larger landholdings quickly became evident. Partly this resulted from peasants falling behind in their credit repayments; more important, perhaps, was the lack of appropriate mechanisms for ordinary farmers to make legal claim to the land they had cleared and, conversely, the exploitation of land registration procedures by village notables, wealthy peasants, indigenous officials, entrepreneurs, and Europeans. In the virtually unoccupied areas reclaimed from swamp to the west and south, the French deliberately sought to create a rice plantation economy by auctioning off large blocks of land to Europeans and especially to absentee Vietnamese who worked them on the basis of share tenancy. Living from rents and debt repayments, these landlords left the profits from rice milling, transporting, dealing and export almost entirely in the hands of Chinese merchants based in Saigon-Cholon. In contrast to the early predominance of petty smallholders in lower Burma, it was usually the case in the Mekong delta that immigrant peasants began their careers as tenants rather than owners, with no reasonable hope of being able to improve their condition. This important difference apart, however, the fate of peasants in the Mekong delta followed the same general course as in the Burma delta—a combination of decreasing resources, rapidly expanding population, declining terms of trade for rice, dependence upon rural credit, all leading inexorably to impoverishment and landlessness. By 1930, 2.5 per cent of landholders owned 45 per cent of the cultivated land, while only one peasant household in four possessed any land at all. The great majority of peasants in the delta were either tenant farmers or landless agricultural labourers. Indeed, in one recently settled province in the far south in 1930, two-thirds of the cultivated land was in the form of holdings of more than 50 hectares.

In Siam, in response to the Bowring treaty of 1855 which forced Siam to become a participant in the broader world economy, large new areas of rice land in the central plain were opened up for peasant rice cultivation. The volume of Siam's rice exports grew more than twenty-five times between about 1860 and 1930. Thanks mainly to the labour invested in waterworks construction and land reclamation by Chinese wage labourers and Siamese smallholders, the area under rice tripled, expanding from the central plain to the north and northeast. The rapid expansion of rice production and export, however, was not accompanied to a significant degree by the intractable social polarizations evident on the rice frontiers of lower Burma and Cochinchina. This was partly because the Thai nobility were oriented to commerce by their unofficial sponsorship of (and integration with) Chinese entrepreneurs during the nineteenth century, accustomed to feeding off the wealth produced by trade, and distracted by the centralizing efforts of the Thai monarch; they found relatively little attraction in controlling extensive rural landholdings. As well, the capital available for development was mostly home-grown and thus relatively insubstantial, so that development was significantly less rapid, widespread and thorough than in the case of Burma or Cochinchina and potential resources in land remained in abundance. Moreover, because agricultural expansion took place in areas contiguous to the existing centres of activity, peasant pioneers were not dependent strangers in a new land but simply more distant neighbours of their kin, and privy to existing support networks which provided the credit they needed for development. The result was that, except in areas reclaimed under government sponsorship—notably the Rangsit region northeast of Bangkok developed by the private Siam Canals, Land and Irrigation Company from 1889 and sold off to well-connected speculators—absentee landlordism, tenancy, indebtedness and dependency did not become such predominant features of Siam's rice economy as they did elsewhere. Rice trading, transport, and milling became and remained the preserve of the Chinese, often financed by the Siamese nobility; the export business was shared between Western and Chinese brokerage firms with only minimal Siamese participation.

Tin Mining in Malaya

In the western Malay states, the 'rush to be rich' occasioned by growing world demand for tin from about 1850 had produced eager and chaotic squabbling and violence between Chinese entrepreneurial groups organized in secret societies, between them and the Malay chiefs who controlled the tin lands, and between the Malay chiefs themselves who fell into contestation over claims to revenues from tin. This invited a British 'law and order' response from 1874 which in turn provided the political, legal and administrative circumstances for accelerated development. With British intervention, exploitation intensified further; by 1895, the western Malay states were responsible for 55 per cent of world tin production as against 11 per cent in 1874. Increasingly, too, the brokerage role of local Malay chiefs in production was bypassed as Straits investors, no longer dependent upon their political authority (partly because the chiefs were by now frequently and heavily indebted to them), dealt directly with Chinese mine operators who assumed virtually complete control of the tin fields. Apart from their technological skills in mining, drainage and smelting, the dominance of tin mining by Chinese merchants and mine-owners was a function of superior corporate business practices (such as the *kongsi*), socially lubricated capital and marketing networks, and their ability, through wealth and the strategic use of clan organizations and secret societies, to recruit and control ever larger numbers of cheap indentured labourers from southern China. These workers were funnelled through Singapore by 'coolie brokers'; they had come to the tin fields to escape war and starvation at home, to create a new, if temporary, life in Southeast Asia, and eventually to return, newly prosperous, to their homeland. Something like five million Chinese arrived in Malaya in the nineteenth century, and a further twelve million in the first four decades of the twentieth. The nineteenth-century immigrants were mostly tied to three-year contracts legally sanctioned by a discharge ticket system to control mobility; their wages paid for their credited passage, their food (often provided under a 'truck' system), their opium consumption and gambling, and allowed where possible for remittances to family in China. The immigrant participants in this 'pig trade' suffered appalling living conditions and very high rates of morbidity and mortality from malaria, beri-beri, dysentery and industrial accidents; annual death rates of mine workers were sometimes as high as 50 per cent.

Smallholder Rubber in Malaya and Sumatra

Smallholder production for the world market attained probably its most lucrative form in the development of the smallholder rubber industry of Malaya and Sumatra. Taking advantage of the introduction of *Hevea brasiliensis* from Brazil via Kew Gardens in London, peasant cultivators, profiting from the demonstration effect of highly capitalized Western rubber plantations which yielded enormous profits, planted huge areas of rubber trees in individually small plots in west Malaya and in south and east Sumatra: by 1940, for example, 715,000 hectares of Sumatra were under smallholder rubber. The crude latex (or coagulated rubber sheets) which the growers produced was placed on the world market through Chinese marketing chains linked to Singapore. In Malaya, the boom years of rubber in the early twentieth century provided a powerful incentive to peasant smallholders to produce rubber rather than investing their skill and labour in rice-growing to feed the growing population of coolie labourers working on nearby Western plantations, much to the chagrin of British officials who tried various admixtures of inducement and sanction (such as the 'no rubber' condition applied to the use of certain categories of land) to discourage smallholder rubber. In Sumatra, initial development was slower, but the extent of smallholder rubber grew sevenfold between 1920 and 1930 at a time when Malaya, in a bid to turn around a price slump after the post World War I boom, had subjected itself to production restrictions under the Stevenson scheme (1922).

The most interesting aspect of smallholder production was the manner in which peasants integrated rubber growing into already existing cycles of food production. This normally took two forms. The first, most common in Sumatra where smallholdings developed well away from the sites of Western plantation agriculture, was an adaptation of swidden cultivation, whereby agriculturalists cleared stretches of forest and planted food crops, moving on to other sites when the land became too exhausted for food production after two or three crops. Now they planted rubber trees in the disused cropping area. In this jungle environment, the rubber tree proved a great ecological success; planters simply returned to the site to tap the trees when they had matured after about seven years. The alternative method, favoured in Malaya, involved sedentary cultivation. Peasants devoted a portion of their established land to rubber trees. While they waited for the crop to mature, they continued their normal subsistence-oriented lives as rice growers; upon crop maturity, rubber production became a valuable and non-disruptive adjunct to subsistence farming. Under both these régimes, the flexibility of part-time rubber production perfectly suited cultivators who had little capital and who were unprepared and unwilling to commit their futures wholly to the uncertainties of the world rubber market. Smallholder rubber cost little in terms of initial outlay, the risks to subsistence were minimal, labour investment between initial planting and tapping was negligible, and most important of all, cultivators could defer production until the market was at its most favourable. When rubber prices were low, peasants lived on their subsistence; as they rose, it was a simple matter to turn on the latex tap again.

By the end of the colonial period, smallholders in the Netherlands East Indies had more land under rubber trees than did that country's plantation sector, and produced almost as much rubber. In Malaya, they produced almost one-third of rubber exports. This massive contribution to the rubber industry changed the lives of smallholders significantly. The sudden influx of cash from rubber rapidly increased the standard of living of those peasants involved. In Sumatra, for instance, peasant incomes doubled or tripled within a very short time; the new flows of disposable cash were spent on improving houses, building mosques, travelling to Mecca, buying imported textiles and other consumer goods, and sometimes reinvesting in the expansion of areas under rubber. Some smallholders became extensive growers, so that they and their families could not tap all their trees themselves and had to employ rubber tappers who worked in return for a half-share of the product. This relatively high payment indicates a significant demand for labour in these developing areas, and the earnings to be made from rubber tapping produced a large spontaneous immigration to the rubber areas of Sumatra. The prosperity of rubber smallholders relative to that of peasants in Java involved in more controlled and servile modes of colonial production is reflected in income tax data: in 1929, less than 3 per cent of Javanese households earned more than 300 guilders per annum, while the corresponding figure in the outer islands was 19 per cent.

Despite this, there was no widespread structural change in peasant society as a result of the smallholder rubber boom. The role of peasant producers remained limited. They were commonly no more than producers of latex, eschewing involvement in rubber processing or marketing and spending their income on consumer goods—food, cloth, bicycles, sewing machines. Their produce, either latex or sheeting, was passed on to Chinese middlemen who transmitted it to large (usually) Western exporters. While in the Netherlands East Indies substantial Indonesian commercial networks in competition with Chinese had developed by the mid-1920s, even becoming involved in rubber exporting, these were exceptional. Most Malay and Sumatran rubber planters remained peripheral to the world markets they supplied; they remained rice-growing, village-dwelling peasants who also happened to plant and tap rubber trees.

Sugar and Abaca in Luzon

Unlike the Burma and Mekong deltas, the central Luzon plain was already the subject of developing cash crop exploitation for the world market before the mid-nineteenth century. As the pace of economic development quickened after about 1850, the Filipino élite, and particularly the Chinese mestizo element which was gradually merging into it, managed to gain control of huge areas of the central Luzon plain, laying claim to large estates (*hacienda*) for the production of rice as well as tobacco, cattle and sugar. At the same time, peasants migrating in large numbers to the interior of the plain from the regions around Manila in the south and from the Ilocos areas of northwest Luzon claimed and brought under cultivation large areas of land in a fractional, piecemeal and gradual manner. The contest between these two groups for control of the plain's land resources was decided rapidly and conclusively in favour of the élite. Sometimes they managed this by purchasing estates from the original holders or from the government itself. Again, as elsewhere in Southeast Asia, their knowledge of land law and legal procedures, together with their abundant wealth and manipulation of connections, enabled them to lay claim to large holdings and make those claims stick. The most important method of large land acquisition, however, was through the extension of credit to smallholder settlers. Under the mechanism known as *pacto de retroventa*,[6] Chinese mestizos lent money against the security of land titles; one was so successful that he expanded an original holding of 250 hectares to control scattered holdings of some 5000 hectares. The rapidly expanding production of sugar in central Luzon from the middle of the century onwards, stimulated by international demand and facilitated by technological improvements in the form of steam-powered mills, was organized around the *hacienda* institution.

Tenancy was the core of this system. The tenants contracted with landholders to pay a share of the income from the sale of processed sugar as rent for the use of land. Where tenants were scarce and where ample opportunity existed for them to transfer their allegiance to another patron, rents tended to be fixed and low; moreover, tenants enjoyed such favours as free firewood and the right to grow vegetables rent-free on dwelling plots. Under these circumstances, the tenant was 'the planter-capitalist's industrial partner responsible for managing his own farm'.[7] By the turn of the century and thereafter, however, the conditions of tenancy had swung

---

[6] This was a contract under which a landholder handed over his title to a buyer for a specified price with an option of repurchasing the land at a later specified time.

[7] Alfred W. McCoy, 'A queen dies slowly: the rise and decline of Iloilo city', in McCoy and De Jesus, eds, 325.

very much in favour of the landlord. Central Luzon became more tightly attached to the world economy, especially after the American takeover and the general opening of United States markets (notably the Payne–Aldrich Tariff Bill of 1909 which allowed 300,000 duty-free tons of Philippine sugar into the US market); this, together with the intensification of colonial control, the spread and enforcement of Western concepts of ownership, increasing and improving mechanization of cane production and process- ing, and the rapid growth of population, all contributed to the consolida- tion of the *hacienda* system and created an impoverished and indebted peasantry saddled with increasingly inequitable share tenancies rather than fixed rents. By the late 1930s, around two-thirds of the cultivated land of central Luzon was farmed by tenants, and much of it was owned by absentee landlords.

Abaca, from which was produced the rope and cordage increasingly demanded by the industrializing West for rigging and binding, was grown predominantly on the large landholdings of local élites in the region of Kabikolan in southeast Luzon, and harvested and processed by a unique combination of peasant wage labour and sharecropping. Although abaca prices were acutely sensitive to cyclical industrial booms and downturns, especially in the United States, the trend line of exports through the nineteenth century was always steep (though gradually flattening), rising from 432 tonnes in 1825–9 to 12,599 tonnes in 1850–4 and 115,985 tonnes in 1900–4. By that time abaca provided about two-thirds by value of Philippines exports.

PHASE TWO: FROM LIBERALISM TO MANAGEMENT

The characteristic feature of the liberal state was its ability to create and maintain circumstances conducive to greatly enhanced traffic in inter- national commerce—evidenced, for example, in a tenfold growth in the nominal value of Philippines exports between 1855 and 1902. Its logic had required the abolition of production and marketing monopolies on export goods and a significant curtailment of customary revenues in kind, espe- cially those levied in the form of corvée labour. Unlike earlier régimes, the liberal state was not afraid for political reasons of encouraging diverse and extensive private economic initiatives. Nonetheless, the state lacked the political and administrative power to manage its subjects efficiently and directly; moreover, in contrast to the monopolist régimes of the early nineteenth century and before, the state's direct profit from the new economic arrangements it had sponsored was meagre. One source of state revenue was duties imposed on the export of produce to Europe, North America and other parts of Asia and import duties on the industrializing West's consumer items, both of which could be levied relatively easily and cheaply as produce and commodities were funnelled through ports under the state's direct control. However, these alone could not fill the revenue void caused by the abandonment of monopoly, nor could they be exploit- ed too hard for fear of prejudicing the trade which generated them. What helped most of all to sustain the state's finances in this intermediate period of relative politico-administrative impotence was its ability to capitalize on the vastly increased buying power of a vastly increased and frequently mobile population, both the products of liberal policies. As with its production strategy, the state resorted to an existing institution, in this case the revenue farm system, adapting and expanding it to fill new needs in a changed environment. Under these new circumstances, revenue farming provided states with a very cheap means of gathering revenue from commerce, consumption and leisure which would otherwise have remained uncollected, without inhibiting economic expansion. In Siam in the reigns of Rama III and Rama IV, for example, imperialist pressure for free trade, together with increasing competition in the China trade, had gradually forced the kings to relinquish their trade monopolies; their response to this financial loss was to skim off a portion of the surplus created by increased economic activity within Siam by farming out to courtiers, local chiefs and Chinese merchant entrepreneurs the right to collect new or reorganized forms of state taxation and to control monopolies on such activities as opium smoking and gambling. This was a more efficient method of collection than the old decentralized tribute system, and it resulted in a spectacular multiplication of revenue from consumption and leisure activities: revenue from these farms grew twenty times in the four decades after 1851. Around the same time, Malay rulers, no longer able to enforce their monopoly on the sale of tin, imposed and farmed out duties on its transit along the river systems they controlled. After 'intervention', the revenue farms put out by the government, mainly to Chinese tin-mine operators, for the collection of import duty on opium and for gambling, alcohol and pawnbroking, provided the state with one-third of its revenue. In other Malay states not yet under British political control such as Kedah and Terengganu, revenue farming was at least as important to rulers anxious to enlarge their revenues (and thus their power) by taxing increasing economic activity; in Kedah, indeed, revenue farms provided more than 90 per cent of the state's revenues around 1900. In Java, the opium farms leased out by the Dutch to Chinese entrepreneurs since the 1830s reached their peak of profitability in the 1870s and 1880s, building on the economic animation promoted by the Cultivation System even as they helped compensate the state treasury (providing as much as one-fifth of its revenue) for the income forgone with its dismantling. In Cochinchina, the French let out the right to sell opium as early as 1861, first to two Frenchmen and later to a Chinese consortium.

But revenue farms were not just an ancillary means of revenue collection and, as sometimes happened, a convenient means for rulers to obtain cheap loans from suppliant farmers. They served two other vital roles as well. First, they were themselves an indispensable component of the liberal drive for economic development. Revenue farming in the Federated Malay States, for instance, helped finance and sustain tin mining. The major Chinese tin miners who generally held the farms used them as a means of lowering their labour costs by regaining from their workers a considerable proportion of what they had paid out in wages; this increased their profits when tin prices were high, and saw them over difficult patches when prices dipped. Indeed, the revenue farms served to enhance production by providing incentives to mine operators to increase the number of workers at their mines who could produce tin and at the same time consume opium or gamble. In a similar way, revenue farming provided a stimulus for export production in the countryside in Siam, particularly since the great bulk of farm revenue came from opium smoking and gambling, activities in which the Chinese labouring class figured prominently. It made their labour cheap, kept them indebted and kept them working. Second, the revenue farms were the single major source of state revenue in many of Southeast Asia's states by the late nineteenth century, partly through their ability to extract money relatively painlessly from alien and mobile populations who would otherwise have been difficult to subject to taxation. This phenomenal success provided the financial wherewithal for constructing the operating mechanisms of the modern state, such as expanded bureaucracies, roads and railways, armies and police forces, allowing for the vertical and horizontal extension of state control characteristic of the second phase of management.

Around the turn of the century, all these legacies of liberalism made for the ripening of conditions—economic, ideological, political, administrative—which allowed the structural imperatives of modern Western imperialism to play themselves out fully. The result was the creation in Southeast Asia of modern centralized states, with the will and the means to manage, exploit and 'improve' their subjects systematically, rather than simply oversee, motivate or cajole them.

THE MODERN STATE IN SOUTHEAST ASIA

The organizational principles and practice of these new states differed from those of their predecessors in five major ways. First, bureaucracies grew enormously in size with the management requirements of the new order. This was partly because the numbers of European civil servants expanded; in Indochina, for example, they doubled in the four years after 1907 as a consequence of Governor-General Doumer's creation of a separate and overarching 'federal' administration to oversee the affairs of the Indochinese states. But the greatest growth was found in the number of indigenous officials who filled positions in the middle and lower ranks of government service. Official numbers swelled with the incorporation of previously independent or semi-independent political entities into the colonial state—for example, the absorption of what is now Laos into French Indochina in the 1890s or the southern Philippines into the American colonial state based on Manila.

Second, the scope of bureaucracy became far wider than before. In 1855, for example, the central administration of the Netherlands East Indies had been divided into five departments: Finance; Revenue and Lands; Produce and Civil Stores; Cultivations; and Civil Public Works. Thus 'the general administration in those days resolved itself into a financial administration and care of the country came down above all to care for lining the treasury'.[8] By 1911, however, there were seven departments with a much broader range of functions: Justice; Internal Administration; Education and Worship; Civil Public Works; Finance; Agriculture, Industry and Trade; and Government Enterprise. In Burma at the turn of the century, a series of bureaucratic reforms saw the creation of a number of functionally specific areas—jails, hospitals, land revenue and registers, excise, justice—which had previously been only vaguely distinguished; hand in hand with this went the creation of a host of other administrative institutions to promote economic and social development—for forestry, agriculture, veterinary affairs, fisheries, communications, education, credit, public health. This elaboration indicates the broadening of what government saw as its interests and responsibilities. Unlike its colonial and indigenous predecessors, the new colonial state, as well as the royalist state in Siam, was interested not just in embodying revered values, keeping the peace and promoting revenue and income, but in a whole range of activities which were aimed both at controlling and benefiting the peoples it now considered its 'subjects'. Thus, in the Netherlands East Indies, government expenditures increased by about seven times between the 1860s and the end of the colonial period; indeed, they outstripped revenues to such an extent that the government very often ran at a deficit during the three-quarters of a century before World War II, making up the shortfall by floating international loans which left it with a consolidated debt of more than a thousand million guilders by the 1920s. In Siam, government expenditure grew at an annual rate of nearly 14 per cent through the 1890s; 45 per cent of expenditure in the early twentieth century was spent on defence and internal administration. In the general budget of Indochina, expenditures rose from 17 million piastres in 1899 to 108 million in 1931.

Third, the expanded size and broader scope of government produced an intensity in governance which had never previously been experienced by Southeast Asians. There were more officials doing a much greater range of jobs, and they were doing them more frequently, more regularly and much more efficiently. This growing control was, moreover, facilitated by competition among indigenous élites at all levels for state patronage; their efforts to curry favour tended to build a culture of mutual denunciation which was sadly destructive of their own roles and identities but splendidly consonant with the state's requirements. One scholar describes the process thus:

> To follow the development of the colonial régime is to follow the inexorable progress of cadastral surveys, settlement reports for land revenue, censuses, the issuance of land titles and licences, identity cards, tax rolls and receipts, and a growing body of regulations and procedures. . . . Nets of finer and finer official weave caught and recorded the status of each inhabitant, each piece of land, each transaction, each activity that was assessable. . . . there is little doubt that, compared to the kingdoms they replaced, they left few places to hide.[9]

[8] Ph. Kleintjes, cited in A. D. A. de Kat Angelino, *Colonial Policy*, Chicago, 1931, II. 51.
[9] James C. Scott, *The Moral Economy of the Peasant: Rebellion and Subsistence in Southeast Asia*, New Haven, 1976, 94.

According to Furnivall, the celebrated scholar-official of Burma, 'even up to 1900 the people saw little of any Government officials, and very few ever caught more than a passing glimpse of a Western official. By 1923 the Government was no longer remote from the people but, through various departmental subordinates, touched on almost every aspect of private life.'[10]

Fourth, all this government activity no longer placed such a premium on the refined manipulation of personal ties and followings but required a new style of administration, characterized by clearly defined, formal and impersonal institutions, specificity of bureaucratic function, regular procedures, and huge amounts of paper. It demanded Western-style administrative skills and formal Western education, and Westerners' approval. In 1913, for example, the Dutch colonial government introduced the requirement that those who were to be promoted to the highest indigenous rank of Regent in the colonial bureaucracy had to have a minimum of formal Western education and had to be capable of speaking and understanding Dutch. In Vietnam in 1903, a knowledge of French was made a prerequisite for admission to the mandarinate in Tonkin and Annam, and in 1919 the anachronistic Confucian civil service examination system was finally dispensed with. In Siam, modern education rather than ascribed rank increasingly became the passport to promotion and senior appointment within government service. Throughout most of Southeast Asia, the old system of managing local Chinese communities through their own headmen (*Kapitan China*) either fell into disuse or was altogether abandoned, to be replaced by direct and formal control. Such developments also brought with them a major transformation in the basis of political legitimacy. One's right to rule was no longer a function of divine anointing, or extraordinary wealth and display, or possession of the palace or regalia, but rather of secular administrative efficiency, formalized order, and getting things done. The political potency of the old values was receding in the face of new needs and new demands.

Fifth, the shape of rule was transformed from a fragmented and localized sprawl into a centrally controlled, regular and compact hierarchy. In Siam, for example, Chulalongkorn's reform of tax farming after 1873 was not simply aimed at increasing the efficiency and regularity of revenue collection, but also at curbing the powers of semi-independent aristocrats, powerful families and provincial chiefs to whom he had previously farmed out revenue-collection rights in the transitional period of state formation. The reduction of their revenue powers starved them of their followings and made them dependent upon, rather than just supporters of, the state. At the same time, the personal administrative fiefdoms of members and clients of the royal family gave way to twelve formal and functionally specific departments, organized on Western—indeed, colonial—principles. In their recently 'annexed' territories, the new Southeast Asian states gradually and carefully set up their own administrations to incorporate (and control) already existing indigenous bureaucracies; thus, in the

---

[10] John S. Furnivall, *Colonial Policy and Practice: a Comparative Study of Burma and Netherlands India*, New York, 1956, 77.

Khorat plateau in what is today northeast Thailand, regional lords (*chao muang*) were transformed into salaried provincial governors. By degrees, such local lords were often replaced by the centre's own appointees. This process of centralization was perhaps symbolized most starkly in the transformation of legal practices and systems. In the Indies, for example, Dutch persistence and ingenuity attempted to codify the permeable, locally variant and constantly evolving *adat* law; in doing so, they corrupted its essential mutability, but this was a small and unnoticed price to pay for the knowledge by which the Dutch hoped to control the frustrating variety of their new subjects. Especially in areas of commercial significance, village land, the control of which had previously been based on loose, communal arrangements of usufruct, was transformed into a commodity item by new laws which ensconced a notion of private, individual right, providing protection and incentive for increased production. In the realm outside the village, so as to reinforce and sustain their political dominance and smooth the path of economic development, Westerners imposed or inserted their own versions of law—in their eyes fair, rational, impersonal, humane, independent—above or in place of older formal legal systems such as the Vietnamese code or the Islamic codes of the Malay states which were seen as manipulated or arbitrary or venal; and they instituted formal police forces (and jails), as well as encouraging the emergence of professional advocates, to oversee their implementation and operation. As a result, according to one scholar of Cochinchina, 'justice became less accessible, less certain and more costly'.[11] Indigenous law and, indeed, the religion from which it issued, was shuffled off into the residual category of the 'personal', to take care of those necessary but unimportant things which did not affect the colonial purpose, to remind Southeast Asians of their cultural inferiority and immaturity, and to provide a facade of undisturbed 'custom'. Religion, itself increasingly subject to state supervision, was to be a matter for 'priests', not law-makers and rulers.

This growing intensity and purpose of government activity were most obvious—and most forcefully felt—in the realm of taxation. From the consolidation of the new states until the Great Depression, taxation receipts, now payable in cash rather than kind, increased sharply. In Cochinchina, for example, in the wake of Doumer's fiscal and administrative reorganization, tax revenues rose from 5.7 million piastres in 1913 to 15.7 million in 1929. In the Netherlands East Indies, the amount collected grew from 57.3 million guilders in 1900 to 361 million guilders in 1928; one Dutch official, surveying the revenue system, felt moved to assert in the mid-1920s that Java's peasants were being taxed to the limit. In Siam, revenues rose from 15.4 million baht in 1892 to 117.4 million in 1927. In the Philippines, the value of internal revenue collections rose by 170 per cent between 1906 and 1916. Such increases were a function of heightened efficiency in collection (as in the systematization of Java's land rent system in the early twentieth century) and a broadening of the tax base which tighter control allowed, as well as the continuing growth of

---

[11] Milton E. Osborne, *The French Presence in Cochinchina and Cambodia: Rule and Response (1859–1905)*, Ithaca, 1969, 268.

export-oriented economic activity and the population's magnified dependence upon it; under these circumstances, taxation was both a prod and a stimulus to increasing production. A notable indicator of the changing nature of governance in this realm was the growth of revenue from direct personal and company taxation and the levying of import and export duties, in contrast to the decline of income from the sale of government products, and from indirect taxes and revenue gathering, particularly revenue farms.

A revolution in financial and commercial practices accompanied this administrative transformation. Of major importance were the gradual restriction and then rapid termination of revenue farming, especially the lucrative opium farms. Paradoxically, the growth of centralized and powerful states, partly paid for by revenue farming, rendered it an anchronism. The instability of tax farms made them 'ultimately volatile and unhealthy for the economy',[12] not to mention politically dangerous; the state now had the wherewithal to collect revenues directly and on its own account. In Indochina between 1897 and 1904, the French established state monopolies on the sale of opium, alcohol and salt; this confirmed and at the same time centralized earlier and generally unsuccessful local French initiatives to abolish revenue farming, and greatly increased the weight of these consumption taxes so that they formed the major revenue item for the French colonial state. As in Siam, this development was at least partly political in the sense of curbing local and sectional pretensions to wielding independent and unsupervised power over the population. Contemporaneously the Dutch abolished the farming out of opium and pawnbroking and replaced them by government monopolies and licences, as did the British in Malaya with opium and gambling.

Other less dramatic but nonetheless important changes were also afoot. Governments constructed regular, stable and national currency systems, pegged to the gold standard in most places shortly after 1900 and expressed as paper money, to replace the enormous variety of coins of different weights and standards. To sustain and monitor the currency, they established national banks. Increasingly, they organized or sponsored (usually inefficiently, inconveniently and thus ineffectively) the provision of credit for the small-scale needs of peasants and petty traders and manufacturers, such as mutual loan associations in Cochinchina and people's banks in Java.

In the private sphere, previously peopled by adventurous individual merchants and entrepreneurs, banks and commercial houses—mostly Western but Asian ones as well—sprouted in the centres of colonial control and in Bangkok to act as agents for government, providers of credit and other facilities to private investors and shippers and insurers of goods. Nowhere was this activity more noticeable than in the development of the agency houses of Singapore; they flourished on the virtues of vertical integration, investing in local production, organizing and overseeing the

---

[12] Hong Lysa, *Thailand in the Nineteenth Century: Evolution of the Economy and Society*, Singapore, 1984, 129.

floating of new companies, providing management expertise for plantations, importing and exporting commodities, granting insurance, and
lubricating their operations with credit. They were the beachheads of
corporate enterprise, the local agents and managers of a vast financial
network ultimately controlled from the boardrooms of Europe and North
America.

Hand in hand with this enormous administrative and financial endeavour came the construction of roads, bridges, offices, railways, new
ports and port facilities, shipping services, irrigation works, telegraph
services and other infrastructure designed to bring government hard up
against the people, to 'pacify' them, to develop and monitor their productive capacities, to siphon out the commodities demanded by the West, and
to profit more efficiently from them. It was no coincidence that the first
state railway in Java connected the rich sugar regions of east Java with the
great port of Surabaya, nor that the first tracks laid on the western Malay
peninsula (from 1885) linked the separate tin-mining regions laterally to
coastal ports and later pushed north and south to integrate expanding
rubber plantations. In Burma, the state-subsidized Irrawaddy Flotilla
Company and the newly constructed railways (2500 kilometres of line by
1914) provided cheap and easy transport for rice exports and consumer
imports. Between 1900 and 1935 in Indochina, more was spent on economic infrastructure development than on any other single item in the colonial
budget, providing almost 3000 kilometres of railways, canals and waterworks, vast areas of reclaimed land, ports, offices and a remarkably
extensive system of metalled roads. Even the maladministered and demor-
alized Spanish régime (boasting fifty governors-general in the fifty-two
years after 1835) managed to establish an embryonic modern transport
infrastructure in Luzon, including a railway tying the central plain to
Manila. A developed and controlled polity and a developing economy
were two sides of the same colonial coin, something exemplified by the
development of Indies inter-island shipping by the Koninklijk Paketvaart
Maatschappij in the early twentieth century and the expansion of the
Siamese railway system into the north and east of the country.

Plantations and Mining

All these developments provided the conditions for a wholly new form of
economic activity: production which was relatively capital-intensive, pri-
vately financed, corporately managed and technologically advanced. Its
most common manifestation was the modern plantation, a system of
production which was the symbol and the direct result of intrusive high
colonialism. Large and powerful concerns, sometimes indigenous but
generally of European or North American origin (for example, Harrisons &
Crosfield, Michelin, US Rubber, SOCFIN), usually working under long-term
leases and benefiting from colonial infrastructures and land improvement
measures, put vast areas of hitherto virgin Southeast Asian countryside
under export crops. In Malaya alone, in response to the extraordinary
growth of the motor-vehicle industry in the West, the plantation rubber

area grew from 2400 hectares in 1900 to almost 570,000 hectares by 1921, the result of an investment of over £70 million. Attempts to define this mode—'a capital-using unit employing a large labour force under close managerial supervision to produce a crop for sale'[13]—conceal the great diversity with which plantation systems operated in Southeast Asia. Plantations on the frontier most closely approximated the stereotyped ideal. They were developed in sparsely populated and often virgin regions of Southeast Asia for the cultivation of crops like rubber, sugar, oil palm and tobacco, radically transforming vast forest environments into neatly segmented and orderly arrays of fields with ecological repercussions that have yet to be properly appreciated. In the grey and red lands north and northwest of Saigon, powerful French companies built extensive rubber plantations, pouring in huge sums of speculative money in the 1920s: between 1925 and 1929, investments in rubber totalled 700 million francs and the area under crop increased from 15,000 to 90,000 hectares. The land was worked by indentured Vietnamese, most of them from the poor and overpopulated north. A similar pattern evolved in Cambodia, where rubber plantations worked by Vietnamese labourers under the control of large French companies dated from 1921. In the outer islands of the Netherlands East Indies, plantation agriculture became the focus of colonial economic activity from the late nineteenth century on. In the fabled plantation area of the east coast of Sumatra, there arose great plantations of tobacco (grown under a shifting régime), rubber, palm oil, tea and sisal in virtually unsettled areas which required the importation of huge numbers of indentured coolie labourers to service them. The coolies came originally from China through an immigration bureau established by the Deli Planters Association, but most, by around 1915, were from Java. In Malaya, rubber, starting from virtually nothing in the 1890s, rapidly came to dominate the country's agricultural export economy, replacing Chinese shifting cultivation of gambier and pepper; to secure the labour they needed, Malayan plantations used some Chinese labour but mostly relied on importing 'free' southern Indian workers. In the Philippines, the hub of sugar production moved gradually from the early 1880s from Luzon, with its *hacienda*–smallholder complex of production, to Negros, where true plantations emerged around the end of the century. Chinese mestizo planters, previously entrepreneurs in the once booming, now fading, Iloilo textile industry on neighbouring Panay, carved out large *haciendas*, often by means of fraud and sometimes force, from existing peasant smallholdings. Their activities were financed by large foreign firms which dominated sugar exports; their workforce comprised debt-bonded labourers and seasonal workers, organized in work gangs, who grew and harvested cane for delivery to large modern steam-powered centrifugal mills, called centrals, which were rapidly replacing the numerous light steam and cattle-driven mills in the 1910s and 1920s. The Java sugar industry—gradually moving from government control to private enterprise in the forty years after 1850—contrasted in organizational style and environmental setting with the frontier plantations. Set in the lush and heavily populated rice

---

[13] Eric R. Wolf, *Europe and the People without History*, Berkeley, 1982, 315.

districts of north, central and especially east Java, the industry was based on hiring peasant wet-rice land for cane growing for periods ranging from three to (after 1918) 21½ years. Peasants were granted access to their land between cane crops to grow rice and other staples. Cane was grown, harvested and transported by hired hands—often, indeed, the land-holders themselves—under close factory supervision, and manufactured into sugar at technologically advanced mills mostly owned by Dutch limited companies. Having endured the difficulties of depression and crop disease in the 1880s, the industry moved from a style of individual enterprise control to one of corporate management and, with huge capital inflows, began a phase of rapid expansion from the turn of the century, doubling its cropping area between 1900 and 1929.

Notwithstanding the value of scientific inputs in improving seed and rootstock, cultivation techniques and processing, the profitability of such concerns lay essentially in their recruitment and tight control and super-vision of large numbers of workers to clear and prepare land, plant and tend the growing crops, harvest them on maturity, and work in processing centres on the estates. Recruiting labour was the central problem. Not only were plantations generally in remote and lightly populated regions, but managers often found it impossible to obtain the services of local peasants. Thus frontier plantations depended almost wholly on recruitment from afar, sometimes employing private recruiting agencies to deliver them the numbers they needed, and sometimes relying on their own efforts. In Vietnam, the great reservoir of labour lay in the crowded lowlands of Tonkin and Annam; by the late 1920s, some 17,000 workers per annum were introduced into the plantations from those regions. They generally worked under indigenous foremen (*cai*) who recruited them, managed their affairs and subcontracted their services to plantation managers. In Malaya, Chinese workers were in short supply and Indians deemed more docile for plantation work; estate-based Tamil foremen-recruiters, called *kangany*, travelled to southern India, usually to places whence they them-selves had come, and recruited villagers—often their kin—for periods of service by advancing credit and promises. After 1907, recruitment was financed by a government-sponsored fund to which all plantations con-tributed. In 1910 alone, 91,723 Indians arrived in Malaya, and the figure peaked in 1913 at 122,583; smaller proportions of Chinese and Javanese were also employed. Javanese from the crowded villages and towns of central and northeastern Java were drawn to Sumatra by similar methods, but under indenture. Between 1913 and 1925, 327,000 contract coolies departed Java for the plantations and work sites of the outer islands. To service the Negros sugar plantations, estate foremen recruited permanent or seasonal workers from the western regions of neighbouring Panay (fallen on hard times with the demise of the Iloilo textile industry), or caught up dispossessed local smallholders by playing on their need for credit.

Most recruits were males in their twenties and thirties, although some-times, as on Malayan rubber estates, they brought their families with them. A much smaller proportion of young females was also recruited and frequently forced into prostitution. Like the Chinese of an earlier period, all these labourers came to make their fortunes and return home (although large numbers did remain as settlers, especially in Malaya and east Sumatra). They were generally housed in barrack-type accommodation in a discrete area of the plantation, although this tended to give way to individual dwellings as the proportion of female workers increased (in 1938, 37 per cent of east Sumatra's plantation labour force was female) and as permanent labour settlements were established. Their lives were ordered (and sometimes ended) by their closely supervised work. Their wages were low (for women only half to three-quarters those of men), and what little disposable income remained men often spent on gambling and prostitutes; systematic indebtedness was a useful means for plantation managers to maintain their workforces. With appalling living conditions, disease was rampant and death never far away; in 1927 in Cochinchina, one in twenty plantation workers died, and local death rates were often much higher than that. This was double the overall mortality rate for the colony, and among a population of workers supposedly in the prime of life. To ensure a docile or at least compliant workforce, plantation managers could call upon the authority of the state, embodied in such legislation as the Netherlands East Indies Coolie Ordinances of 1880, 1884 and 1893, which imposed fines, imprisonment or extra labour obligations for those who transgressed the conditions of their contracts; less formally they employed physical beatings and financial penalties, or exploited ingrained habits of regimentation. Nonetheless, brutal mistreatment and mean conditions sometimes led workers to attack supervisory personnel and, intermittently, to conduct strikes. 'They are men, so are we. How can we accept that they continually beat us?', remarked Nguyen Dinh Tu, a participant in the 1927 assassination of a French overseer at the Phu-Rieng plantation in Cochinchina.[14] Desertion was quite common; 4484 coolies—around one in ten of the workforce—ran away from Cochinchina plantations in 1928.

Under the new management-oriented régimes of high colonialism, resource extraction, like agricultural production, took on wholly new forms. By the turn of the century in the Malayan tin industry, the rich surface tin deposits for which Chinese labour-intensive methods of extraction had been appropriate were close to exhaustion, and labour was becoming more expensive with the end of the opium revenue farms, and more mobile with demand rising elsewhere. These problems blunted the edge of Chinese competitiveness and, allied to increasing European dominance of tin smelting and the appearance of huge and expensive bucket dredges from 1912, saw control of the industry flow more and more from Chinese into Western hands. The failure of the Chinese to adapt was partly a result of the fact that dredges required huge capital sums which Chinese were either unable or, more likely, disinclined to procure for this purpose, and partly because the colonial government provided Westerners with large land leases and geographical and geological advice to make this expansive form of mining workable and profitable. The result was that by 1937 dredges produced half Malaya's tin. A trend to highly capitalized and

[14] Cited in Martin J. Murray, *The Development of Capitalism in Colonial Indochina (1870–1940)*, Berkeley, 1980, 311.

mechanized mining was not, however, evident everywhere. In Vietnam, where coal production had quadrupled to 2 million tonnes by 1930, only 6 per cent of Tonkin coal production was mechanized at the end of the 1930s.

Oil production, in contrast to tin, relied from the very outset on capital-intensive operations; as a result, the oil industry, established in the vicinity of such places as Yenangyaung (central Burma), Palembang (southeast Sumatra), Balikpapan (east Borneo), Seria (Brunei) and Miri (Sarawak) came to be the monopoly of a very few large international companies such as Royal Dutch-Shell, Standard Oil and Burmah Oil. Similarly, the timber industry, equally demanding of capital to exploit remote sites in such locations as northern Burma, northern Siam and British North Borneo (even when employing traditional extraction techniques and local ethnic minorities as workforces), became largely the preserve of a small number of large Western firms such as the Bombay–Burmah Trading Corporation.

ASPECTS OF SOCIAL CHANGE

Southeast Asia's gradual incorporation into a global system of commerce, together with the consequential accelerating impetus for new forms of state control, economic development, and invigorated local, regional and international trade, reshaped patterns of social life in the region in momentous ways. The social change typical of the period, however, was not a matter of simple, discrete and direct responses to specific events; rather, it evolved from conjunctions of developments that were sometimes interconnected and mutually reinforcing and sometimes contradictory and ambiguous, all stimulated and sometimes dictated by the general pattern of economic growth. One useful way of unravelling the complexities of this social transformation is to examine, against the general contours of change already outlined, especially its last and dominant phase, how these conjunctions affected those aspects of Southeast Asians' lives—their reproductive activities, their places of residence, their occupations and modes of work, their gender, their states of health—that affected them most deeply.

People: Growing and Moving

One of the most readily obvious changes which coincided with Western-inspired economic change was rapid population growth. The classic case of rapid and sustained population growth is, of course, Java, where a population of between three and five million at the end of the eighteenth century had grown to 40.9 million by 1930, a rate approaching 1.9 per cent per annum. But statistics from other parts of Southeast Asia show similarly spectacular growth: in Malaya, a population of 250,000 in 1800 had risen to 3.8 million in 1931. In the Philippines, one of 2.5 million in 1830 had grown to 16.5 million by 1940. Burma's population more than doubled between 1891 and 1941. The component parts of French Indochina grew at rates around 2 per cent per annum from the late nineteenth century on. Siam witnessed a similar rate of increase after the turn of the twentieth century.

In some settings, especially where plantation modes or labour-intensive resource extraction were common, a considerable proportion of this growth came from immigration. As early as the 1820s, the Chinese population of west Borneo was estimated at between 30,000 and 50,000. Especially from the mid-nineteenth century, Chinese flocked to the Malay states as indentured labourers or 'paid immigrants' and perhaps as many as three million Indian Tamils were brought to Malaya as rubber workers in the early decades of the twentieth century. Under less iniquitous circumstances Chinese (not to mention Mons, Khmers, Laotians and other ethnic groups) were encouraged through the nineteenth century to settle in Siam, and Chinese flowed into the Philippines in such numbers that, despite persistent counterflows home, the Chinese population rose from around 6000 in 1840 to 100,000 by 1890. Malays from Sumatra, Java and other parts of the archipelago migrated in large numbers as free settlers to the largely empty western Malay peninsula from the late nineteenth century onwards. Indians flocked into lower Burma, especially after the beginning of the twentieth century, to work stints as labourers; Indian traders, moneylenders and prostitutes landed with them. About 2.6 million Indians migrated to Burma between 1852 and 1937; by 1931, 10 per cent of lower Burma's population was Indian.

Immigration alone, however, cannot explain the rates of growth which, despite some earlier scholarly scepticism, seem to be remarkably high, to stretch over long periods of time, and thus to constitute a dramatic new phase in Southeast Asia's demographic history. Nor can Southeast Asian states' greater efficiency in controlling, incorporating, settling and enumerating disparate and distant populations. Attempts to explain the mechanism of this surging growth and to discover what sustained it have polarized around the views that either increased fertility or reduced mortality were responsible. Arguments for increased fertility generally attribute population expansion to indigenous attempts to reduce the state's labour impositions by augmenting the available workforce through natural means or, alternatively, to the development of circumstances that promoted higher fertility, such as a large-scale transformation from shifting to sedentary cultivation or a more settled and certain future. The mechanisms adumbrated to explain higher fertility also vary. Some look to a significant decline in female celibacy, others to reduction in female age at marriage; one ingenious suggestion locates the mechanism for increased fertility in shorter periods of breast-feeding and amenorrhea caused by greatly increased labour demands upon women. Those who propose reduced mortality cite the reduction of warfare and especially the devastating consequences which flowed from it (crop destruction, disease, the capture or flight of populations), increased nutrition, better standards of health care and even perhaps a transition to endemicity of previously epidemic diseases. The key to a solution seems to lie in identifying the characteristic demographic pattern before the period of intensive colonial rule. From the scanty research thus far performed, it appears that the prevailing trend was one of regularly high natural fertility interspersed with frequent periods of catastrophic mortality which were for the most part the result, direct and indirect, of warfare (as, for example, in the depopulation of Kedah resulting from the Siamese attack of 1821). If this was so, it seems difficult to adduce argument and evidence that a rate of fertility which was already very high could be expanded to an extent sufficient of itself to explain the high and sustained rates of growth of the nineteenth and twentieth centuries. At the very least, there is little evidence to suggest the widespread adoption of behaviour which might increase fertility to a higher and demographically significant plane, such as earlier or more frequent marriage, the forsaking of previously widely used and effective fertility-control practices, or increases in coital frequency. By the same token, however, apart from the imposition of peace there is little evidence, either precise or suggestive (and sometimes evidence quite to the contrary) of higher levels of nutrition or radically changed environments more conducive to health which might be adduced as positive support for the reduced mortality thesis. Under such circumstances, the most plausible picture is perhaps one of a significant reduction in mortality, possibly augmented by a small increase in fertility resulting from more settled and regular times. Since a dearth of appropriate data renders the relevant variables intractable to satisfactory empirical evaluation, it seems unlikely that a solution will emerge that goes much beyond this.

Population growth was spectacular, as was the large-scale introduction of new ethnic groupings. However, a similarly profound demographic trend, internal migration, has lain almost unnoticed and its impact little investigated. One reason for this is that colonial governments (as well as the Siamese élite) treasured a stable and docile workforce just as much as their predecessors did. Characteristically, they sought to register and immobilize sedentary cultivators, to domesticate wandering swidden cultivators as rice farmers who could be counted and regularly taxed, and to play down exceptions to their purpose. Their efforts at control were only partially successful, because despite an enduring stereotype of the territorially-rooted peasant household, mobility rather than permanency seems to have been a keynote of peasant life in this era as well as in earlier ones; indeed, the opening of new economic opportunities accelerated mobility. There were a number of great peasant migrations. The opening of the Burma delta through the later nineteenth century attracted huge numbers from the dry zone; thus in 1901, 10 per cent of lower Burma's 4.1 million people was made up of people born in upper Burma, an important ingredient in the process of 'Burmanizing' the Irrawaddy delta region. The opening of Siam's central plain attracted large numbers of peasants from the northeast. In Vietnam, the long southward movement of Vietnamese reached its conclusion with the opening up of the Mekong delta lands under French rule; thousands of Vietnamese moved into Laos and Cambodia as well (there were 60,000 of them in Cambodia by 1908). In the Philippines, the vast plain of central Luzon attracted and was gradually brought under the plough by immigrants from the Manila region and from Luzon's northwestern edge. The east Java frontier was pushed back by people from the northeast coast and the thickly settled volcanic valleys of central Java; this was part of a more general pattern of movement which left more than one Indonesian in ten living outside the region of his or her birth in 1930.

As well as these dramatic movements, there was a persistent and probably rapidly accelerating 'background' movement, often of a circular or sojourning nature. Everywhere, as the pace of commercialization increased and transport infrastructure improved, seasonal wage labour flourished, bringing peasants in great numbers from the Khorat plateau of upper Burma to harvest rice in the lands around Bangkok or the Burma delta, or from Panay to cut cane on Negros sugar plantations. As many as 50,000 Tonkin peasants regularly sought seasonal work in the region's coal pits. Itinerant labour gangs traversed the Cochinchina ricefields in search of harvesting work. Statistics on railway passenger traffic convey something of the intensity of this moving around; Malaya's railways, for example, carried 4.8 million passengers in 1904 and 14.7 million by 1916, while Burma's carried 8.4 million passengers in 1896 and 27 million by 1928. Social customs and obligations, as well as opportunity and oppression, helped to feed the persistent movement. Thus in lower Burma there was a great deal of internal migration within the delta region itself, partly caused by the practice of equal splitting of inherited lands among the family offspring; one member would frequently buy out the others, who then proceeded to the frontier to establish themselves anew on larger holdings. Again, people often fled to new regions to escape from debts and obligations incurred in longer-established areas of the delta. In Luzon, deteriorating tenancy conditions encouraged mobility as peasants searched for more secure and satisfactory arrangements; one unreflective *hacendero* later complained that 'peasants around here were forever moving around before the Japanese occupation. I don't know why, but they did.'[15] Peasants in the Federated Malay States at the turn of the twentieth century have been characterized as 'restless people in search of elusive fortunes'.[16] Patterns of incremental movement were evident everywhere as people slowly and relentlessly radiated out from points of settlement to form satellite communities, mostly as household units rather than pioneering individuals. Alien minorities were no exception to this pattern; whereas 92 per cent of Chinese in the Philippines were resident in Manila in 1848, the figure was only 48 per cent by 1894. All these movements of people, ranging from dramatic and permanent surges to bit-by-bit reclamation and modest local commuting, contrived to transform radically the landscape and ecology of previously sparsely inhabited and thickly forested plains.

Villagers

The characteristic flux of populations annoyed and perplexed governments who sought ever more closely to control their peoples. In general, they attempted to do this by investing the village community with state

[15] Cited in Benedict J. Kerkvliet, *The Huk Rebellion: a Study of Peasant Revolt in the Philippines*, Berkeley, 1977, 26.
[16] Lim Teck Ghee, *Peasants and Their Agricultural Economy in Colonial Malaya 1874–1941*, Kuala Lumpur, 1977, 55.

power, in order to supervise their subjects more closely. The village, previously a rather loose amalgam of peasant households, often with no fixed territorial attachment, and subject to a competing array of patrons, became an administrative institution of the state. In Burma, the British were puzzled at what they saw as the vague, personal and untidy style of administration provided to lower-level communities by local traditional chieftains, *thugyis*. Their response was to 'create' the village as an artificial administrative entity, often in the form of an arbitrary amalgamation of formerly discrete settlements. In Cambodia, when the French found no institutionalized villages (as they understood them), they responded by inventing 'artificial proto-villages'[17] called *phum*. A similar though not quite so fundamental process of artifice was evident in Java as well. Such changes in administrative mentality were reflected in the spatial organization of villages. Mobile, vaguely integrated, higgledy-piggledy settlements slowly became firmly attached to specific sites, their dwelling compounds fenced, their houses compacted together in more or less orderly patterns, their rights to surrounding fields and forests ever more precisely demarcated.

Previously, village politics, like those of the larger state, had been built around the notion of consensus, a broad understanding of the limited rights and powers of the village leadership group over against those of the village community. Under the press of the developing and ambitious state, however, leadership tended to become focused in one person, a village chief, and the authority he held came not from community consensus but from the increasingly intrusive state. Under the régime of the Cultivation System in Java, for example, the village chief was required, regularly and frequently, to make demands which would previously have been unacceptable. In this situation, the importance of consensus, of mediating and balancing between the two poles of the village and the state, fell into disuse. In order to maintain his position (and the lucrative rewards which went with it, such as a percentage of the taxation receipts he collected and a controlling hand over land allocation), the chief came more and more to rely on the coercive power of the state, and less and less on his own political ability. This meant, in fact, that his formal power (and the privileges that went with it) increased, but also that because that power was so dependent on the state he became estranged from his villagers; while the rank of village chief was never officially a governmental position, in practice it became so. In the frontier environment of Cochinchina, where peasant communities were less spatially integrated and authority correspondingly more diffuse than in long-settled and heavily populated regions like Java and Tonkin, a similar thrust in French policy had rather more confusing results. As the French attempted to bring the village under administrative control, they tended to saddle the ruling body of the village, the council of notables, with a huge range of specific administrative tasks and roles, and to transform the village chief, previously no more than the executor of the council's decisions, into a power figure in his own right. Because of the more 'open' nature of villages in Cochinchina,

---

[17] Alexander B. Woodside, *Community and Revolution in Modern Vietnam*, Boston, 1976, 129.

however, power remained relatively unconcentrated. Authority within Cochinchina's villages had customarily been a function of age, learning and especially the wealth that came from controlling land. But the French interference laid such burdens upon village life that the 'natural' leaders of the village were reluctant to take up an office which was full-time, unsalaried and expensive, and which harmed their relations with other villagers. This meant that those who took up village office were often less esteemed than those they replaced—'the more ambitious and unscrupulous'[18] members of the village, as one writer puts it, who relied for their power totally on the backing of French force, and who used their office as a means of advancement. For example, they might allow fellow villagers to clear virgin land, and then lay claim to it themselves, because they controlled the village-level process of making land claims. The result was an acute crisis in village government, in which those who had customarily provided leadership went their own way, and those appointed by the French generally used their office in an exploitative rather than protective manner.

As commerce grew in scale and intensity and as land increasingly became a commodity in its own right, the new or enhanced configurations of authority both above and within villages resulting from the greater reach of state power were reflected in a mountingly uneven and exploitative distribution of productive resources among peasants. At the top, there emerged a group of large landlords, frequently and increasingly of the absentee variety, who had capitalized on their attachment to the state to assume control of much of the village's land. Beneath them was a layer of households who possessed enough land to provide for their own upkeep. Beneath them lay a large component of villagers—as much as 70 per cent of the village population in the case of Tonkin, often more than 60 per cent in Java—who had insufficient land to sustain themselves, or no land at all. The lot of this last group was an ever more insecure and impoverished style of life; to make ends meet they relied on tenancy, field-labour paid in cash or kind and, increasingly, in off-farm work: small-scale industry, such as the manufacture and marketing of handicrafts, petty trade, and especially the varieties of wage labour thrown up by developing economies. Many of these people fell into or approached a meagre, proletarian mode of life.

What was novel about this situation was not inequality nor privation nor exploitation—these had always been natural aspects of village life—but rather their permanence and pervasiveness. The new centralized state drove further, deeper and more efficiently into village life than any of its predecessors. Characteristically nervous about 'unrest', it deprived villagers (those at the bottom of the heap as well as those above them who now perceived their interests as unacceptably compromised) of their previous ability either to negotiate tolerable livelihoods with a range of competing potential patrons or to flee their antagonists altogether. As time went by, as the old physical frontier disappeared and as the new political frontier was confirmed, the avenues for evading impositions or redressing

[18] Murray, 427.

perceived wrongs were narrowed and almost eliminated.

The result was that peasants' attempts to protect their livelihoods and styles of life, while not necessarily increasingly in volume, took on a more organized, public and confrontationist style and tone. 'Everyday resistance' endured, as it always will—earthy jokes at the expense of a landlord, small-scale theft, strategies of absenteeism or footdragging, isolated arson, the adoption of various forms of religious cults, the use of folk theatres or other forms of art and culture as protest vehicles. But the range of such measures was continually circumscribed more tightly by a state which could construct efficient intelligence services and which made a virtue of punishing those it saw as dangerous to 'public order' so as to set an example to others. Under these circumstances, attempts at withdrawal or refusal to acknowledge the state's authority—as with the frequent cases of social banditry and, best known of all, the Saminist movement of north-central Java—resulted, paradoxically, only in confrontation. Peaceful organized protest—associations for mutual aid, both material and spiritual, petitions, marches, demonstrations, even strikes—could be ignored or smugly tolerated. Most often it was easily and arrogantly dismissed by targeting ringleaders, threatening force, or buying off dissent. In the end, peasants were frequently moved to physical violence in a final and desperate means to redress what they perceived as intolerable oppression. Sometimes this took the form of uncoordinated and spontaneous outrage, as in the assassination of the tax-collecting Resident Bardez by Cambodian peasants in 1916. In its more developed modes—such as the Muslim communist rebellion of 1926 in west Java, the millenarian nationalist Saya San movement of lower Burma in 1930–1, and the defiance of the 'red soviets' of Nghe An and Ha Tinh in northern Annam of the same period— resistance was often shaped and hardened by disaffected non-peasant intellectuals. In the short term all these movements were tragic and futile, trampled unforgivingly by the technological and political superiority of the state.

City Dwellers

The village and the countryside were the characteristic focuses of Western-inspired economic development; they were the production sites for primary produce and resources. Change, however, affected not only the sites of production, but also the places from which production was directed, the newly developed colonial capitals and Bangkok. Under the new régime of Western-inspired production and trade, the two great tasks of cities were commerce and territorial administration, combined in ways that had never previously been possible in Southeast Asia. The cities of the high colonial period possessed, unlike their classical antecedents, the skills and technology to marry both these functions effectively.

One way of appreciating urban change in this period is to analyse a freeze-frame of Southeast Asian cities at the zenith of their transformation. In 1930, there were sixteen cities with populations of 100,000 or more. They can be divided into three groups: first, the 'old' indigenous capitals of

Mandalay, Bangkok, Hanoi, Yogyakarta and Surakarta, mostly modelled on the principles of the old sacred city; second, old colonial cities with their origins in the merchant capital era of the Western presence, cities founded or settled by Westerners essentially as trading posts: Batavia, Semarang, Surabaya, Manila, Penang and Singapore; third, the new colonial cities of Rangoon, Saigon, Kuala Lumpur, Palembang and Bandung, cities which owed their importance to being sites of the commercial expansion which marked this period of high colonialism. Comparing this freeze-frame to one taken a century or so before reveals a number of crucial developments. Pre-eminence had passed from the old sacred city to the city based on commerce—Mandalay gave way to Rangoon, Yogyakarta to Batavia, Hué to Saigon. A city's vitality was a function of its unrelenting commercial orientation; with the exception of Kuala Lumpur and Bandung, the new colonial cities were port cities, and even these two exceptions owed their size to their commercial significance. Commerce and territorial administration had been welded together; capitals now stood at the termini of infrastructural grids through which produce was moved out of the interior, and administrative control of the hinterland established, maintained and enhanced.

More spectacular than this change in the functions of cities was the late, rapid increase in their sizes. Before the last part of the nineteenth century, urban populations in Southeast Asia generally grew more slowly than rural ones, a reflection of the limited, perhaps stultifying, effect of Western merchant capital on urban development. The development of state territorial control and more pervasive forms of economic activity, however, saw the beginnings of rapid and continuing urbanization; now all the major cities grew in population much faster than the rural areas that surrounded them, partly because of relatively poor conditions in the local (and international) countryside, and partly because the city seemed to promise a better life of expanding economic opportunities. Thus, for example, Batavia's population increased at an average annual rate of 5.5 per cent between 1905 and 1930, and Bandung's at 5.2 per cent; over the first three decades of the twentieth century, Bangkok's rose at an average annual rate, respectively, of 3.5 per cent, 4.0 per cent and 4.0 per cent. Rangoon's population grew by a factor of 3.5 between 1872 and 1921. In Malaya in 1911, one person in ten lived in a city of more than 10,000 inhabitants; by 1931, it was one in seven. In the Philippines, the level of urbanization rose from 12.6 per cent to 21.6 per cent between 1918 and 1939.

Such growth in numbers manifested itself in the spatial expansion of cities, rendering them considerably larger than their pre-colonial and early colonial predecessors. This occurred not just because economic activity and population growth expanded, but also because Westerners tended to move out from the centre of the city and establish their residences in more commodious and expansive regions on the peripheries. In Batavia, for example, the Dutch established a large residential suburb, evocatively named Weltevreden ('contented') on the southern outskirts of Batavia, away from the congested and disease-ridden old port centre; in Surabaya, large areas to the south were established for the exclusive habitation of Europeans. This practice tended to expand city boundaries, so that previously rural settlements often found themselves part of the urban environment; in 1927, for instance, the city of Semarang included 137 villages within its boundaries and took up an area larger than 100 square kilometres.

Westerners dominated city space. In Bandung in 1930, for example, they made up 12 per cent of the population but occupied more than half the urban space. Maps of other colonial cities reveal a similar disproportion with large areas set aside for Westerners' offices, residences and recreation (clubs, race tracks, cricket grounds). Their dominance was partly reflected, too, in the rigid racial compartmentalization of the city—Westerners in one quarter (the most salubrious), Chinese in another, Arabs in another and various ethnic indigenous subgroups in others—something already present in pre-colonial times but exacerbated and refined under more intensive colonial rule. Colonial governments, especially in Java and also Manila (where the Spanish believed it was 'healthier' to keep the races apart), often forced ethnic groups, especially Chinese, to live in separate areas, so better to police their activities and to protect the indigenous people from their alleged rapacity. By the same token, segregation was sometimes the result of historical circumstance—Kuala Lumpur's China-town was the site of the early Chinese tin-mining camp—and sometimes it arose because ethnic groups in cosmopolitan cities tended to congregate together where they could share language, and profit from family or clan support. Discrimination based on ethnicity and relative poverty also ensured that city populations were unevenly distributed. Despite the expansive dimensions of cities in the high colonial era, their centres tended to be exceedingly densely populated. The suburbs were occupied by peasants whose urban status sprang from administrative accident; by squatter immigrants combining urban employment with market gardening; and by wealthier (mainly Western) people who could afford to commute to the city centre every day. Most occupants of cities, however, were poor, too poor to live far from where they worked, so that as the population of cities grew, more and more people packed more and more tightly into the inner urban commercial cores. In Bandung, for example, the area of urban kampongs decreased by 25 per cent between 1910 and 1937, but the population rose from around 45,000 to about 160,000; one part of Semarang had a population density of 1000 people per hectare. The excruciating congestion was exemplified in a report from Surabaya of a dwelling which measured 3 metres by 8 metres, was 1.7 metres high, and which housed 23 workers. In another house 120 workers were crammed, each of whom paid three cents a night for the privilege. In Singapore, the lodgings of rickshawmen were often owned by rickshaw owners; they sometimes contained (if that is the appropriate word) 16 people in one room or, again, 175 in a house. Over a thirteen-year period, the number of tenants in one house in Singapore rose by more than 300 per cent.

While the focus of the colonial city was commerce, it was commerce of a limited kind. In the industrializing urban centres of nineteenth-century Europe, cities produced goods, employment, and income, and exercised a modernizing influence in the surrounding areas; in contrast, the Southeast Asian cities were agents rather than actors in the process of production.

Although all these cities had some industry—metal, cigarette, furniture, tile and batik factories, coconut-processing plants, cement works, printeries, railway maintenance yards—such activities were ancillary to the real focus of the city's life and existed to service machinery, to process agricultural goods or manufacture small-scale commodities which were cheaper than or not competitive with imports. There was no call for substantial industry where the industrialized West already enjoyed a tremendous advantage in terms of technology, capital, social organization and amenities. More particularly, the rulers and merchants of these cities had little desire to encourage industrialization which would compete with imports from metropolitan Europe, nor did they wish to encourage a demand for urban wage labour which might vie with the requirements of mines, plantations and smallholder food production. Least of all did they want the political problems which might arise with the growth of a clamorous indigenous middle class or a discontented proletariat. Consequently, the role of the city in late colonial Southeast Asia was not that of an industrial dynamo but rather a channel, pushing the products of its hinterland on to the world market and distributing Western consumer imports and Westernized administration into the hinterland.

The peculiar nature of the Southeast Asian capitals led (with such notable exceptions as Batavia and Hanoi) to the phenomenon of the primate city. This was not in itself, it must be added, a new feature of Southeast Asian urbanization. Directing economic development and the process of administrative integration and control, and channelling the fruits of its activities on to the world market, the capital came to dominate each state, with its size at least twice as great as the next biggest city. Bangkok, indeed, became the greatest primate city in the world: in 1940 it was fifteen times bigger than Siam's next biggest city, Chiengmai. In these capital cities were concentrated the various component parts of this endeavour; the major offices of the bureaucracy, the head offices of banks, agency houses and shipping and insurance firms, the ports and great warehouses, the centres of education (such as they were), the termini of the transport networks. Some of these cities became so huge that they contained a significant proportion of the population of the whole nation, a paradoxical realization of the pre-colonial concept that the central city *was* the nation.

An emphasis on urban morphology tends to distract attention from the lives and fates of the people who inhabited these cities, particularly the less fortunate ones. Apart from Westerners, they fell into three general categories. There was an élite comprising the traditional aristocracy, absentee landlords and powerful members of non-indigenous groups, especially wealthy Chinese. Below them in the social hierarchy came an indigenous middle class which, while growing rapidly—especially in the Philippines where Western education was relatively widely available —was proportionately only a tiny segment of the total indigenous population; it was peopled by government white-collar workers, private merchants and entrepreneurs, and professional people like teachers, doctors and engineers. The great mass of the urban population, however, was made up of the working class, those who made their living through manual labour. A large number of them were either immigrants to the cities or the immediate descendants of such immigrants, and sometimes they came from far afield, often making the capital city an alien enclave—Indians in Rangoon, Chinese in Singapore and Saigon and, to a lesser degree, in Bangkok and even Phnom Penh. Only one-third of Rangoon's 1931 population had been born in the city; more than half Batavia's 1930 population was born outside the city; in Manila, over one-third of the population increase of the city between 1903 and 1939 came from immigration. Alongside those permanently settled in the cities were the considerable numbers of circular migrants—comprising perhaps as much as 40 per cent of the adult indigenous population—who normally resided in the countryside and came to the cities for temporary or seasonal work. Characteristically, they worked at their urban occupations for two or three months before returning to their rural environment.

Many members of the working class found employment in formal occupations, which were characterized by wage labour, regular hours and a certain degree of security. Some worked as construction labourers; some worked in factories, producing such things as embroidery, cigars, cigarettes and sandals. Many more worked in formal service industries, as train or tram drivers or conductors, domestic servants and cooks, repairmen, waitresses, dock workers. A very large number, perhaps even the majority, did not have formal employment at all, but worked in the so-called informal sector, as rickshaw pullers (20,000 of them in Singapore in the early twentieth century), pedicab drivers, roadside barbers, or prostitutes, or selling food and drink at the roadside or along railway tracks, or recycling rubbish from dumps. The characteristic feature of work in the informal sector was that it was highly labour intensive and consequently less productive than formal employment; it tended, then, to reinforce and entrench the poverty of its practitioners.

The most remunerative jobs in the formal manual workforce—as car mechanics, electricians, bus drivers—went to older, more literate males.[19] Poorly paid jobs, such as domestic service, went to those who were youngest and least literate, that is, those most likely to be newly arrived in the city; they were disproportionately occupied by women. Again, people working in the informal sector tended to be younger and less literate than those employed in the formal sector. Female employees had high rates of job turnover, probably because of childbearing and childrearing duties. Most manual workers were also subject to persistent bouts of unemployment or underemployment. The importance to newcomers of personal contacts and networks for gaining employment, informal on-the-job training and a place to live meant that career trajectories were notable for their lack of vertical mobility and sometimes for their ethnic or regional character: a young female who began employment as a domestic servant might in later life find employment as a washerwoman or cook or peddler, none of which required much literacy; less literate male servants would frequently move on to become porters or dockworkers or market vendors; an illiterate

[19] This section is mostly based upon Daniel P. Doeppers, *Manila, 1900–1941: Social Change in a Late Colonial Metropolis*, Quezon City, 1984.

servant could not generally aspire to become a relatively well-paid tram conductor. For this reason, ethnic and locality groups tended to be concentrated in certain occupations and certain residential areas.

Enduring poverty manifested itself most obviously in the squalid living conditions of manual workers in all colonial cities in Southeast Asia. Very few members of the urban working classes owned their own houses and land; most had to pay high rents for miserable conditions, without sanitation, refuse disposal facilities or drainage. Often accommodation was shared with others. Most suffered seriously and often mortally from the baleful effects on their health of such conditions, and morbidity and death were exacerbated by heavy exertions and poor or inappropriate nourishment.

Although many city dwellers were materially poor and indebted, retained strong links with their rural origins, and were strangers to urban life, they did not necessarily form a culturally lost or misplaced group. To replace the social life and supports they had left behind in the countryside, they often created energetic and highly organized urban proletarian cultures, expressed in such things as a multiplicity of community self-help groups like the *sinoman* of Surabaya, oral information networks, folk theatre like Iloilo's *zarzuela*, and local newspapers (read aloud in groups). Much of this energy was eventually directed into labour unions to improve wages and conditions at work sites and ultimately and naturally (as workers began to appreciate the structural reasons for their poverty and hardships) into variants of nationalism. In this way, the colonial city, the key symbol and means of Western dominance, became the site from which the ending of that dominance was engineered.

Entrepreneurs and Traders

The development of government enterprise and, later, sophisticated banking, merchant and agency institutions by Western concerns was one of the major aspects of Western dominance in Southeast Asia in this period. The commercialization they fostered penetrated deeply into the indigenous world to tap the wealth of agriculture and resources at the base of society. Under the Cultivation System, for example, peasants were moved to labour for the Dutch exchequer not just through physical or moral coercion but also to acquire the cash income to meet their taxation demands, pay debts and purchase the goods they increasingly came to need and desire. The exponential growth of rice production in the lowland river basins of mainland Southeast Asia and of smallholder rubber in Malaya and Sumatra was similarly fuelled by the need to meet taxation, service debt and purchase commodities; in Siam, for example, consumer goods consistently made up more than 70 per cent of all imports, drawn in to meet the demands of smallholding peasants. The trend towards regional crop specialization also fuelled demand for enhanced commodity merchandising; the attachment of the Bikol region to intensive abaca production, for instance, made it a permanent rice deficit area after 1850. Throughout Southeast Asia, incentive and need fuelled production;

money flooded into villages, accentuating individualism and providing a powerful stimulus to the growth of petty commerce.

In most parts of Southeast Asia, the means through which the village, the mining camp and the plantation were tied to the world economy was the various tiers of Chinese entrepreneurs and middlemen. The wealthiest and most influential of them, men like Loke Yew of Selangor and Oei Tiong Ham of Semarang, enjoyed close working relations with Western capital and government (or with the royal élite in Siam, where they were sometimes ennobled and incorporated into the regional bureaucracy). They operated as tax-farming entrepreneurs through much of the nine-teenth century and thereafter as compradores, collecting and managing goods and business for Western financial and agency institutions and importers and exporters. Some became exceedingly successful independ-ent merchant capitalists in their own right, accumulating vast fortunes in the process: Yap Ah Loy, for example, the Kapitan China of Kuala Lumpur from 1868 to 1885, owned 150 houses in Kuala Lumpur as well as substantial mining and plantation interests. Connected to these men through complex arrangements of credit, and often by kinship and clan links as well, were multiple networks of Chinese agents and petty traders, who carried consumer items and cash into the countryside and exchanged it on exploitative terms for the produce of the hinterland: rice, rubber, tobacco, sugar, abaca. The lowest formal link in the chain was the little Chinese retail store set in the village or small town, its modest appearance contrasting sharply with its vital economic importance, and its every inch crammed with consumer items. These stores (*sari-sari, kedai, toko* were three of the names they went under) provided peasants and workers with credit to finance their crops, replace their tools, and celebrate their festivities, and consumer goods (textiles, metalware, non-local foods) to keep them going. In return, shopkeepers obtained the promise of a later repayment, at substantial interest, on their investment, in the form of either a portion of the harvest or a cash payment. Chinese penetration, indeed, went even lower than the retail store. Peripatetic petty traders visited indigenous periodical markets and even individual village pro-ducers, disbursing goods and credit and collecting produce to pass up the export chain. In this way, local trade came to be dominated by the Chinese.

Explaining Chinese pre-eminence in these aspects of commerce has always been difficult and controversial, all the more so because the vast majority of Chinese in Southeast Asia enjoyed little success of any sort, commercial or otherwise, and were frequently fortunate to escape the experience of Southeast Asia with their lives. Contemporary Western observers customarily attributed Chinese success to such 'inherent' qual-ities as preparedness to endure hard work and discomfort and devious cunning, characteristics in which 'natives' were thought to be seriously deficient. More appropriate explanations, however, look to the social structure and commercial organization of overseas Chinese communities and the long history of Chinese trade with Southeast Asia. Organized in tightly-knit and carefully controlled language, clan and kinship groups, sometimes organized as secret societies and guilds, Chinese communities provided identity and support to both newcomers and old hands. They were a source of capital, credit, connections, labour power and markets. These things, not to mention the patronage Chinese enjoyed from Western and Siamese élites, were the building blocks of Chinese economic predominance. By contrast, indigenous entrepreneurship was fragmented, lacking in capital and commercial links, and often stunted by the forced diversion of the most powerful and able members of indigenous society into colonial bureaucracies; it could offer only the weakest opposition.

Developments in Burma provided something of a contrast to this pattern. On the one hand, domestic agricultural credit was dominated by Chettiars; to their well-established and trusted links with the Western banks and companies who provided them with operating capital, Chettiar moneylending firms coupled a longstanding tradition of expertise in credit provision and bookkeeping, sustained and elaborated by tightly sanctioned family and community networks that passed on their knowledge and business structures generation after generation. On the other hand, however, the Chettiars did not generally involve themselves directly in collecting produce and marketing consumer goods. This was left to the Burmese themselves, usually fuelled by Chettiar credit; despite competition from Indian and Chinese middlemen, they played a major role in the domestic economy as up-country rice millers, paddy brokers and petty commodity merchants, advancing credit, collecting produce, and distributing consumer goods from Indian and Chinese wholesalers to peasant producers.

Slaves, Bondsmen, Coerced and 'Free' Labourers

Notwithstanding the occasional existence of small pockets of early capitalist enterprise and wage and contract labour, such as the use of Chinese workers on canal construction in Siam during the reign of Rama III, the characteristic feature of the way most Southeast Asians organized scarce labour in the early nineteenth century was their preference for slavery and forms of bondage. This probably reached its pinnacle in the Siamese practice of tattooing dependants. Through the course of the nineteenth and early twentieth centuries, albeit gradually and unevenly, both these forms gave way to more 'modern' forms of organization.

Slave trading was abolished in English possessions in 1807; slavery as such was abolished by the Dutch in the Indies from 1860 and by the French in Cambodia in 1884. In Siam, King Chulalongkorn proclaimed a gradual phasing out of the practice in 1874. Slavery's demise, however, was much less a result of legislation (humanely intended or otherwise) than of changing social and political realities across the region. In Java, its decline in the eighteenth century had been partly a consequence of the gradual disappearance of a previously prosperous indigenous commercial class as a result of Dutch economic strangulation; in short, few people could now afford the luxury of maintaining slaves. At the same time, the growth of an impoverished peasantry had devalued the importance of formal slaveholding since, in circumstances of increasing state control, labour could be acquired more readily and cheaply through other means such as labour taxation. In Siam, the major forces at work were perhaps more complex. They involved the presence of large numbers of wage-labouring Chinese; the desire by the royal élite to centralize political control in its hands, a process which required that non-royal élites in both capital and regions be disqualified from independent control of large numbers of what Bangkok now considered to be 'its' subjects; and the need to increase the supply of peasant rice farmers for the purposeful development of rice monoculture, by now the great motor of the Siamese economy. The French reforms in Cambodia were a thinly disguised attempt to destroy the patronage style of Cambodian politics, reduce regional leaders to impotence and dependence, and affirm their own unambiguous control. More generally throughout Southeast Asia, the development of 'law and order' made redundant the services of personal retainers or bodyguards, while with the expansion of economic opportunity, bondage became a less attractive option for peasants. It is notable, however, that where economic and political environments were not conducive to reform—particularly in regions where Western-inspired efforts at centralization and economic development were sporadic or slight, such as the more remote parts of east Borneo and Magindanao in the early twentieth century—slavery stubbornly endured despite sporadic efforts to eradicate it.

Economic development and the elaboration of state control similarly provided conditions for the gradual elimination of the many varieties of traditionally coerced labour, many of which differed only in degree from the styles of slaveholding long practised in Southeast Asia. Where economies were increasingly reliant upon regular peasant production of commodities like rice and sugar, the maintenance of recurrent labour imposts upon peasants constrained them from these productive tasks, and sometimes reinforced their loyalty to provincial élites; it was counterproductive to state revenues and politically dangerous to boot. Moreover, in circumstances where landlessness and impoverishment were growing, as in Java, economic need transformed peasants into reliable wage labourers. Thus it was that, from the last part of the nineteenth century, service demands for the indigenous élite and state corvée labour were gradually phased out in Java, the latter replaced by a head tax. In Siam, the obligation of peasants to provide three months or more of their labour for the king was eliminated in 1899 and a money tax put in its stead. It was, perhaps, for similar reasons that corvée obligations were considerably lower in Cochinchina than in Annam or Tonkin.

It would be wrong, however, to assume that markets and modern state formation definitively and naturally led to the superseding of all forms of 'unfree' labour. As if to demonstrate that the general process of emancipation was not a lineal progressive movement from slavery to the 'freedom' of wage labour, old forms of bonded or coerced labour endured: corvée's abolition in Vietnam came only gradually after 1937, and it continued into the 1930s in the outer islands of the Netherlands East Indies. Moreover, new ones were developed, particularly by Westerners themselves who sought to people labour-scarce plantations with foreign indentured labourers bound under penal contracts to work for three-year periods; indeed, the conditions of such servitude were much harsher than those generally suffered by slaves in early centuries. Outcries occasioned by the revelation of abuses brought formal reform in the shape of a somewhat grudging abandonment of indenture—the British in Malaya abolished Indian indenture in 1910 and Chinese in 1914, while the Dutch legislated to remove its last vestiges in the Indies only in 1942. Despite this, the methods of labour recruitment and control suffered relatively little change. In Malaya, for instance, Chinese indenture was replaced by private recruitment or by the lodging-house system where Chinese could be recruited on arrival—in both cases, the labourer's indebtedness brought him or her under an employer's control rather than just into his employment.

To the end of the colonial period, there was little real evidence of a transition to a system of free wage labour. While opportunities for wage labour expanded greatly—for example, two-thirds of Indochina's rural population relied on some form of wage labour to make ends meet—the characteristics of a bonded society remained. This was evident even within the new and modern environment of the city, flushed with immigrant landless peasants desperate for a livelihood. Workers remained personally attached to agents, managers and foremen who contracted them out as labour gangs; low wages and poor conditions proliferated; the use of debt obligations as a means of direct economic coercion endured; opportunities for vertical or horizontal employment mobility remained limited; ethnic and familial networks determined occupation; and a real wage-labour market refused to emerge. Economies structured along colonial lines could not afford to have it any other way.

Women

Southeast Asian women customarily enjoyed comparatively higher status than those in many other regions of Asia. Even the Chinese-influenced Le legal code of Vietnam, for instance, endorsed a significant measure of property and inheritance rights for females; again, women in central Luzon could inherit, buy, sell and pass on land in their own right. Southeast Asian women did not incur seclusion or separation (with the partial exception of women of high-born class), and enjoyed substantial esteem as carers, organizers, providers, financial managers and spiritual intermediaries within the household and village. It was significant that whatever savings a peasant household might have accumulated were frequently held in the form of female jewellery. Sexual equality was most nearly approached in poorer families where all had to contribute substantially for the unit to survive. Nonetheless, women generally did not approach the status of males. The structured inequality of the sexual division of labour awarded women the major share of domestic duties (cooking, washing, cleaning, spinning and weaving the household's clothing, collecting firewood and water) and a considerable array of tasks outside the home (transplanting and harvesting crops, pounding rice, manufacturing handicrafts, selling and purchasing goods at market). Women were perennially prey to the whims of better-off men, and at times of crisis it was their daughters who were sold off as slaves and prostitutes.

The demands and effects of the period of Western domination affected women in complex and sometimes ambiguous ways. Demeaning attitudes to women allowed Westerners, particularly in the years before their political dominance was complete, to have easy recourse to prostitutes, house servants and concubines. Paradoxically, however, these women frequently achieved substantial influence by exploiting the accidental roles they acquired as cultural mediators of the strange new world encountered by their Western partners. More important than this transitional role, however, was the manner in which Western economic power contrived to change significantly the place of women in the social and domestic order of things.

This transformation was perhaps most marked in the realm of textile production. Colonialism's twin goals were to increase agricultural production from Southeast Asia and to use the region as a market for the products of industrial Europe, machine textiles most of all; these were linked in a mutually supportive and particularly disruptive way as far as women's roles and perceptions were concerned. Clothing for a Southeast Asian family had nearly always been spun and woven by the women of that household: virtually every Western traveller's account of Southeast Asia in the early nineteenth century refers to a loom in every household. Through the later nineteenth century, however, the enormous growth in peasant consumption of cheap European manufactured textiles bit deeply into household production and even into more commercialized textile industries like the remarkably successful enterprise based on Iloilo. Peasants and urbanites were increasingly purchasing cheap European cloth at market rather than weaving it in their own houses. In Java, an early example of the trend, the value of imported textiles rose from 3.8 million guilders in 1830 to 13.1 million guilders ten years later; in Burma by 1930, around three-quarters of the country's textiles were imported, while the nominal value of cotton manufactures imported into Siam rose seven times between 1864 and 1910. Vietnam, where the French established their own manufacturing industry, was the only exception to this pattern.

The key to this development was that the levies and tasks required of peasant societies in general were greatly increased: they included demands on males for corvée or paid labour for infrastructure development; more intensive or extensive cropping or the enhancement of household income in other ways in order to cater for a rapidly growing rural population; and the need to increase agricultural production for the market to pay taxes and buy consumer goods. In these circumstances, female labour could be put to comparatively better use in other tasks than slow and laborious weaving. Women increased their already considerable inputs into domestic agriculture, in part to compensate for male absences; they sought greater income from agricultural labour or petty trade; and they gained employment in the off-farm wage-earning sector (domestic service and factory work were two popular spheres). In other words, in an economic régime where cash was relatively freely available and the terms of trade favoured crop production and ancillary industry, it made better economic sense to the household for women to be employed in these ways.

A similar displacement of women from time-honoured duty, in this case the pounding of rice, occurred with the introduction of mechanical rice milling. This development resulted from improvements in steamship technology as well as the opening of the Suez Canal; the consequent rapid transport allowed rice to be clean milled (making it lighter) and to reach a far-off destination without the risk of spoiling. Thus, while there were just 13 commercial rice mills in Lower Burma in 1869, there were 83 by 1900 and 538 by 1930. The result for women was a considerable contraction of employment in this sphere.

In one scholar's view, displacement of this sort reduced women's social status; it caused something of a deterioration in their cultural identity; and it prejudiced their economic position vis-à-vis men.[20] This is a true assessment, but it over-emphasizes the negative. More and more women were driven by opportunity or need from their domestic milieu of agricultural production and exchange. Pressed hard against the ragged edges of social and economic change, they sought work wherever they could in both formal and informal sectors, often with considerable success. They comprised a surprisingly large proportion of the wage-labour sector, especially in light manufacturing work such as embroidery or cigar rolling where they were deemed to be more reliable, careful, docile and dextrous (and, of course, cheaper) than men, and increasingly in mines and on plantations as well. Yet their income, despite its importance to the household unit, was poor (usually around half that of men) and perceived as ancillary; their status was low, their positions dispensable. The best-paying and most prestigious jobs went to men; as the urban workforce grew and modernized, and as competition for work increased, it seems likely that jobs occupied by women declined in status, conditions and remuneration, and perhaps in number as well. Notwithstanding all this, however, these developments had an incipiently emancipatory flavour. As two (male) Vietnamese Marxists put it in 1938:

> In order to survive, women are now forced to leave families to work in factories and mines. Daily they rub shoulders with men and toil as men do, and thus come to understand their true value. Knowing that they must work to eat, women no longer simply *follow* their fathers and mothers, *follow* their husbands and sons, as though they were in a state of perpetual bondage.[21]

The Sick and the Dead

Before the beginning of the nineteenth century, Westerners were generally highly impressed with the physical well-being of Southeast Asians.[22] Thereafter, they began to comment increasingly unfavourably upon Southeast Asians' health, their lower rates of longevity and their smaller

[20] Norman G. Owen, 'Textile displacement and the status of women in Southeast Asia', in Gordon P. Means, ed., *The Past in Southeast Asia's Present*, Ottawa, 1978.
[21] Cuu Kim Son (Tran Duc Sac) and Van Hue (Pham Van Hao), cited in David G. Marr, *Vietnamese Tradition on Trial, 1920–1945*, Berkeley, 1981, 242.
[22] This section draws substantially on the essays in Norman G. Owen, ed., *Death and Disease in Southeast Asia: Explorations in Social, Medical and Demographic History*, Singapore, 1987.

physical stature. In retrospect, these changing appreciations reveal less about Southeast Asians' health than about rapidly increasing Western vitality. The average age at death for Southeast Asians then and earlier was around twenty-five or thirty years of age; infant and child mortality were certainly very high, and once people had survived past the age of five they could probably expect to reach the age of fifty or fifty-five. Southeast Asians suffered from a wide range of diseases: malaria, typhoid fever, tuberculosis, venereal diseases, and possibly bubonic plague as well. Typical of pre-modern, pre-industrial societies, the most frequent causes of death by illness were infective gastro-intestinal diseases or fevers.

So tenuous a grip on life affected their behaviour in ways one can only surmise: parents' knowledge that many of their children would not survive infancy surely affected fertility patterns, while the relatively short span of years available to most people must have influenced fundamentally their beliefs and how they organized and managed their social and working lives. In general, Southeast Asians attributed diseases to two frequently intertwined causes. The first was personal spiritual forces—spirits, demons, ghosts—which attacked individuals or communities. The second, most common in Vietnam but evident elsewhere as well, was behaviour not in harmony with the preordained order of things. These understandings governed the way Southeast Asians responded to disease; just as they were always ready to seek the causes of their ailments at a variety of levels in a syncretistic way, so this multi-layered approach was carried over into the realm of curing. So, for example, to fend off the horrifying cholera epidemic of 1820 in Bangkok which killed about one-fifth of the city's population, the king proposed a whole series of actions which were meant to cover every contingency: cannons to be fired off all night to frighten away the spirits, special formulas sung and religious processions held to ward them off, and everyone to stop work and engage in merit-making to placate them. Since the proximate variables which could cause illness and death were so numerous, and since they were impossible to identify with any precision, there was no sense of there being a single correct treatment for a particular ailment; people customarily took refuge in a range of different methods to cure themselves, sometimes concurrently, sometimes sequentially—drugs, prayer, holy water, consulting various medical practitioners, adopting a more moral style of behaviour. What helped in one case might not necessarily help in another: in Vietnam, for example, the time at which the sickness or injury occurred was crucial in deciding the outcome and the form of treatment.

The accelerating intrusion of the West in Southeast Asia through the nineteenth century had no directly devastating effect upon the health of the indigenous population, as it did in Australia and Africa. Westerners introduced no new diseases, at least none on a scale to be socially or demographically significant, because Southeast Asia's long involvement in international commerce had already opened it to international disease. On the other side of the ledger, however, Westerners' efforts to improve Southeast Asians' health were unhelpful, with the notable exception of the vaccination campaigns (begun in Java in 1804) which eventually reduced smallpox to an insignificant disease. The Dutch, like the Siamese, had no answer to cholera which was introduced into Java in 1821 and which often had a case mortality of 60 per cent; the best they could come up with was opium-based drinks that were little more than panaceas. American medical therapy was similarly unsuccessful in combating the Philippines cholera epidemic of 1902–4. Indeed, the Western presence probably had damaging indirect effects on health standards. Demands on the subject population's labour and food supplies led in some cases to poverty and malnutrition, and consequently lowered resistance to infection from existing pathogens. Again, the development of infrastructure and the increasing commercialization of agriculture which came with Western-inspired economic growth allowed for the far easier spread of pathogens, particularly to virgin populations which had previously been isolated from them and among whom, consequently, the effects of infection were particularly disastrous. Deforestation for crop production, mining, and public works, as well as the expansion of artificial irrigation, promoted the incidence of malaria. Increased commercial rice milling made polished rice more readily available for non-agricultural workers, and a surge of beri-beri resulted. Finally, the expansion of urban centres provided an extraordinarily unhealthy environment, with cramped and unhygienic housing and insufficient clean water and sanitation; in the first decade of the twentieth century, the death rate among Indonesians in Batavia was 64 per 1000; during epidemics, it went as high as 400 per 1000 in some parts of the city.

For much of the nineteenth century the colonial impact on indigenous health was probably minimal and possibly damaging. In contrast was the period of high colonialism, when Westerners seemed dominant on every front—political, technological, economic. Their sense of superiority, as well as their need for political legitimacy, commonly embodied the notion of a paternalistic duty to look after the people whom they were destined to rule: the application of 'imperial medicine' was one component of this attitude. Imperial medicine was particularly interested in controlling, by medical research and eradication campaigns, the most spectacular manifestations of ill-health, epidemic sicknesses. The continued outbreak of such epidemics was an affront to Western dominance; moreover they had serious economic consequences because they killed so many labourers and rendered so many others incapable of work. A second thrust of imperial medicine was to improve sanitation and general hygiene; by the early twentieth century, significant progress in medical science had brought a recognition of the relationship between environment and disease: between pooled water and malaria, drinking water and cholera, poor sanitation, bare feet and hookworm. A third area of activity was in the training of indigenous doctors, nurses and midwives. However, notwithstanding the establishment of medical schools such as STOVIA (School tot opleiding van inlandsche artsen) in Batavia, the number of people trained was pitiably small; they were generally clustered in the main towns, and socially alien to most of the population; moreover, the medicine they practised was unfamiliar and expensive. In Penang in 1930, there were only fourteen trained midwives for a population of 190,000; Vietnam in

1930 boasted one Vietnamese auxiliary doctor or pharmacist for every 67,000 people; in Lombok in 1931, three qualified doctors served a population of 790,000. A fourth area of activity was to provide routine inspections and medical and educational services. Clinics were established to combat venereal disease. Drug dispensaries were opened in towns to provide medication for the population. In Malaya, a network of infant-welfare centres was established to provide medication and advice for mothers and their children. There were also, of course, hospitals, but where these catered for indigenous people rather than Westerners they were turned to only as a last resort, confirming 'their reputation for burying rather than curing people'.[23]

Overall, the impact of Western medicine in Southeast Asia after the beginning of the twentieth century was mixed. During the influenza pandemic of 1918, which has been described by one author as 'probably the greatest single natural disaster ever to hit this earth',[24] and which killed about 1.5 million Indonesians, Dutch medicine could treat only symptoms and was helpless to control the progress of the disease. In Malaya between 1910 and 1930, half a million people died of malaria, despite great advances in scientific knowledge of the disease's cause. Nonetheless, Western medicine eventually made important strides towards understanding and containing major diseases such as beri-beri, cholera and malaria by vaccines and drugs and better control of the environment. Infant mortality rates, especially the dreadfully high ones encountered in cities, were significantly reduced, at least in some parts of Southeast Asia. Despite these triumphs, the effect on general mortality rates seems to have been limited. As far as morbidity is concerned, one can only guess that its incidence also declined somewhat. One reason for this apparent lack of success was that medical strategies were designed to cure and control rather than to prevent. Imperial medicine was essentially interventionist in character; it sought to stop or control particular manifestations of disease, especially spectacular ones, rather than to change the root conditions which allowed those diseases—as well as 'background' ills like infantile diarrhoea and tuberculosis—to emerge and flourish. A second reason was the lack of appropriate resources in money and personnel. Budgetary constraints on 'welfare' items—except, as on the plantations, where there were obvious and demonstrated connections between spending, health and profit, something that emerged only around 1930—ensured that progress was partial and halting.

Westerners

If numbers alone were the measure, the Western presence in Southeast Asia in this period was insignificant. The development of Westerners' influence and power was at first gradual and finally rapid and comprehensive by the turn of the twentieth century. In contrast, their numbers

[23] Susan Abeyasekere, 'Death and disease in nineteenth century Batavia', in ibid., 199.
[24] Colin Brown, 'The influenza pandemic of 1918 in Indonesia', ibid., 235.

remained proportionately tiny, for instance 0.4 per cent of the total population of the Netherlands East Indies and 0.18 per cent of Indochina's population. A more appropriate indicator of emerging Western dominance—political and economic—was the changing organization of their social existence. In the early and mid-nineteenth century, the West, in those places where it enjoyed at least formal territorial control or substantial commercial influence, was represented not only by stolid grey officialdom but also by a colourful collection of freebooting adventurers, inventive evangelists, romantics, crooks and eccentrics. To get where they needed and obtain what they wanted—and sometimes just to keep their lives and minds in a hostile environment—Westerners had to adapt themselves to the styles and practices of the region. They were obliged to compromise in the face of superior authority and numbers, and to manage and exploit commercial and social structures as they found them. Thus it was with Speedy of Larut or Bozzolo of Upper Perak, not to mention the numerous Scotsmen who proved extraordinarily effective in appreciating and working the Southeast Asian system.

All this changed with the achievement of political supremacy by the new states. Control, once attained, had to be maintained, and this meant the fabrication of a new myth of authority. Thus developed the claim of Westerners to innate cultural, technological and moral superiority over the peoples and societies they ruled; a superiority manifested and sustained by the importance attached to prestige, to 'maintaining standards', to keeping one's proper distance from the subject population. This had numerous important repercussions. It meant the thinning from government service of the flamboyant individualist who disdained accountability, to be replaced by 'properly' organized and standardly trained bureaucrats whose patronizing attitudes and mountainous paperwork often meant they understood 'the native' less intimately than their predecessors. It meant the development of a relatively homogeneous, prosperous and insulated enclave society of Westerners, organized above all around the ritual of the club, where one could 'drop one's guard' without prejudice to prestige. It meant the influx of Western wives (when Western men could afford to take them), a development which itself reinforced the sense of separateness and dominance; where Western men could not afford to support wives, the Asian concubine was replaced by the Asian prostitute, and mestizo culture evaporated under the heat of formal racial separatism. In some places, notably the Netherlands East Indies, it meant that Westerners began to consider the colony as their home rather than a place of sojourn. Most interesting and paradoxical of all, it increased the anxiety and constrained the freedom of action of Westerners, particularly when indigenous voices (mostly Western-educated ones) began feebly questioning the future of Western political dominance; witness the bored, lonely and unsettled lives of wives entrapped by the social and political demands of their environment, and Orwell's police officer who, against his best instincts, felt forced by a hooting crowd of Burmese to shoot the elephant.[25]

[25] George Orwell, 'Shooting an Elephant', in Sonia Orwell and Ian Angus, eds, *The Collected Essays, Journalism and Letters of George Orwell*, London, 1968, I. 235.

The Prosperous, the Poor, and the Underdeveloped

Material prosperity and underdevelopment are not always and necessarily mutually exclusive; in the short term, and in some places on a more permanent basis, colonial-style production frequently brought prosperity to indigenous societies. Thus, despite the demands made on their land, labour and other resources, Javanese peasants who grew sugar for the Dutch under the Cultivation System were considerably better off than they had been before 1830. The extra purchasing power from crop payments and wages served to enhance their commercial contacts beyond the village itself; increasing prosperity expressed itself in expanding purchases of salt and European cloth, in higher levels of consumption of rice and meat, and in a much busier commercial life. Those who grew, harvested and stripped abaca in Kabikolan similarly enjoyed nearly a century of hitherto unknown (though sometimes irregular) prosperity as a result of the rapid growth in demand for cordage fibre in the West. Peasants growing rubber to augment rice cultivation in Malaya or Sumatra profited from new and more regular sources of income. The rolling back of the frontier of lower Burma by Burmese rice smallholders was based on the realization that increased production brought greatly increased prosperity and heightened social mobility.

Nonetheless, at the outbreak of the Japanese war, most Southeast Asians were poor and many of them were falling ever deeper into poverty, losing their land and suffering from a declining availability of foodstuffs. To explain the existence and persistence of poverty, some observers have adumbrated a wealth of cultural inhibitors to economic development among Southeast Asians. These included 'natural slothfulness' or at least passivity; aversion to risk and a parallel need to invest surplus in informal and unproductive social and spiritual insurance; religious strictures on usury and wealth accumulation; and an overwhelming submission to the uncertainties of fate. Explanations of this type, however, beg questions about the origins and endurance of these alleged patterns of behaviour, especially given persistent evidence of Southeast Asians' enthusiastic responses to material incentive in colonial times, not to mention the zest with which they have recently taken to capitalism.

The key to Southeast Asian poverty lies rather in the fact that the widespread prosperity engendered by Western-inspired economic growth did not lead to fundamental structural change in the economies and societies of the region. Of those Southeast Asians who profited from investment in crop production or mining, few showed much interest in converting their wealth into upward social mobility or radically different varieties of economic pursuit. Those who succeeded in these activities— sometimes making extraordinary fortunes—did not have the political power nor probably the desire to change or develop the structure of the economy. However, the peculiar structure and nature of production was in its essence inimical to the longer-term interests and prosperity of the vast majority of Southeast Asians.

There were two mutually reinforcing components in this scheme of things. The first was that Southeast Asia's comparative advantage in the

international economy lay in the production of a narrow range of unpro-
cessed or simply processed raw materials: rice, sugar, tin, coal, oil, rubber,
timber, fibre, tobacco; moreover the particular comparative advantage of
each component state tended to narrow the range of goods produced even
more severely. Economies structured in this way were highly susceptible
to damaging cyclical price fluctuations: partly because of the relative ease
with which competition from other sources of supply could be mounted,
and partly because they depended on the health and needs of the more
developed economies which purchased their goods. Such was the trend
endured from the late nineteenth century onwards: depression in the
1880s and 1890s, recovery in the decade after 1900, the disruption of World
War I, a short-lived boom, and a downward spiral into the Great Depression. To make things worse, superimposed on this picture was a general
downturn in the international terms of trade for these commodities from
the early twentieth century onwards. For the same general reasons, these
forms of production did not have the capacity to provide long-term
expanding profits for their producers or investors. They were also constantly subject to supersession: sometimes for economic reasons, like the
expanding world production of cheaper forms of fibre, replacing Bikol
abaca; sometimes at the whim of fashion, as in the Western preference for
cigarettes rather than cigars wrapped in Deli's exquisite leaf.

Consequently, investors, both indigenous and foreign, sought to outlay
as little as possible in fixed capital and to recover it from profits with the
utmost rapidity. Where production was based around elaborating existing
systems of peasant labour organization—for example rice in lower Burma
or on the Mekong delta, or sugar in Java and central Luzon, rubber
smallholding in Malaya and Sumatra—it settled into static forms that
depended upon an increasingly intensive exploitation of those labour-
intensive and poorly capitalized systems. Investors devoted their attention
to increasing the size of the pie (through lateral extension of cropping) and
their slice of it (through increasing rents and crop shares) without building
up any substantial long-term flexibility or self-sustaining capacity. Technology, as in the introduction of steam-driven centrifugal sugar mills,
steam rice milling or the application of the results of scientific research on
agriculture, was meant to make the prevailing systems of production more
efficient rather than raising production to a new and higher plane. The
admittedly beneficial spin-offs from this development in the form of small-
scale ancillary industries—transport, machine shops, packaging—were
similarly elaborations on an existing theme. This meant, of course, that
once the structural limits of this method of production were reached,
peasant welfare inevitably nose-dived. This happened when, for example,
reclaimable land began to run out or became more marginal, or the number
of residents seeking employment increased rapidly, or irrigation systems
decayed, or prices fell abruptly.

The second and more important component, of course, was that these
were Western-dominated economies. They were, in the last analysis,
intended for the benefit of the metropolitan power and its allied interests.
Improved prosperity was available and obtainable for Southeast Asians if
its pursuit did not collide substantially with the economic interests of the

metropolitan state. The colonized status of Southeast Asia's economies manifested itself in various ways. One was the 'colonial drain', repatriating profits from entrepreneur investments (these were estimated at $US3007 million in 1930) which might otherwise have been reinvested in productive enterprise. A variation of this, especially in the Philippines, was the diversion of wealth to an indigenous entrepreneurial class which invested in conspicuous consumption, and there was also the repatriation of earnings by sojourning Chinese and Indian labourers. A second was taxation systems which bore most heavily upon poorer indigenous classes, effectively subsidizing the Western sector of the economy. Yet another was policy decisions which discriminated against peasant enterprise, such as banning smallholder sugar production for Western factories in Java in 1923 because of the threat it was seen to pose to the Western-controlled industry; or casting the major burden of lowering production on to smallholders in the Malayan rubber restriction of the 1920s ('a total sell-out of peasant interests',[26] according to one writer); or regulating to prevent smallholders growing tobacco in the vicinity of the east Sumatra plantations. Peasant production could survive side by side with Western capitalist enterprise while economies grew and while there was still slack to be exploited, but it was immediately dispensable if it competed too well. A fourth manifestation of the colonial nature of such economies was the introduction of harmful tariffs. Those in French Indochina served to subsidize metropolitan manufacturers at the expense of the indigenous population; Indochina imported more goods from France and its other colonial possessions than any other country. United States tariffs discouraged Americans from investing in Philippines processing industries. A fifth manifestation was the pattern of domestic expenditure. Characteristically this invested heavily in sustaining the state (bureaucratic expansion to control and tax the population, transport inputs for defence purposes) and servicing the existing economic structure (ports, roads, railways for the transit of export goods) rather than productively investing in education, manufacturing or the technology of peasant agricultural production such as seeds, fertilizers and irrigation. This was perhaps most notable in Siam where the élite saw little short-term personal gain from such improvements. Colonialism and colonial-style production were organized to perpetuate the circumstances which made it profitable, not to ensure an economically independent and sustainable future for the indigenous population. Under these circumstances, even such well-intentioned efforts to 'protect' Southeast Asians from the effects of economic change as the Malay Reservations Act of 1913 served rather to confirm their status as poor, dependent and peripheral.

THE GREAT DEPRESSION

Since about the middle of the nineteenth century, the economic life of the Southeast Asian colonies and Siam had been structured around supplying

---

[26] Lim Teck Ghee, *Peasants and Their Agricultural Economy*, 144.

food and raw produce to world markets; the wealth that had accrued to those in charge had been a function of their ability to sell these products on world markets at profitable prices. This unsophisticated and undiversified structure had survived numerous crises visited upon it by the vagaries of the world market, but these were as nothing compared to the Great Depression, which devastated the markets of virtually all the products upon which Southeast Asia's economies were based. World commodity prices tumbled: the average wholesale price of Java sugar fell from 13.66 guilders per quintal in 1929 to 9.60 guilders in 1930, reaching a low of 5.61 guilders in 1934; rice prices in Cochinchina declined from 7.15 piastres per quintal in 1929 to 1.88 piastres in 1934; rubber prices on the London market from 10.25 pence per pound to 2.3 pence between 1929 and 1932. Thus the value of exports—the economic lifeblood of the colonies—declined precipitously in the years after 1929. In the Federated Malay States, the value of rubber exports fell from 202 million Straits dollars in 1929 to 37 million in 1932; in the same period, the value of tin and tin-ore exports dropped from 117 million dollars to 31 million. The value of Indochina's rubber exports fell from 62 million francs in 1930 to 27 million in 1932. In the Netherlands East Indies, the value of agricultural exports declined from 1237 million guilders in 1928 to 294 million by 1935. The Philippines, protected by its special access to American markets, avoided the worst effects of the slump until the United States imposed import quotas on Philippines commodities in the mid-1930s.

Declining exports seriously affected the revenues and activities of the colonial states and Siam. The state revenues of the Federated Malay States and the Netherlands East Indies, for instance, were roughly halved between 1929 and 1932, as was the size of the general budget of Indochina. Nevertheless, governments were initially unaware of the seriousness of the situation, and were generally slow to react. It was only when it became clear that this depression was something entirely new in both its severity and its duration that governments began seriously to cast about for solutions. In the economic area, the main thread of their efforts involved attempts to protect their primary-product export industries so as to ensure their survival. This meant joining world-wide schemes such as the Chadbourne Plan for sugar and the International Rubber Regulation Agreement which sought to limit production and thereby raise prices. These measures were largely successful in their aims, but they could do little more than provide long-term solutions to problems that were being immediately felt, especially as government expenditures could not at once be cut back proportionately. In some cases, indeed, colonial policies exacerbated problems caused by the Great Depression. The Indies government, for example, in deference to the policies of the metropolitan government, steadfastly refused to devalue its currency until 1936 and had to compete for declining markets with nations which had devalued much earlier.

Private commercial concerns suffered even more severely; because they could not sell their products, or could sell them only at ridiculously low prices, their incomes virtually disappeared. As a result, many companies were simply wiped out; in Java, only 45 of the 179 Western sugar factories continued to operate, while the area planted to cane fell from 200,831 hectares in 1931 to 27,578 in 1935. Some enterprises were more fortunate than others; in Indochina, rubber companies received large doses of aid from the government to see them through their problems. Through the region, most companies managed to survive, usually by cutting back heavily on their costs of production. In the Malayan rubber industry, for example, more effective machinery and higher-yielding plants were introduced, the number of expensive European supervisors cut back, wages, salaries and commissions reduced; by 1932, the costs of the highest-cost producers were only five-eighths of those of the lowest-cost producers in 1929. Operating costs on east Sumatra's rubber plantations were halved between 1928 and 1932 by increasing the efficiency of tapping systems and rubber processing.

The effects of this reduced activity, reduced income, and the range of economizing and support measures struck at every level of Southeast Asian society. The number of Western government officials was reduced (in the Malayan civil service, for instance, from 270 in 1929 to 213 in 1935); further recruitment was stopped; and salaries were reduced sometimes by as much as 25 per cent. Companies were much more ruthless in cutting costs than government; in Malaya, between 30 and 40 per cent of the planting community was retrenched between 1930 and 1933, while half the 1700 European employees on east Sumatra's plantations were dismissed. These people were repatriated or, alternatively, provided with government or community support to prevent them falling into a penury that might prejudice Western prestige. Indigenous employees of government bureaucracies and private companies also suffered significant wage cuts and severe levels of retrenchment. Where those dismissed were able to find work, it was often far beneath their accustomed station; many were forced to return to the countryside from which they had originated. Paradoxically, those who retained salaried employment—usually more senior and experienced men—often prospered because the cost of living fell much more quickly and precipitately than their salaries: the real income of Filipino civil servants, for instance, doubled between 1929 and 1932. Their spending power sometimes manifested itself in countercyclical booms in spheres like the construction industry. The income differential between such people and the bulk of the population increased markedly in these years. It was also true that some indigenous workers moved up the social scale as they replaced more expensive Western or Chinese employees in bureaucratic and service industries.

Non-Western unsalaried employees did much less well, although the extent of their impoverishment has probably been overstated. Most regular wage labourers were employed in mines and plantations. Those not under indenture were the first victims of retrenchment. In Malaya between 1930 and 1932, nearly 200,000 Indians and 50,000 Chinese plantation workers were repatriated at the cost of the Federated Malay States government. Moreover, poor employment prospects led many foreign labourers to leave the country voluntarily. All told, more than 240,000 more South Indians left Penang (the port of arrival and departure for Indians) than arrived between 1930 and 1933, and between 1931 and 1933, nearly a quarter of a million more Chinese left Singapore than arrived. Between

1930 and 1934, the number of estate workers in east Sumatra fell from 336,000 to 160,000, with most of those dismissed repatriated to Java. Those who remained on such enterprises, whether 'free' or indentured, had to make do with wages which gradually fell to half those of 1929, reduced working hours and sometimes even unemployment: the wages paid to non-Europeans on east Sumatran tobacco plantations, for instance, fell from 29.4 million guilders in 1929 to 10 million guilders in 1934. Their struggle to make ends meet was eased by the fact that the cost of living also dropped appreciably—in some places and times to half its pre-depression level—but many still had families to feed in circumstances where there was little or no ancillary work for wives and children. They took up substitute activities to see them through—fishing, hunting, or cultivation of rice and vegetable crops to provide extra sources of food and income, often on urban outskirts or on allotments made available by the plantations.

The years of depression brought two important changes in the social composition of plantation and mine labourers. The first was the development of a much more balanced sex ratio. In Malaya, for instance, where there were 225 Chinese men for every 100 Chinese women in 1931, by 1939 the ratio was 144 to 100. The change sprang partly from ordinances that restricted the inflow of male Chinese from 1933 but left female immigration untouched until 1938; moreover, unemployed females were not repatriated. Foreign workers who had refused repatriation began to think of themselves as permanent residents of Malaya, and sent for their wives to join them. In Sumatra's plantation belt, a similar trend towards more equal sex ratios was evident, reflected in a more family-oriented style of residential accommodation; this was a response, perhaps, to the decline of indenture and the consequent need for plantations to establish a permanent retinue of settled workers rather than transient, difficult labourers. The second aspect of change was the rapid decline in indentured service in those areas where this form of recruitment was still practised. Whereas 76 per cent of labourers on east Sumatran plantations had been indentured in 1929, all but 7 per cent were 'free workers' by 1934.

Smallholder producers had periodically prospered from the rapid growth in international demand, especially in industrial produce. By 1929, 41 per cent of the Netherlands East Indies' rubber output came from smallholders, as did 96 per cent of its kapok, 45 per cent of its tobacco, 73 per cent of its coffee, and 22 per cent of its tea. Everywhere, however, the depression cut deeply into incomes from cash cropping. Where small-holders competed for markets with Western plantation agriculture, legislation restricting production burdened peasants much more than the estates, leaving them few options to sustain their incomes. Even where ecological conditions were favourable for it, there was no point in smallholders trying to diversify their cropping patterns because the prices available for the whole range of cash crops were disastrously low; in the absence of alternatives, many continued to produce their accustomed cash crops at high levels despite crashing prices. In the great rice-producing deltas, the depression served to confirm and entrench existing modes of life. In Cochinchina, the rapid drop in rice prices after 1929 affected landlords just as it did peasants. Landlords themselves were usually large users of credit from urban rice markets and moneylenders; they had commitments to meet, and the only way they could meet them was by reducing production costs and increasing production. They dismissed large numbers of wage labourers and cut the wages of those who remained: perhaps as many as 40 per cent of the wage labour force was sacked, and the salaries of employed workers were halved in the first few years of depression. The result was that half a million hectares of rice land remained uncultivated in 1934. Despite this, the amount of rice exported actually rose during the depression, a reflection of more exploitative collection of produce by landlords. Such pressures served also to accelerate the existing trend towards land alienation and concentration, and the growth of a substantial tenanted class. In lower Burma, too, the most obvious sign of rural distress was the huge climb in the rate of land alienation. The proportion of land held by non-agriculturalists climbed from 31 per cent in 1930 to nearly 50 per cent by 1935; Chettiar moneylenders, previously keen to eschew landholding in favour of liquid capital, controlled 25 per cent of lower Burma's cropped area by 1937. Many of those who lost their land took up as tenants, just as conditions were making tenancy increasingly insecure. Tenants owned nothing of substance and depended for their survival on the flow of credit; unable to service debts with rapidly falling rice prices, they were frequently forced from their holdings which landlords rented out to new tenants under much harsher conditions. Landless labourers found themselves competing for an ever-shrinking number of jobs. According to one estimate, rice consumption in Burma fell by nearly 25 per cent in these years as the amount of rice exported grew at the expense of the domestic consumption. In contrast to these dislocating developments on the Mekong and Irrawaddy deltas, distress and deprivation were much less evident in Siam's central plain. As we have seen, the pace of expansion in rice cultivation had been much slower because of a relative lack of capital and a less elaborate and formal credit network. The factors of production in the rice economy, particularly land, remained relatively undeveloped and there was, accordingly, much more slack: there were many more options which could be exploited at times of need.

Java's situation was somewhat different from the previous cases because, by the twentieth century, peasant participation in the export economy was much less direct than in, say, Burma or Malaya where an owner or cultivator could sell the product of his labour for cash. Few Javanese peasants produced export goods for sale on their own initiative and sold them to middlemen; their involvement with export cropping, large though it was, was mediated through the Western-controlled economy where foreigners initiated and directed the productive process. Under such circumstances, peasants for the most part were dependent servants of Western enterprise rather than active participants in the colonial economy itself; they had, then, little or no control over their fates when the Great Depression hit. Their situation was made all the worse by the fact that Java's domestic economy (as distinct from its export economy) was already stretched critically tight. Rapidly increasing population and a declining availability of land had pushed ever larger numbers of people out of the village in search of either full-time or part-time employment; increasingly, peasant society was unable fully to support all the people it produced, and Western agricultural enterprise had come to sustain large numbers of them. Java's sugar industry, for example, provided permanent employment for tens of thousands of Javanese, and seasonal and temporary employment for three-quarters of a million of them, as well as providing huge sums for land rental. Income from such sources had provided a level of welfare which would not otherwise have been available. Its virtual removal in the depression years (payments for land rental and wages by the sugar industry declined from 129.6 million guilders in 1929 to 10.2 million in 1936) cast the Javanese back on already inadequate domestic resources. There was, however, little sign of the increasing land polarization evident elsewhere, in part because of the peculiar structure of rural credit in Java. The general pattern of peasant adaptation was a significant intensification of domestic agriculture. Peasants expanded the area under cultivation (partly by utilizing the substantial areas previously under Western export crops, particularly sugar) and, more important, they used available land much more intensively: the cropping ratio of wet-rice land increased from 1.31 in 1928 to 1.41 in 1937, while dryfield cropping was substantially elaborated. The employment this generated within villages, together with shifts in the allocation of village labour, helped to absorb most of the people released from Western enterprises.

Later episodes like the subsistence crises of 1944–5 in the Philippines and Vietnam were probably more troubled and painful for their victims than the years of depression; there were, moreover, significant regional variations in the degrees of hardship suffered through the early 1930s. Overall, however, it was a time of considerable distress for rural Southeast Asians, with widespread unemployment or underemployment, a substantial decline in the amount and quality of food available for consumption, and a general fall in living standards. The latter was expressed in terms of reduced expenditures on leisure, religious and other celebrations, non-consumables, and travel, and perhaps even a decline in marriages. While all were exposed to difficulties, the poor were hit hardest. According to one estimate from Indochina, landless wage labourers and those who had land but were forced to seek occasional wage work, often far from home, made up two-thirds of the rural population and 'form[ed] a miserable mass of workers who only satisfy their hunger at the time of plentiful work or during the harvest'.[27] Hardship bred frustration which often vented itself in crime and banditry and, in Burma, communal violence against Indians.

CONCLUSION

By the late 1930s, Southeast Asia was showing signs of severe strain. The duration and intensity of the Great Depression had made manifest in the clearest terms the unsophisticated, narrow, structurally stagnant and

---

[27] Rene Bunout, cited in Murray, 615.

dependent nature of the region's economies. In the Western-dominated drive to integrate them into international circuits of commerce, they had been cast as pliant invalids; the great majority of Southeast Asians who relied on them were left with their livelihoods compromised. In this scheme of things, they could be sustained only so long as Western-inspired export production supported them, and when that support evaporated in the years of depression the restricted and unbalanced nature of their relationship with the global economy became clear.

Meanwhile, other structural flaws were appearing. The economic development of Japan in the commercial life of Southeast Asia, with its genuine industrial capability, its ability to produce cheap goods of reasonable quality such as textiles and bicycles, its aggressive marketing, and its unpegged yen, served notice that Western control of imports was no longer assured. By 1934, Japan had outstripped Europe as a supplier of imports to the Netherlands East Indies, holding nearly a one-third share of that sector. In the context of the Great Depression, and in the face of Japanese and other commercial infiltration, the long-held dogma of free trade was coming under severe attack. In the Indies, this first exhibited itself in the creation of regulations in 1933 to control the import of rice into Java and, later, into other parts of the colony; this was an attempt to stop the Indies being used as a dumping ground for surplus Asian rice and to upgrade the Indies' rice production capability by keeping prices at relatively high levels. The measures, however, soon extended to protection against Japanese manufactures such as cement, cloth, utensils and light industrial products. The French in Indochina and the British also had recourse to similar policies.

Hand in hand with this development, the notion that colonial possessions were not just convenient appendages for the metropolitan powers was also gaining strength. The Great Depression had brought home with some urgency that the interests of mother country and colony were not necessarily identical, and that the commercial needs of the former could have serious detrimental effects upon the economy of the latter. Indeed, the Governor-General of Indochina was moved to remark in 1937 that 'it is impossible to conceive that Indochina should remain forever in a state of economic vassalage, under the pretext that it must not compete with French products either in France or at home'.[28] The experience of the depression had shown how the subservience of colonies to metropolitan interests had left their economies with dangerously limited bases, and thus exposed to socially devastating conditions over which the colonies themselves had no control. Thus, the need to diversify activities by moving away from a concentration on the provision of food crops and raw industrial materials to the development of a more elaborate industrial base became more thoroughly accepted. Among the most spectacular examples of this was the extraordinary growth of the west Java weaving industry in the mid- and late 1930s: it made use of vastly improved mechanical and handlooms (the numbers of handlooms in use grew from 500 in 1930 to 35,000 in 1940), it employed huge numbers of women in factory and

---

[28] Cited in Joseph Buttinger, *Vietnam: A Dragon Embattled*, London, 1967, I. 185.

(part-time) cottage industry, and it produced four-fifths of the Indies' needs in woven sarongs.

Where this pattern might have led is impossible to know, for the age of colonialism in Southeast Asia had nearly run its course. Over the previous century and a half, in the context of revolutionary changes in the world's economic and social order, Southeast Asia had been thoroughly transformed by its incorporation into the emerging global system of commerce. Around 1800 its physical resources and environment were pristine, their value unrealized and barely exploited; its people, small in number, diverse in culture, were scattered among innumerable polities of varying sophistication and uneven economic stature. By 1940, there was a wholly new Southeast Asia. It was fixed fast to global commerce. Its polities were simplified according to the centripetal pattern of the modern nation-state while subservient to more powerful Western states. Its economies were organized to reflect this new conception and distribution of power. Its demographic, cultural and ecological patterns were irreversibly altered, frequently in detrimental or dislocating ways. The ambiguous and often contradictory legacies of these years of elemental change guaranteed that succeeding generations of Southeast Asians would face a trying and combative future.

BIBLIOGRAPHIC ESSAY

Most general studies that discuss this period, such as D. G. E. Hall, *A History of South-East Asia*, London, 1955, John F. Cady, *Southeast Asia: Its Historical Development*, New York, 1964, and, the best and most stimulating of them, David J. Steinberg, ed., *In Search of Southeast Asia: A Modern History*, New York, 1971, rev. edn, 1987, are showing their age. There are numerous country studies of varying quality, including M. C. Ricklefs, *A History of Modern Indonesia*, London, 1981; Barbara W. Andaya and Leonard Andaya, *A History of Malaysia*, New York, 1982; David Joel Steinberg, *The Philippines: A Singular and a Plural Place*, Boulder, 1982; David P. Chandler, *A History of Cambodia*, Boulder, 1983; David K. Wyatt, *Thailand: A Short History*, New Haven, 1984: they provide useful introductions, but their concerns are mostly political rather than economic or social. Until quite recently, the dearth of serious research on the history of social and economic change meant continuing reliance on such classics as J. S. Furnivall, *Netherlands India: A Study of Plural Economy*, Cambridge, UK, 1944; Charles Robequain, *The Economic Development of French Indo-China*, London, 1944; J. Russell Andrus, *Burmese Economic Life*, Stanford, 1948; James C. Ingram, *Economic Change in Thailand since 1850*, Stanford, 1955; G. C. Allen and Audrey G. Donnithorne, *Western Enterprise in Indonesia and Malaya*, London, 1957; and G. William Skinner, *Chinese Society in Thailand: An Analytical History*, Ithaca, 1957.

Over the last couple of decades, progress has been made on a number of fronts using different techniques of analysis to uncover or reinterpret Southeast Asia's experience. One popular approach has been the analysis of a specific industry or crop and of the ways it influenced those who serviced its various needs. Important works of this sort include Wong Lin Ken, *The Malayan Tin Industry to 1914*, Tucson, 1965; Cheng Siok-Hwa, *The Rice Industry of Burma: 1852–1940*, Kuala Lumpur, 1968; Michael Adas, *The Burma Delta: Economic Development and Social Change on an Asian Rice Frontier, 1852–1941*, Madison, 1971; John Drabble, *Rubber in Malaya 1876– 1922: The Genesis of the Industry*, Kuala Lumpur, 1973; Ed. C. de Jesus, *The Tobacco Monopoly in the Philippines: Bureaucratic Enterprise and Social Change, 1766–1880*, Quezon City, 1980; R. E. Elson, *Javanese Peasants and the Colonial Sugar Industry: Impact and Change in an East Java Residency, 1830–1940*, Singapore, 1984; and Norman G. Owen, *Prosperity without Progress: Manila Hemp and Material Life in the Colonial Philippines*, Quezon City, 1984. Often closely allied to this approach has been regional history, allowing closer and often more fruitful investigation of social relations than national- or industry-level studies permit. Stimulating examples of this are John A. Larkin's classic, *The Pampangans*, Berkeley, 1972; James Francis Warren, *The Sulu Zone*, Singapore, 1981; Shaharil Talib, *After Its Own Image: The Trengganu Experience 1881–1941*, Singapore, 1984; and the summaries of regional research contained in Alfred W. McCoy and Ed. C. de Jesus, eds, *Philippine Social History*, Quezon City, 1982. Another popular object of analysis, encouraged by the desire to write 'Asia-centric' history and to enquire into Southeast Asian poverty as well as to draw out the poorly documented fates of the bulk of the region's people, has been the notion of 'peasant'; work in that area has led to spirited controversy, initiated in particular by James C. Scott's *The Moral Economy of the Peasant*, New Haven, 1976, and extended by Samuel Popkin's *The Rational Peasant: The Political Economy of Rural Society in Vietnam*, Berkeley, 1977, and numerous other commentaries: for example, a symposium on 'Peasant Strategies in Asian Societies: Moral and Rational Economic Approaches', JAS 42, 4 (1983). For similar reasons, there have been important developments in urban studies: Alfred McCoy's work on Iloilo (summarized in *Philippine Social History*); John Ingleson, *In Search of Justice: Workers and Unions in Colonial Java, 1908–1926*, Singapore, 1986; James Francis Warren, *Rickshaw Coolie: A People's History of Singapore*, Singapore, 1986; and Daniel P. Doepper's fascinating study of career trajectories in *Manila: 1900–1941: Social Change in a Late Colonial Metropolis*, Quezon City, 1984. Notable, too, in this context, is David G. Marr's study of Vietnamese intellectual life in the early twentieth century, *Vietnamese Tradition on Trial, 1920–1945*, Berkeley, 1981. Related questions of population growth, mobility and morbidity have been discussed in Norman G. Owen, ed., *Death and Disease in Southeast Asia: Explorations in Social, Medical and Demographical History*, Singapore, 1987.

Other work has focused on changing bureaucratic structure as a key to understanding changing conceptions of power and hierarchy, perhaps most revealingly in Heather Sutherland, *The Making of a Bureaucratic Elite: The Colonial Transformation of the Javanese Priyayi*, Singapore, 1979, and 'The Taming of the Trengganu Elite', in Ruth T. McVey, ed., *Southeast Asian Transitions: Approaches through Social History*, New Haven, 1978, and also in Alexander B. Woodside, *Vietnam and the Chinese Model: A Comparative Study of Vietnamese and Chinese Government in the First Half of the Nineteenth Century*, Cambridge, Mass., 1971; Onghokham, 'The Inscrutable and the Paranoid: An Investigation into the Sources of the Brotodiningrat Affair', in *Southeast Asian Transitions*; Jan Breman, *The Village on Java and the Early Colonial State*, Rotterdam, 1980; Jean Gelman Taylor, *The Social World of Batavia: European and Eurasian in Dutch Asia*, Madison, 1983; Akin Rabibhadana, *The Organization of Thai Society in the Early Bangkok Period, 1872–1873*, Ithaca, 1969; and Constance M. Wilson, 'The Nai Kong in Thai Administration, 1824–68', *Contributions to Asian Studies* 15 (1980).

Changing labour, ethnic or gender relations in the context of broader economic transformations have been explored in Edgar Wickberg, *The Chinese in Philippine Life: 1859–1898*, New Haven, 1965; K. S. Sandhu, *Indians in Malaya: Immigration and Settlement, 1786–1957*, Cambridge, UK, 1969; John Butcher, *The British in Malaya 1880–1941: The Social History of a European Community in Colonial South-East Asia*, Kuala Lumpur, 1979; Ann Laura Stoler, *Capitalism and Confrontation in Sumatra's Plantation Belt, 1870–1979*, New Haven, 1985; and numerous articles by G. R. Knight, including 'Peasant Labour and Capitalist Production in Late Colonial Indonesia: The 'Campaign' at a North Java Sugar Factory, 1840–70', JSEAS, 19, 2 (1988). Dependency theories and structural varieties of Marxist thought have encouraged study of the organization of production; apart from Martin J. Murray's monumental *The Development of Capitalism in Colonial Indochina (1870–1940)*, Berkeley, 1980, this strand has been particularly noticeable in work on Thailand, such as Chattip Nartsupha and Suthy Prasartset, eds, *The Political Economy of Siam, 1851–1910*, Bangkok, 1981, and Hong Lysa, *Thailand in the Nineteenth Century: Evolution of the Economy and Society*, Singapore, 1984. More recently, attempts to understand the region as a dynamic and interconnected whole and to establish a firmer understanding of the transformative role of the state have led to the analysis of revenue collection and farming as analytical devices; notable pioneering works include Carl Trocki, *Prince of Pirates: The Temenggongs and the Development of Johor and Singapore*, Singapore, 1979; James R. Rush, 'Social Control and Influence in 19th Century Indonesia: Opium Farms and the Chinese of Java', *Indonesia*, 35 (1983); John Butcher, 'The Demise of the Revenue Farming System in the Federated Malay States', MAS, 17, 3 (1983); and Ian Brown, *The Elite and the Economy in Siam, c. 1890–1920*, Singapore, 1988. Invaluable sets of statistics have been published in the series of W. M. F. Mansvelt and P. Creutzberg, eds, *Changing Economy in Indonesia*, since continued by other scholars, and Constance M. Wilson, *Thailand: A Handbook of Historical Statistics*, Boston, 1983.

CHAPTER

4

RELIGION AND ANTI-COLONIAL MOVEMENTS

The period from the mid-nineteenth to the early twentieth centuries in Southeast Asia was one of increased turmoil concomitant with intensified European penetration, political consolidation by the dominant states, and the economic transformation of the countryside. European records of this period evidence a multitude of resistance movements, popular rebellions, acts of insubordination and other assertions on the part of the colonial 'other'. Since wars and rebellions have always been the stuff of which traditional histories have been written, it should be of no surprise that many of the charismatic leaders and their movements in the present study have already been mentioned in the general histories of Southeast Asia. But, in general, they have not been treated in their own terms; they figure as momentary interruptions of the grand sagas of colonial conquest, nationalism, modernization or state construction. In colonial records these phenomena are simply 'disturbances', sometimes 'aberrations', their perpetrators reduced to the status of dacoits or fanatics often led by crazed monks, popes, and prophets. Post-colonial writers, on the other hand, have appropriated such movements for their narratives of nationalist opposition to colonial rule.

More recently, such movements have been viewed as primitive precursors of modern, more successful, sociopolitical movements. Harry Benda must be credited with establishing a hierarchy of types that has provided subsequent scholars with a persuasive means of classifying the otherwise confusing and regionally-diverse data. The most primitive form of peasant movement, of which the 1890s Samin movement in Java is cited as an example, is characterized as rural-based, backward-looking, lacking organization, spontaneous and irrational. The most advanced are urban-based, progressive, organized, and consciously political. Benda points to the 1930s Sakdal movement in central Luzon as gearing towards the latter form since it had an educated, nationalist leader and a party structure, as well as a distinct independence goal.[1]

The evolutionary perspective that has been brought to bear on the nineteenth-century peasant unrest already knows the end-point—modern movements—toward which they were presumably 'groping'. What this

[1] Harry J. Benda, 'Peasant movements in colonial Southeast Asia', in *Continuity and Change in Southeast Asia*, New Haven: Yale University Southeast Asia Studies Monograph Series no. 18, 1972, 221–35.

perspective does is to bring these movements into line with a theory of human emancipation and social change, rather than enable us to listen to them and give them their due. The concept of 'millenarianism', it must not be forgotten, was developed during the era of high colonialism when cargo cults and the like were reduced to irrational and ultimately subhuman forms in order to suppress them more easily.[2]

Rather than reduce diversity and difference to general types like 'primitive', 'millenarian', and the like, our task ought to be the pursuit of the different meanings of such concepts in different contexts. Instead of merely classifying peasant movements and reducing them to techniques for coping with the hardships of life, we might ask how they were informed by thought: their shapes of the future, notions of community, and perceptions of change and leadership. Here is where religions can be seen to function as crucial matrices for peasants' interpretations of their experience.

In many of these stirrings from the countryside, religion can be seen to have provided both a language for articulating discontent and the social forms for mobilizing adherents against their perceived enemies. By 'religion' we do not mean an unchanging corpus of key doctrines and practices or the classical statements that define a particular belief-system. Once implanted in Southeast Asia, the universalizing faiths became localized as Thai, Filipino, Vietnamese, or whatever. Core doctrines entered into play with older local preoccupations, such as ancestor worship, invulnerability magic, healing, worship of village and mountain spirits, and ideas of power. Furthermore, as these localized religions functioned in popular movements they were already readings 'from below' in line with the material and symbolic interests of the subordinate classes. A distinction should be made between official interpretations of religion that tend to emphasize the fatedness, immutability or unchangeability of the social order, and popular views that acknowledge the possibility of change and reversal in the social order.[3] Images of ordered Southeast Asian hierarchies and state systems are presented in officially-sanctioned monuments and documents, but these must be seen as constructions posited and consolidated in relation to potentially subversive millennial and utopian visions.

The millennial strains inherent in the various dominant religions of Southeast Asia produced not just a counterculture, but a counterstructure as well to the dominant polities. The possibility of interpretations involving the subversion of the existing order is inherent in the doctrines and traditions themselves. The processes of localization and assimilation by subordinate groups have led to certain, often minor, themes in these religions coming into play at times of rebellion, or being built up by cult and sect leaders into an ideological or ritual system that was perceived to

---

[2] Benedict R. Anderson, 'Millenarianism and the Saminist movement', in *Religion and Social Ethos in Indonesia*, Clayton, 1977, 48–9.

[3] See James C. Scott, *Weapons of the Weak: Everyday Forms of Peasant Resistance*, New Haven, 1985, 332–4; Reynaldo C. Ileto, *Pasyon and Revolution: Popular Movements in the Philippines, 1840–1910*, Quezon City, 1979, ch. 1; Andrew Turton, 'Limits of ideological domination and the formation of social consciousness', in Turton and Shigeharu Tanabe, eds, *History and Peasant Consciousness in South East Asia*, Osaka: National Museum of Ethnology, 1984, 63–5.

threaten the legitimacy of the state or the official interpretations of the faith. The sects and movements that will be discussed here should be viewed as emanating from traditions perhaps less visible but no less vibrant than dominant, state-sponsored ones. In view of the difficulty in obtaining or comprehending statements from within the movements themselves in such a broad study as this, there are bound to be obvious disparities in the depths to which we can take our discussions of individual movements and regions. It is thus important to keep in mind the above-mentioned perspectives which are being brought to bear on the subject, despite the limitations of the sources.

THE RELIGIO-POLITICAL LANDSCAPE

The sensational and prolonged anti-colonial movements of the late nine-teenth century—e.g. the Can Vuong movement, the Katipunan rebellion, the Aceh War—can be understood only in terms of the internal dynamics of the societies that produced them. Resistance, evasion, assertion, with-drawal, and even self-immolation were possible modes of action in South-east Asian societies even prior to the crises of the late nineteenth century. In this section, we examine the tensions between centres and peripheries, and the cultural systems—which we call 'religions'—that facilitated state-building as well as provided the idioms of resistance to the state. Quite often, as we shall see, the individuals who led groups of pupils, adepts or ordinary villagers against the colonial forces were the very same ones who had been opponents, critics or simply shadowy 'others' of rulers and officialdom. Despite the differences in doctrinal content between, say, Thai Buddhism and Filipino Christianity, the religio-political terrains in which they operated were very similar, leading to striking regularities in the style of anti-colonial resistance throughout Southeast Asia.

The Thai polity, to take our first example, was built upon an accepted tradition of contracting and expanding mandalas. The empire of Rama I in 1809 consisted of a large number of power centres which can be imagined as a series of concentric circles, only the 'inner core' of which, close to Bangkok, can be said to have been ruled directly at the outset. The actual processes by which the Chakri kings transformed such a polity into a modern territorial state in response to a changing geopolitical order is treated elsewhere in this volume. What concerns us here is the nature of the popular resistance to such centralizing moves.

Buddhist states in Southeast Asia had always been plagued by centri-fugal tendencies and internal unrest. The nature of the mandala system itself, in which local and subordinate identities were never erased, con-tributed largely to this. But the political geography was also complicated by the presence of individuals or groups dwelling in forest hermitages or wandering about holy mountains. This activity was an extension of the early Buddhist practice of 'going forth', distancing oneself from society in order better to achieve the strict disciplining of mind and body demand-ed by the eightfold path. Around the more charismatic forest-dwellers have formed cults or associations, the aim of which was usually the self-fulfilment of the adepts, although at times these cults were charged with a more political mission.

The role of holy men, men of great merit (*phumibun*) in the founding of Thai kingdoms and settlements and the strengthening of 'official' Buddhism is well known. As monasteries grew, so did their dependence on the generosity of the rich; on the other hand, the legitimacy of kings rested in great part on their fulfilment of the precepts of the *dhamma*, the body of teachings zealously guarded by the *sangha*. The triangular relationship between the *dhamma*, *sangha*, and monarch enabled the state-centre to appropriate much of Buddhist activity for its own ends. As much as possible, holy men were kept under the supervision or surveillance of officially recognized abbots.

Village monasteries and temples, however, tended to be ambiguous signs of central control, potentially subversive under charismatic abbots. Because the *sangha* was also a grass-roots phenomenon to which lay people became attached at some point of their lives, it was the vehicle for the dissemination of popular Buddhist literature and practices. The everyday preoccupation with the accumulation of merit is evidenced in the popularity of accounts of the former lives of the historical Buddha. Another favourite theme of such literature was the coming of the future Buddha, the Maitreya, and his glorious reign. The sanctuaries of monasteries all over Thailand are decorated with wall paintings, many of which are inspired by the *Traiphum*, a text which promotes expectations of coming *cakkavatti*, men of great inner power, and the Maitreya.

Official Buddhism continually sought to co-opt ideas and expectations of the coming of a righteous ruler and saviour, often fused in one person. Millennial expectations were 'short-circuited' by the Chakri kings' assumption, in the folk mind at least, of Bodhisattva status: they were the men of greatest merit in the kingdom, approximating the *cakkavatti* ideal. While the court appropriation of karmic theory tended towards the stabilization of the existing sociopolitical order, the absence of a caste system in Burma and Siam nevertheless created a tension between social experience and religious expectations as far as karma was concerned. An individual's high karma, and consequent abundance of merit, could be demonstrated in various ways—such as the performance of healing and magic—and shared with or transferred to others. While kings sought as much as possible to reserve this role for themselves, in actual fact villagers often turned to alternative and more localized men of merit for leadership.

The Thammayut movement, founded by Mongkut around 1833, is often seen as part of Siam's drive to modernize, to adapt Buddhism to the age of science. This movement, though, should also be seen in terms of bolstering the power of the centre by arresting the proliferation of popular Buddhist texts, or at least controlling the public consumption of such. By marginalizing the potentially subversive, millennial side of Buddhism, the dynastic state would be strengthened. However, the Thammayut movement appealed mainly to the Thai middle class. The popular Buddhism, through which villagers continued to organize their experience, contained a potential critique of the monarchy and offered alternative figures—

phumibun and *phuwiset* (person with extraordinary power) around whom they could gather particularly in times of natural calamities, profound political changes, or intensified economic demands of the state.

The politico-religious terrain in Burma was much the same. Since the time of Anawrahta in the eleventh century, the establishment of the *dhamma* ran parallel to the unification of kingdoms. Kings often had to suppress renegade groups of monks and the persistent worship of indigenous spirits called *nat*, eventually reaching a compromise by incorporating the latter into popular Buddhism. More than the Siamese, the Burmese kings exercised considerable control over religious affairs through their sponsorship of an ecclesiastical hierarchy headed by a Thathanabaing, a title which literally meant 'lord or owner of the Buddhist religion'. In theory the primate exercised authority through a chain of command reaching down to the head of the village monastery. But because monks were, after all, individual ascetics who had not vowed obedience to any superior, royal and ecclesiastical control over them was ambiguous.

The tensions that perennially existed between the officially backed hierarchy and individual monks and sects arose also from the fact that, to villagers, supposedly animistic and anti-Buddhist figures such as the *weikza* (a magician, one who has overcome death and has supernatural powers) were not really much different from monks in an advanced stage of meditation and merit-accumulation.[4] The invulnerability, curative powers, and prophetic wisdom of *weikza* and *pongyi* alike made them attractive to villagers and townspeople fleeing from corvée exactions and other hardships or simply seeking a more meaningful existence. Undoubtedly, as in Siam, the transformation of such groups of teachers and followers into more militant movements can be attributed at least partly to the popularity of Buddhist texts which provided villagers with images of the coming Maitreya and the ideal Buddhist ruler (*Setkya-min*, a Burmanization of *cakkavatti*).

The popularity of Burmese kings lay in part in their ability to identify themselves with these potent figures and the ideal conditions of existence they represented. King Kyanzittha (r. 1084–1112), for example, announced that the era of rule he inaugurated would mirror the magnificence of heaven. Not only would the highest moral order prevail, but there would be freedom from all sickness and pain, calamity and misfortune. 'Even the poor old women who sell pots and potlids . . . They shall become rich . . . Those who lack cattle shall have plenty of cattle . . . Even poor people who have difficulty in getting food and clothes shall wear gold ornaments.'[5] Much of the attraction of popular Buddhism obviously lay more in such promises of the satisfaction of earthly wants, than in an escape from them. It is thus not surprising that King Bodawpaya (r. 1781–1819) should have proclaimed himself as the Buddha Mettaya (Maitreya), destined to be a world conqueror. His successor Bagyidaw used the title Setkya-min, while Bagyidaw's heir apparent was actually named Setkya-min.

[4] Stanley J. Tambiah, *The Buddhist Saints of the Forest and the Cult of Amulets*, Cambridge, UK, 1984, 315.
[5] Cited in Emmanuel Sarkisyanz, *Buddhist Backgrounds of the Burmese Revolution*, The Hague, 1965, 60.

The other side of the Burmese kings' identification with millennial Buddhist figures was their continual attempts to purify the faith and to suppress heretical movements. In the eighteenth century King Hsinbyu-shin persecuted a heretical sect called the Paramats, while his successor Bodawpaya occasionally executed heretics. Purification of the order im-plied not merely an attack on monastic indiscipline, but a drive to unify a *saṅgha* that tended to fracture into many contending sects, with the ensuing danger that such groups might articulate grievances against the throne. The threat such sects offered to the king could be compounded if they aligned themselves with some pretender to the throne, or *min-laung* (lit. king-to-be, embryo king) who happened to claim special powers.

The crisis of the Konbaung dynasty, brought about by internal rivalries compounded by British threats and conquests, encouraged precisely the dispersal of the *saṅgha* and the flourishing of small, increasingly militant, groups led by monks, *weikza*, and *saya* (experts in esoteric lore). Millennial expectations gravitated towards these figures, particularly after the loss of the centre of the realm and the physical disintegration of the Konbaung polity. The very sorts of holy men, cult centres, and popular energies that the Thai kings managed to contain and draw towards the centre became, as we shall see, the sources of resistance to the politico-economic order imposed by British rule in Burma.

As we move to the eastern part of mainland Southeast Asia, we find Confucian rulers experiencing very much the same problems as their Buddhist counterparts. Having overcome the Tayson centres of rebellion and established themselves at Hué in the beginning of the nineteenth century, the Nguyen emperors were finally able, for the first time in history, to unify the north and the south, and even to establish control over the Cambodian court at the expense of the Thai. But the Confucian state's control over the vast empire was plagued with problems from the start. Gia-long's reliance on French support resulted in the spread of Catholic missions which would eventually provoke religious conflicts among Vietnamese villages. The incorporation of the south, with its Cham and Khmer traditions, posed the complex problem of integrating diverse ethnic and religious groups into an idealized Confucian political and moral order. And as always, there was resistance posed by the strong autono-mous tradition of the villages, which were tantamount to religious congre-gations centred on cults of guardian spirits.

Although the official religion of Vietnam was, like China's, an amalgam of the 'Three Teachings'—Confucianism, Taoism and Buddhism—the need for national integration spurred the scholar-gentry to fashion the Nguyen polity more in accordance with the Confucian ideal. This involved the closer integration of villages in the central polity through the grant of patents to village guardian spirits—the imperial document to be housed in the main shrine (*dinh*). National integration also spurred a continuation of the old and well-documented 'war' on Buddhism. Since Buddhist monks had often served as advisers to their patrons in secular matters, and since monastic centres often served as havens for disaffected nobles and peasants alike, the war on Buddhism was meant to neutralize poten-tial sites of rebellion against the Nguyen court. The Buddhist monkhood was pressured into adhering to the monastic ideal of withdrawal from the world of men. And as far as they could, without alienating the peasantry, the scholar-gentry attacked the superstition and fanaticism which they associated with popular Buddhist and animist practices. Emperor Minh-mang himself was visibly contemptuous of such beliefs as invulnerability magic. In 1834, to disprove the Thai faith in amulets, he tied one to the neck of a duck, shot at it himself, and reported the duck's death.

The emperors and mandarins of traditional Vietnam thus saw themselves as the guardians and agents of a superior, secular civilization both surrounded, and threatened from within, by barbarism. However, their drive to impose this Confucian order was punctuated by rebellions and other acts of resistance. It is estimated that 105 separate uprisings occurred during Gia-long's reign (1802–19), and 200 during Minh-mang's (1820–40). Specially in the north, where the Tayson rebellion, Chinese invasion, floods, typhoons, crop failures, and official abuses all wreaked their havoc, many villages were abandoned. Drifting peasants contributed to a spate of rebellions, led by bandits who were often advised by men of scholarly background. Remote sacred mountains provided bases of operations, and the popular imagination was fired by the appearance of omens promising a new and better society in the aftermath of rebellion.

One source of instability was intrinsic to the system itself. The legitimacy of the Vietnamese state rested on the emperor's possessing the mandate of heaven and ruling through purity of example. The Confucian-educated élite composed of mandarins and scholars generally looked up to the emperor as the exemplar of moral behaviour, and transmitted to the populace at large the values of obedience to superiors and veneration of the ruler. However, as in other parts of Southeast Asia, this élite could function as an ambiguous sign. In troubled times, such as after serious floods or famines, the mandate of heaven could be perceived to be lost by the emperor, leading to popular unrest. In such situations local scholars, in particular, because of their close ties with villagers in their roles as teachers, scribes and physicians, could lead rebellions against the reigning monarchy.

Confucian scholars did not derive their power and influence from the accumulation of merit or virtue, as did Buddhist monks. They were simply superior men acting in accordance with Confucian ideals. Vietnamese villagers, however, never ceased to be attracted to individuals who could tap the power of spirits and gods. Partly this was due to the failure of the examination system centred at Hué to produce enough scholar-gentry to achieve a uniform Confucianization of society—a situation particularly serious in the south. Since, in the Confucian ordering of things, common people had no religious function, they continued to be attracted to practitioners of the Taoist, Buddhist and other religions who offered, aside from notions of personal salvation, practical skills in healing, divination, geomancy and so forth. The officially sanctioned belief in an impersonal heaven always existed in tension with theistic beliefs in ancestral and guardian spirits.[6] In some areas of traditional Vietnam, challenges to

[6] Charles F. Keyes, *The Golden Peninsula*, New York, 1977, 201.

the authority of the state were mounted in the name of a spirit or god, such as a Bodhisattva, who was perceived to have greater power than that of the emperor. If the state was triumphant, then here was proof that greater power resided in heaven rather than with spirits and gods.

One theistic belief that greatly perturbed the Confucian court from the early nineteenth century on was Christianity. The conversion to French Catholicism of whole Vietnamese villages—by 1848 there were 68,000 converts—was tantamount to a challenge to the Confucian social order itself. Of course, the panoply of Christian beliefs was itself subjected to a certain amount of 'Vietnamization'. Popular culture was given an added dimension through the Gospel story, the sacraments, and other basic elements of the Christian faith. But in relation to the totalizing Confucian order, Christianity was subversive. Christians were oriented to the after-life; they counted time in linear fashion from Christ's birth; they recognized a potentate in Rome; they dressed and behaved differently. In areas affected by this new religion, 'canton teachers' were recruited from among local scholars to lecture on Confucianism. In the second half of the century the persecution of Vietnamese converts and priests, coupled with mission-ary ambitions, were to a great extent responsible for the massive French intervention.

In the southern part of Vietnam (Nam Bo) Christianity was only one of several religions competing for the allegiance of the populace. This was a frontier area which the Confucian court sought to populate and incorpo-rate into the realm. These two aims were not exactly compatible: in seeking to attract manpower to the area, the court found it necessary to refrain from policing the religious beliefs and practices it suppressed elsewhere. In any case, because land-ownership tended to be valued more highly than a bureaucratic career in the south, rising families did not generate enough scholar-gentry to do the policing. For various reasons Nam Bo, especially its western part bordering on Cambodia, became a haven for defrocked monks, political dissidents, heretics, bandits, Chinese secret society elements and a diverse immigrant population, all of which could carry on their 'proscribed' rituals. Sects and movements inherently subversive of the existing order thus often began there and spread beyond their confines through the work of itinerant apostles.

By the 1850s, Vietnamese authorities were quite alarmed by the growth in the region of a popular religious tradition called Buu Son Ky Hong (Strange Fragrance from Precious Mountain). The name is derived from the characters inscribed in the amulets distributed by the sect leader Doan Min Huyen, who held the title of 'Buddha Master of Western Peace'. The Buddha Master had put together themes and practices culled from different religious currents among the Vietnamese, Khmer, and Chinese 'floating' populations. He and his disciples were 'holy men' who could prophesy the future and perform rituals, medicinal curing, divination, and the like. Like the *phumibun* and *weikza* of the Buddhist polities, apostles of the sect formed small groups of adherents without much organizational structure and concerned mainly with self-cultivation in accordance with the Buddha Master's precepts. At times of unrest, however, these groups had the potential of feeding into a wider rebellion or anti-colonial movement.

Much of the Buddha Master's attraction lay in his ability to provide more specification to eschatological ideas already familiar to the populace. 'The Low Era is at an end' was the slogan of Buu Son Ky Hong in the nineteenth and early twentieth centuries. Upon a time base of cycles of eras (High, Middle, Low), the end of each marked by cataclysmic events, the Buddha Master based his specific prophecies. The world was reaching the end of a cycle, an apocalypse would occur, and the Maitreya Buddha would descend to initiate a new era and cycle. The attractiveness of the Maitreya's advent can be gleaned from the following prophecy:

> When the Buddha descends into An Giang,
> The people of the Six Provinces will know an easy life.
> Every home will have things in plenty,
> Everywhere will be peaceful and happy,
> The roads to Heaven will be wide open,
> We will follow in the steps of emperor Shun and the Sages,
> There will be harmony in the Three Spheres.[7]

The message of the Buddha Master was understood by a population that included ethnic Khmers, Vietnamese, and Chinese who lived in a kind of no-man's-land beyond the control of the centres of state power at Phnom Penh and Saigon. This region of unrest in fact also constituted the southern and eastern edges of the Cambodian mandala. Since the seventeenth century the Nguyen overlords of the south had intruded into space formerly under Cambodian control, starting with the occupation in 1620 of Saigon (still known to Cambodians today as Prey Nokor). Large chunks of territory and thousands of ethnic Khmer were subjected to progressive Vietnamization for over two hundred years. Vietnamese intervention extended to the throne itself, forcing the Cambodian royal family to split into pro-Thai and pro-Vietnamese elements. Dynastic squabbles and foreign invasions diminished whatever control the throne had over the countryside. Thus, in the eighteenth and early nineteenth centuries, much of the countryside was under the control of 'holy men' (*nak sel*) endowed with magical powers and able to tap the millennial strains of popular Khmer Buddhism.

The *nak sel* were particularly active in the southeastern borders, where anti-Vietnamese feelings were particularly intense. In the first half of the nineteenth century intensified Vietnamese control over this region sparked several rebellions against the throne. In 1820 a monk named Kai declared himself king in the vicinity of a sacred mountain in southeastern Cambodia called Ba Phnom. The economic grievances are clear: Kai was rebelling against the exactions of the Vietnamese who had been in virtual control of the court since 1811. Politically he sought to displace the feeble monarch and restore the potency of the centre. But what actually drew

---

[7] Cited in Hue Tam Ho Tai, *Millenarianism and Peasant Politics in Vietnam*, Cambridge, Mass., 1983, 29.

adherents to his cause was his possession of special powers deriving from his great merit, his connection with the sacred mountain, his distribution of amulets, and his millennial message of a new and pure society free of the Vietnamese. A mixed Vietnamese-Khmer force sent against Kai failed because the Khmer commanders deserted with their troops and turned against the Vietnamese. Eventually the rebellion was crushed by a purely Vietnamese contingent.

The receptivity of Khmers in southeastern Cambodia and Nam Bo to the preachings of the Buu Son Ky Hong apostles in the 1850s can be attributed more specifically to the turmoil occasioned by a massive anti-Vietnamese revolt from 1840 to 1847. High-ranking officials (*onkya*) had interpreted the Vietnamese exiling of the Cambodian queen and her entourage, and the confiscation of her regalia, as the virtual dismantling of the monarchy. Vietnamese actions aimed at rationalizing the Cambodian administration were seen as attacks on the very foundations of the Buddhist state and social order. The *onkya*-led revolt that ensued was similar in many respects to the Burmese guerrilla warfare against the British following the Konbaung dynasty's fall in 1885. No overall leader emerged. Although estimates of rebel strength ran to thirty thousand men, these were fragmented into hundreds of small bands armed mostly with knives, cross-bows and clubs.

It seems an inescapable conclusion that millennial ideas informed the response of Khmer villagers to the call of the *onkya*. Originating along the east bank of the Mekong, the revolt had spread farther inland and to parts of southern Vietnam inhabited by Khmer—terrain over which *nak sel* had great influence. Who were leading the small band of rebels? And why were they pitting their puny weapons against the Vietnamese war machine? The disappearance of the queen and her regalia would have been interpreted as a sign of the approaching Low Era. Monks were undoubtedly involved, for it was the Buddhist order itself, patronized by the monarch, that was threatened with extinction. As one rebel wrote, 'We are happy killing Vietnamese. We no longer fear them; in all our battles we are mindful of the three jewels [of Buddhism]: the Buddha, the law, and the monastic community.'[8]

The ending of the rebellion was, not surprisingly, marked by the restoration of the monarchy under Thai sponsorship, and with Vietnamese acquiescence. The elaborate ceremonies that took place in 1848 signified the restoration of Theravāda Buddhism as the state religion. Monasteries were subsequently rebuilt and monks encouraged to assume their 'normal' roles in society. But all this activity merely confirms that what had transpired in the recent past was the loss of official Buddhism's control over the monks in the countryside, many of whom were in fact identical to the *nak sel* rebel leaders. Despite these restorative gestures, Khmer monks and disciples of the Buddha Master would continue, in the decades to come, to provide leadership and inspiration for movements aimed at bringing about the ideal Buddhist polity in the face of alien intrusion.

---

[8] Cited in David Chandler, *A History of Cambodia*, Boulder, 1983, 131.

As we move to the island world of Southeast Asia, the religio-political terrain becomes somewhat more complex. One is struck by the diversity of the Malayo-Indonesian world owing to the varying degrees of accommodation with Hindu, Buddhist and Islamic influences, the dichotomy between coastal-commercial and inland-agrarian principalities, and the different levels of state formation that had been reached by the end of the eighteenth century. The Philippines seems to be altogether different, owing to centuries of Spanish colonization and the widespread adoption of Christianity. Despite such complexities, however, certain regularities can be discerned. Pilgrimage sites, rural prophets, gurus, millennial messages, and invulnerability magic all had their role to play in opposition to the establishment. One finds in them pronounced slippages between older ideas of power and the universalizing faiths of Islam and Christianity. The Philippines, it turns out, is no exception to the rule.

In studies of the Indic states of Java, the bulk of the attention has been paid to the *negara*, the site of the royal palace and shrine, the axis of the universe and thus the very source of power of the kingdom. The interior of Java can be visualized as a conglomeration of such power centres whose influence and authority rose and fell in a succession of periods of order and disorder. Local chiefs and villagers became incorporated into one or another *negara*, depending on which was in the ascendancy, as evidenced in its ruler being in possession of the *wahju* (divine radiance).

In the peripheries of the Javanese kingdoms where the power of the centre was weakest, we can identify another set of élites, of individuals powerful in their own right yet outside the sociopolitical order. In pre-Islamic times these were the hermits and sages (*resi*, *adjar*) who inhabited remote mountain sides and caves. They had withdrawn from society to live a life of isolation and asceticism in order to penetrate the secrets of the universe and acquire the powers of a seer; they were able, among other things, to call attention to the state of decay of a kingdom. Because of their prophetic powers, *adjar* were respected and feared by rulers. They were also attractive to other seekers of knowledge, who became their pupils. And in times of crisis, they could be the foci of rebellious activities. The hermit tradition is conveyed to villagers through the *wayang* shadow play, in which the advice of an *adjar* is sought because he is able to offer alternative views that might otherwise be missed. At times these alternatives pointed to messianic ideas, such as the appearance of a *ratu adil* (just king).

With the advent of Islam and colonial rule, the traditional *adjar* largely disappeared. Since the conversion to Islam in the Javanese interior had been achieved without destroying the basic features of the old Indic polity, the new Islamic-titled rulers simply harnessed the doctrines and functionaries of Islam to enhance the power of the state or centre. But the official appropriation of Islam, which would carry over into the Dutch colonial period, was confounded by the presence of independent, rural religious leaders who played a role quite similar to the *adjar* of old. The *kyai* (venerated teacher of Islam) established reputations and followings in *pesantren*, or schools, often located in remote villages beyond the administrative control of the state. There were also the gurus or masters of Sufi brotherhoods called *tarekat*, which mushroomed in Java and parts of Sumatra in the nineteenth century. In times of crisis these Islamic teachers, leading bands of their pupils, would emerge from their isolated *pesantren* and *tarekat* to play a role, albeit temporary, in the collapse of an old order and the emergence of a new.

The popular appeal of the *kyai* went beyond his Islamic learning and holiness. Many of the best-known *kyai* were also healers and prophets. They were deemed to be men of immense potency, which was dispensed to their adherents in the form of invulnerability and cures. They also operated in a cultural milieu that could readily interpret unusual occurrences, such as volcanic eruptions and foreign intrusions, in terms of a Javanese amalgam of Hindu and Islamic ideas of time. The message of the *kyai* could, and often did in the nineteenth century, mesh with beliefs in the imminent coming of the *ratu adil*, the just king who would institute an age of justice and plenty after a period of decline; or with the appearance of the Mahdi who would bring a temporary end to suffering and oppression by restoring order and founding a new kingdom.

Before the Dutch incorporated the *priyayi* (Javanese hereditary aristocracy) into the colonial bureaucracy from the mid-nineteenth century on, there was tension but not really a chasm between court *priyayi* and religious figures beyond the state's control. It was part of the aristocratic tradition for the youth to withdraw from *kraton* life at some point of their lives, in order to engage in study, meditation and asceticism in isolated places under the guidance of sage-hermits and Islamic teachers. Aristocrats often negotiated the pilgrimages to holy graves alongside travelling *santri*, the 'students of religion', thus coming into contact with prominent Islamic teachers as well as crowds of ordinary pilgrims. As with all passages through sacred sites in Southeast Asia, the Javanese practice of visiting holy places fitted very well into scenarios of rebellion. This is exemplified in the career of Prince Dipanagara, chief protagonist in the Java War fought against the Dutch (1825–30). Dipanagara had in previous decades spent much time wandering about the hills in the environs of Yogyakarta, visiting shrines, caves and other holy places. Such activities would have been undertaken by him, and interpreted by other Javanese, as a way of strengthening his inner being in preparation for some difficult and historic task. At the same time, some of his wanderings would, at the very least, have made groups of teachers and pilgrims in those holy sites aware of the issues that informed his acts of defiance against the Dutch.

Though led by a scion of the Yogyakarta royal family, the Dipanagara rebellion attracted all levels of Javanese society to its cause. But it was not necessarily the interests of the *priyayi* that the peasant rebels sought to defend against colonial intrusion. Through his links with religious figures and centres in the countryside, his act of defiance came to be interpreted by the society at large in moral and even millennial terms. It was outside a cave where Dipanagara had often meditated that the standard of revolt was raised in 1825. He claimed to be a champion of Islam, not merely of its formal institutions but in the sense of purifying the whole of Javanese society that had become degraded by the presence of the Dutch and their collaborators. By assuming the title of Sultan Erucakra, which is a name of the *ratu adil*, he gave concrete form to the society's widespread familiarity with images of struggle and change as transmitted through popular art forms such as the *wayang*. Not just the *kyai* and their adherents, but even bandits and peasants as well, recognized in Dipanagara the fulfilment of their aspirations.

After the war, the anti-feudal policies of the Dutch were abandoned and the *priyayi* became increasingly part of the colonial edifice. The courts were stripped of their vast territorial holdings and became reduced to 'ritual establishments'. Dipanagara's was thus the last of the *priyayi*-led rebellions. Meanwhile, the conditions were created after 1830 for the heightened involvement of *pesantren* and *tarekat* in protest movements. The expansion of the civil service and the colonial penetration of rural areas threatened the traditional religious leaders while providing them with a wider base of economically-dislocated villagers from which to draw adherents. In an attempt to control the directions of popular religiosity after the Java War, the Dutch and *priyayi* administrators organized a parallel religious bureaucracy with prescribed roles from the regency down to the village level. This, however, served only to increase the resolve and solidarity of the independent *kyai* and *ulamā*. In the spate of minor anti-colonial uprisings that immediately followed the Java War, some of which looked to Dipanagara's return, leadership was mainly in the hands of *kyai* and other holy men, rather than scions of the nobility. The increasing identification of *priyayi* with Dutch rule is evidenced in an 1843 uprising led by Amad Daris, a commoner, who sought to expel all officials from Java and inaugurate a new era in which the hierarchical social order would be overthrown.

In the coastal-commercial states of the archipelago, the *ulamā* and their *pesantren* played an even more crucial role in unrest and resistance. The idea of kingship evolved quite differently in these coastal principalities: not, as in interior Java, from a divine-kingship model with the palace as the centre of the universe, but from the notion of ruler as the regulator of commerce in the market, and the Protector of Islam. The Acehnese sultan, for example, did not symbolize the overriding unity of the Acehnese people. Islam, however, was used to strengthen his position vis-à-vis the district chiefs. His relation to Islam made the sultan culturally superior, a magical figure even, but without real power.

The Acehnese *pesantren* were always separate from the villages and were even economically self-sustaining. The *ulamā* were not rivals of the chiefs, and challenged the latter only on moral or reformist grounds. In normal times, *pesantren* simply coexisted with the villages, making no attempt to impose themselves on the flawed society around them. Yet they were potent foci of unrest. In the first place, villagers could be attracted to the *ulamā* for the 'wrong' reasons: because they had power to command a blessing or a curse, to cure sickness, and to provide invulnerability. But on a wider scale, men were attracted to the *pesantren* because of the opportunity offered them to leave their villages and kinfolk behind in order to unite as Muslims. The *ulamā* himself symbolized this movement towards supra-kinship unity. Furthermore, in times of unrest or when action was necessary to purify and defend the Faith, the *pesantren* offered an avenue towards an alternative form of existence in Paradise. This, as we shall see, made the *ulamā* a powerful leader of resistance against the Dutch.

Beginning in the nineteenth century, attitudes of Islamic teachers towards their secular surroundings and the intrusions of the colonial state were shaped to a large degree by radical developments in the wider Islamic world. The pilgrimage (hajj) was a conduit for reformist impulses that initially shook Mecca in 1803 when it was invaded by the Wahhabis, a militant group from the deserts of eastern Arabia. The Wahhabis preached the return to the pure teachings of the Koran and the tradition of the prophet. They declared a jihad (holy war) on lawlessness, irreligion, and heresy—a kind of Islamic puritanism. Pilgrims from Southeast Asia could not but be impressed by this revitalization of their faith. Although they rejected some aspects of reform that clashed with popular practices—such as the worship of saints and holy places—many hajjis (pilgrims from Mecca) returned to their communities bent upon combating corruption and imposing strict Islamic laws.

The new Islamic orthodoxy had direct political repercussions as well. Previously the pilgrimage could readily be incorporated into a *raja*-centred polity; it was an extension of the royal domain, enhancing popular perceptions of rulers as 'Shadows of Allah on Earth'. By the nineteenth century the pilgrimage was nurturing other ideas of where political and communal life ought to be centred—such as Islamic law, or national identity. This development coincided with the Dutch and English consolidation of their claims to the archipelago. The effects were particularly dramatic in the relatively more complex polities of Java and Sumatra. Since the *priyayi* and other traditional aristocracies eventually collaborated with the Dutch, the reformist attack on 'official' Islam (i.e., that patronized by the aristocrats) was readily broadened into an anti-colonial struggle. As the militant reformists saw it, not only was official Islam in an abysmal state, but the Dutch *kāfir* (unbelievers) were actually working through the system to establish their control.

The first major outburst informed by such sentiments occurred in the Minangkabau region of Sumatra. Early in the nineteenth century Minangkabau pilgrims initiated what came to be called the Padri movement (from Pedir, whence most of them had sailed for Arabia). The Padris gained control of many *tarekats* based in the foothills of Merapi and other mountains, fortified them and put them on a war footing. Their goals were to cleanse the lowland communities of such practices as cockfighting, gambling, and alcohol consumption, and uniformly implement the Islamic legal code; their attempts were resisted by the royal family and many local communities. Declaring a *jihad*, the Padris at times resorted to the use of armed groups of teachers and students to effect their reforms. Eventually, they clashed with the Dutch who, aided by the royal family and some chiefs, were determined to wrest control of the coffee trade which was then in the hands of the Padris. Hostilities began in the early 1820s and did not really end until 1838.

The Padri war illustrates how a religious impulse from the outside—reform Islam—was able to radicalize existing *tarekat* and *pesantren*, thus transforming groups of teachers and pupils into insurgent armies that fought the 'corrupt' Islam of the villages as well as the expanding colonial state. There would be more such confrontations, particularly after the opening of the Suez Canal in 1869—increasing the traffic to Mecca—and the advent of the high colonial period. It must be borne in mind, however, that the terrain on which hajjis preached determined the character of the movements as much as the reformist ideals did. As more and more peasant villagers were drawn into such movements, particularly on Java, millennial expectations and demonstrations of magical power became the overriding concerns.

As stated earlier, the religio-political terrain of the Christianized Philippines was not much different from those of 'traditional' or pre-colonial states elsewhere in Southeast Asia. Spanish colonial rule had delineated cities, towns (pueblos) and provincial boundaries within an administrative structure that looked good on paper. In actuality, a mandala-type situation existed wherein the prestige and power of the parish priest and indigenous town élite (*principalía*) determined a pueblo-centre's hold over the peripheries. Up to fairly late in the century, there was ample scope for non-pueblo elements—called hermits, bandits, wanderers, curers, heretics and the like—to operate almost at will, attracting people to them during periods of natural calamities or annual pilgrimages, or forming permanent communities beyond the pueblos. The movement of people away from the Spanish centres could be due to a variety of reasons ranging from exorbitant tax and corvée demands to the rumoured calls of a prophet to prepare for a coming new era.

Each Spanish religio-political centre, located in the church-*convento* complex, in effect had a rather less visible and less structured 'other' that mimicked its ritual practices while retaining many of the features of pre-Spanish religion; it competed for manpower, and in times of crisis flared up in rebellion. The more intense manifestations of an 'other side' to the Spanish ordering of Indio life were to be found in areas difficult to penetrate by the police and army, and a multitude of them existed in the nineteenth century. Even such a heavily 'Hispanized' region as central Luzon had the sacred Mount Arayat at its centre, and was bordered by the Zambales mountains to the west and the Sierra Madre to the east. Almost every major island had tall mountains—some of which were regarded as sacred—the slopes of which served as havens for individuals or communities fleeing from pueblo control or simply wishing to practise alternative lifestyles, as hermits or sectarian adepts.

Officially, the spread of Catholic doctrine among Filipinos of all classes was supposed to tie them to the Spanish-Christian world. The Spanish priest was the agent of the Christian god, whose superiority to the local sorcerers and spirits was repeatedly demonstrated during the period of conversion. The institutionalization of the Catholic faith in the colony coincided with the birth and growth of pueblo centres, and a native élite that saw themselves as children of Mother Spain. However, the popularization of Catholic teachings through hymns, poems, dramas, and particularly the epic of Christ's passion, death and resurrection (*Pasyon*) produced a popular view of the world in which the human and divine dimensions could not be kept entirely separate. Thus, there became available for appropriation such figures as that of *Kristo* (Christ), a man of power (*kapangyarihan*), yet lowly and humble, the leader of a group of ordinary men and women who are infused with a knowledge far superior to that of the learned priests of the establishment. While functioning to integrate the indio into a social and ritual circuit leading upwards to the parish priest and the Christian god, the *Pasyon* also created the possibility of *separation* from family and pueblo life to heed the call of a sorcerer, prophet, or rebel and 'head for the hills', to die for this leader's cause and thus to see heaven. A conception of the biblical unfolding of time was also introduced: a notion of the eras (*panahon*) of the Father, Son and Holy Spirit, the winding down of the latter marked by catastrophic events preceding the apocalypse and the return of Christ the King. Prophets were expected to be able correctly to read the extraordinary events in human time in terms of this over-arching conception of changing eras.

Such non-official readings of the Christian master text provided the ideological conditions, at least, for certain forms of opposition to the Spanish colonial order. Often, these radical movements were originally Church-approved sodalities and confraternities which changed their character under the influence of prophetic leaders and extraordinary circumstances such as famines and the appearance of comets. The most sensational of these was the Cofradía de San José (Confraternity of St Joseph) which began in 1832 as one of dozens of sodalities throughout the islands devoted to the practice of piety and the performance of works of charity. But under the leadership of Apolinario de la Cruz, an articulate lay brother attracted to Catholic mystical literature, the Cofradía expanded and began to function as a separate church. As small groups of its preachers and adherents continued to sprout all over the southern Tagalog region, the Cofradía was proscribed by the Spanish church in 1840. This native holy man and prophet was drawing whole congregations away from the official church. Furthermore, it was discovered that portraits of Apolinario depicted as a saint were being venerated at secret meetings.

Apolinario retreated to the slopes of Mount Banahao, a sacred mountain, where he managed to attract thousands of lowlanders to join him in forming an independent commune that would prepare for the impending cataclysm and the new church that would arise from the ashes. His success can be attributed in part to the Spanish friars themselves. They had implanted in the region a religious vocabulary that the Tagalogs infused with their meanings. To his brethren Apolinario promised superior knowledge, equality, material abundance, victory over illness and even over death. Take, for example, the following excerpt from a devotional text written by a friar:

> That day most eagerly awaited
> becomes even more joyful
> should the source of fulfillment
> be seen with our eyes.

All goodness and truth
that people aim for
but never quite attain
will be granted in heaven.

... High-born or low,
rich or poor,
all will look alike
this is God's vow.[9]

A note in Apolinario's copy states: 'This is what will be seen by those who ascend beginning 19 February 1840.' Familiar images of Paradise beckoned villagers to join this particular event. Apolinario himself was recognized early in his career as a saintly figure, then later as a Tagalog Christ and, finally, king—a title he vigorously denied ever arrogating to himself. At the same time, he had the 'traditional' attributes of a curer and a practitioner of invulnerability magic.

The violent suppression of the Cofradía did not stamp out the movement. Survivors of the revolt simply withdrew to their villages or to isolated settlements in the hills, secretly continuing to adhere to their beliefs and practices and spreading the tradition to other islands to the south.

One crucial factor that made such sects attractive was the Spanish failure to develop a satisfactory corps of native clergymen. If Apolinario de la Cruz had not been barred from entry into the Franciscan order, the illicit Cofradía would probably not have developed. In the late eighteenth century a serious shortage of Spanish priests had forced the archbishop to ordain native Filipino priests. But by the 1820s their increasing numbers and intellectual sophistication had become a matter of grave concern to the Spanish clergy, who imagined the native priests leading their flock against Mother Spain. By the 1830s the tide had turned against the Filipinos, and more and more of their parishes were turned over to the Spanish orders. Not surprisingly, a Filipino priest was incriminated in the Cofradía rebellion of 1841. As the rift between Filipino and Spanish priests deepened through the rest of the century, it was bound to instill a religious dimension to anti-colonial agitation from *within* the pueblos themselves.

ANTI-COLONIAL MOVEMENTS FROM 1850

The second half of the nineteenth century saw an acceleration of the European imperial advance into Vietnam and Burma, the imposition of a 'protective' net around the Malay states, and territorial and bureaucratic consolidation in Siam, the Netherlands East Indies and the Philippines. Political independence was surrendered in varying degrees to the Europeans, as economies were increasingly tied to the global economic system

[9] Cited in Ileto, 49.

centred in Europe; villages experienced the steady penetration of the money economy as well as central administrative and fiscal control. Such revolutionary transformations in the politico-economic order were accompanied by a series of disasters like cholera epidemics, armed invasions, and fluctuating commodity prices leading to a depression in the 1880s. Given the intensity of the changes taking place around them, Southeast Asian villagers during this period showed a readiness to follow individuals who could organize their experience and point to a better future. Whether led by kings, gentry, religious teachers or sage-prophets, whether they called for armed resistance or withdrawal from society, the popular movements that emerged reveal striking similarities in form, a reflection no doubt of the religious experience that animated the bulk of them.

Siam would at first glance appear to be exempt from the phenomenon of anti-colonial resistance. In a broader sense, however, the Chakri kings were practising a form of colonialism when they transformed their realm in the image of the European colonial states elsewhere. Faced with foreign economic penetration and the loss of royal trade monopolies after the signing of the 1855 Bowring treaty, the Chakri kings were compelled to intensify the production of rice and other crops for export, as well as exploit their teak and tin reserves. The need to streamline the economy, and to collect taxes and duties efficiently, necessitated the consolidation of boundaries and the direct control of far-flung provinces. Always the worry was that the British and French would enlarge their domains at Siam's expense.

In the process of transforming the basically feudal, *mandala* polity into a centralized, bureaucratic one, the former tributary states and semi-autonomous provinces were forced into line by commissioners sent from Bangkok from 1874. This form of internal colonialism not only eroded the power of local ruling families, but imposed hardships on villagers through the rapid dismantling of their subsistence economy and the imposition of various taxes in cash, collected mainly by Chinese agents. Under such circumstances, not surprisingly, several revolts or assertions against Bangkok broke out in various parts of the kingdom.

Around August 1889, there were various protest actions against the new taxes in the north around Chiengmai, a region with a centuries-old identity as the site of the Lannathai kingdom. A month later, a peasant rebellion broke out led by Phaya Phap (Phraya Prapsongkram), a petty official linked to the Chiengmai royalty. Significantly, Phaya Phap used to be called *Nan* Techa, *Nan* being a title held by a person previously ordained as a Buddhist monk. His ability to mobilize up to 3000 peasant followers (mostly Khoen people), including a large number of Buddhist monks, in open rebellion against the Thai and Chinese was no doubt due to his ability to articulate their discontent within a popular religious idiom. He was perceived to be a man of extraordinary powers, owing to his great accumulation of merit. He shared his invulnerability to enemy bullets with others through the ritual of bathing in sacred water. In normal times, he would have been one of dozens of holy men surrounded by adepts in search of self-fulfilment. But in this particular context he articulated popular expectations of a new era: he was expected to reign as the ideal

Buddhist king of a revitalized Chiengmai that was independent of Bangkok and free of taxes.

Similar reactions to Thai practices occurred in the northeast and in Laos. Beginning in 1899, there were reports of *phuwiset* and *phumibun* distributing sacralized water and medicine to peasants and performing various purification rituals. Most of these white-robed ascetics had had monastic experience; some had been forest dwellers and hermits, others had the ability to cure. They prophesied imminent disasters such as howling windstorms and darkness for seven days and nights. Some remarkable transformations were to occur: pebbles would become gold and silver, while gold and silver were to become pebbles; gourds and pumpkins would become elephants and horses, and so forth. The *phumibun* preached that the people should be pure of heart and join them in order to be saved or to become rich. Monks and ordinary villagers alike began to gather around these charismatic figures, often prefixing their names with the honorific 'Ong'. By 1901 the *phumibun* or 'holy man' phenomenon had escalated; the total emerging in 1902 alone numbered well over 100. By this time it was clear to the Thai and French authorities that the *phumibun* and their followers were intent upon defying the new politico-economic order and establishing their own kingdom. As these movements became threatening, Thai officials called them by the pejorative term *phi bun*.

Most of the 1901–2 *phumibun*-led movements did not lead to armed clashes with the state. The large groups of people who gathered around the holy men were taught to observe the Buddhist precepts, not to cause harm to others. However, the simple fact of their separateness from the official Buddhist *saṅgha*, plus the tendency of *phumibun* to be ordained with semi-divine status, was subversive enough of the established order.

The threat to the state was multiplied when millennial expectations were generated among the populace. The case of a *phumibun* named Ong Keo illustrates this. In several wats of the Saravane region in southern Laos there appeared, in 1901, white cotton panels depicting Ong Keo as a *thevada* (god) enjoying the blessings of a Buddhist paradise—suggesting the invocation of the Maitreya tradition. Himself an Alak tribesman, Ong Keo initially attracted mainly the Kha hill people of southern Laos to his movement, but eventually large numbers of Lao joined as well. The following year, the Lao on the Thai side of the border also became involved. They were led by Ong Man, a lieutenant of Ong Keo, who publicly declared himself *Phaya Thammikarat Phumibun*, a celestial being descended from heaven to save mankind from sin.

At this point, in 1902, the *phumibun* phenomenon had reached the point of armed rebellion. Each fighting unit was led by a *phuwiset* who wore multicoloured robes in monkish fashion, his head wrapped around with palm leaves inscribed with magical formulae. In March Ong Man's forces captured the Thai governor of Khemarat, but they were eventually defeated by the repeating rifles and powerful cannon of the Thai army. In late April, the forces of Ong Man and Ong Keo surrounded the French Commissariat in Savannakhet, convinced that they were in no danger since the French militia's ammunition would turn into frangipanni flowers. When the French did open fire, a hundred and fifty of them were killed. Ong Keo was later shot dead after he was lured to the negotiating table.

The *phumibun* movements that directly challenged the state, or were perceived to be doing so, were quickly suppressed by the vastly superior Thai and French forces. But this does not mean that the ethos that sustained these movements also disappeared. After all, the king of Siam himself claimed the status of *phumibun*. The difference between him and the others was that only he was empowered by the state to share his merit. Significantly, the captured rank and file were made to drink the water symbolizing their allegiance to the Thai king. But how could there be any guarantee that some other *phumibun* would not come along to capture their imagination and loyalty?

The problem for the Chakri kings was that, in the eyes of the ordinary villager, power resided not just in the rich and the mighty, but in poor, forest-dwelling ascetics as well. Whether they liked it or not, these recluses attracted followers and seekers of wisdom, and were often invested with attributes which they themselves denied. Such was the case with a monk named Siwichai, from the province of Lamphun in the north, who had the title *khru ba* (venerated teacher). Having emerged from a period in the forest, Siwichai founded a new monastery atop a hill outside his village where he taught the ways of the forest-dwelling tradition. Soon he began to attract large numbers of people from the provinces of Lamphun and Chiengmai—not just Thai but Karen, Meo and Muser as well. His reputation grew by leaps and bounds; soon he was rumoured to have the unusual powers characteristic of a Bodhisattva.

By the end of the nineteenth century, *Khru ba* Siwichai had become more than just a venerated ascetic and teacher. Stories of his various acts of defiance against the enroachments of the national *sangha* were becoming caught up in the wider narrative of the north's attempt to preserve its identity and heritage. The issue that provoked most concern was the government's attempt in 1902 to integrate monks and wats into a single, unified organization controlled from Bangkok. Since resistance was articulated in the Buddhist idiom, it is not surprising that there should be widespread rumours—which Siwichai apparently refused to discourage—that he was a Bodhisattva: the appearance of this sort of figure would have signalled the coming of a new era of righteous rule for the north. Like Phaya Phap farther to the north, and the *phumibun* rebels in the northeast, Siwichai had become a vehicle for the articulation of popular sentiments against the internal colonialism practised by the Chakri dynasty.

The 'disturbances' and uprisings in Siam during this period pale in comparison with those in Burma and Vietnam, which experienced a direct foreign invasion. Since the British and French represented alien cosmologies which threatened the Buddhist and Confucian orders, widespread resistance could be generated through appeals for a 'holy war' to preserve the integrity of a civilization or to restore its greatness. Let us first examine Burma, where the British dismantling of the kingdom of Burma provided the setting for resistance in the idiom of popular Buddhism.

The destruction of Konbaung Burma proceeded in three stages. Finally, in November 1885, the British captured Mandalay and early the following year annexed the rest of the kingdom to the empire's Indian province. The gradual loss of royal authority in the south beginning in 1824 had the effect of widening the gap between the monarchy's claims to actualizing the ideal Buddhist state, and the reality of its decline under the British onslaught. The less the actual ruler displayed the characteristics of a *cakkavatti*, or Setkya-min, the wider the space was for royal or Setkya-min claims to be made by other men of merit and power such as *weikza, saya* and monks. Furthermore, the series of wars, military defeats, and foreign occupations could not but have been viewed in terms of the Buddhist conception of history—as signs of the age of world decline, which would be followed by a new age. Thus, the retreat and fall of the Konbaung dynasty, while causing dislocation and a sense of loss, also pointed towards a future in which the kingdom and a perfect Buddhist society would arise, and the Future Buddha—the Maitreya—would finally descend. This ideological context helps explain the forms and intensity of popular resistance to British occupation.

It was after Burma's losses in 1824 that the Setkya-min claim became a potent force for galvanizing peasant uprisings. King Bagyidaw's heir apparent, as we have seen, was a prince actually named Setkya-min who was executed under the next king in 1838. But there were rumours that this prince was actually saved by the magician Bo Bo Aung, and was going to reappear at any time to restore the greatness of the Buddhist kingdom. The folk expectations of a return of Setkya-min were subsequently tapped by a series of claimants to his identity and mission. In January 1839, the very use of the name Setkya-min by a certain Maung Tsetkya enabled him to collect followers for a revolt in Pegu, a predominantly Mon area. This phenomenon was repeated several times, despite severe repression in the offending districts by the Konbaung forces.

The appearance of Setkya-mins and other Buddhist messiahs became intensified after the annexation of lower Burma in 1852. Although this may be attributed mainly to the British-Indian presence, a contributing factor was the withdrawal to Mandalay of many of the more ecclesiastical monks—i.e. those who recognized the Thathanabaing's authority and the king's patronage. This left the supervision of Buddhism in the villages to independent, local *sangha* which could very well have supported the Setkya-min claims of rebel leaders. In any case, the recognition of such figures largely rested upon the populace. In 1858, a mere fisherman, who had received a portent, was recognized as the Mettaya (Maitreya) destined to expel the *kalas* (Western strangers, barbarians) from Rangoon. His followers then proceeded to capture the local colonial commissioner. Two years later, a Future Buddha (Paya-Alaung) appeared, threatening the British position in Toungoo. Although these revolts were quickly put down by the superior British-Indian forces, the sentiments that propelled them endured. In 1861–2 the German ethnologist Bastian heard Burmese songs which seemed to be about a prince of victory who was expected to drive out the invaders.

Just before the third and final war with the British, King Thibaw himself donned the armour of world conqueror, announcing to all of his subjects that he would march forth with his army to expel the English heretics and *kalas*. His mission to uphold the honour of religion and country would, he said, 'gain for us the notable result of placing us on the path to the celestial regions and to Nirvana, the eternal rest'.[10] Thibaw's fight ended in disaster, but the framing of the struggle in Buddhist terms ensured a continuance of popular resistance despite the loss of the monarchy. It took another five years of campaigning from 1886 to subdue the country. At one point, the British deployed an army of 32,000 troops and 8500 military police against various guerilla groups.

The British conquest entailed the exiling of the king and the removal of the royal throne from Mandalay Palace to a museum in Calcutta. The British knew that this would mean for the Burmese the collapse of a whole cosmological and moral order anchored in the royal capital. As a senior monk expressed it in a *ratu* poem:

> No more the Royal Umbrella,
> No more the Royal Palace,
> and the Royal City, no more . . .
> This is indeed an Age of Nothingness
> 'Twere better we were dead.[11]

Indeed, this was widely perceived as the end of an era, for at the end of a Buddhist World Age, the throne is the last part of the whole world to disappear. But the British strategy underestimated the forces that could be generated by this period of dislocation and uncertainty in between world ages.

The fall of the centre saw a flurry of activity from various claimants to a restored throne. Some, like the Myinzaing and Limbin princes, had established ancestries, but many others were pretenders with dubious claims to royalty. British reports mention, without going into much detail, individual foci of resistance who went by the names of Buddha Yaza (Buddha Raja), Dhamma Yaza (Dhamma Raja), or Setkya Mintha (Setkya Prince). In the past, the Burmese state had harnessed the notion of *cakkavatti* to legitimize its conquests and reigns. Now the field was open to practically anyone who could successfully claim to be an Embryo or Future Buddha who would restore the traditional Buddhist monarchy. Having a direct, genealogical link to the old royal family was an advantage, but in the end what mattered most were one's leadership qualities and ability to address millennial expectations. District chiefs (*thugyi*), *weikza*, *saya* and *pongyi* were able to gather bands of fighting men around them by demonstrating their possession of inner power and claiming to hasten the coming of the new Buddhist age.

The role of monks and ex-monks was crucial in the resistance movement. The British attempted to neutralize the monks by acting through the Buddhist ecclesiastical authority in the same way the kings had done. But although the Thathanabaing offered to preach submission to the British if his traditional authority was upheld, in fact he no longer commanded the

---

[10] Cited in Donald Smith, *Religion and Politics in Burma*, Princeton, 1965, 84; and Ni Ni Myint, *Burma's Struggle against British Imperialism*, 1885–1895, Rangoon, 1983, 42.
[11] Cited in Ni Ni Myint, 42

respect of the majority of monks, his proclamation being regarded as a betrayal of the cause. All over upper and lower Burma men in yellow robes were reported to be advising rebel leaders, or actually bearing arms at the head of guerrilla bands. Among those who rejected the Thathana-baing's advice to surrender to the British was U Parama, a Shan. The Thathanabaing had appointed him the district *saṅgha* official for the Hsipaw region in the Shan States. But he joined the Myinzaing prince's resistance movement, then on the latter's death joined the faction of the Limbin prince, who made him 'Thathanabaing of the Shan States'. Even when Limbin surrendered in 1887, U Parama continued to hold out until he was captured. The significance of his rejection of the Thathanabaing is not just that he was against the British takeover, but that the fall of Mandalay, the old centre, had created the possibility of the peripheries— in this case, the Shan States—reasserting themselves.

There were some colourful rebel monks whose careers drew more than the casual mention in British records. In 1886 U Ottama, who had cast off his yellow robe, unsuccessfully attacked Salin, in Minbu District, with more than 3000 men. He established a small principality of his own north of Minbu and controlled it until the end of 1888, when British counterin-surgency measures succeeded in depriving him of village support. The military police found him, with only one follower, sitting despairingly by the Chaungdawya pagoda. Then there was U Kelatha, a self-proclaimed Setkya-min, who with eighteen followers attacked Fort Dufferin in 1887. Now this fort was actually the old Mandalay palace which U Kelatha attempted to occupy in order to cosmologically turn the tide of war against the British. Finally, there was the ex-monk U Po Lu who declared himself a *min-laung* (king-to-be) and led a ragtag band of peasants into Sandoway in 1889. Assisting him was a blind monk renowned as an expert in invul-nerability charms.

Effective police action by the British saw to it that these uprisings were contained and finally suppressed. Conflating all such disturbances to the category of 'dacoity'—a tactic used by the colonizer all over Southeast Asia—was one way of excluding such activities from the realm of 'normal' politics. As the British consolidated their gains, they encouraged the development of a new, non-hereditary, urban-based and Western-educat-ed élite; from this group would spring the nationalists of the twentieth century. The monkhood, now more fragmented than ever, had to relin-quish much of its educational role beyond the village and was encouraged to confine its activities to 'religion'. However, the expectations that an ideal Buddhist king—a Setkya-min, perhaps, or Buddha Yaza—would someday restore Burma's greatness never really faded in the rural areas. In the following century armed uprisings continued to break out in the old areas of Setkya-min activity. And when urban nationalists arrived in the villages to preach their anti-colonial message, their success would depend very much on tapping Buddhist notions of change.

The French occupation of Vietnam differed significantly from the British occupation of Burma in that the Confucian court was not the object of destruction. By gradually turning the monarchy into a facade, however, the French upset the harmony between heaven and earth that the emperor ritually sustained. Resistance to French rule was evoked in the name of the emperor, who stood for an idealized existence on earth; in this sense, one can speak of a millennial dimension to the event. For the sectarian movements in the south, the slippage between Confucian appeals and the Buddha Master's prophecies spawned another flurry of activity that would remain fairly constant through to the next century.

The French forward movement began in September 1858, when an invasion force sent by Napoleon III seized Da Nang. Early the following year the Gia Dinh defence complex around present-day Saigon (Ho Chi Minh City) fell. In late February 1861 the defence complex at Ky-Hoa, outside Gia Dinh, was overrun by the French. After this battle, the formal, organized Vietnamese defence deteriorated progressively. The French wove a net of treaties and concessions around the court at Hué, continued to recognize it as the legitimate source of local authority, then propped it up against those who angrily turned against the imperial collaborators.

Meanwhile, popular resistance in the Mekong delta, under the banner of the Popular Self-Defence Movement, developed mostly under the leadership of local scholar-gentry and landowners who ignored the Hué court's compromise dealings with the French. That elements of the scholar-gentry should become foci of resistance was to be expected, given the popular regard for them as the 'soul' (*linh hon*), the spiritual locus of society in times of great crisis. Truong Dinh, for example, could count on a fighting force of about a thousand tenants and peasants armed with spears and swords. The pompous title he adopted, Binh-Tay Sat-Ta Dai Tuong (Western Pacifying, Antiheresy General), bespeaks the Confucian order which he sought to uphold against the Catholics and barbarians.

The *nghia quan* - 'righteous armies' or partisans—of Truong and others repeatedly ambushed French strongholds and rivercraft, assassinated collaborators, and taunted court representatives to go out and fight the enemy. Among the populace there circulated the now famous eight-character epithet: 'Phan and Lam sell out the country; the court doesn't care for the people.'[12] The guerrilla partisans, however, drew a careful distinction between the actual, reigning king and the moral principle of loyalty to the monarchy. While condemning the court, they repeatedly pledged loyalty to the monarchy as an idealized institution. In the past, the defence of this political and moral order often demanded the sacrifice of their lives in fighting Chinese invasions. This became part of a tradition of martyrdom. As the great poet Nguyen Dinh Chieu wrote of the peasants killed fighting the French near Saigon in 1861: 'You are dead, but temples and shrines have been erected for your cult, and your name shall be cherished by thousands of generations to come.'[13]

The seemingly interminable resistance in the delta, and the breakdown of mandarin rule, were largely responsible for the French decision to seize all of its provinces and establish direct rule in 1867. The departure of most of the patriotic scholar-gentry after 1867 did not, however, usher in

---

[12] Cited in David G. Marr, *Vietnamese Anticolonialism*, Berkeley, 1971, 32.
[13] Cited in Alexander B. Woodside, *Community and Revolution in Modern Vietnam*, Boston, 1976, 29.

the tranquillity expected by the French. For while scholars drew upon Confucian ideals to mobilize the peasants behind the throne, a good many of the armed partisan units, even under the Popular Self-Defence Movement's banner, were actually religio-political or sectarian in nature. Confucian scholars and emergent Buddha-Masters had found common ground in the anti-colonial struggle. The French realized this when their attention was drawn in 1867 to the person of Tran Van Thanh, who had been an officer in the regular army but later emerged as the leader of the Dao Lanh sect which was determined to continue the fight.

Tran Van Thanh had built up his base near the border with Cambodia, where he communicated with the spirits, practised healing, and distributed amulets to his hodgepodge of followers who had come from all parts of southern Vietnam. The Buu Son Ky Hong tradition, ever powerful in this region, was expressing itself in a distinctly anti-colonial form. It is significant that the struggle here transcended ethnic divisions. Tran's closest ally was a Cambodian monk and 'holy man' named Pou Kombo. The French by 1864 had gained a firm foothold in King Norodom's court. In 1865 Pou Kombo rallied the Khmers in eastern Cambodia and southern Vietnam around him by claiming to be a grandson of King Ang Chan, who would restore the greatness of the kingdom. At one point his followers numbered ten thousand and even threatened the court at Udong. He and Tran Van Thanh together raided French military positions in Chau Doc until Pou Kombo's death in 1867.

In 1872, the Hué court, which in the past would have attempted to neutralize the sect's influence, sent Tran Van Thanh a banner bearing the characters *Gia Nghi* (Resolute and Righteous)—a signal to step up the struggle. But the following year the French killed Tran, exposing his body for three days to demoralize the sect. Unfortunately they had not reckoned on the popular belief in reincarnation. The Dao Lanh apostles spread the word that Tran had merely disappeared from the world of the living. In the midst of a cholera epidemic followed by the threat of famaine in 1877, an apostle announced that a spirit had told him that the time had come to expel the French. This spirit would descend from heaven and actually lead the faithful into combat and make them invulnerable. The embodiment of this spirit was a certain Nam Thiep.

Nam Thiep was able to unify the Dao Lanh groups and mount a rebellion in 1878. He announced that the Low Era was ending, and that the reign of the Emperor of Light (i.e. the Maitreya) was being established. Peasants armed with bamboo spears and amulets attacked French garrisons, only to be driven back decisively by rifle fire. But this did not faze Nam Thiep, who in 1879 proclaimed himself a living Buddha and built a new community on Elephant Mountain, in the region of the Seven Mountains.

The year 1882 must have been a particularly ominous one for the peasant populace of the region. Rumours spread of the French occupation of Hanoi and their operations throughout the Red (Hong) River delta. Then late in the year the cholera struck, and a comet appeared in the sky. These events triggered fresh expectations of a cataclysm. The comet was interpreted by Dao Lanh preachers as a sign of the impending French departure. Not surprisingly, various sects began to mobilize, swelling the population of Nam Thiep's base on Elephant Mountain. Khmers, Vietnamese, and Chinese alike could be counted among the adherents. However, no long-term plans were made for a revolt, the assumption being that the court would send in reinforcements and the rest of the populace would join in as groups of sectarians traversed the villages.

Like his predecessor Tran van Thanh, Nam Thiep became involved in Cambodian affairs in 1885. Soon after the French had succeeded in pressuring King Norodom into signing a treaty that, among other things, installed French Residents in provincial cities and threatened to dismantle the Cambodian feudal order, a rebellion broke out under the leadership of Prince Si Votha, Norodom's half-brother. Significantly, the provincial élite was able to rally popular support by comparing French treatment of Norodom with the way the Vietnamese had treated the Cambodian royal family in the past. In other words, the French were seen to be threatening the very foundations of the Buddhist polity and social order. In such a situation, as in Burma around that time, claims to power by someone with dynastic links would have fused with popular beliefs in the coming of a messiah Buddha who would restore the political, economic and religious integrity of the kingdom after a period of disorder. This may also explain why Nam Thiep was enthusiastic about supporting Si Votha's cause, to the extent of enlisting Dao Lanh members in the Cambodian forces. The rebellion began to subside only when the French allowed King Norodom to travel around the countryside to convince the insurgents that the reigning monarch was still in control of the centre.

With the Cambodian rebellion over by 1886, the Vietnamese volunteers returned to their base. At this point, however, the French noted an increase in sectarian activity coinciding with the circulation of decrees calling for the population to rise in support of Emperor Ham Nghi. Peasant restiveness was, in fact, noted all over Vietnam and must be seen in the overall context of the collapse of the monarchy.

The death of Tu Duc in 1883 had precipitated a crisis of succession, which enabled the French to negotiate a treaty turning Vietnam into a French protectorate. On 5 July 1885 the boy Emperor Ham Nghi fled the capital and called for an all-out struggle to expel the French. The numerous scholar-gentry and peasants who had been organizing local resistance in previous years without royal sanction were elated to find their ruler amongst them. This did not mean that other members of the royal family ceased their collaboration with the French. However, henceforth the succession of kings on the Hué throne would be regarded as mere puppets by the anti-French activists and their peasant supporters. With the centre spiritually empty, resistance could galvanize, in the traditional manner, around the person of the 'real' king, or around various pretenders to the throne.

The circulation throughout Vietnam of the edict of Can Vuong (Loyalty to the King) considerably widened the terrain of anti-French resistance. Now, for example, central Vietnam, Ham Nghi's base, was in turmoil as well. The history of the Can Vuong movement is too complex to be detailed here. The pertinent question to ask is why ordinary villagers responded to this royalist, scholar-gentry affair. The edict provides some clues: while it was addressed mainly to the scholar-gentry, it also had great emotional impact when read or interpreted to the populace at large. 'With luck,' it said, 'Heaven will also treat man with kindness, turning chaos into order, danger into peace, and helping thus to restore our land and our frontiers. Is not this opportunity fortunate for our country, meaning fortunate for the people, since all who worry and work together will certainly reach peace and happiness together?'[14] We get the sense here that popular participation in the movement was a way of restoring the harmony between heaven and society that was so crucial for prosperity and happiness. Without a proper emperor, there was no one to mediate between heaven and earth through the proper performance of rituals, no one to assure that agriculture, society and state were properly attuned to the workings of fate.

In a sense the Can Vuong movement was also a popular, religious one. Tenants and peasants who joined the scholar-gentry can, of course, be seen as merely fulfilling their traditional duties towards their intellectual and social betters. However, the scholar-gentry also represented, at the local level, the link between the human and divine planes of existence. The political situation after 1885 would have been construed by many as the imminent end of the dynastic cycle, precipitating a tumultuous period during which the mandate of heaven might shift to another claimant. And this was precisely one of those times when the scholar-gentry assumed leadership of popular movements. But the scholar was only one type of figure around whom the peasantry traditionally gathered. To those informed by Buddhist notions of history, the very same events—the Can Vuong manifesto even—would have intensified perceptions of the Low Era. Thus the attraction of messianic figures like Nam Thiep.

There is a Javanese parallel to the French co-optation of the Vietnamese court aristocracy and the stiffening of resistance towards the centre which this engendered. The identification of the *priyayi* and their 'official Islam' with the Dutch during the second half of the nineteenth century exacerbated the tensions between centres and peripheries in Java, whose history during this period is filled with accounts of disturbances, illicit gatherings, and uprisings. Some of these were located in areas haunted by the potent spirits of past kingdoms; such were the 'illicit' gatherings around the graves of the Mangkunegara dynasty on Mount Lawu's slopes. A desire for wholeness in this age of colonial economic penetration and political reordering made millennial appeals and messianic figures attractive; at the very least, groups of people could seek to withdraw from the colonial order and its money economy in order to maintain their self-worth. To Dutch officials, at least, the most serious threat came from the Islamic figures who wandered about preaching jihad and the imminent arrival of a new era. As the Dutch *kāfir* presence intensified, village Koranic schools and *pesantren* increased in number, injected with anti-colonial sentiments by *ulamā* and hajjis circulating through a network of *pesantren* and *tarekat*.

14 Cited in Marr, 50–1.

The spread of anti-colonial sentiments can be traced in part to the intensification of the pilgrimage to Mecca. The liberal policies following the dismantling of the Cultivation System in the 1870s brought increasing wealth to those able to respond to new economic opportunities. For these fortunate ones, success was to be capped by fulfilling the last religious duty: the pilgrimage. Despite restrictions placed by the Dutch, the numbers of pilgrims increased dramatically after the opening of the Suez Canal in 1869. Although only a select few stayed long enough to study under a great teacher and be initiated into a *tarekat*, even the masses of pilgrims could not but be transformed by the experience of the pilgrimage. In Mecca they mingled with co-religionists of all classes and races and learned about the crisis being faced by Islam as a result of Western expansion.

Hajjis returned to their towns and villages aware of the need for purification, renewal, and even outright assertion against the colonizer. It was common to find hajjis and their circles of followers constituting small communities within the wider Muslim community and yet set apart from it through their puritanism, austerity, and condemnation of *adat*. A notable example in the 1850s was Hajji Mohamad Rifangi who started a movement of sorts, called the Budiah movement, among the rural populace of Pekalongan and Kedu residencies. There was nothing outwardly 'anti-colonial' about this movement, but the members' withdrawal from the collective social and religious life of their villages, plus Hajji Rifangi's constant disruption of 'official' religious services in the Kalisalak mosque, were subversive enough to local officials, who secured his exile to Ambon.

Reformist and pan-Islamic sentiments spread by the hajjis had the potential of being translated into mass action. For the majority of Javanese, the last two decades of the century saw a drastic decline in living standards. This, combined with ever more regulations and tax exactions from a more efficient bureaucracy, made the peasantry receptive to appeals for a rejection of the colonial order. As stated earlier, however, such appeals were never received in pristine form, for they had to operate within a field of older expectations and traditions. The activities of itinerant hajjis prior to the 1888 uprisings in Banten are illustrative. When Hajji Abdul Karim, a guru in the Kadiriah *tarekat*, returned to Banten in 1872, he not only established a religious school in his home village but travelled through Banten, holding purification rites, *dhikr* (short prayers with ritualized body movements) and processions. In the religious revival that ensued, he came to be regarded as a saintly figure with curative and invulnerability powers, his prestige outshining the local *priyayi* officials. He predicted an imminent jihad, the arrival of the Mahdi and the 'Last Judgement'. Says the Dutch Islamicist Snouck Hurgronje, 'Every evening hundreds eager for salvation flocked to where he was staying, to learn the *dhikr* from him, to kiss his hand and to ask *if the time were at hand* and how long the Kafir government would continue.'[15]

Other holy men, all hajjis, circulated through the branches of the Kadiriah *tarekat* in the Banten region, propagating the message of jihad

---

[15] Cited in Sartono Kartodirdjo, *The Peasants' Revolt of Banten in 1888*, 's-Gravenhage: Martinus Nijhoff, 1966, 180.

and the coming of the Imam Mahdi to packed audiences in the mosques, at the same time dispensing or selling amulets, rosaries and copies of the Koran brought back from Mecca. When hostilities broke out in Cilegon in July 1888, the ragtag rebel army was composed largely of peasant disciples or devotees of the *kyai* who marched against superior government forces, convinced that they were invulnerable in waging the holy war. In less than a month the rebellion was crushed, but the spirit of revolt was not extinguished. Despite the indiscriminate persecution of hajjis, Islamic teachers and mystics continued to circulate surreptitiously throughout the *tarekat* and *pesantren* networks; bands of gurus and pupils re-emerged from time to time threatening new insurrections.

The impact of the pilgrimage and orthodox Islam in shaping popular opposition to the Dutch-*priyayi* colonial order is clearly demonstrated in other Javanese movements and disturbances, and need not be mentioned individually here. It needs to be stressed, however, that colonial officials tended to exaggerate the Islamic element in the various movements and 'disturbances' they discovered. When, for example, a certain Djasmani was arrested together with his armed band in the residency of Kediri, there was an attempt to link him to the Banten rebellion then raging. Actually, he had absolutely no connection with hajjis or *tarekat*, his aim being to establish a new kingdom and be proclaimed Sunan Hrutjokro or Sultan Adil. Another popular leader, Kasan Mukmin, did visit *pesantren* and famous *kyai* but was not recognized by religious leaders with authority. He was regarded as an ordinary curer (*dukun*), yet to his enthusiastic followers in the 1903 revolt he was an incarnation of Imam Mahdi. There were numerous sectarian movements that had nothing to do with Islam, but were manifestations of a much older search, through Javanese mystical practices (*kebatinan*), for equilibrium and fulfilment in a world gone out of kilter.

The difficulty of neatly classifying Javanese resistance to colonialism shows up in the Samin movement. From about 1890 Surontiko Samin, an illiterate villager, began to attract a following in the Blora regency. No notice was taken of this movement until about 1905, when local officials reported the Saminists' withdrawal from common village activities. More seriously, they either refused to pay taxes or regarded payments as voluntary contributions. They also insulted the local *priyayi* officials by replying in *ngoko* (low Javanese) during interrogation. The government could not quite gain a clear picture of the movement. Samin's teachings were interpreted differently by individual gurus and their followers. There were said to be expectations of a new era and the *ratu adil* or Erutjakra, and Samin himself was to assume the title of *raja* while two followers would get names from *wayang* mythology. But these attributes of a 'typical' Javanese messianic movement were denied by the leaders, and appear rather to have been various readings of the movement's aims by followers or outsiders.

It is clear that the Saminists rejected outside interference, government restrictions and demands, and the money economy. Furthermore, their religious beliefs had much in common with Javanese mystics—such as, for example, their notion of 'God is within me.' But although they did not mount an armed insurrection, their movement was plainly subversive. Whilst their immediate targets appeared to be the *priyayi*, Chinese middlemen, and European officialdom, in a wider sense they were opting out of the whole social order based on the Islamized *abangan* village, with its normalized traditions and hierarchies. They refused the ritual mediation — such as at weddings — of Islamic officials, not out of doctrinal difference but because they eschewed altogether the notion of an official hierarchy.

In a situation wherein new alien ideologies were penetrating the Javanese hinterland, it is not surprising that Christianity, too, would figure in uniquely Javanese forms of protest. Conversion to Christianity, of course, implied submission to Dutch rule in most cases. It was the religion of the Dutch, and conversion was seen as *masuk belanda* ('entering Dutch society'). However, as in the Philippines, Christianity could lead to dissatisfaction with colonial rule and offer an idiom of resistance to it. In 1817 Protestant converts in Maluku (Moluccas) led by an Ambonese Christian soldier, Thomas Matulesia (known as Pattimura), rose against the Dutch; they invoked biblical themes to legitimize their action. In the Batak region, as we shall see, the Christian God was seen as a source of power to counter missionary hegemony. The relative paucity of Christian-inspired protest movements can perhaps be attributed to the Dutch reluctance to allow missionary proselytization, especially in Java. It was only after 1850 that the government reluctantly granted permission to missionary organizations to operate in some residencies.

The most remarkable example of nineteenth-century Javanese adaptation to Christianity and the latter's use as a vehicle of protest was the Sadrach movement in central Java. Sadrach might be regarded as a typical rural religious leader trained in Javanese and Islamic mystic traditions. In the late 1860s, however, he discovered in Christianity a superior *ngelmu* (faith or knowledge). He won a following by displaying his superiority to other gurus. By the 1870s he was regarded as *guru kuasa*, a 'powerful teacher,' as well as a famous healer (*dukun*); he used Christian formulae in addressing his followers. Large groups came under his leadership. Some were of *santri* background, some *abangan*. The gathering of various Christian groups around him partly fitted into the pattern of *guru* and *murid* (teacher and pupil). By 1887 Sadrach's circle involved seventy local and seven regional groups. This congregation was independent of the Christian church, the members being loyal to Sadrach personally as in the case of pupils in a *tarekat*.

Javanese messianic expectations found specific expression among a good number of Sadrach's followers in the *ratu adil*, who was none other than Christ. Sadrach himself was expected to participate in the restoration of Javanese society and the expulsion of foreigners. In fact, Sadrach should be counted as one of several Javanese religious leaders who resisted Dutch dominance — specifically that of the church and the missionary orders — at that time. Eventually he was denounced by Dutch missionaries as a false teacher, and intense efforts were made to integrate him and his flock into the official church.

The Dutch forward movement in Sumatra had begun in Minangkabau in the 1820s, precipitating, as we have seen, the Padri War. In the 1850s and 1860s, Dutch 'pacification' efforts extended to Palembang, Jambi and other small states where opposition to the Dutch and their local allies was fanned by hajjis and local *ulamā*. The Dutch advance northward brought them to Batak country and to Aceh, where the most spirited and long-lived resistance took place.

Batak resistance to colonial rule centred on the Si Singa Mangaraja ('great-king-kind-of-lion') figure. Although Batak traditions acknowledge the existence of such a dynasty, the Si Singa Mangaraja was not normally a political figure among the Batak. He was revered as a divine king and an incarnation of Batara Guru. He had the ability to summon rain and control rice-growing, to drive evil spirits away, and so forth. His main political function was to maintain harmony among the Batak people as well as stable relationships with the outside world. When the Padris spilled over from Minangkabau territory in the 1820s, the tenth Si Singa Mangaraja (Ompu Na Bolon) became the symbol of Toba Batak unity against the intruders.

The economic and political transformation wrought by the Dutch presence in the Toba area tested the power of Si Singa Mangaraja. Also, missionary activity from the 1850s began to divide the local chiefs, some of whom had come to terms with the new religion in order to consolidate and extend their power. Although not personally opposed to the Christian missionaries, Si Singa Mangaraja XI and his son (the twelfth) were pushed by anti-missionary chiefs and Acehnese agents into confrontation with the Dutch. In 1878, Si Singa Mangaraja XII held a religious ceremony to unify his people, and then went off to fight the Dutch in what amounted to a holy war. Defeated, he consolidated his forces and struck again in 1883, with Acehnese aid. This time the Dutch wounded him, destroyed his most important shrine, and drove him off his land. He was killed in a skirmish in 1907.

The Batak, however, believed that the Si Singa Mangarajas did not die but just disappeared. Even upon Si Singa Mangaraja XII's death, his *tona*, (real or imagined commands) and those of his son Raja Buntal were still widely obeyed. Moreover, the call to restoration of this legendary god-king inspired Bataks from all over the region, not just the Toba, to join sects and movements which often turned against Dutch rule. From 1890 on, the Batak region experienced the rise of the Parmalim, Na Siak Bagi and Parhudamdam movements, all proclaiming the restoration of Si Singa Mangaraja's ideal kingdom.

In the Parmalim (from the Batak *malim*, 'to be different from others') movements, Si Singa Mangaraja spoke through various local gurus. However, by this time many Christian concepts and names—God, Jesus and the Virgin Mary being prominent—had entered into the vocabulary of the movement. Although their God was the same as that of the Dutch, the Parmalim preached that they offered a superior means of access to the Supreme Being Jehovah. Parmalim groups refused to accept the terms of subordination imposed by the Dutch government, so from around 1890 various Parmalin gurus promising God's protection and Si Singa Mangaraja's reappearance, were able to gather disaffected Batak around them to protest against the Dutch measures. The inevitable suppression of these movements did not extinguish Parmalim beliefs which, however, underwent revision in an attempt to tap the power of the Europeans. Conversion to Christianity practically decimated its ranks in the early 1900s.

The Na Siak Bagi ('man suffering from misfortune') movement took a slightly different turn. Si Jaga Simatupang, a prominent leader of the later stage of the Parmalim, preached a return to the Toba High God, Muladji Na Bolon, as their source of power. However, this revival was heavily influenced by Christian moral injunctions. Si Jaga, who assumed the name Na Siak Bagi, convinced his followers that the poor and humble were to share in God's power, and that even Si Singa Mangaraja might appear to them in humble garb. By 1910 Na Siak Bagi had attracted a wide following, including a few chiefs, and people came to him for amulets and to undergo rituals of purification. Many thought of him not just as a messenger of their High God, but as a new Si Singa Mangaraja himself. The Dutch, rightly perceiving Na Siak Bagi as a potential focus of rebellion, had him arrested in November of that year.

The only serious challenge to the Dutch consolidation of Sumatra came at the hands of the Acehnese. Aceh was wealthy, organized, well armed, and fully determined to remain independent. The Dutch force that first invaded Kota Raja (Banda Aceh) in 1873 was driven out. And when Kota Raja was finally occupied the following year, the sultan and much of the populace fled to the hills to begin a guerrilla war that formally ended only in the early 1900s. The parallels with Burma after the British capture of Mandalay, or the Philippines after the United States army overran Malolos, are striking. The loss of the capital, the centre, triggers a more bitter and prolonged conflict because charismatic local leaders and their followers enter the fray, releasing the tremendous though often short-lived energies of a populace experiencing a violent transition between two eras. In the Aceh War the familiar themes of pan-Islamism, jihad, millennial expectations and *ulamā* leadership are clearly manifested. Although the Ottomans never really provided the assistance expected of them, their moral support and that of Muslim centres throughout the archipelago sustained the Acehnese through the first two decades of the war. Also, events like the Russo-Turkish War of 1877-8, the Mahdist rebellion in the Sudan, and the passage of a Turkish warship through Singapore in 1890, were perceived as signs of forthcoming success in the protracted jihad.

Clearly, the tenacity of the Acehnese resistance can be attributed to the efforts of the *pesantren*-based *ulamā*, the most distinguished among them being Teungku Cik di Tiro. By the time guerrilla warfare commenced in 1881, he had taken over leadership from the *hulubalang* or *uleebalang* (hereditary chiefs) and their religious officials. The *ulamā* constructed ramparts in the mountains, collected 'holy war contributions', and even succeeded in reconquering areas which were returned to the *hulubalang*. What constituted the basis of their popular appeal? The *ulamā*, who counted among them Arabs of Hadhramaut Sayyid descent, were the links to the reformist and anti-colonial currents in the Islamic world. Committed to the goal of a revitalized Islamic community, they and their pupils lived in perpetual tension with the chiefs and ordinary villagers, who had other visions of their own. It was the circumstances of war that enabled the *ulamā* successfully to draw peasants away from their traditional kinship obligations, in order to unite as Muslims. But even then, what appealed most to the guerrilla fighters was not the image of a community of believers but the fulfilment of their desires in a heavenly existence. As the *Hikayat Prang Sabil* (Epic of the Holy War) put it,

> The blessings of God are unlimited for those who serve,
> who fight the *prang sabi*.
> To those He gives Paradise full of light,
> Seventy heavenly princesses.
> More than can be counted He gives ...
>   You will get a new face, a young one ...
> God will give you wealth and life ...[16]

By 1903 the royal family and the *hulubalang* had been completely subdued. But the guerrilla war continued in the form of attacks by small bands under the guidance or outright leadership of *ulamā*. These *muslimin* (Muslims), as the Acehnese called them, were prepared to die a martyr's death rather than submit to the rule of *kāfir*. It was only in 1913 that the two main centres of resistance were broken, by which time tens of thousands of Acehnese had died in the war. The Dutch attempted to neutralize further outbreaks by propping up the authority of the *hulubalang* as district chiefs, in the same way that they established collaborative ties with the Javanese *priyayi* chiefs and the Minangkabau *penghulus*. At the same time, the *ulamā* were to be restricted to purely religious affairs. This strategy, however, merely deepened the divisions, aggravated by the war, within Acehnese society. Up to the 1930s local *ulamā* continued to attract groups of followers around them. Together they would recite the forbidden *Hikayat Prang Sabil*, take an oath of resistance, and then go off to attack some Dutch outpost. At times, individuals took this path to Paradise by attacking Dutchmen in the towns, a phenomenon the Dutch called *Atjeh-moord*.

Dutch expansion into Kalimantan (Borneo), a response to the growing presence of the Englishman James Brooke and his successor, produced significant resistance in the west and southeast of the island. In 1859 Pangeran Antasari, a prince from a branch of the Banjermasin royal house that had lost out in an internal power struggle, rose against the Dutch and their client ruler. Although major hostilities had ceased by 1863 (Antasari was killed the previous year), the conflict persisted up to 1905. Antasari was fortunate in having by his side a popular peasant leader called Sultan Kuning, who was a healer and practised invulnerability magic. The Banjermasin War was, in fact, another holy war. At one point

[16] Cited in James T. Siegel, *The Rope of God*, Berkeley, 75.

the movement's centre was located in a village which was perceived as a transplanted Mecca. Small bands of men armed with charms and cursing the *kāfir* would emerge to attack the Dutch working in the nearby coal mines. Not only did the rebels hope to revive Banjermasin's past glory: they looked to a future without taxes and where all their wishes would be fulfilled.

In the peninsular Malay states the tensions between 'official' and 'rural' Islam which often fuelled anti-colonial resistance in Java and Sumatra was largely absent. The political structures of the small riverine principalities never evolved to such an extent that an elaborate hierarchy of religious officials was ever deemed necessary. Religious authority thus resided largely with whomever among the rural *ulamā* were seen fit to exercise it. By the end of the century, these *ulamā* were being brought into the new religio-legal bureaucracy then developing in the court centres under British protection. This relatively benign reorientation of *ulamā* activity towards the new, British-supervised order may explain the absence of widespread resistance movements in the Malay states. However, it would be a mistake to equate this with universal acceptance of the new system. The relative absence of millennial movements in the Malay peninsula points to a basic problem in dealing with the interconnection of religion and unrest: we only get to know about the subject when it becomes embodied in a movement or disturbance that becomes visible and threatens the state. Rumoured prophecies, visits by itinerant preachers and curers, unprescribed rituals, irreverent language—such manifestations of 'resistance' tend to evade documentation.

At the more visible level, the late-nineteenth-century intensification of the Mecca pilgrimage did have a pronounced impact upon religious life in Malay communities. The spread of *tarekat* such as the Naksyabandiyya and Kadiriah, coupled with pan-Islamic anti-colonial sentiments transmitted via Singapore, ensured the circulation of millennial visions and prophecies in the margins of the Islamic court centres. The potential was there for these images to be drawn upon for religious mobilization against an intruder or overlord. Resistance to Thai suzerainty is a case in point. In the early 1800s, following Siam's conquest of Kedah, a protracted jihad was declared on the Thai infidels. By the turn of the century, the Chakri consolidation of its territorial claims vis-à-vis the British resulted in a redrawing of lines which left Pattani, by 1909, as the only Malay state within the Thai ambit. The incorporation of this famed 'cradle of Islam' into the Thai state beginning in 1902 met with resistance from the disempowered nobility and particularly the *ulamā*. From 1903 *ulamā* and their followers engaged in tax boycotts and other acts of insubordination. In 1910 public offices were burned down by a group led by To'Tae, an elderly mystic claiming invulnerability. The following year, the Thai authorities with difficulty put down another uprising led by a certain Hajji Bula. By far the most widespread uprising occurred in 1922, when *ulamā* successfully appealed for a jihad against the Buddhist régime.

The British success in working gradually through the traditional leadership probably explains why anti-British uprisings were rare in the Malay states. However, there were at least two instances where open conflict, with religious overtones, did break out. One was in Sabah where local opposition to new taxes imposed by the North Borneo Company found expression in Mat Salleh's rebellion which began in 1895 and simmered till 1905, taking on the aspects of a jihad. Mat Salleh's use of Islamic standards as well as symbols of royalty attracted a wide following. To Muslims he was the Mahdi, the coming saviour.

A more significant movement against British control occurred in Pahang. Only grudgingly did the sultan accept the presence of a British Resident, and even then the interior chiefs refused to concede. Things came to a head in 1891 when the Resident persuaded Sultan Ahmad to sign a decree depriving a district chief, Dato Bahaman, of his title. The latter came out in open defiance, initiating a series of armed confrontations known as the Pahang War. Pan-Islamic anti-colonial appeals were in evidence at this point. However, the rebel chiefs always claimed that they were defending the ruler's interests. It was Sultan Ahmad's tacit support that gave the movement much of its initial momentum, attesting to his role as the moral and religious centre of Pahang Malay life. This role subsequently came under threat owing to collaboration with the British. As Sultan Ahmad bowed to British pressure, Bahaman and his allies were perceived as the defenders of their heritage against infidel threats. The rebels came to be influenced by a Terengganu holy man, Ungku Sayyid Paloh, who imbued the movement with the spirit of jihad.

During the second half of the nineteenth century, the Spanish colonial state attempted to establish uniform control over the territory it claimed. In part it had the same problems as the other European powers which were drawing the boundaries of Southeast Asia. The army encountered resistance from some of the semi-independent hill peoples of the northern Luzon Cordillera, while the navy was barely able to capture the Muslim capitals of Jolo and Cotabato. Spanish accounts of the wars in the south, beginning with the campaign against Sulu in 1851, are quite clear about the religious dimension as seen from both sides. As a Dominican friar put it in 1876: 'The war against Jolo is now a just war, a holy war in the name of religion.'[17] The *ulamā* of Sulu, naturally, were proclaiming the same cause, calling for its support as an expression of loyalty to the Sultan. The holy war also raged in Mindanao, where Datu Utto had rallied the Magindanaoan chiefs of the interior against the advancing Spaniards. The independent areas showed many signs of an Islamic revival spearheaded by hajjis and foreign-trained *ulamā*, some of Arab origin. Thus, the Spanish conquest of the major towns meant little to a populace that was becoming ever more conscious of its Islamic identity in the face of a direct Christian assault.

The intensity of Islamic fervour in Mindanao and Sulu was brought home to Spanish soldiers and missionaries through the phenomenon they named *juramentado* ('one who has taken an oath'), known as *sabil ullah* to the Sulus. The *juramentado* were groups of men who fearlessly threw themselves upon companies of Spanish soldiers—or Christian civilians

---

[17] Cited in Cesar A. Majul, *Muslims in the Philippines*, Quezon City, 1973, 292.

in marketplaces—inflicting great damage until each one was killed. Although there are few *pesantren* and no *tarekat* on record in Sulu and Mindanao, a close examination reveals that *juramentados* were groups in the *tarekat* tradition. The adepts underwent a period of fasting and meditation under expert *ulamā* or *pandita*. They were then initiated into the teachings of the *parang sabil* (holy war), and offered a vision of Paradise that they would enter upon death. The *juramentado* phenomenon intensified as the sultans increasingly failed to hold their own against the better-equipped Spaniards.

While the 'Moro Wars' captured headlines in the Manila press, the Spanish establishment was actually more preoccupied with consolidating the Christianized territory they supposedly had held for over 250 years. With the loss of much of America and Spain itself in crisis, the colony had to be economically self-sustaining and potential trouble had to be eliminated. In a sense Manila's problems were the same as Bangkok's. The last of the old royal monopolies were abandoned and various port cities,— notably Manila, Iloilo and Cebu—were subsequently opened to international commerce. British, French and United States capital joined up with Spanish and mestizo interests to open new areas to commercial crop cultivation. Such ventures, aided by the new network of ports and roads and the termination of Moro slave-raiding, allowed people in heavily populated areas to migrate to unsettled territory. Unfortunately, few of these pioneers ended up as independent farmers. The funds advanced to them by mestizos and foreigners in order to establish themselves almost certainly dragged them into a cycle of debt, a problem specially acute in the sugar-producing areas. As elsewhere in Southeast Asia where capitalist agriculture took root, peasants took the brunt of declining commodity prices. And as elsewhere, they were increasingly attracted to leaders who promised them a new and better era.

Quite common from the 1860s on were combined police and church actions against illicit gatherings, both in the towns and in the hinterland. What were these proscribed groups up to, and how did religion function in their assertions against the colonial state? Among the dozens of movements discovered in Luzon, let us take just three examples. In 1865 three men addressed at various times by such appellations as *Dios* (God), *Kristo* (Christ) and *Maestro* (Teacher) were reported to be circulating in the Camarines provinces, southeastern Luzon. At secret gatherings in various homes, including a few of the wealthy, people gathered to hear one or the other of the trinity speak about certain doctrines contained in a sacred book. Claiming to have descended from heaven and based on nearby Mount Isarog, they promised to cure sufferers of the cholera and smallpox, relieve the land of locust plagues, and create an abundance of food.

In 1870, the Spanish discovered that a certain Januario Labios had stirred up townspeople around Mount Banahao, in the southern Tagalog region, by claiming to have communicated with the spirit of the dead rebel Apolinario and the Virgin Mary, who had instructed him to rebuild the Cofradía de San José and revive its religious rituals. Those who responded to the call would be rewarded with heavenly bliss in the after-life, but meanwhile they would enjoy independence and freedom from tribute.

Labios, like his model Apolinario, was drawing people away from the town centres toward a 'New Jerusalem'—a complex of sacred caves and springs—in Mount Banahao's foothills. When the police arrested Labios, they found in his possession several notebooks of Tagalog writings about the life of Christ, and some medicinal prescriptions.

The third Luzon example takes us to the provinces north of Manila. Beginning in 1887, Gabino Cortes, a man 'of very small fortune', started to preach to the peasants around Mount Arayat that a worldly catastrophe was imminent. By getting together in small groups to pray and perform communal rituals, they would receive divine protection as well as an abundance of wealth. Considerable numbers of mainly poor peasants from Pampanga and Bulacan provinces gathered in the homes of Cortes's disciples. Since they were dedicated to nonviolence and, after all, recited Christian prayers, the local authorities decided to leave them alone. Gabino, however, was no ordinary lay preacher. Stories circulated that he possessed a magic ball, given to him by an old man on the mountain, with which he could cause money, food, and male attendants to appear. When he was crowned king in 1888, the subversive nature of the movement became all too apparent, and the civil guard moved in to disperse it.

The Visayan islands experienced much the same sorts of assertions against the colonial order. After the great cholera visitation of 1882 and the appearance of a comet in that same year, Spanish officials in Samar and Leyte provinces became preoccupied with a rash of 'disturbances' in inland settlements only recently incorporated into the colonial state. Certain sites—distant from pueblo centres—where images of Catholic saints were venerated for their healing and other miraculous powers, were found to be quartering groups of pilgrims who had come originally to fulfil certain vows made in order to be saved from the cholera. The problem was that these groups of people, who claimed to be there to pray, engage in trade, or merely to satisfy their curiosity, were being won over by itinerant preachers who distributed miraculous cures and prophesied a cataclysm and the coming of a new era.

The rumours that coincided with the appearance of these *Dioses* (Gods) reveal some of the preoccupations of the crowd. Isidro Reyes, who was arrested in early 1884 for promising magical cures, was believed to be a messenger sent by God to announce the coming of a Bisayan king. There was to be a great catastrophe, such as the sinking of the islands or the end of the world. Various groups led by gods or saints armed themselves with primitive weapons and retreated to the hills to await the appearance of a new city ruled by their own king, under a new era in which ancient customs and dress would be revived and the prices of goods would decline. Leaders distributed amulets and magical prayers (*oraciones*) to render protection from enemy bullets and the cholera. In November 1884 three to four hundred rebels attacked Borongan, a major town, but their knives and clubs were no match for Spanish bullets. Police operations, supported by Spanish priests and the local *principales*, continued until 1886.

Just who were these *Dioses*? In the Visayas they were practically identical to the *babaylan*, male and female sorcerers dating back to pre-Spanish society. The *babaylan* had always been around since the conquest, as the shadowy rival of the Catholic priest, attracting people to their haunts beyond the pueblo where they practised their sorcery which in time accommodated many of the symbols and rituals of Catholicism itself— hence their continued attraction to the wider populace. Towards the end of the nineteenth century, the *babaylan* became particularly active among peasants in the islands of Panay and Negros who were suffering from massive indebtedness and from the vagaries of the world economy. Spanish reports of the 1880s, in particular, provide the identities of dozens of men and women arrested for gathering people into 'illicit associations' which practised illegal curing and sorcery, refused to pay taxes, and so on.

Among those with more substantial documentation is Ponciano Elofre, better known as Buhawi (Waterspout, God of the Four Winds), who attracted Spanish attention in 1887 when people from all the towns along the southeastern coast of Negros started trekking to his independent community in the adjacent mountains. Buhawi had all the trappings of a *babaylan*: curing powers, invulnerability, the power to change shape, command of fire, flood and rain. Lest these attributes be regarded in some sort of binary opposition to Christianity, there is also strong evidence that Buhawi had been a devout Catholic, fond of religious processions, and never without a cross hung around his neck. Buhawi's massive following originated as a small, private novena prayer group, which expanded as word spread about his special powers and talents. But there was something else about his message that was attractive: his prediction that the world would be destroyed by a great flood and cast into utter darkness. Those who did not heed his call would perish. Thus Buhawi also came to be called 'The Redeemer' by his followers.

Like the 'holy man' phenomenon in Siam, the movements described above were centred on extraordinary religious leaders: preachers, prophets, gods and Kristos. Their utterances circulated among a populace familiar with traditional animist practices, as well as with figures in the Old and New Testaments who bridged the gap between the divine and human planes of existence. The millennial strains are evident: these men and women pointed to a coming change of era, as heralded by such signs as epidemics (particularly the cholera), comets, and hardships caused by a collapse in the world sugar price.

As the century wore on, the Spanish pueblos themselves became the sites of unrest. While undoubtedly the majority of Spanish priests outside the friar estates continued to be respected, if not revered, the continued ejection of Filipino priests provoked racial tensions that would grow to national proportions. In 1862, there were only twelve parishes left for some 400 secular priests, mainly Filipinos. Brief periods of liberal government, coupled with the influx of the ideas of the Enlightenment specially after the opening of the Suez Canal, accelerated the demands of the native priests for equality. Spanish reaction was firm and unrelenting, from surveillance in the late 1860s to the actual execution of three reformist priests in 1872.

The inadvertent creation of a triad of Filipino martyr-priests gave a more 'national' focus to the popular movements that followed. Even the above-mentioned *Dioses* movements in the Visayas called on followers to pray for the soul of one of the slain priests, Father Burgos. The involvement of ordained priests in some of these religio-political movements is clear, if not yet fully documented. Certainly Filipino priests would be actively involved in the massive rebellion of 1896, and in the resistance to United States occupation from 1899 their behind-the-scenes exhortations would produce comparisons with Indian medicine men.

The rebellion of the Katipunan (Highest and Most Venerable Association of the Offspring of the Land) in 1896 is usually seen as the climax of a liberal awakening, when Enlightenment ideas imbibed by Europeanized Filipino intellectuals since the 1880s finally became translated into a mass movement. When viewed 'from below', however, the religious dimension of this movement is unmistakeable. In exhorting the lower classes to participate, the Katipunan leadership juxtaposed events of colonial history with biblical images of the Fall from Eden; joining the rebellion was interpreted as a redemptive act; the rallying cry *kalayaan* ('liberty') reverberated with meanings of a return to a condition of wholeness and prosperity. Furthermore, the execution in December 1896 of the celebrated propagandist Dr José Rizal gave the movement a martyr to focus on. Rizal's own words and behaviour ensured that his final hours would be interpreted in terms of Christ's passion and death, a story familiar to every Christianized Filipino. And sure enough the image of a 'Filipino Christ' was seized upon equally by the revolutionary leadership and independent sectarian leaders. Henceforth, Rizal would be incarnated in many a peasant rebel leader until well into the next century.

By 1897 the Katipunan uprising was widely interpreted as a sign of an impending change of eras. True, the pueblo élites in all but a few provinces around Manila remained aloof from the fray or loyal to Spain. But, significantly, all over the islands those illicit associations in the peripheries of the pueblo centres re-emerged to fight the Spaniards. The descendants of the Cofradia on Mount Banahao—now the 'Katipunan of San Cristobal'—with their saints and magical ropes, attacked the Spanish garrison at Tayabas. The movement of Gabino Cortes resurrected as the Santa Iglesia of Felipe Salvador. The followers of Buhawi became a Katipunan under the leadership of Papa (Pope) Isio. One movement—the Guardia de Honor—originally recruited to defend friar interests against the 1898 republic, became imbued with millennial expectations and was broken up by the Americans. Movements such as these led by prophets, saints and curers certainly saw the war years as part of the great cataclysm preceding the end of the world. By the end of the century, then, the religio-political movements of earlier decades had largely reappeared as 'nationalist' ones. Yet they remained distinct from, and subversive of, the 1898 republican order and the mainstream independence movements during United States rule.

The wars of conquest now largely over, the early twentieth century is generally viewed as a new period marked by various manifestations of the 'modern'. The privileged native actors are now the urban-educated élites speaking the languages of progress and national unity. The organizations which they established are readily contrasted with the more 'traditional' and 'backward-looking' movements characteristic of the previous century. Yet the latter continued to thrive in their rural environments during the period of high colonialism. Not only that, but the course of 'modern' movements was profoundly shaped by older terrains and discourses.

As the Americans discovered in the aftermath of the Philippine war (1899–1902), military victory and the co-optation of the élite did not terminate the event called 'the revolution'. Macario Sakay, a veteran of the Katipunan secret society and sometime actor in passion plays, continued the resistance in Luzon until 1906. Priests of the Philippine Independent (Aglipayan) Church which had broken off from Rome in 1902, preached on the theme of the 'unfinished revolution' to congregations which continued to grow through the 1910s. In Aglipayan and other sectarian churches throughout the islands there evolved a religious iconography which juxtaposed Christian and revolutionary figures. A messianic figure was generated in 1910 when the exiled General Artemio Ricarte promised to return with the aid of the Mikado's fleet, bringing independence. Secret societies allegedly under Ricarte's direction attempted to rise upon the outbreak of the Great War in 1914.

Among the most effective resistance leaders of this period were the curers, sorcerers and sectarian preachers of old who now promised to obtain that magical condition called 'independence'. In the Visayas, Papa Otoy and Papa Isio held out until 1907. Felipe Salvador, variously hailed as king, pope or Christ by his peasant followers, continued his proselytizing in central Luzon until his capture in 1910 after he had occupied a town in the belief that the appearance of Halley's Comet signalled the advent of independence. But, after Salvador's execution, others readily filled the void. The proliferation of rural sects went largely unnoticed until the early 1920s when police fought skirmishes with sectarians led by a preacher known as Lantayug, who claimed to be a reincarnation of Rizal. Thousands of peasants from the eastern Visayas and northern Mindanao had converged on the island of Bucas Grande, where the 'Eternal City' was to emerge after the holocaust. The sect refused to pay taxes, rejected the Catholic Church, and threatened to confiscate the property of the rich. A similar set of events unfolded in Negros and Panay where, in 1921, Flor Yntrencherado declared himself Emperor of the Philippines, as well as a reincarnation of the martyred priest José Burgos and a successor to the patriots of 1898. Like all the others, Yntrencherado vowed to finish the revolution and realize the utopian dream of 'independence'.

The situation was little different elsewhere in Southeast Asia. In Burma the *pongyi* largely ignored or resisted government attempts to institutionalize a system of monastic schools wherein English subjects would be grafted onto the traditional, mainly religious, curriculum. The British thought the 'backward' *kyaung*, or village schools, to be the losers, since the brightest and most ambitious students gravitated towards government and mission schools. On the other hand, this meant that from 1900 to 1920 the *kyaung* remained largely free of state interference. Peasants circulating through them continued to be reminded of the impermanence of alien rule and the return of kings who would protect Buddhism and restore unity and prosperity. Another locus of resistance was the semi-secret sect or *gaing*, where *weikza* and *saya* practised the traditional arts of sorcery and curing, powers which made them potential 'embryo kings' or *min-laung*. The Filipino Rizals and popes had their Burmese equivalents in *min-laung* and Setkya-mins—such as the *min-laung Buddhayasa*, Nga Myin, who in 1907 attacked the police station at Sedaw, or the *min-laung* Maung Than who underwent the ceremony of accession in 1910 and forthwith attempted to attack Shwebo. Rumours periodically surfaced of *min-laung* prophecies, and the police had to break up crowds gathering at sites where the birth or the return of a king was expected.

The Dutch administrators were no less preoccupied with 'disturbances' in their domains. The *ulamā*-led resistance in Aceh continued to smoulder through to the 1920s. In west Sumatra the *guru tarekat* and mystics, heirs to the Padris, were largely behind the anti-tax rebellions of 1914. Between 1915 and 1917 the Batak countryside again responded to leaders bearing the potent title 'Si Singa Mangaraja', but this time drawing inspiration from Islamic prayer and purification rituals. The Parhudamdam, as this latest Batak movement was called, urged a holy war against the Dutch, yet was entirely separate from other Islamic movements of the time. Java, of course, had its fair share of unrest centring on expectations of the *ratu adil*. Kyai Dermadjaja was typical: an itinerant santri who received mystical training in various *pesantren*, attracted a circle of disciples, and proclaimed himself *ratu adil* in 1907. His followers went bravely to battle expecting the *wayang* figures Togog and Semar to aid them, just as in the Philippines the aid of heroes of *awit* (metrical romance), Bernardo Carpio and Don Juan Tiñoso, was invoked during the revolution.

Similar hopes for the restoration of ideal kingship animated Vietnamese popular movements, particularly in the south. Despite the French hold over the court, it continued to provide signs that the cosmic order it represented would return. In 1912 the Confucian revolutionary Phan Boi Chau, who had earlier canvassed the sentiments of sectarian preachers in the Mekong delta, founded the monarchist 'Revival Society' (Quang Phuc Hoi) and formed an interim revolutionary government with exiled Prince Cuong De at the helm. In 1915 the prince's army moved out from bases in China to attack some towns in the north, but was badly defeated. The following year, the young Emperor Duy Tan, heeding the advice of a Taoist scholar, mounted a coup against the French which quickly ended with his arrest in a Buddhist temple south of Hué. Duy Tan was, in fact, just one of three Vietnamese emperors who were deposed and exiled by the French between 1885 and 1926. Such gestures of resistance were of immense significance to villagers looking to the old centre for sustenance and hope.

Not surprisingly, peasant rebels in the Mekong delta responded to the monarchist signals in their own way. As in Burma, the de facto absence of the emperor opened up the field to any pretender promising a new order. Around 1912 a mystic and healer, known as Phan Xich Long (Phan the Red Dragon) and claiming to be a descendant of deposed emperor Ham Nghi, called for an overthrow of the French, precipitating an attack on Saigon in 1913 by his white-garbed followers. In 1916 the delta experienced another wave of rebellions, this time centred on the monk Bay Do who lived on

Forbidden Mountain. Whether or not there was a connection with Emperor Duy Tan's coup, as the French suspected, the Maitreya myth circulating at this time certainly presumed a monarchical order: 'How have you paid the Four Debts since you have not even fulfilled a tenth of your duties? How can you pretend to be faithful toward the King and toward your father and mother? . . .'[18]

In a sense, the colonial wars of the previous century had never ended. The ethos of resistance continued to be nurtured in concealment, taking the shape of uprisings only when the state excessively intruded into village life, or when signs of cataclysmic change appeared—Halley's Comet, the Great War, the Great Depression, or even something local like the major flood of 1926 in Terengganu or the 1927 eruption of Mount Canlaon in Negros. Rizal and other heroes of the revolution were worshipped in sectarian chapels from Mount Banahao in Luzon to Bucas Grande in Mindanao. From Shwebo in central Burma emerged a series of embryo kings who urged non-payment of taxes and attacks on British government offices. As late as the mid-1930s photos of the deposed Emperor Duy Tan were being venerated in a temple on Forbidden Mountain. Manggadua in downtown Batavia—the very heart of the Dutch empire—was the locus of saint worship focused on holy graves which served as the catalyst of certain *ratu adil* movements. These sites were part of extensive circuits of communication traversed by troubadour singers, seekers of esoteric knowledge, itinerant curers and fortune tellers, and ordinary pilgrims. At certain junctures flourished secret societies, cults, peasant associations, and circles of teachers and followers where 'independence' or 'freedom' was experienced in communal relationships, mutual help arrangements, the practice of martial arts, religious rituals, and the like. Even entire villages, usually under the sway of anti-colonial *pongyi, kyai*, or priests, could be sites of hidden resistance.

In most, if not all, of these cases, the emergence of a righteous and just leader was the catalyst of rebellion. The past had been mythologized as a condition in which society revolved around ideal kings and selfless patriots. Popular hopes of their reappearance signified the lack of a spiritual centre, a source of power, in an age of economic dislocation and alien rule. One would, therefore, expect to encounter fewer instances of popular anti-colonial movements in societies where the monarchies retained their vitality, as in Siam and, to a lesser extent, Cambodia and the Malay states.

The ghosts of a lost past certainly did not haunt the Thai kings, who successfully assumed the roles of protector of religion, helmsman of the state, and national talisman. Vajiravudh, in a 1911 speech, saw himself as possessor of the power of the nation, using it for the benefit and happiness of everyone. To the Thai peasant, such statements only confirmed the view that the king was the fount of merit and energy. Even the occasional Thai-led *phuwiset* rebellion, such as that which occurred near Saraburi, north of Bangkok, in 1925 did not challenge the centrality of the monarch: it was to him that the rebel leader Ai Kan presented his grievances, all

---

[18] Cited in Hue Tam Ho Tai, 75.

stemming from foreign interference in Siam's economic life and religion. More extensive *phumibun*-led movements there certainly were, but these developed in the northeastern provinces where artificial boundary lines had pushed into the Thai sphere peoples who naturally looked to Vientiane. Thus during the 1924, 1933 and 1936 uprisings the coming of the Maitreya was seen as a prelude to the re-establishment of a Lao kingdom.

Like their Thai counterparts, the Cambodian kings continued to be the symbols of national identity, protectors of Buddhism and, at the village level, semi-divine figures. But French protection was bound to exact its price. Excessive colonial demands on corvée labour and taxation particularly from 1912 on, spawned rural unrest which peaked in 1916 when tens of thousands of peasant demonstrators converged on Phnom Penh, compelling King Sisowath to address angry crowds outside his palace. Later, he travelled through the most disturbed rural areas by automobile in order to evidence his power and reassure the population. Not unlike Norodom during the 1885 rising, Sisowath by his royal presence managed to calm the protesters, for it was *Luong*, the king, and not the French from whom they expected relief. But where the royal gaze failed to reach, there were attacks on plantations, government offices, and foreigners. As in the past, monks and holy men were often the instigators of such actions. Predictably, the southeast provinces were almost certainly 'disturbed' by holy men with links to the sects based across the border in Cochin-China. In fact, in 1927 thousands of Cambodian peasants were reported to have trekked to the Cao Dai centre at Tay Ninh—before the French closed the border—in order to prostrate themselves before a statue of a prince on a white horse whose imminent reincarnation would mark the renewal of the Cambodian kingdom. There were expectations, after all, of a saviour-king who would replace the pro-French one at Phnom Penh!

The nature of British protection—non-interference in religion and custom, encouragement of courtly grandeur—meant that the world of the Malay sultans and their subjects remained largely intact. Peasants, furthermore, were shielded from the export economy and its concomitant dislocations through the importation of Chinese and Indian labour. But there were limits to peasant toleration of colonial demands, and to the restraining influence of the sultan and his entourage of Islamic officials. The 1915 uprising at Kelantan began on the fringes of the sultan's authority where hajjis and imams—representing non-official Islam—continued to exercise local leadership. The rebels sought the expulsion of foreigners and a change in the tax system. They were emboldened by the conviction that Britain was losing the war in Europe, and by the fact that their leader Hajji Mat Hassan, alias To' Janggut, was *keramat*—a holy man armed with supernatural powers. Neighbouring Terengganu experienced even more intense conflict a decade later. In the upriver regions, rural religious teachers, *sayyid* (descendants of the Prophet) and *keramat* persons had always provided an alternative focus to the sultanate in times of crisis. Thus when a peasant revolt, provoked by new land restrictions, erupted in 1928 it was framed in terms of a holy war against the *kāfir*. A new sultan and other officials would replace those who had become colonial servants or *orang neraka*, people of hell, as one Hajji Drahman put it.

Thus far we have looked at protest movements originating in older sites of unrest and opposition to the centre. But one obvious phenomenon of the early twentieth century was the emergence of urban-based leaders and movements with increasingly strident nationalist voices. Colonial régimes, in their liberal phases at least, considered sectoral representation in their fledgling Assemblies and Legislative Councils an important aspect of native progress and encouraged or at least condoned it within limits. The new, educated élites, on the other hand, grabbed these opportunities to voice their aspirations. Now in appealing for unity through their newspapers and rallies, urban organizers soon found themselves grappling with, and usually drawn into, more deeply rooted idioms of change. In the Philippines by 1909, Partido Nacionalista stalwarts Manuel Quezon and Sergio Osmena had become adept at tapping memories of the 1896 revolution and transposing this to the electoral struggle. When the Sarekat Islam first began to spread throughout Java in 1913, its most eminent propagandist, Oemar Said Tjokroaminoto, used familiar images from the *wayang* and Islam to call for native solidarity in the attainment of progress and equality with the Dutch. In Burma during the 1920s, the urban leaders of the General Council of Burmese Associations (GCBA), backed by the General Council of Sangha Samaggi (GCSS, the monks' association), took their message to the countryside, forming rural nationalist associations called *wunthanu athin*. In writings and speeches directed to village audiences, references to the life and teachings of the Buddha were regularly interspersed with the *wunthanu* political message.

Partido Nacionalista, Sarekat Islam and GCBA rallies were huge and colourful affairs. Politicians and organizers spoke of progress and unity, harangued against discrimination and unfair laws; there was talk of 'freedom', '*kemerdekaan*', '*independencia*' and the like. To the illiterate majority in attendance what often registered were images of Paradise, the earthly nirvana (*lokka nibban*), a just and moral order, a world in perfect harmony with Heaven's laws, a future with no taxes and no corvée labour. The drifts of meaning often turned millennial: imminent independence, the 'Djayabaya prophecy' concerning a Javanese liberator, the restoration of Burmese kingship. As these memorable rallies became the subject of rumours, the politicians themselves were seen in an entirely different light. Tjokroaminoto was thought to be none other than Prabu Heru Tjokro, the awaited *ratu adil*. Quezon, arriving from the United States in 1916 after having lobbied successfully for eventual self-rule, was hailed as the redeemer bringing independence. U Chit Hlaing, the GCBA president, was followed around by adherents holding aloft a golden umbrella, and was greeted by peasants with a royally caparisoned elephant.

The legal mass movements, of course, were in no position to sanction moves that might actually subvert the political status quo. Quezon and Tjokroaminoto—in close contact with their colonial patrons and advisers—were anxious to prevent popular energies from diverting their organizations from the goals of native progress *cum* loyalty to the mother country. Furthermore, participation in colonial politics promised a stable career and personal rewards to the bulk of the new, Western-educated élites. Certainly, in the Philippines campaigning for independence did not preclude the accumulation of wealth. In Burma many prominent leaders of the central GCBA soon stood for election to the Legislative Council, effectively quitting their roles in boycott and non-cooperation activities. Even the rehabilitated Buddhist primate—now an ally of the British—tried in vain to prevent *pongyi* from engaging in political agitation. Thus, while politicians generally capitalized on millennial expectations to win the crowds, their actions tended to fall short of their words and this made them vulnerable to criticism from radicals who also employed religious ideas in their arguments.

A blistering critique of the politicians Quezon, Roxas and Osmena runs through the literature of Philippine peasant movements from the Ricartistas of the 1910s to the Sakdal of the 1930s. The tapping of revolutionary memories in electoral campaigns had its limits, since peasant leaders from Pedro Calosa in Luzon to Lantayug in Mindanao were doing the same thing in claiming to be messengers or outright reincarnations of Rizal and Bonifacio. The difference is that, consistent with the careers of past heroes, they lived out their convictions by defying the state. As Calosa put it, they rebelled in 1931 in order to show the Americans that there was 'no town, no matter how small, without *real* people'.[19] 'Real' meant, as the Sakdalistas repeatedly stated, having a *loob* (inner being) that matched the *labas* (externalities). Quezon and company were 'accused' (*sakdal*) of hypocrisy rather than genuine inner commitment. 'The leader of a subject country', the newspaper *Sakdal* declared, 'should be the first in making the sacrifice ... No liberty was ever obtained happily ... nobody ever triumphed without passing over Golgotha and being nailed at the cross of Calvary.'[20]

Tjokroaminoto, as well, came under attack for his personal ambitions and alleged mismanagement of funds. A more serious charge was made in the early 1920s by militants, some prominent *ulamā* and *kyai* among them, that the Partai Sarekat Islam, Central Sarekat Islam, and Muhammadiyah were merely using the appeal to Islamic unity in order to camouflage their retreat from the struggle. Hajji Mohammad Misbach, a leading *pesantren*-educated *muballigh* (Islamic propagandist), in his attacks drew a distinction between *Islam sedjati* (true Islam) and *Islam lamisan* (pseudo-Islam), or between *mukmin* (the faithful) who sacrifice everything for God and *munafik* (hypocrites) whose claim to be *mukmin* is only for show. Islamic propagandists in Banten, Minangkabau, Aceh, and Terengganu echoed the same refrain.

At the local branches of the Partido Nacionalista, Sarekat Islam and GCBA, the programmes of the central organizations were not necessarily adhered to. Strikes and demonstrations were mounted without official permission by more radical leaders, who eventually gravitated towards less compromising organizations like the Democrata, Indische, and of course the Socialist and Communist parties. Some of the branches were really secret societies and sects which had adopted the forms of the 'modern' organizations. Such was the case with Thet Kywe, leader of eleven *wunthanu athin*, who proclaimed himself the Setkya min-laung in 1922.

[19] Pedro Calosa interview, in David R. Sturtevant, *Popular Uprisings in the Philippines, 1840–1940*, Ithaca, 1976, 274.
[20] Cited in *Tribune*, 12 May 1935; copy in the US National Archives, file 4865–93, BIA.

It could be the other way around, of course: Western-educated radicals used traditional forms to gain a mass following. In 1927 the French-educated lawyer Nguyen An Ninh started to organize peasants in his home province of Gia Dinh, using rituals and oaths patterned after the Heaven and Earth secret society, and promising a more equitable sharing of wealth. By 1928 he had attracted a sizeable following made up of people who commonly joined sects. To his dismay, however, he found that some members wanted to become mandarins, and he himself was venerated as a divine figure. The French, nonetheless, tagged the movement as 'communistic' and suppressed it. A similar experience befell Patricio Dionisio, a Filipino lawyer and journalist who in 1927 formed a patriotic society to propagate, through legal means, the goals of the 1896 hero Andres Bonifacio. His rhetoric was akin to that which pervaded Partido Nacionalista rallies, yet by reviving the rituals and symbols of the Katipunan secret society Dionisio struck a chord among peasants all over Luzon during the Depression years. By 1931 Dionisio's attempts to restrain his Tanggulan Society proved futile; talk of armed rebellion prevailed and the inevitable arrests followed. With the dissolution of the Tanggulan, most of the members simply drifted towards other, rising groups such as the Sakdal, Socialist and Communist parties which also spoke of the 'unfinished revolution' and the 'new era' on the horizon.

The success of Socialist and Communist parties in establishing mass memberships from the mid-1920s on can be attributed to the 'adaptationists' among the organisers who allowed party principles to be carried by 'traditional', mainly religious, idioms of protest. The extremely popular *Pasyon of the Workers* (or 'Red Pasyon'), for example, composed in the mid-1930s by Socialist Party member Lino Dizon, used the story of Christ's life and death as a springboard for an attack on wealthy landlords, the government, the institutional church, and capitalism. In Java and Sumatra, which witnessed widespread PKI (Partai Komunis Indonesia) rebellions in 1926–7, a turning point was reached when Islamic teachers like Hajji Misbach and Hajji Achmad Chatib embraced the cause. They preached that the trials devised by God in this day and age took two forms: capitalism, which promoted greed and distance from God, and imperialism, which threatened the world of Islam. Interspersing their arguments with Koranic passages, they stressed the religious meaning—proving one's faith—of resisting the *kāfir* government and its local allies. To the dismay of doctrinaire party leaders, the *ulamā* even called for the holy war to be waged, since capitalism was seen as being no different from Satan. But such 'excesses' had to be tolerated, for the hajjis, *ulamā* and *kyai* who preached revolution were highly respected—some even revered for their secret knowledge. In Aceh, Minangkabau and Banten, the mosque, *tarekat*, and *pesantren* became—as in the past—centres of revolutionary activity.

The Indochina Communist Party (ICP) also succeeded in organizing large numbers of peasants in the 1930s and thereafter. The cultural explanation for this is not hard to find: peasants accustomed to sorcerers or holy men predicting the future decreed by heaven did not have much trouble accepting the Marxist notion of a historical process that would guarantee victory to the revolutionaries. After all, this was the teaching of cadres who behaved in a manner reminiscent of the village Confucian scholars, whether in crusading against corruption, displaying a superior morality, or practising stoicism in the face of adversity. The mandate of heaven was envisioned as passing from class to class rather than from dynasty to dynasty; images of the civilizing action of this mandate even pervaded the language that articulated the notion of 'socializing landed property' (*xa hoi hoa*). In the Mekong delta, where Confucianism had been weak, the apostles of the Buu Son Ky Hong and other folk Buddhist sects, and to a lesser extent the Cao Dai, had nonetheless paved the way for some communist successes. Decades of anti-colonial agitation and periodic expectations of the Maitreya had made the sectarians receptive to suggestions of violent and total change, in the aftermath of which would emerge a society without greed, taxes and alien rulers.

The establishment of communist organizations over older terrains of rebellion meant that the ensuing uprisings tended to take on a life of their own. The rebellions in Java and Sumatra by all appearances were fought as jihads and *parang sabil* by peasants nursing their red party membership cards like precious amulets. The arrests of key PKI organisers in Banten throughout 1925–6 meant that when the revolt started in November 1926, the *ulamā*, aided by men of prowess called *juwara*, were indeed the *only* leaders around. The revolt took on meanings quite different from what the party intended; *kemerdekaan* meant freedom from taxes, but it could also signify the establishment of an Islamic state, or the restoration of the old sultanate. Like their poorly armed compatriots in Minangkabau, Aceh, and elsewhere, the Banten rebels were mowed down by Dutch reinforcements. The defeats everywhere testified both to the firepower of the state and the failure of Communist Party policy. But from another perspective, the outcome was not unexpected; the rebels were, as the Acehnese put it, *muslimin*—men who had put their faith in God and died a martyr's death.

There was a similar slippage between the party and the mass membership in the Nghe-Tinh 'soviet' movement of 1930–1. All sorts of contradictory actions were taken in the name of socialism. The ICP had to admit its difficulties in dealing with 'superstitions and anachronistic customs' in Nghe-Tinh itself. In the south, the communist cadres guiding fraternal organizations called 'Committees of Action' found it next to impossible to extinguish millennial expectations among the rank and file. As soon as government repression began to take its toll in 1931, peasants abandoned the committees and sought refuge in the sects. When a charismatic figure in Huynh Phu So appeared, the committees in traditional Buu Son Ky Hong areas practically turned over their mass membership to the Hoa Hao sect.

In the context of what was happening elsewhere in Southeast Asia, the 1931 Saya San rebellion does not seem to be all that 'fantastic' and 'backward'. Saya San was the perfect leader of a Burmese mass movement. He had been an itinerant fortune teller, curer (*se saya*), *gaing* member, practitioner of invulnerability magic, and sometime *pongyi*, before joining the GCBA in 1924. In other words, he had traversed the older terrain of resistance before joining a modern organization. His concerns in the GCBA focused on the rural miseries caused by taxes and police abuses.

Like other truly committed activists elsewhere in Southeast Asia, he witnessed with dismay the abandonment of militant action by the élite—the central GCBA leaders in this instance—prodding him to form his own Galon association to resist the collection of head tax. By 1930 the ingredients of a mass uprising were all there: unbearable taxes, plummeting paddy prices, a great earthquake that shook lower Burma in May. A great cataclysm was about to happen, and Saya San stepped in to fulfil the scenario. He proclaimed himself a *min-laung* and, subsequently, Setkyamin; he adopted the whole paraphernalia of kingship, the most significant of which was the building of a palace to serve as the new centre, the source of potency of the realm. Once the rebellion was launched in December 1931, it spread rapidly and without much central control over twelve of Burma's twenty districts, with *pongyi* and *saya* making up the bulk of local leadership. This was no longer just a tax revolt, but a holy war against the enemies of Buddhism and the monarchy. Aeroplanes and machine guns were needed to turn the tide of rebellion in mid-1931, by which time around 1300 rebels had been killed.

It could be said that Saya San was merely turning back the clock, that his revolt was disorganized, ill equipped and doomed to failure. But such a verdict is based on a certain view of what constitutes success, and involves locating the rebellion within a linear history that moves towards our 'modern' present. Alternatively, the rebellion can be understood in its own terms—as a religious experience, perhaps, or an intense moment in the lives of its participants. In this light, we might ponder the meaning of that memorable event during the Banten 'communist' rebellion, when five hundred poorly armed rebels emerged from the Labuan mosque dressed entirely in white, except for a black-clothed septuagenarian waving a flag bearing a quotation from the Koran: 'With God's help everything can be achieved.'[21] Little, in fact, separates these rebels from Salud Algabre, a Sakdal organizer in Cabuyao, who said of her experience in the 1935 rebellion: 'That was the moment. Everything led up to the uprising. That was the high point of our lives. . . . No uprising fails. Each one is a step in the right direction.'[22]

BIBLIOGRAPHIC ESSAY

Several comparative and theoretical studies of rebellion have made extensive use of Southeast Asian materials. The earliest example of this, written in 1965, is Harry Benda, 'Peasant movements in colonial Southeast Asia', in *Continuity and Change in Southeast Asia*, New Haven: Yale University Southeast Asia Studies, 1972. The Saya San rebellion and the Nghe Tinh soviets are case studies in James Scott, *The Moral Economy of the Peasant*, New Haven, 1976. In neither work is the role of religion particularly noted. However, Scott explores the culture of popular protest in 'Protest and profanation: Agrarian revolt and the Little Tradition', *Theory and Society*, 4, 1–2 (1977). And Michael Adas, *Prophets of Rebellion*, Chapel Hill, 1979,

[21] In Michael C. Williams, *Sickle and Crescent: The Communist Revolt of 1926 in Banten*, Ithaca: Cornell Modern Indonesia Project, 1982, 55.
[22] Algabre interview, in Sturtevant, 296, 299.

underlines the importance of millennial visions for the Diponegoro and Saya San rebellions.

That peasant consciousness and ritual action can be given at least equal play in a Marxist analysis is demonstrated in Andrew Turton and Shige-haru Tanabe, eds, *History and Peasant Consciousness in South East Asia*, Osaka: National Museum of Ethnology, 1984. Here, Tanabe uses the 1889–90 Chiengmai rebellion as a case study of peasant ideological practice. Other relevant chapters are Chatthip Nartsupha's on the ideology of 'Holy Men' revolts; Masaya Shiraishi's on rural unrest in early Nguyen Vietnam; and Joel Kahn's on the 1927 communist uprising in west Sumatra.

The best introductions to the religio-political terrain of the Buddhist states are Stanley Tambiah, *The Buddhist Saints of the Forest and the Cult of Amulets*, Cambridge, UK, 1984, and Charles Keyes *The Golden Peninsula*, New York, 1977. For Thailand, specifically, see Yoneo Ishii, *Sangha, State and Society: Thai Buddhism in History*, trans. Peter Hawkes, Honolulu, 1986. On Buddhism and popular religion in Burma, see Melford Spiro, *Buddhism and Society*, 2nd edn, Berkeley, 1982; and E. Michael Mendelson, *Sangha and State in Burma*, Ithaca, 1975.

Other studies of the 'Holy Man' rebellions besides Chatthip Natsupha's are Ishii, *Sangha*, ch. 9; John Murdoch, 'The 1901–1902 Holy Man's rebel-lion', JSS, 42, 1 (1974); and Charles Keyes, 'Millennialism, Theravada Buddhism, and Thai society', JAS, 36, 2 (1977). For the Laotian side of these rebellions see Francois Moppert, 'Le révolte des Bolovens', in Pierre Brocheux, ed., *Histoire de L'Asie du Sud-est: Révoltes, Réformes, Révolutions*, Lille, 1981. Popular perceptions of Khru Ba Siwichai are examined in Charles Keyes, 'Death of two Buddhist saints in Thailand', *Journal of the American Academy of Religion*, Thematic Studies, 48, 3–4 (1982).

Accounts of the Burmese resistance to British-Indian occupation tend to be dominated by British perspectives. Nonetheless, some useful introduc-tions are John Cady, *A History of Modern Burma*, Ithaca, 1958; and Trevor Ling, *Buddhism, Imperialism and War*, London, 1979. The millennial aspects are best brought out in the sympathetic study by Emmanuel Sarkisyanz, *Buddhist Backgrounds of the Burmese Revolution*, The Hague, 1965. Ni Ni Myint, *Burma's Struggle Against British Imperialism, 1885–1895*, Rangoon, 1983, further uncovers the Burmese side of the story.

Sarkisyanz, *Buddhist Backgrounds*, is still the most illuminating work on Burmese religion and nationalism. Donald Smith, *Religion and Politics in Burma*, Princeton, 1965, is more lucid but overly dwells on Burmese Buddhism's failure to adjust to the 'modern' world. A wealth of informa-tion, though skewed towards the élites, is found in U Maung Maung, *From Sangha to Laity: Nationalist Movements of Burma, 1920–1940*, Canberra: Australian National University Monographs on South Asia, 1980. The Saya San rebellion finds a place in all of the abovementioned works. Patricia Herbert's paper, 'The Hsaya San rebellion (1930–1932) reappraised', Clayton: Monash University Centre of Southeast Asian Studies, 1982, portrays Saya San as less of a *minlaung* than a mainstream nationalist, but for an opposing view see T. Ito, 'Pre-Saya San peasant uprisings in colonial Burma', paper presented to the 31st International Congress of Human Sciences, Tokyo, 1983.

FROM c. 1800 TO THE 1930s

The tradition/revolution nexus in Vietnam is succintly presented in Keyes, *Golden Peninsula*. Paul Mus's seminal ideas on the subject can be gleaned from John McAlister and Paul Mus, *The Vietnamese and their Revolution*, New York, 1970. If one can ignore its dated exaltation of scientific thinking, the chapter on Confucianism and Marxism in Nguyen Khac Vien, *Tradition and Revolution in Vietnam*, Berkeley: Indochina Resource Center, 1974, is an excellent introduction to the culture of the scholar-gentry class. Alexander Woodside sensitively reflects upon the modern transformation of this élite in *Community and Revolution in Modern Vietnam*, Boston, 1976, which marks a pinnacle of sorts in wartime attempts to understand the Vietnamese 'enemy' on its own terms.

The limits of state control in Nguyen Vietnam are analysed in Masaya Shiraishi's chapter in Turton and Tanabe, as well as in Hue Tam Ho Tai, *Millenarianism and Peasant Politics in Vietnam*, Cambridge, Mass., 1983. The latter is a fascinating study of the persistence of the Buu Son Ky Hong tradition, in the light of which Vietnamese—and to some extent Cambodian—anti-colonial movements are reassessed. A more top-down approach is taken in David Marr's indispensable sourcebook, *Vietnamese Anticolonialism, 1885–1925*, Berkeley, 1971. Most of the abovementioned works address the vital but problematic relationship between the communist movement and more deeply-rooted mentalities among both gentry and villagers.

David Chandler, *A History of Cambodia*, Boulder, 1983, presents a useful overview of Khmer manifestations of unrest. But the 'Holy Man' phenomenon is better described in Chandler's 'An anti-Vietnamese rebellion in early nineteenth century Cambodia: Pre-colonial imperialism and a pre-nationalist response', *JSEAS*, 6, 1 (1975). For detailed accounts of the 1916 demonstrations see Milton Osborne, 'Peasant politics in Cambodia: The 1916 Affair', *MAS*, 12, 2 (1978); and Alain Forest, 'Les manifestations de 1916 au Cambodge', in Brocheux, *Revoltes*.

As an introduction to the historical complexities of Indonesia, Claire Holt *et al.*, eds, *Culture and Politics in Indonesia*, Ithaca, 1972, has stood the test of time. Benedict Anderson's chapter, 'The idea of power in Javanese culture' offers a convincing explanation of charisma and centre–periphery relations. Also important are the chapters by Sartono Kartodirjo on agrarian radicalism in Java and Taufik Abdullah on Minangkabau. Peter Carey offers the best accounts of Javanese millennial expectations focused on Diponegoro; see his 'The origins of the Java War (1825–30)', *English Historical Review*, 91 (1976), and 'Waiting for the "Just King": the agrarian world of south-central Java from Giyanti (1755) to the Java War (1825–30)', *MAS*, 20, 3 (1986).

Post-1830 assertions against Dutch–priyayi rule are examined in Sartono Kartodirjo, *Protest Movements in Rural Java*, Singapore: ISEAS, 1973, which, however, is marred by an attempt to locate Javanese movements in an evolutionary series. Sartono's earlier work, *The Peasants' Revolt of Banten in 1888*, 's-Gravenhage (*Verhandelingen van het Koninklijk Instituut voor Taal-Land- en Volkenkunde*, Deel 50), 1966, is a classic in the field. On the Samin movement, see the pathbreaking study by Harry Benda and Lance Castles, 'The Samin movement', in *Continuity and Change*. The limits of their analysis are underlined in Benedict Anderson's provocative essay, 'Mille-narianism and the Saminist movement', in *Religion and Social Ethos in Indonesia*, Clayton: Monash University Centre of Southeast Asian Studies, 1977. On the incorporation of Christianity into Javanese religion, see Ph. Quarles van Ufford, 'Why don't you sit down? Sadrach and the struggle for religious independence in the earlist phase of the Church of Central Java (1861–1899)', in R. Schefold *et al.*, ed, *Man, Meaning and History*, The Hague, 1980. The *ratu adil* theme appears in nearly all studies of Javanese protest movements, but nowhere does it figure more centrally than in Bernard Dahm, *Sukarno and the Struggle for Indonesian Independence*, trans. Mary F. Somers Heidhues, Ithaca, 1969, which also looks at the Sarekat Islam.

A useful guide to the major uprisings and wars throughout the Dutch East Indies is Merle Ricklefs, *A History of Modern Indonesia*, London, 1981. Christine Dobbin, *Islamic Revivalism in a Changing Peasant Economy in Central Sumatra, 1784–1847*, London, 1983, is the authoritative work on the Padri Wars. On Batak resistance see Lance Castles, 'Statelessness and stateforming tendencies among the Batak before colonial rule', in *Pre-colonial State Systems in Southeast Asia*, Kuala Lumpur: Monographs of the Malaysian Branch of the Royal Asiatic Society, 1975; and the comprehen-sive study by Masashi Hirosue, 'Prophets and followers in Batak millen-arian responses to the colonial order: Parmalim, Na Siak Bagi and Par-hudamdam, 1890–1930', Ph.D. thesis, Australian National Univeristy, 1988. The most comprehensive account of Acehnese resistance to the Dutch is Anthony Reid, *The Blood of the People*, Kuala Lumpur, 1979. James Siegel, *The Rope of God*, Berkeley, 1969, links social structure and categories of perception to the Aceh war.

The classic study of the communist-led rebellion in west Sumatra is B. Schrieke, *Indonesian Sociological Studies*, part one, The Hague, 1966. On east Java see Michael Williams, *Sickle and Crescent: The Communist Revolt of 1926 in Banten*, Ithaca, 1982. The main shortcoming of these works is their lack of attention to language and discourse. This problem is brilliantly overcome in Takashi Shiraishi, *An Age in Motion*, Ithaca, 1990, which deals with popular radicalism in Java from the rise of the Sarekat Islam in 1912 to the rebellions of 1926.

The spread of pan-Islamic sentiments in the archipelago is documented in Anthony Reid, 'Nineteenth-century Pan-Islam in Indonesia and Malay-sia', JAS, 26, 2 (1967), and William Roff, 'South-East Asian Islam in the nineteenth century', in *The Cambridge History of Islam*, II, Cambridge, UK, 1970. On the 1915 Kelantan uprising, see Ibrahim Nik Mahmood, 'The To' Junggut rebellion of 1915', in William Roff, ed., *Kelantan*, Kuala Lumpur, 1974; and J. de V. Allen, 'The Kelantan rising of 1915: some thoughts on the concept of resistance in British Malayan history', JSEAS, 9 (1968). The 1928 Terengganu rebellion is treated extensively in Heather Sutherland, 'The taming of the Trengganu elite', in Ruth McVey, ed., *Southeast Asian Transitions*, New Haven, 1978. However, a better perspective 'from below' is provided in Shaharil Talib, *After its Own Image: The Trengganu Experience, 1881–1941*, Singapore, 1984.

Islam's role in mobilizing resistance to Thai suzerainty is detailed in Surin Pitsuwan, *Islam and Malay Nationalism*, Bangkok: Thai Khadi Research Institute, 1985. For the analogous case of resistance to Spanish conquest in Mindanao and Sulu, the best introduction is Cesar Majul, *Muslims in the Philippines*, Quezon City, 1973. Samuel Tan takes the story up to the American invasion in *The Filipino Muslim Armed Struggle, 1900–1972*, Manila: Filipinas Foundation, 1977.

Centre–periphery relations in the Spanish Philippines are discussed in Reynaldo Ileto, 'Outlines of a non-linear emplotment of Philippine history,' in Lim Teck Ghee, *Reflections on Development in Southeast Asia*, Singapore: ISEAS, 1988. The Cofradia de San José is treated extensively in Reynaldo Ileto, *Pasyon and Revolution: Popular Movements in the Philippines, 1840–1910*, Quezon City, 1979; and Setsuho Ikehata, 'Popular Catholicism in the nineteenth-century Philippines: The case of the Cofradia de San José', in *Reading Southeast Asia*, Ithaca: Cornell University Southeast Asia Program, 1989, 109–88.

David Sturtevant, *Popular Uprisings in the Philippines, 1840–1940*, Ithaca, 1976, provides an extensive coverage but falls prey to stress-strain and linear classification theories. The Dios-Dios phenomonen in Samar is described in Bruce Cruickshank, *Samar: 1768–1898*, Manila: Historical Conservation Society, 1985. Western Visayas movements are examined in Don Hart, 'Buhawi of the Bisayas: The revitalization process and legend-making in the Philippines', in Mario Zamora, ed., *Studies in Philippine Anthropology*, Quezon City, 1967; and Alfred McCoy, '*Baylan*: Animist religion and Philippine peasant ideology', in David Wyatt and Alexander Woodside, eds, *Moral Order and the Question of Change*, New Haven: Yale University Southeast Asia Studies, 1982.

The religious aspects of the 1896 revolution are discussed in Ileto, *Pasyon*; his 'Rizal and the underside of Philippine history', in Wyatt and Woodside, *Moral Order*; and John Schumacher SJ, 'The religious character of the revolution in Cavite, 1896–1897', *Philippine Studies*, 24 (1976). In *Revolutionary Clergy*, Quezon City, 1981, Schumacher thoroughly documents the Filipino clergy's role in nationalist movements to 1903. Post-1910 peasant radicalism is treated in McCoy, '*Baylan*'; Reynaldo Ileto, 'Orators and the crowd: Philippine independence movements, 1910–1914,' in Peter Stanley, ed., *Reappraising an Empire*, Cambridge, Mass., 1984; and Brian Fegan, 'The social history of a central Luzon barrio', in Alfred McCoy and Ed. de Jesus, eds, *Philippine Social History*, Honolulu, 1982. The Sakdal movement occupies a chapter in Sturtevant, *Popular Uprisings*; however, new ground is broken in Motoe Wada, 'The Sakdal movement, 1930–34', *Philippine Studies*, 36 (1988).

CHAPTER

5

NATIONALISM AND MODERNIST REFORM

Throughout Southeast Asia, the early twentieth century produced reformist activity directed toward altering established practices, whether indigenous or colonial in origin. This modernist impulse accepted the need for change, recognized benefits to be gained from some of the new arrangements introduced under colonial régimes or by Western advisers, and generally worked within the framework of bureaucratic systems of administration, creating organizations and promoting principles that owed little or nothing to indigenous traditions and much to ideologies and techniques introduced from outside the region. Many modernist reformers had Western educations and held ideas concerning how governments ought to be run that were similar to the views of the officials whose régimes they opposed. They often had somewhat less in common with the mass of the people, for the most part semi-literate peasants, in whose name they professed to act.

One strain of modernist activity led to the formation of governments for the states that succeeded colonial régimes after 1945, and part of the task of this chapter is to explain the role of modernist political movements in events leading up to the creation of these successor states. Such movements are conventionally called nationalist, but most of them represented nationalism of a particular sort, based on territories containing heterogeneous populations rather than on groups of people with shared cultural characteristics. A second strain of political activity represented the interests of collectivities with good nationalist credentials. The members of these groups thought of themselves as part of a larger whole sharing a common language, religion, or culture ('imagined communities' in the terminology of Benedict Anderson[1]), but they did not form independent states and their unsatisfied nationalist aspirations would remain a source of political conflict in post-colonial Southeast Asia. There was also modernist reform in Southeast Asia which did not pursue independence and showed little interest in political nationalism, but addressed religious or social concerns, generally through measured social programmes, occasionally in religiously inspired revolutionary activity.

What lay behind this reformist impulse? The answer can be traced to

[1] Benedict Anderson, *Imagined Communities: Reflections on the Origin and Spread of Nationalism*, London, 1983, 15–16.

several more or less concurrent developments. One was the provision of education to small but growing segments of the local population, for it was this educated group, tiny though it remained, that provided leadership and new ideas throughout the region. Other sources of impetus included increased mobility and improved communications facilities; the introduction of Western-style bureaucratic administrations; the inspiration provided by reformist activity elsewhere, first in Japan and later in China and India; a growing race consciousness on the part of colonial officials; and the spread of anti-colonial ideologies. Finally, the policies adopted by colonial régimes toward local political activity had much to do with the tactics and objectives of reformers, and the timing of developments.

The significance of education in the development of reformist movements can be seen in the fact that virtually every major indigenous political thinker and leader in Southeast Asia during the first half of the twentieth century received, by the standards of the time, an exceptional education. Most obtained what might be called 'Western education', referring to the teaching of skills—basic literacy and arithmetic and sometimes craft-related techniques as well—in a classroom, and the awarding of certificates which qualified the holder for certain types of employment. Students who continued their education in Europe often encountered a curriculum and a university environment that stimulated political awareness and introduced them to Western concepts of nationalism, democracy, socialism and constitutionalism. Many became painfully aware that the political ideals and aspirations of the peoples of Europe or America were far from being realized in their homelands. Moreover, while higher degrees in principle opened opportunities at higher levels of bureaucracy, senior posts were monopolized by Europeans and the local aristocracy, and in many instances a formal or informal 'colour bar' prevented non-Europeans from advancing in the civil service.

Government educational programmes were closely related to the motives that lay behind Western intervention in Southeast Asia. Economic and strategic considerations were of fundamental importance, though public explanations of imperialism tended to emphasize humanitarian motives. Frank A. Swettenham captured the situation nicely when, having written that British intervention in Malaya was 'a duty forced upon England' and 'imperative from motives of humanity alone', he added that it was also certain to be 'highly beneficial to British interests and British trade'.[2] One important function of education was to train subordinate administrative and clerical staff for government offices and commercial houses. Social Darwinism, which pictured a world in which some races were advanced and others backward, provided an additional motive for education by introducing the idea that more advanced (that is, Western) nations had a duty to assist less advanced nations, a concept reflected in slogans such as the White Man's Burden and the *mission civilisatrice*. The Malay peninsula in the 1880s, according to Hugh Clifford, was 'in the Middle Ages, surrounded by all the appropriate accessories of the dark centuries',[3] and

---

[2] Frank A. Swettenham, *British Malaya*, London, 1907, 174.
[3] Hugh Clifford, *The Further Side of Silence*, New York, 1916, 40.

Britain was attempting 'nothing less than to crush into twenty years the revolutions in facts and in ideas which, even in energetic Europe, six long centuries have been needed to accomplish'.[4] Drawing on this perception, Western régimes justified intervention by taking on the role of parent or teacher, providing education and working to bring local communities closer to the 'modern', or Western, world.

In most colonies, these ideas never reached the level of fully developed administrative policy and most colonial governments carried out very modest programmes of education. The principal exception was the American administration in the Philippines which made public education widely available, reflecting the egalitarian educational philosophy of the United States, and also a fervent desire in some quarters to prepare Filipinos for self-government on a democratic model as quickly as possible in order to be rid of the risks and obligations of colonial rule. Elsewhere in Southeast Asia, the need to economize and the fear that education would create a troublesome class of people who held diplomas but were unemployable slowed the development of education. Educational expansion was also impeded by a lingering romantic notion that extolled the virtues of cultures unspoilt by civilization, and led to efforts to protect communities against disruptive intrusions.

As the twentieth century progressed, non-government education became an important focus of nationalist sentiment. Religious schools, particularly Muslim *pesantren* or *madrasah*, and in some places private secular education programmes, taught practical skills, but many also promoted nationalist feeling, at least indirectly. Colonial administrations were acutely aware of the dangers which unfettered educational institutions might pose. French authorities closed the independent and nationalist Dong Kinh Free School shortly after it was founded in Hanoi in 1907; Britain imposed tight controls on Chinese schools in Malaya; and the Dutch authorities passed a number of restrictive measures to regulate private education in the Netherlands East Indies.

The receptivity of Southeast Asian peoples to Western education varied. The obvious efficacy of European technology posed a challenge that could not be ignored, and those concerned with self-strengthening welcomed the chance to gain access to that technology. However, the need to master a foreign language and operate within a foreign culture in order to go beyond the elementary level of study was a major obstacle, while costs were beyond the reach of most of the population.

The relationship between Western education and the political development of Southeast Asia is easily traced, since nationalist leaders came from this background and drew many of their ideas from European political traditions. More difficult to assess is the extent to which those who opted for Western education were unusual individuals. The question whether exceptional people acquired Western education, or whether Western education produced exceptional people, is probably unanswerable, but a great many of those who formed the new élite came from the lesser aristocracy

---

[4] Hugh Clifford, 'The east coast', in *Stories by Sir Hugh Clifford*, ed. William R. Roff, Kuala Lumpur, 1966, 11.

or its equivalents, and there must be a strong suspicion that education provided an outlet for talent and ambition.

Although education was important to the process of introducing new ideas, other sources also played a critical role. Southeast Asian travellers, among them traders and seamen, young people who left their homelands seeking work and experience, and Muslims who participated in the hajj or studied in the centres of Muslim learning, contributed to the pool of ideas. European administrators themselves added new political understandings, as did others from outside the region, a broad category that included missionaries and traders, immigrant labourers, trade union organizers and Comintern agents.

Improved transport and communications contributed significantly to the development of political thought. Two leading nationalist figures, José Rizal in the Philippines and Raden Adjeng Kartini in Java, shaped their thinking in part through letters exchanged with correspondents in Europe. In many parts of Southeast Asia the rate of basic literacy was fairly high owing to instruction given as part of religious training, and information spread rapidly through print media. Radio broadcasts and increased mobility further facilitated social interaction and exposure to new ideas.

Western-style bureaucratic systems of administration, introduced to the region in the last half of the nineteenth century, brought major innovations, centralizing authority to an unprecedented degree and eliminating many of the traditional prerogatives of indigenous leaders. The changes resulted in increased and more stable revenues for the state, as well as more efficient (and less flexible) ways of collecting taxes. They allowed the state to become involved in a wider range of activities, and to legislate in areas previously left to the workings of local custom.

Modernist reformers recognized the utility of bureaucracies and, while they objected to many features of colonial rule, their intention was generally to take over rather than to eliminate the mechanisms of the colonial state, and to turn them to new purposes. This approach distinguishes modernist reform from two other sorts of opposition to colonial rule, the one a defence of the old régimes and traditional methods, the other consisting of millenarian religious movements and peasant uprisings. Both traditionalist and millenarian opponents of colonial rule objected to the intrusive administrative procedures that accompanied Western domination, but neither mounted a serious threat to any established government. When nationalist reformers eventually came into power, they retained these aspects of colonial rule.

Events elsewhere in Asia and the world were a source of inspiration for modernist reform. The example of the self-strengthening movement in Japan greatly influenced anti-colonial activity in Southeast Asian territories, as did later nationalist struggles in China and India and within the region itself. Japan, where the Meiji restoration was followed by a reformist movement which borrowed from abroad to defend indigenous traditions, inspired many political activists in Southeast Asia, notably in

Vietnam and the Philippines. Japan's victory in the Russo-Japanese War of 1904–5 had an extraordinary impact in the region, since it represented the triumph of an Asian over a Western power. The nationalist struggle in China also served as a model, particularly after Japan abandoned anti-colonialism to improve relations with the European powers in the wake of the Anglo-Japanese Alliance of 1902 and the Entente Cordiale of 1904, and embarked on its own course of imperialist expansion. The 1911 revolution placed China under an administration sympathetic to nationalist causes elsewhere, and the country subsequently provided a refuge for a number of political exiles from Southeast Asia.

Developments outside Asia, particularly World War I and the Great Depression, also greatly affected Southeast Asian politics in the decades leading up to the Pacific War. Direct Southeast Asian involvement in the European conflict was limited: a German cruiser, the *Emden*, raided Penang in October 1914; the Straits Chinese contributed substantial sums of money to the British war effort; the French government requisitioned Vietnamese labour to serve in Europe. A few Burmese labourers were sent to Iraq, while Siam (Thailand) entered the war on the side of the Allies in July 1917, despatching a small expeditionary force to the European front. Indirect effects of the war were of greater importance. The unprecedented scale and carnage of the hostilities served to undermine any pretensions that Western civilization possessed inherent moral superiority, while on a more concrete level, Britain and France, despite emerging as victors, both suffered a serious (and, it would prove, irreversible) erosion of economic and military power. The war led directly to the Russian Revolution, which in turn transformed Marxism-Leninism from a somewhat abstract European ideology into a force on the Asian political scene, with the rapid formation of embryo communist movements in the Dutch East Indies, China, and other parts of the region. The war also brought about the breakup of the great multinational empires of Europe and Eurasia (Austro-Hungarian, Ottoman, and Russian) along roughly ethnic lines, giving self-determination and the nation-state formally sanctioned recognition as the accepted basis of the international political order. And on an ideological level, the fifth of President Woodrow Wilson's famous Fourteen Points asserted that on colonial questions 'the interests of the populations concerned must have equal weight with the claims of the government whose title is to be determined'—a partial recognition of nationalist aspirations accepted by the colonial powers in principle if not, as Ho Chi Minh discovered at Versailles, in practice.

The Great Depression, with its disruption of capitalist trading networks, profoundly affected colonial or semi-colonial commodity producers as well as the more industrialized nations. The prices of rice, rubber, tin, coffee, sugar and other major Southeast Asian exports fell drastically, driving down both government revenues and personal incomes. In Burma, Vietnam, and the Philippines the economic hardships of the early 1930s contributed to outbreaks of rural violence, while the economic crisis was also a major factor in the 1932 coup which ended the absolute monarchy in Siam. However, the effects of the depression were uneven in Southeast Asia: the impact fell mainly upon areas where the colonial period had brought into being a commercialized export-oriented agriculture or commodity production linked to world markets, notably the extended river deltas of Burma, Siam, and Vietnam, and parts of Malaya, the Dutch East Indies, and the Philippines. More remote areas, where a semi-subsistence mode of production still prevailed, were less affected by the economic crisis, and consequently by the political repercussions which accompanied it.

Racial consciousness is deeply embedded in Asian history, but it took on new significance during the early twentieth century. European visitors to Southeast Asia in the seventeenth century approached Asians as equals, displaying an openness and readiness to learn that was often lacking in the nineteenth century, when scientific and industrial developments had produced a technological gulf between Europe and the rest of the world. Even nineteenth-century accounts of colonial life portray a relatively easy mixing and camaraderie between the limited number of Europeans resi-dent in the region and the local population. By the early twentieth century a substantial increase in the number of European officials had begun to make it possible to emulate a European lifestyle, a tendency reinforced by the arrival of significant numbers of European women in the colonies. Europeans and Asians increasingly met only in their working capacities, and then often in an unequal relationship.

New ideologies further enhanced the significance of race. Social Darwinism provided a 'scientific' explanation for racial inequality, and nationalism brought race into matters of state. Discrimination on racial grounds was a grievance upon which nationalist politicians could readily capitalize, and it provided a useful focus for their programmes.

Anti-colonial ideologies derived from a number of sources, and sometimes promoted inconsistent goals. The term 'nationalism' is commonly used to characterize much of the opposition to Western rule, but the equating of nationalism with anti-colonialism, although enshrined by long usage, obscures important distinctions. Some anti-colonial movements (notably those based on Islam and socialism) promoted transnational ideologies and were intrinsically hostile to nationalism, while others represented the interests of non-national groupings, such as the aristocracy or traders or those professing a certain faith.

In nineteenth-century Europe, 'nationalism' referred to the idea that humanity was divided into discrete groups—peoples or communities distinguishable by differences of language, religion, culture, and physical appearance—and to the argument that these 'nations' should be the basis of sovereign states. The doctrine also implied that the nation, the people, as the ultimate source of power and authority, should participate in the governing of the state through representative institutions. Nationalism of this sort did not provide an appropriate model for a stable political order in areas such as Southeast Asia, where a profusion of groups that differed in language, religion, culture and physical appearance intermingled. It was, however, the most successful political idea in nineteenth-century Europe and, since imperialism in Southeast Asia violated all the basic tenets of nationalism, it had obvious attractions for opponents of colonial rule.

The defects of nationalism as a political ideology for Southeast Asia were apparent. Some reformers saw socialism or religion, doctrines which transcended ethnic and cultural differences (and opposed the way nationalism divided the working class, or the community of believers), as better foundations upon which to build in the future. Marxism provided a comprehensive explanation and critique of imperialism, along with a rationale for action and an assurance of success in the long term, but the confrontational style adopted by communist parties was alien to the cultures of the region, and control of the communist movement by Moscow seemed suspiciously like imperialism in another guise. Marxism's hostility to religion, although played down by exponents within the region, also limited its appeal.

Religion and culture were another source of opposition ideas. For many people, the most objectionable feature of colonial rule was that it involved the subjugation of Muslims, or of Buddhists, to non-Muslims or non-Buddhists. The payment of taxes and other levies, although sometimes harsh, may have been little different from what the population had endured under indigenous rule, but the spectacle of non-believers, of barbarians, ruling the state and failing to respect indigenous custom was new. It provided a clear symbolic expression of a world that needed to be changed. However, from a tactical point of view one fundamental consideration was that the colonial régimes were (or appeared to be) militarily too strong to be dislodged by force, particularly since efficient intelligence services enabled the colonial authorities to act against opposition groups while they were in a formative stage. And if the anti-colonial struggle was to be carried out in the political sphere, the idea of nationalism, which enjoyed legitimacy in Europe and was accepted in principle by many colonial officials, offered greater leverage than socialism or religious movements which lacked powerful constituencies in Europe and were viewed with intense suspicion by colonial administrations.

Anthony D. Smith has suggested that nationalist movements require: 'an easily identifiable territory and location' together with 'a single political authority and bureaucracy'; a population sharing both a 'myth of common origins and history' and other distinctive cultural features such as language or skin colour; and an urban intelligentsia acting as the bearer of the nationalist idea. In Southeast Asia, as in many colonial contexts elsewhere, the territorial basis for nationalist movements (along with the unified political authority and the centralized bureaucratic administration) was largely provided by the colonial powers, a situation characterized by Smith as 'territorial nationalism', or 'nationalisms without nations'. In these circumstances, a nationalist movement 'arises among heterogeneous populations [and] is based upon the territorial unit in which they are forcibly united and administered, usually by a colonial power',[5] while the people concerned 'possess no common and distinctive cultural identity to

[5] Anthony D. Smith, 'Introduction: the formation of nationalist movements', in Smith, ed., *Nationalist Movements*, New York, 1977, 5, 9.

protect . . . The main aim is to take over the alien's political machinery and adopt his administrative unit as the basis of the projected "nation".'[6]

The territorial divisions produced by colonialism in Southeast Asia coincided neither with indigenous political units nor with groups possessing myths of common origins and distinctive cultural features. Borders sometimes divided groups which shared national characteristics, and nearly always embraced various groups which did not. As a consequence, nationalism based on a common cultural identity, and anti-colonialism among those subject to a colonial state, were distinct and sometimes conflicting concepts.

Instances of what Smith calls 'ethnic nationalism', political activity undertaken by culturally distinct populations, also occurred in the region. Examples include the Thai of the Chao Phraya basin of central Siam, the Muslims of southern Thailand and the southern Philippines, and the Malays in British Malaya. In British Burma some non-Burman or non-Buddhist peoples developed ethnic nationalist movements and opposed integration with other communities living in the territory.

In the Netherlands East Indies, ethnic nationalism was largely subsumed by territorial nationalism, although local, ethnically-based organizations developed before the Japanese Occupation, and ethnic loyalties produced a divisive regionalism after independence despite official emphasis on unity and an Indonesian identity. Within the Philippines, too, ethnic loyalties derived from dialects or cultures remained potent, but posed little threat to the unity of the state except in the Muslim south, where the Moros combined ethnic and territorial nationalist appeals. Non-territorial ethnic nationalisms also emerged in Southeast Asia, based on groups of people distinguished by cultural features but lacking a clearly defined territorial base, among them the Chinese, Indian, and Karen communities.

Some populations which did possess shared cultural characteristics ultimately came to identify themselves with territorial nationalism and attempted to co-opt it as their own. The Burmans in British Burma, the Khmer in Cambodia, and the Vietnamese, and after 1945 the peninsular Malays, tended to give territorial nationalism an ethnic flavour and to define other peoples within their territories as ethnic minorities.

Governments within the region, most of them colonial administrations, varied greatly in their degree of tolerance for indigenous political activity. At one extreme the United States régime in the Philippines co-operated with an elected Filipino legislative body which actively promoted the cause of independence. In the Netherlands East Indies the Dutch administration adopted the so-called Ethical Policy at the start of the twentieth century which officially encouraged local involvement in administrative affairs, and in 1918 launched a partially elected parliamentary body, the Volksraad. However, the Volksraad was limited to an advisory role, and the government permitted only modest criticism, suppressing organizations that ventured beyond these limits. British administrations in Burma and Malaya also operated legislative councils with some local participation but

---

[6] Anthony D. Smith, *Theories of Nationalism*, London, 1971, 216–17.

provided no latitude for effective opposition to the régime from this source. The French in Indochina were intolerant of all but the mildest expressions of dissent. Where political activity went beyond what a government was willing to countenance, colonial régimes dismantled organizations, banished and imprisoned leaders, and effectively stifled opposition. By acting before opposition movements had built up momentum, colonial administrations usually managed to prevent the mounting of major challenges to their authority.

Anti-colonial groups faced a difficult choice in deciding whether to seek reforms by co-operating with colonial administrations, or to refuse co-operation and face the possibility of suppression. Filipino political parties co-operated, but also had a growing measure of real power, and any advocate of non-cooperation would have been in the invidious position of opposing a Filipino administration. Elsewhere in the region the question whether to co-operate with colonial administrations to achieve reforms was a divisive issue, but by the 1920s and 1930s the failure of colonial régimes to address suggestions raised by reformers had led more and more to confrontation, and to increasingly repressive counter-measures.

Beyond these general considerations the character of modernist reform movements varied according to local circumstances, and must be discussed individually. Attention will first be given to movements that were territorially based, directed at taking over control of a colonial régime, and then to movements that were ethnically based. Finally, reference will be made to loyalist activity that does not fit neatly into either category.

TERRITORIAL NATIONALISM

The Philippines

The first major modernist movement directed against colonial rule in Southeast Asia developed in the Philippines. Its origins lay in issues related to the Catholic faith shared by a majority of Filipinos and the Spanish. The initiative for political reforms came from younger, educated members of the élite, the *ilustrados*, who were inspired by the ideals of European liberalism and sought political participation through democratic institutions.

During the 1890s a revolutionary movement to secure independence from Spain developed, but the decade ended with the United States displacing Spain as a colonial power within the archipelago. Under American rule the Philippines differed from the rest of Southeast Asia in two fundamental ways. First, the Americans gave Filipinos a substantial and increasing role in the administration, as part of a stated policy to grant the colony independence at an early date. In connection with this policy, the government made education widely available in order to develop a populace capable of involvement in public affairs and able to participate in democratic institutions of government. Second, the Filipino élite owned large tracts of land, giving them a base of power and wealth outside the government, and a clear stake in sustaining the country's agricultural export economy.

The population of the Philippines occupied numerous islands, and was further fragmented by mountainous terrain. These physical divisions were reinforced by linguistic differences, regional loyalties and religious conflicts. During the nineteenth century, however, a shared 'national' identity began to develop, and a small number of people became politically active in the cause of bettering the political and social situation of the Philippines as a whole.

Some historians have attempted to place this change earlier, pointing to a long series of conspiracies and uprisings during the Spanish period as evidence of a nascent Filipino nationalism. The interpretation was rejected as long ago as 1889 by the nationalist leader José Rizal on the grounds that such revolts were isolated and directed against local grievances, and that Filipinos became conscious of themselves as a nation only during the nineteenth century.

Why did a Filipino identity emerge at this time? Rizal traced the change to a new Spanish attitude toward the population of the archipelago. While the Filipinos had once been treated 'as a subject, but not an inferior people', during the nineteenth century Spaniards began to show contempt for the Filipinos. According to Rizal, 'They made the race itself an object of insult. They professed themselves unable to see in it any admirable quality, any human trait',[7] and this insult, directed at the entire 'Indio' population, gave rise to a 'national' response.

One key episode in generating Filipino political consciousness was a mutiny at the Cavite Arsenal in 1872 and its aftermath. The mutiny lasted only two days and was easily suppressed, but Spanish authorities claimed it was part of a larger conspiracy and used the opportunity to crack down on various proponents of liberalization. The government imprisoned or exiled a number of Filipino priests, and three dissidents—Fathers José Burgos, Mariano Gomez, and Jacinto Zamora—were sentenced to death. The executions, by garrotte and carried out publicly, had a deep impact that was far from what the Spanish administration intended. Many considered the priests innocent of the charges laid against them, and the Archbishop of Manila refused to defrock them, lending credence to the idea that the three men had been executed to intimidate others who might be moved to challenge Spanish authority.

The executions shifted the focus of what had been a grievance against the friars to the Spanish administration as a whole, and following this event a political movement took shape among the Filipino élite, and particularly among the small group of Filipinos studying in Spain. Because their principal activity consisted of drafting articles and pamphlets calling attention to conditions in the Philippines, this initiative is known as the Propaganda Movement. The best-known writings produced by the group were a fortnightly newspaper called *La Solidaridad*, which appeared be-

---

[7] Quoted by Horacio de la Costa, SJ, 'Rizal's political ideas', in his *The Background of Nationalism and Other Essays*, Manila, 1965, 33–4.

tween 1889 and 1895, and two novels (*Noli Me Tangere* and *El Filibusterismo*) written by Rizal.

In general, the objectives of the Propaganda Movement reflected the ideals of nineteenth-century liberalism. They included equality before the law for Filipinos and Spaniards alike, and political rights for Filipinos comparable to those enjoyed in Spain. Far from advocating independence, the Propaganda Movement sought recognition of the Philippines as a province of Spain with representation in the Spanish parliament, the Cortes. Rizal wrote in a private letter in 1887 that 'in the present circumstances we want no separation from Spain; all we demand is more care, better instruction, better officials, one or two representatives, and more security for ourselves and our property.'[8] In an article in *La Solidaridad* he put the matter more colourfully, writing of 'the stainless patriotism and the loyalty of the Filipinos who since [the sixteenth century] have been joined to Spain, not for reasons of religion nor of traditionalism but, at the beginning, for reasons of high political convenience, and later, for love, for affection for the Mother Country'.[9]

Filipino demands generated sympathy in Europe but the friars resident in the Philippines, drawing on anti-liberal statements in the Syllabus of Errors issued in 1864 by Pope Pius IX, rejected the proposals. In 1889 Gregorio del Pilar, the editor of *La Solidaridad*, took a stronger line in urging assimilation of the Philippines with Spain. Rizal, however, was revising his position and increasingly diverged from this viewpoint, looking instead toward working for change within the Philippines itself: 'The error all make in thinking we can help here [in Europe], far away, is a great mistake indeed. . . . The field of battle is in the Philippines; there is where we should be.'[10]

Rizal returned to Manila on 26 June 1892, and on 3 July helped set up an underground organization called the Liga Filipina to work for unity, mutual protection, and reforms. Less than a week later he was arrested by the Spanish authorities, who sent him into internal exile in Mindanao. Within a few months, the Liga Filipina was dissolved. One faction continued to support Del Pilar's propaganda work in Europe, but another helped establish a secret society known as the Katipunan, which laid the groundwork for an insurrection that broke out in 1896 against Spanish rule.

The Katipunan was founded and led by a former Liga Filipina member named Andres Bonifacio (1863–97). For its structure and symbolism, the organization drew heavily on Freemasonry, indigenous mysticism, and Catholicism. Politically, the Katipunan worked to secure independence, and prepared for violent revolution to achieve this objective. Rizal declined to support this endeavour, arguing that conditions were not yet right, but plans went ahead. Fighting broke out on 26 August 1896 when the plot was revealed to the Spanish authorities. The government responded by trying and executing Rizal for his supposed involvement.

---

[8] Cited in John N. Schumacher, SJ, *The Propaganda Movement: 1880–1895*, Manila, 1973, 226.

[9] 'How to deceive the native land', *La Solidaridad*, II (15 May 1889), 72–3, reproduced in José Rizal, *Political and Historical Writings (1884–1890)*, Manila, 1989, 27–30.

[10] Schumacher, 223.

The Katipunan proved ineffective against Spanish forces, but Emilio Aguinaldo (1869–1963) had some success in Cavite and emerged as a rival to Bonifacio for leadership of the revolutionary cause. The two agreed to resolve the issue through an election, which Aguinaldo won. Bonifacio refused to accept the outcome and, accused of treason, was executed by followers of Aguinaldo.

On 1 November 1897, the revolutionary movement, located at Biak-na-bato in Bulacan Province, established a government and promulgated a constitution to formalize independence from Spain. Spanish forces continued to achieve successes, but the colonial government, concluding that the defeat of Filipino forces was likely to lead to protracted guerrilla warfare rather than peace, negotiated a settlement. The Pact of Biak-na-bato stipulated that fighting would cease, that rebel forces would surrender their arms, and that Aguinaldo and his supporters would receive a payment of three million Mexican dollars and leave the Philippines. This extraordinary agreement reveals the weakness of the Filipino forces, constantly harassed by the Spanish and unable to attract the backing of the landed Filipino élite, the *principalia*, whose wealth and control of manpower would have appreciably strengthened the revolutionary cause. The terms were not wholly carried out by either party, but Aguinaldo did depart for Hong Kong, only to return with American forces which invaded the Philippines in 1898 following the outbreak of the Spanish–American War.

Back in the Philippines, Aguinaldo, with growing support from the *principalia* now that success appeared to be at hand, issued a decree setting up a government to replace that established at Biak-na-bato, and on 12 June 1898 proclaimed Philippine independence. A congress convened at Malolos prepared a constitution for the Philippine Republic. This document, promulgated on 21 January 1899, embodied a bill of rights which barred arbitrary arrest or detention; prohibited taxation except by a legally authorized body; guaranteed Filipinos 'the full enjoyment' of 'political and civil rights'; established rights of *habeas corpus*, property, and domicile; and guaranteed freedom of expression and association. The Malolos administration also adopted measures (such as a civil marriage law) aimed at reducing the powers of the friar-dominated Catholic Church, and on 23 January, the day the Philippine Republic was inaugurated, President Aguinaldo issued a decree expelling all regular Spanish clergy from Philippine territory. The Malolos constitution also declared forfeit all properties of the religious corporations, claiming them for the government. However, the republic soon found itself at war with the United States, a struggle which it ultimately lost, and these measures were not carried out.

Relations between American and Filipino forces around Manila, already uneasy, deteriorated in early February and fighting broke out between the two sides. At the time, ratification by the US senate of the Treaty of Paris, drafted to settle the Spanish-American War and providing for cession of the Philippines to the United States, had been delayed owing to protracted debates between pro- and anti-imperialist interests. With the outbreak of hostilities, the Senate proceeded to ratify the treaty by a narrow margin, making the Philippines an American colony. Fighting continued until 1902, but the Americans were substantially in control by 1900.

The character of the Philippine revolution has aroused heated debate. Large numbers of Filipinos supported the cause of the republic, but questions have been raised concerning whether popular participation resulted from mobilization by élites using patronage networks, or was a free expression of popular feeling—a revolt of the masses. If the latter, there is also a question whether the inspiration lay in nationalism, folk beliefs, or Catholicism. John Schumacher has suggested that no single explanation will apply to all participants, an observation in keeping with the evidence and with common sense. He rejects generalizations concerning the behaviour of social classes during the revolution on grounds that élite characteristics and behaviour varied widely, and that mass support for the conflict was tempered in some instances by hostility toward the élite.[11] Another criticism has been advanced by Reynaldo C. Ileto, who argues that some historical accounts impose a spurious continuity on events, placing the Katipunan in a sequence of developments leading to the formation of a Philippine Republic with a Western-style constitution. Ileto suggests that those 'who swelled the ranks of the Katipunan had certain ideas about the world and their places in it, ideas quite different from those of the "better classes" of society', and that some of these ideas survived the transition to élite, *principalia* leadership under Aguinaldo, forming an undercurrent of political thought directed toward national rebirth and redemption that persisted under American rule.[12]

While fighting was still under way, a Philippine Commission carried out a fact-finding exercise. A second commission, with William Howard Taft as chairman, was appointed in September 1900 and established civil government in July of the following year. Initially, the second Philippine Commission served as the country's legislative body, but the Philippine Organic Act of 1901 accepted the principle of Filipino participation in government, and in 1907 a new arrangement was introduced which gave lawmaking powers to a bicameral legislature consisting of the Philippine Commission and a Philippine Assembly made up of Filipino delegates selected from the provinces.

From the beginning Filipinos occupied positions of authority as municipal officers and provincial officials, and two political parties took shape during the first decade of American rule. The Partido Federalista was instrumental in securing a peace settlement in the Philippine–American War, but it adopted an assimilationist posture—advocating American statehood for the Philippines—that cost it popular support. Although the Federalistas shifted their stance in 1907 (adopting the name Partido

[11] The issues are debated in Milagros Guerrero, 'Understanding Philippine revolutionary mentality', reviewing *Pasyon and Revolution: Popular Movements in the Philippines, 1840–1900*, by Reynaldo C. Ileto, *Philippine Studies* 29 (1981) 240–56; Reynaldo C. Ileto, 'Critical issues in "Understanding Philippine revolutionary mentality"', ibid., 30 (1982) 92–119; and John N. Schumacher, SJ, 'Recent perspectives on the revolution', ibid., 445–92.
[12] Reynaldo Ileto, *Pasyon and Revolution: Popular Movements in the Philippines, 1840–1910*, Quezon City, 1979, 99, 139.

Nacional Progresista), a newly formed Partido Nacionalista, which backed immediate independence, dominated the new Philippine Assembly, and remained pre-eminent in Philippine politics throughout the period of American rule.

Despite the activities of opposing political parties and superficial resemblances to political arrangements in the United States, Philippine politics became a clash of contending personalities within a dominant one-party system. Theodore Friend has written of this period that 'the Philippine political party was unideological and only loosely institutionalized, tending to form around charismatic persons rather than special programs'.[13] The key figures were Manuel L. Quezon, Sergio Osmeña, and Manuel Roxas. Osmeña, an aloof and cautious man, initially dominated the Partido Nacionalista, but during the 1920s the colourful and temperamental Quezon outmanoeuvred him, becoming the leading political figure, and the country's first president when the Philippine Commonwealth came into being in 1935. The younger Roxas, an ambitious and aggressive man, entered politics during the 1920s as a protégé of Quezon, who secured for him the position of Speaker of the House in 1922. Roxas later aligned himself with Osmeña, completing an uneasy triumvirate at the top of the Philippine administration.

A Democratic Party victory in the 1912 United States presidential election portended faster progress towards political change, and President Woodrow Wilson stated in 1913 that United States policies should be formulated 'with a view to the ultimate independence of the Islands and as a preparation for that independence.'[14] Filipinization of the government administrative services proceeded apace under Governor-General Francis Burton Harrison (1913–20), placing substantial power in Filipino hands, and in 1916 the Jones Law established an administrative structure modelled on that of the United States, with a strong executive (for the time being the American governor-general with an appointed Cabinet) and an independent judiciary alongside the bicameral legislature, the Philippine Commission being replaced by an elected Senate. The Jones Law stated that the United States would recognize independence for the Philippines 'as soon as a stable government can be established therein', a declaration of good intentions that left much latitude for negotiation and disagreement.

With independence promised in principle, the outstanding question was when it would be granted. Nationalism remained an emotive issue and politicians made what capital they could out of the demand for early progress in that direction, though public opinion so clearly favoured independence that no significant disagreements were possible on this central point. Historians have, however, questioned the devotion of the Partido Nacionalista to achieving this goal. Lewis E. Gleeck Jr, for example, argues that when independence seemed to become a real prospect under Harrison, the Partido Nacionalista employed 'two different policies,

---

[13] Theodore Friend, *Between Two Empires: Philippine Ordeal and Development from the Great Depression through the Pacific War, 1929–1946*, New Haven, 1965, 27.

[14] This statement is quoted by J.S. Furnivall in an unfinished manuscript published posthumously under the title *Experiment in Independence: The Philippines*, Manila, 1974, 24.

one of independence for public consumption, and another of autonomy under American sovereignty and protection, in private'.[15] Publicly the party pursued the issue by sending a series of independence missions to Washington, beginning in 1919 with one led by Quezon. But the 1920s brought Republican administrations that did not wish to press ahead with independence, and Leonard Wood, the governor-general for most of the decade (1921–7), took steps to reassert American control of Philippine affairs. He had as a result a stormy relationship with Quezon.

The Great Depression produced a difficult situation for nationalists in the Philippines. Philippine sugar and tobacco competed with domestic production in the United States and its possessions elsewhere, and there was a strong lobby in the United States seeking to place Philippine imports on an equal footing with those from foreign countries. Under pressure from this quarter, a number of members of the United States Congress moved to offer full and immediate independence to the Philippines. However, the proposals envisaged subjecting imports from the Philippines to American tariffs, a potentially disastrous provision given that over 75 per cent of Philippine exports went to the United States, and that the depression had severely reduced the demand for tropical agricultural products world-wide.

The response of the Filipino leadership was to negotiate a transitional period when a Filipino administration would take responsibility for the affairs of the country, and tariffs would be increased gradually to allow the economy to adjust. There has been much criticism of the policies pursued during the 1930s. Some historians have accused the élite leadership of the Partido Nacionalista of betraying Filipino nationalism to benefit their social class. In the words of Norman Owen, 'wealthy agriculturalists succeeded in defining their own interests as those of the Philippines'.[16] This case rests on the fact that the Filipino élite was composed of landowners who derived the major part of their income from agricultural exports, and stood to lose if the country did not have free access to the United States market. However, had Filipino leaders agreed to the more radical independence proposals, the sudden loss of the United States market for agricultural exports would surely have had a deleterious effect on the general welfare of the country.

Personal considerations also helped shape the tactics of leading politicians. In 1933 the United States Congress overrode a veto by President Hoover to pass the Hare–Hawes–Cutting Act, providing for independence after a ten-year transition period. During this time a Philippine Commonwealth constitution was to be drafted and elections held, while on the economic side quotas would be imposed on duty-free Philippine exports to the United States, and a graduated tariff would be introduced. Independence was to take effect automatically after ten years, but the United States

[15] Lewis E. Gleeck, Jr, *General History of the Philippines, Part V, I: The American Half-Century (1898–1946)*, Manila: Historical Conservation Society, 1984, 97.
[16] Norman Owen, 'Philippine economic development and American policy: a reappraisal', in Norman G. Owen, ed., *Compadre Colonialism: Studies on the Philippines under American Rule*, Ann Arbor: University of Michigan Center for South and Southeast Asian Studies, 1971, 113.

would retain commercial rights and military bases in the Philippines. Quezon opposed this legislation, ostensibly because of the provisions relating to military bases but in large part because it had been negotiated by Osmeña and Roxas, and he wanted to be personally responsible for independence. Following Quezon's lead, the Philippine legislature rejected the Hare–Hawes–Cutting Act, and Quezon then renegotiated the agreement, achieving slight modifications, and accepted the Tydings–McDuffie Act on much the same terms the following year. Quezon's faction triumphed in elections held in 1934 to select delegates to the Constitutional Convention, and the transition period commenced in 1935 with a national plebiscite approving the new constitution and the country's first presidential election, which Quezon won.

In the broader sphere of modernist reform, the Philippines was relatively quiet until the 1930s. With substantial educational opportunities available, with a Filipino Congress writing the laws of the country, and with a predominantly Filipino civil service, there was little scope for opposition nationalist political groups. The Catholic Church, which had been closely identified with the Spanish régime, underwent a somewhat difficult adjustment after 1898. The Church had to submit to the principles of religious liberty and separation of church and state, and to the forced sale of lands held by the religious orders. Moreover, it faced a loss of support to a schismatic religious movement called the Iglesia Filipina Independiente (the Philippine Independent, or Aglipayan, Church), formed by Bishop Gregorio Aglipay in 1902. This Church had its origins in an initiative of the revolutionary period to form a Filipino Church loyal to the Vatican, but later took shape as a body outside the Catholic Church. Initially the Philippine Independent Church attracted about a quarter of the Catholic population.

During the 1930s, in part as a result of the Great Depression, political activity intensified in the Philippines. An opposition movement took shape under the name 'Sakdal', a word meaning 'to accuse' or 'to strike' and the name of a newspaper critical of the Nacionalista administration. The Sakdal leader, Benigno Ramos, a former Quezon protégé, at first directed the movement along orthodox political channels, forming a Sakdal Party that capitalized on divisions within the Nacionalista leadership and contested the 1934 general election with some success. By 1935, however, the transition to the Commonwealth government was strengthening the Nacionalista position, and the Sakdal Party responded with increasingly strong rhetoric and overtures to the Japanese for support. When the government applied repressive measures, Sakdal supporters staged an uprising in early May 1935. Government troops quickly defeated the rebels, destroying the party if not the spirit of Sakdalism.

At the beginning of the decade both a Socialist Party (formed by Pedro Abad Santos in 1929) and a Communist Party (publicly launched on 7 November 1930) had also entered the political picture in the Philippines. The Communist Party was declared an illegal organization in 1931 (a decision confirmed by the Supreme Court in October 1932) and went underground. The socialists concentrated on trade-union activities and peasant causes, and after 1935 recruited supporters of the discredited Sakdal Party into an increasingly effective political movement. In November 1938, Quezon released communist leaders from provincial exile, and the communists joined the socialists in creating a new Communist Party of the Philippines, which participated in a Popular Front against Fascism and did well in the 1940 elections.

Peasant unions, such as the Kalipunang Pambansa ng mga Magsasaka sa Pilipinas (National Society of Peasants in the Philippines), were also a significant force during the 1930s. The unions challenged the authority and supremacy of the landed élite, but it has been argued that in many respects their objectives were conservative or even reactionary, oriented toward preserving or restoring traditional social arrangements that provided welfare guarantees, rather than achieving radical change.

The Filipino Independent Church also took up the cause of the peasant, and Bishop Aglipay stood against Quezon in the 1935 election to select a Commonwealth President. This challenge was not a serious threat, and the Nacionalista leadership drew together to produce a comfortable victory in the election. Their success is conventionally seen as a triumph of Philippine nationalism, but it has also been characterized by Alfred W. McCoy as a triumph of Philippine authoritarianism based on 'a system of clientelist politics' that was to be 'institutionalized and perfected' under the Commonwealth.[17]

Under United States rule, Philippine nationalism was a political weapon deployed by the dominant Partido Nacionalista. Because independence had been conceded in principle by the American régime, opposition groups did not and could not take shape around this issue, but by the same token nationalism did not provide a focus to draw together the disparate groups that made up the Philippine population. Regional sentiments remained important and politicians derived support based on their linguistic and regional identifications. Efforts to devise a national language or other all-embracing national symbols were half-hearted and largely ineffective throughout the American period. While support for the Commonwealth government and for independence was widespread, regional loyalties and the authoritarian pattern of administration would create difficulties in the postwar era.

The Netherlands East Indies

In its early days, the Dutch régime adopted the administrative style of the kingdom of Mataram which preceded it in Java, and made extensive use of members of the Javanese aristocracy as regional administrators. Opposition to Dutch rule likewise drew on indigenous patterns of political behaviour, employing traditional symbols and working toward objectives that fitted within the traditional political order.

---

[17] Alfred W. McCoy, 'Quezon's Commonwealth: the emergence of Philippine authoritarianism', in Ruby R. Paredes, ed., *Philippine Colonial Democracy*, New Haven: Yale University Southeast Asia Studies, 1988, 118–20.

Toward the end of the nineteenth century, the Dutch increasingly replaced this quasi-royal system with a bureaucratic administration, and a new form of political opposition developed. Based in part on racial or 'national' distinctions, it accepted the conventions of statecraft that underlay the colonial government, and competed for the right to participate in or to run the administration. The beliefs and traditions of the archipelago, the mysticism and the cosmology that drew on indigenous as well as Hindu-Buddhist concepts, did not disappear, but they no longer lay at the heart of the political process.

Reformers pursued a variety of goals, including modest cultural assertion, economic development, religious purification, and independence. For the most part the tone was modernist, reflecting dissatisfaction both with Dutch rule and with long-established indigenous practices, and there was an emphasis on the application of reason to solve problems or shape new initiatives, rather than reliance on faith or traditional authority. Inspiration came from a variety of sources, including a reformist tendency within Islam, and the conceptual and technical innovations that reshaped production, trade, and administration throughout the world during the nineteenth century.

Some specialist prewar accounts of nationalism in the Netherlands East Indies exist, but serious writing for a general readership paid little attention to Indonesian opposition politics. Nor was this lack of emphasis wholly unwarranted in view of the modest accomplishments of prewar Indonesian political activity. Bernhard Dahm has observed that a great majority of the population of the Netherlands East Indies knew nothing of the nationalist movement, and the movement itself 'did not constitute a threat to the colonial government'.[18] On the other hand, the Dutch administration was extremely concerned with local political activities during the 1930s, and an extensive and effective system of surveillance contributed to the reformists' lack of success.

The issue of wartime collaboration, and the nationalist struggle against reimposition of Dutch rule after 1945, led to a reassessment of prewar political activity in the archipelago. An Indonesian study of the nationalist movement appeared in 1947,[19] and George McTurnan Kahin published a classic English-language account in 1952.[20] Kahin adopted a chronological approach, briefly describing the history of opposition to Dutch rule before 1900 and then tracing modern nationalism from the early twentieth century, portraying it as the activities of a series of organizations of different ideological persuasions. This portrait of the nationalist movement remains standard,[21] although subsequent in-depth studies have altered perceptions of some of the organizations concerned. However, it seems possible that these divisions have been overemphasized. The nationalist leader Mohammad Hatta considered Indonesian Marxists to be nationalists at

[18] Bernhard Dahm, *History of Indonesia in the Twentieth Century*, London, 1971, 77.
[19] L.M. Sitorus, *Sedjarah Pergerakan Kebangsaan Indonesia*, Jakarta, 1947.
[20] George McTurnan Kahin, *Nationalist and Revolution in Indonesia*, Ithaca, 1952.
[21] Secondary-school texts used in Indonesia provide an account that follows much the same lines as that of Kahin.

heart, and Sukarno glossed over the differences between nationalism, Marxism and Islam. Such interpretations might be said to reflect an imperfect understanding of Marxism or nationalism, but alternatively might be seen as reflecting a deep understanding of Indonesian society, and as illustrating the inadvisability of relying on foreign categories to interpret Indonesian events.[22]

Modernist reform activity in the Netherlands East Indies can be divided into four phases, based on the goals and activities of local organizations and the stance adopted by the Dutch government. An initial phase of co-operative activity between 1900 and roughly 1918 was followed by a radical period, a non-cooperating phase, and in the 1930s by a period of grudging co-operation dictated by restrictive Dutch policies. Alongside this politically oriented activity, there was also a reform movement that largely disregarded the Dutch administration and used education and social welfare activities to work for change.

Reformist activity benefited from the Ethical Policy inaugurated by the Dutch administration in 1901. Designed to redress past injustices, the Ethical Policy brought the introduction of measures to promote economic development, improve health and welfare, and to encourage indigenous participation in professional life and in social and administrative affairs. However, during the 1920s relations between the Dutch administration and Indonesian activists became increasingly acrimonious, and the Ethical Policy was effectively discarded.

During the nineteenth century the influence of the *bupati*, the *priyayi* or aristocrats who served as Regents within the Dutch administration, underwent a decline. In response, some among the *bupati* advocated self-strengthening through education, both for the aristocracy in their capacity as leaders of Javanese society, and ultimately for non-nobles as well, to enable them to participate in the administration of the country. Notable for their efforts in this regard were R. M. A. A. Hadiningrat, *Bupati* of Demak, and his niece, Raden Adjeng Kartini, whose interest in modernization and in education for women made her a nationalist icon after her death in childbirth in 1904.

Indonesians who had obtained an education through the two principal Dutch institutions available to them, the Opleidingscholen voor inlandsche ambtenaren (OSVIA), a school to train native officials, and the School tot opleiding van inlandsche artsen (STOVIA), a school for training native doctors, took the lead in proposing political initiatives. STOVIA graduates in particular felt that their education and work received insufficient recognition, and in May 1908 a group of them formed an organization with the name Budi Utomo (Glorious Endeavour) to promote social reform. The founders, who expressed a wish to help ordinary people, planned to extend their movement throughout Java and ultimately throughout the

---

[22] Drawing on this perspective, Takashi Shiraishi has re-examined political activity in Java prior to 1926 with a view to abandoning conventional categories and considering political groupings not as representing distinct ideologies but as a part of a broad 'movement', or *pergerakan*. See his *An Age in Motion: Popular Radicalism in Java, 1912–1926*, Ithaca, 1990.

Netherlands East Indies, but an older and more conservative element of the aristocracy soon took control of Budi Utomo, diluting its reformist character and stressing Javanese culture and Javanese values.

Three organizations dominated Indonesian reformist activity during the 1910s: Sarekat Islam, created to encourage economic activity among the indigenous Muslim population; Muhammadiyah, a modernist reforming Muslim organization; and the Indische Sociaal-Demokratische Vereeniging (ISDV, the Indies Social-Democratic Association), a radical Marxist group. None of these organizations was ethnically based, although all originated in Java and had their greatest strength there.

Another body, the Nationale Indische Partij, founded in 1912, directed its appeal to all races and called for racial equality, socio-economic justice and ultimate independence. As an organization the group accomplished little, for the government suppressed it within a year and sent its principal leaders, E. F. E. Douwes Dekker, Suwardi Suryadiningrat and Tjipto Mangunkusumo, into exile in the Netherlands. All returned within a few years and played a further role in the nationalist movement, but their fate gave some indication of the limited range of political activity the government was prepared to countenance. The membership of the Nationale Indische Partij regrouped as Insulinde, a predominantly Eurasian organization which had limited appeal in other sectors of the society.

Formally constituted in September 1912, Sarekat Islam grew into a mass movement claiming a membership in excess of two million. The organization proposed to promote a commercial spirit, act as a mutual aid association for members, serve the spiritual and economic interests of the people, and combat misunderstandings concerning Islam. Its key figure was an aristocratic OSVIA graduate, Raden Umar Sayed Tjokroaminoto. Although Sarekat Islam benefited from the modest latitude given indigenous organizations under the Ethical Policy, overt political activity was disallowed, and the movement accordingly adopted a co-operative stance in dealing with the Dutch government. For its part, the Netherlands East Indies administration sanctioned Sarekat Islam activities at the local level but did not authorize a central organization until 1916, by which time local branches had developed to such a degree that they were not amenable to central control.

A charismatic leader, Tjokroaminoto rapidly became a cult figure, and popular identification of him with the messianic Javanese tradition of the *ratu adil* (just king) contributed to the movement's early growth. After 1915 this approach was criticized by, among others, Agus Salim, a member of the Central Sarekat Islam who helped turn the organization towards an increased emphasis on Islam and modernism. In 1917 the Sarekat Islam formulated a Declaration of Principles that focused on Islam as the source of democratic ideas and spiritual education, and stressed a need for intellectual and moral development to enable the people to participate in politics. It also produced an Action Programme which called for transformation of the Volksraad into a true legislature, establishment of regional councils and extension of the franchise.

In the first Volksraad elections, held in 1917, only two nationalist figures won seats, Abdul Muis of Sarekat Islam and Abdul Rivai of Insulinde. The governor-general, who had hoped to draw the nationalist opposition into the political process, subsequently selected other activists to serve as appointed members, including the Sarekat Islam leader Tjokroaminoto, and Tjipto Mangunkusumo. Nationalist representatives formed a bloc called the Radical Concentration, but the Volksraad did not become a major forum for Indonesian opinion and efforts to turn it into a true parliament failed. By the 1920s Indonesian leaders were beginning to favour a non-cooperative approach and withdrawal from the Volksraad.

Around 1918, Indonesian political activity entered a radical phase, owing to a lack of substantive concessions on the part of the Dutch administration and to pressure from ISDV members who joined Sarekat Islam in the latter part of the decade. The Marxist ISDV had been founded in 1914 by Hendricus J. F. M. Sneevliet. Owing to its European make-up and the novelty of its political stance, the group had only limited popular appeal, but Sneevliet attempted with considerable success to acquire a mass base by linking his movement with Sarekat Islam. Although Sneevliet was expelled from the Indies in 1918, ISDV supporters in the Sarekat Islam grew in strength, and became increasingly extreme in their demands, clashing with moderate elements in the leadership. The ISDV was particularly strong in the city of Semarang, and the Semarang branch of Sarekat Islam, under the leadership of two ISDV activists, Semaun and Darsono, pressed for implementation of a programme of revolutionary action.

In 1918 the Dutch administration uncovered a secret revolutionary 'Section B' of the Sarekat Islam, leading in 1920 to prison sentences for various figures associated with it. The episode caused defections from Sarekat Islam, notably among the peasant membership, and also deepened divisions within the organization as a conservative religious faction led by Agus Salim and Abdul Muis began trying to counter radical influence. At the sixth Sarekat Islam Congress, held in 1921, the leadership moved against the ISDV faction, pushing through a resolution that called for party discipline and barred joint membership in Sarekat Islam and other organizations. As intended, the measure resulted in a communist withdrawal.

The ISDV group (which in 1920 had adopted the name Perserikatan Komunis di India, PKI, or the Indies Communist Organization) retained control of a number of local branches and made these the basis of a Red Sarekat Islam, but the Dutch administration was monitoring events and in 1922 began expelling communist leaders from the Netherlands East Indies. Faced with increasingly effective government surveillance, one faction within the PKI laid plans to stage a revolt. Efforts to secure Comintern support failed, and most PKI branches refused to participate, but uprisings took place in Banten in November 1926, and in the Minangkabau lands of west Sumatra early in 1927. Although instigated by the communist leadership, these uprisings owed much to local grievances and, lacking widespread support, were quickly put down. However, in the aftermath the Dutch administration suppressed the PKI so effectively that the party did not again become a political force in Indonesia until after 1945.

The communist uprisings of 1926–7 confirmed the views of those in the Dutch administration who felt the Ethical Policy had gone too far, and effectively ended the ethical period. A new Indische Staatsregeling, in essence a constitution, introduced in 1925 provided added controls, and while nominally giving concessions to the nationalists ensured that power remained in Dutch hands. However, while Dutch attitudes toward Indonesian political activity hardened during the 1920s, under Governor-General A. C. D. de Graeff (1926–31) the Dutch administration maintained a moderate stance. De Graeff's conservative successor, Jonkheer Mr B. C. D. De Jonge (1931–6) was less tolerant of opposition. When Indonesian political activity became increasingly non-cooperative, his administration took strong action, sending the principal figures into internal exile.

Islam provided the rationale for a non-nationalist activism based on the principle that all Muslims formed part of an *Ummat Islam* or Islamic community that transcended political and ethnic divisions, but it served nationalist purposes as well, raising objections to rule by non-Muslims over Muslims and offering the prospect of support from outside the region. However, a substantial proportion of the Muslim population held beliefs that combined Islamic doctrines with elements of local tradition, some arguably in conflict with orthodox Islam. Reformists had attacked this sort of syncretism in the Minangkabau area of Sumatra in the early nineteenth century, precipitating the prolonged and traumatic Padri wars, and anti-colonialism based on Islam inevitably brought such matters to the forefront once again. Divisions within the Muslim community as well as the presence of a significant number of non-Muslims in the archipelago made Islam a questionable basis for national unity, while many reformist leaders saw economic and political modernization as their primary objectives, and had little interest in religious dogma.

Muhammadiyah, formed in Yogyakarta in November 1912 by Kijai Hadji Ahmad Dahlan, was a principal component of the modernist, reform-minded faction known in Indonesia as the *kaum muda* (lit. young group). In the religious sphere, Muhammadiyah attacked heterodox religious practices, the influence of *adat* (customary law) and the associated aristocratic *priyayi* society, and Westernization. The *kaum muda* advocated a purified Islam purged of accretions derived from Indian and Indonesian sources, and applied reason to basic textual materials such as the Koran and the Sunnah so as to deal with contemporary issues. Muhammadiyah, which favoured a religiously-oriented programme of modernization, concentrated on education and social welfare, and generally did not become involved in political activity.

This reformist programme eventually drew a response from those who practised the syncretic form of Islam that had long prevailed in the archipelago. In 1926 this faction, generally known as the *kaum tua* or elder group, formed a rival organization called Nahdatul Ulama (The Rise of the Religious Scholars) to defend established religious practices. Like Muhammadiyah, Nahdatul Ulama tended to stay out of politics during this period.

Sarekat Islam, after its split with the ISDV, attempted to establish itself as a major voice for Muslim interests, but the organization had been compromised by its association with communism. During the 1920s, religiously oriented moderates tended to turn to established non-political groups such as Muhammadiyah, while on the political side, the communists and later a newly formed nationalist organization, the Perserikatan Nasional Indonesia (PNI), seized the initiative. In 1929 Sarekat Islam reconstituted itself as the Partai Sarekat Islam Indonesia, but the organization never recovered the influence or pre-eminence it had once enjoyed.

During the 1920s, reformist activity that concentrated on religious or educational matters but was not overtly political grew increasingly significant, and bolstered the nationalist cause. Education was a concern of Indonesian intellectuals of all persuasions, and grew in importance as Dutch monitoring and suppression of political activity became more intense. Schools and study groups provided a forum for disseminating new ideas and creating a politically aware population, while avoiding direct action that might provoke a Dutch response. One major educational movement, called Taman Siswa or the Garden of Students, was founded in 1922 by Ki Hadjar Dewantoro (the former Indische Partij activist Suwardi Suryadiningrat) who had developed a strong interest in education during his period of exile in the Netherlands. Like Nahdatul Ulama, the Taman Siswa represented an assertion of Javanese identity, combining Javanese culture and a modernist Western-oriented curriculum as an alternative to modernist Islam. Muhammadiyah also devoted a great deal of attention to education, sponsoring schools that taught the ideas of reformist Islam together with practical skills. Reformers in the outer islands similarly used education to spread modernist and nationalist ideas, notably in the Minangkabau area where the Sumatra Thawalib organization established a school system that became an intellectual centre for anti-government activity.

Indonesian students in the Netherlands became politically active during the 1920s. Their vehicle was Perhimpunan Indonesia (the Indonesian Association), which had its origins in a student society formed in 1909. In 1918 the group began expressing nationalist political views, and in 1925 was reconstituted as a political body which, although never large, became a fertile source of ideas and launched many of its members, including Mohammad Hatta—Perhimpunan Indonesia's moving force—Sutan Sjahrir, Soetomo, and Sartono, on careers as political activists. Perhimpunan Indonesia advocated a unified archipelago-wide effort against the Dutch, with non-cooperation as a tactic, and it formulated the concept of 'Indonesia', an essential step in moving away from the colonial 'Netherlands East Indies' and creating a new national identity.

In Europe, Perhimpunan Indonesia worked together for a time with Marxist groups, but the high degree of control exercised over the communist movement by Moscow made Perhimpunan Indonesia members fear that following this path might simply mean the replacement of one form of imperialism by another. In 1926 Hatta, as head of Perhimpunan Indonesia, and the PKI leader Semaun signed a convention under which the two groups would co-operate. The agreement was in effect for only two weeks before the Comintern instructed Semaun to repudiate it, but the arrangement became known to the Dutch security service and coloured its view of Hatta and the Perhimpunan Indonesia.

Another development of the 1920s was the emergence of a second generation of political activists within Indonesia, and of new political organizations that displaced Sarekat Islam as the leading secular nationalist association. The younger leadership, disillusioned with the lack of progress to date, adopted a more confrontational style. Study clubs, the first established in Surabaya by Dr Raden Soetomo, a founding member of Budi Utomo and a Perhimpunan Indonesia member while studying in the Netherlands, provided a common meeting ground for returned students and local activists. The most important of these groups was the General Study Club of Bandung, where the membership included established leaders such as Tjipto Mangunkusumo and Douwes Dekker, and also Sukarno, an engineering student in Bandung when the group was formed in 1925. Sukarno, who rapidly became one of the key nationalist figures in the Netherlands East Indies, argued for unity in opposing the Dutch, and attempted to produce a synthesis of nationalism, Islam and Marxism. However, government pressure had caused the Bandung Study Club to distance itself from Marxism even before the abortive uprisings, and the alliance between secular modernizers in the nationalist movement and the religious faction was always uneasy.

In 1927, the study clubs and returned members of Perhimpunan Indonesia formed a new political organization called the Perserikatan Nasional Indonesia (PNI, the Indonesian National Association) to promote the cause of Indonesian nationalism by fostering unity, eliminating reliance on the Dutch, and working towards independence. The Bandung Study Club took the lead in setting up the organization, and Sukarno occupied a prominent place in its executive body. The Dutch government monitored the situation but for the moment tolerated these developments as a means of containing nationalist sentiment and preventing the growth of extremist tendencies.

John Ingleson has observed that the leaders of the PNI, although describing themselves as radicals, adopted moderate demands:

> There was a noticeable lack of radicalism in the party's social and economic policies, particularly when compared with the platform of the banned PKI. There was nothing which would lose it support among the wealthier Indonesian elite. Scant attention was given to urban workers, there was no mention of peasant rights nor of land reform and no suggestion of any redistribution of wealth or resources after independence, beyond the cessation of Dutch drainage of the economy. This was partly in order to retain as wide a spectrum of support as possible but at the same time it was also a reflection of the essential social and economic conservatism of the PNI leaders.

By way of mitigation, Ingleson notes that government sensitivity in the aftermath of the PKI uprising made a moderate programme expedient to avoid suppression. This moderation notwithstanding, the Dutch security service associated the PNI with Marxism, and accordingly treated it as a very dangerous movement.[23]

---

[23] John Ingleson, *Road to Exile: The Indonesian Nationalist Movement, 1927–1934*, Singapore, 1974, 56–7.

Sukarno, who considered unity to be of paramount importance, was also instrumental in creating a federation of anti-colonial parties called the Permufakatan Perhimpunan-Perhimpunan Politik Kebangsaan Indonesia (PPPKI, the Association of Political Organizations of the Indonesian People). The major political organizations joined this front, but the PPPKI was rent by conflicts (in particular over the appropriateness of a non-cooperative approach, and the role of religion) and played only a minor part in subsequent events.

The nationalist movement did succeed in gaining acceptance for a number of key symbols in the late 1920s. One was a red-and-white national flag, another the national anthem, entitled 'Indonesia Raya'. The movement also pressed for use of Indonesian—based on Malay, the lingua franca of the ports—as a national language, and for new terminology: Indonesia for the Netherlands East Indies, and Jakarta for Batavia. A youth congress that met in 1928 adopted a slogan to the effect that Indonesia comprised one people, one language, one homeland, and this youth pledge provided a rallying cry for the nationalist struggle.

The PNI flourished until the end of 1929, building its organizational base while using Sukarno's extraordinary gifts as an orator to attract mass support. As the membership grew, Sukarno became increasingly bold in his speeches, and the government began to intervene, banning some meetings and forbidding the use of emotive terms relating to freedom and independence at public gatherings. The PNI's growing extremism, which many members opposed, led in December 1929 to the detention of a number of leaders including Sukarno, who was subsequently tried and sentenced to four years' imprisonment, although he was released after serving half the term.

During the 1930s the reformist movement was characterized by grudging co-operation. Dutch authorities under the influence of De Jonge, and the conservative H. Colijn, who became Minister of Colonies in 1933, conceded little to nationalist sentiment and made it clear that non-cooperating groups would not be tolerated. The Dutch security service identified five sources of danger to the colonial régime: extremist movements (indigenous messianic activity); trade unionism; foreign movements (a category that included both international communism and Perhimpunan Indonesia); nationalist and Muslim movements; and the Chinese movement (arising from the influence of political developments in China on Chinese living in the Indies).[24] During the 1920s and 1930s, the government took strong and generally effective action against organizations in all categories.

After Sukarno's conviction, the new PNI leader, Sartono, suspended PNI political activity, and in April 1931 dissolved the organization. Two successor parties were formed. Partai Indonesia (Partindo) attempted to carry on PNI activity under a new name, while the Pendidikan Nasional Indonesia (Indonesian National Education, known as the PNI Baru, or New PNI), a body which reflected Hatta's philosophy, sought to educate a

[24] Theodore Friend, *The Blue-Eyed Enemy: Japan against the West in Java and Luzon, 1942–1945*, Princeton, 1988, 39.

cohort of future nationalist leaders and to cultivate a political base among the proletariat and the peasantry. Upon his release at the end of 1931, Sukarno resumed his attempt to foster nationalist unity through the PPPKI, but he found divisions too deep to overcome and on 1 August 1932 joined Partindo, just twenty-four days before Hatta returned to Indonesia to take control of PNI Baru after spending eleven years as a student and political activist in the Netherlands.

A year later, on 1 August 1933, the government again detained Sukarno, this time banishing him to Flores without a trial. Hatta and Sjahrir adopted a conciliatory approach, but nonetheless were arrested in February 1934 and banished to Boven Digul in New Guinea. By the end of 1934, most prominent anti-colonial leaders had been detained, and non-cooperating nationalism had ceased to be a viable option. For the remainder of the prewar period, the nationalist cause was represented by cautious, co-operating groups such as the Partai Indonesia Raya or Parindra (The Greater Indonesia Party), formed in 1935 by drawing together members of various moderate organizations, and the Gerakan Rakyat Indonesia or Gerindo (Indonesian People's Movement), a nationalist organization sympathetic to socialism which was founded in 1937. Partindo dissolved itself in 1936, and PNI Baru ceased to play a significant role after its leaders were detained.

One of the most important nationalist figures of the 1930s was Mohammed Husni Thamrin, chairman of the PPPKI during the 1930s and head of the political section of Parindra. A close friend of Sukarno and a strong critic of colonial rule, Thamrin was sufficiently co-operative with the Dutch to retain his independence, and as a member of the Volksraad had a forum for openly and effectively criticizing abuses. His death in Dutch custody in January 1941, although due to natural causes, helped to mobilize anti-Dutch opinion in the last months before the Japanese invasion.

The rise of fascism in Europe and Japan during the 1930s altered the political situation, and proponents of a loyalist posture made a number of efforts to reach an accommodation with the Dutch government as war approached. In October 1936 Sutardjo Kartohadikusumo, president of an Association of Native Civil Servants founded in 1929, initiated a petition in the Volksraad addressed to the queen and requesting that an imperial conference be convened to draft a reform programme leading towards Indonesian self-government within a Dutch commonwealth. The Dutch government did not respond until late 1938, and then rejected the petition.

Gerindo, reflecting the growing concern about the growth of fascism in Europe, also offered co-operation with the Dutch internationally against this threat, while pursuing nationalist objectives domestically; but it found the Dutch unreceptive. In 1939 the main nationalist organizations (including Gerindo, Parindra, and Partai Sarekat Islam Indonesia) formed an umbrella group called the Gabungan Politik Indonesia (GAPI, the Indonesian Political Federation). GAPI offered to work with the Dutch against fascism in return for a promise of autonomy for Indonesia, and attempted to get the Dutch to agree to the formation of a true Indonesian parliament, but the Netherlands rejected these proposals. After the German invasion of Holland, the Dutch government-in-exile declined to consider the status

of Indonesia while the war was in progress, and rebuffed further suggestions by Indonesian leaders.

Another development of the late 1930s, and a significant portent for the
future, was an agreement by Muhammadijah and Nahdatul to join forces
in a Council of Muslim parties (the Madjlisul Islamil A'laa Indonesia, or
MIAI). Created to co-ordinate religious affairs, MIAI was soon drawn into
politics and supported GAPI's proposals to establish an Indonesian parliament, but with the proviso that it should be based on Islamic principles.

The involvement of peoples living outside Java in modernist political
reform varied considerably. Many societies in the archipelago fulfil the
classic definition of a nation, possessing unique languages, cultures, and
historical traditions, and some developed nationalist activity based on
these characteristics. In the case of the Minangkabau, one of the most
distinctive societies owing to its matrilineal traditions, regional loyalties
were subsumed by involvement in a broader nationalism, and Java-based
organizations such as the Muhammadiyah and the PKI were well received.
Minangkabau, however, was unusual among territories outside Java in
having a long history of colonial rule (Dutch control dated from the 1820s),
and was exceptionally aware of extra-local events owing to the *merantau*
tradition which took young men away from the Minangkabau heartland to
trade or study elsewhere. By way of contrast, the Acehnese, who also had
a long history of external contacts with traders from outside the archipelago, were preoccupied with local issues and showed no great interest in
political developments in Batavia or elsewhere. Political organizations
formed around Acehnese leaders, and national Indonesian organizations
had little appeal.

Other societies and groups also had parochial concerns that competed
with the political objectives of the small, urban-based, Western-educated
nationalist élite in Java, as reflected in a large number of youth organizations operating during the 1920s (including besides Jong [Young] Java,
Jong Sumatra, Jong Celebes, Jong Bataks Bond, Jong Ambon, and Jong
Minahasa). The Eurasian community, attracted initially to the multi-racial
Nationale Indische Partij which the Dutch suppressed in 1913, subsequently turned to Insulinde, which supported a moderate programme of
reform. The Chinese and Peranakan communities likewise formulated
political programmes, a development discussed elsewhere in this chapter.
Finally, in the Indies as elsewhere, there was an element of loyalist
sentiment. The *priyayi* who served the Dutch administration, the Ambonese in the Dutch military forces, some of the Eurasians in government
service, and the Chinese in the archipelago had good reason to fear
Indonesian nationalism, for it was directed against themselves as well as
against the Dutch.

The Dutch administration itself developed an initiative to shape and
channel reformist sentiment in a benign way. Marxism, secular nationalism and Islamic reform were all directed against both colonial rule and
indigenous traditions within the archipelago. In an effort to counterbalance these movements and build political support, the Dutch promoted
the study of *adat*, or customary law, attempting to transform it into a set of

principles that would provide a foundation for a modern state and society. The Dutch had identified the indigenous aristocracy as their natural allies within Indonesian society, and *adat* had the added value of enhancing the importance of the aristocracy. This approach underlay a postwar Dutch initiative to create a federal Indonesia which would safeguard the interests of less powerful cultural groups within the archipelago, and certainly had some appeal in areas which saw Jakarta-based nationalism as a new form of imperialism.

French Indochina

There is general agreement that nationalism developed in Vietnam considerably earlier than in Cambodia or Laos. When, however, is another question. Particularly in a country such as Vietnam with a long history of active resistance to foreign domination and colonialism, it is difficult to draw a dividing line between traditional patriotism or national consciousness and what may be regarded as modern nationalism. One standard study, covering the period 1885–1925, avoids the problem by using the more elastic term 'anti-colonialism'.[25] Another Vietnam specialist has written that 'if nationalism in the Southeast Asian context means ideologies that simultaneously stress the rediscovery and preservation of a distinctly non-Western cultural identity and the assimilation of modern Western techniques and revolutionary ideas, then Vietnamese resistance to French colonialism before the 1900s was not nationalistic but a compound of xenophobia and Confucian loyalism', adding however that such resistance 'was nonetheless a vital forerunner of Vietnamese nationalism'.[26]

The issue arises out of Vietnam's centuries-old tradition of resistance to attempts to impose Chinese hegemony, and the fact that early anti-French activities often seemed to fit into much the same mould. Divided loyalties, for example, were an old issue, and as the French seized control of Cochinchina in the 1860s, bitter debates engulfed the Confucian literati as to whether collaboration afforded an acceptable alternative to non-cooperation. The moral dilemma was complicated by the fact that in the early years of French advance the imperial court at Hué adopted a compromising, concessionist policy, signing agreements recognizing French authority in various regions, so that in theory at least open resistance to the French meant opposition to court policy as well. Nonetheless the early French advance into Cochinchina in the south and then Tonkin in the north was met with at least sporadic, if not centrally coordinated armed resistance.

The moral dilemma was temporarily resolved in the mid-1880s when a group of hardline anti-French officials seized control of the court and fled inland with the boy-emperor, in whose name an edict calling for a general uprising against the invaders was issued. The French soon placed a more

[25] David G. Marr, *Vietnamese Anticolonialism*, Berkeley, 1971.
[26] Alexander Woodside, in David Joel Steinberg, ed., *In Search of Southeast Asia: A Modern History*, rev. edn, Honolulu, 1987, 312.

pliant member of the imperial family on the throne, and eventually captured and sent into exile his refugee predecessor, thus ending royal sanction for the Can Vuong ('aid the king') movement. Nonetheless this example served as the inspiration for a series of scattered anti-French, and at times anti-Catholic, uprisings in the years to come, the latter directed primarily at Vietnamese who had adopted the Catholic faith.

Such resistance did not prevent the consolidation of French rule over all of Cochinchina, Tonkin, and Annam, under somewhat differing formalistic legal arrangements but in effect amounting to a unitary colonial administration. The task of evolving a coherent colonial policy was made more difficult by the notorious political instability in France itself, which in the half-century from 1870 to 1920 went through two major wars and numerous changes in cabinets and ministers responsible for its Asian empire. The frequent shifts of political line were to some degree reflected in Vietnam itself, with relatively short tenures for top colonial administrators (some twenty governors-general between 1887 and 1920) and long-running debates over such questions as whether cultural policy should aim at 'association' or 'assimilation'. Economic policy was more firmly and consistently pursued: the resources of Vietnam should be exploited for the benefit of France and the empire. This included the development of an infrastructure of roads, railways, ports, and the like; the opening of new lands, particularly in the less-populated Mekong region in the south and southwest, and a great expansion in the cultivation of rice and, at a somewhat latter date, rubber, mainly for export; the recruitment of labour from the densely populated north to work as rice planters or on rubber estates; a limited industrial development in certain products which would not compete with French imports in the local market; and a burdensome tax system that relied heavily on excise taxes on a range of consumer items, including such necessities as salt. While the large plantations were mainly French-owned, Vietnamese with capital and connections also acquired extensive tracts of land, and particularly in the south there emerged a class of indigenous absentee landowners who depended for their well-being on the colonial system. The existence of such a dependent élite inevitably hindered the development of a broadly-based nationalist movement.

In the first decades of the twentieth century, Vietnamese anti-colonialism underwent a gradual transformation as it assimilated and incorporated a variety of foreign influences. At the beginning of the century anti-French agitation was still dominated by 'Confucian scholar activists', of whom Phan Boi Chau (1867–1940) and Phan Chu Trinh (1871–1926) are perhaps the best known. They were much influenced by the abortive late Qing reform movement of Kang Youwei, Liang Qichao and their followers. Through the medium of Chinese-language translations and adaptations (which this early generation read more easily than French) they also came in contact with French liberal thought and such current Western doctrines as Social Darwinism. Another major external influence was the example of Japan, which by its victories in the Sino-Japanese and Russo-Japanese Wars (1894–5; 1904–5) and the 1902 conclusion of the Anglo-Japanese Alliance had clearly demonstrated its emergence as a technologically modern state, able to deal with the Western powers on a basis of equality.

Various pan-Asianist elements, and Chinese reformers living in exile in Japan, encouraged Vietnam to follow Japan's path in adopting Western science and technology in order to throw off Western domination. In particular Vietnamese students were encouraged to study in Japan, and short-lived attempts were made to establish proto-nationalist schools in Vietnam itself.

On several major questions, Phan Boi Chau and Phan Chu Trinh differed. One, which was to prove a divisive issue in Vietnamese national-ism down to the 1950s, was the role of the monarchy. Chau at this stage still favoured retaining the monarchy as a unifying symbol, hoping to find a suitable member of the imperial family willing to provide leadership, at least in name, to an anti-French movement; Trinh, however, was an uncompromising critic of the collaborationist court and an advocate of republicanism. He also, in contrast to Chau, rejected any resort to violence as part of the independence struggle. He was impressed by the liberal aspects of French culture and humanist philosophy (he spent most of the latter part of his life in France), and he had a belief, not shared by Chau, that the French presence in Vietnam could be a positive force if it led to the introduction of progressive aspects of Western civilization and ultimately to concession of the political rights and ideals of the Enlightenment.

The second decade of the century was, on the surface, and despite another abortive plot involving a young emperor, a period of relative calm. France was absorbed in the great conflict in Europe, and in Vietnam a liberal governor-general, Albert Sarraut, who served two terms which together covered nearly half of the decade, seemed to offer hope of progressive policies and gradual change. In this atmosphere there emerged moderate reformers willing to work within the colonial system, constitutionalists, and cultural nationalists. But there were also develop-ments which would prove to be of greater long-range significance. In Asia, Japan began to lose its appeal as a model. Responding to Western diplo-matic pressures, official Japanese policy became increasingly hostile to the presence of anti-colonial activists and students. Japan had annexed Taiwan in 1895 and Korea in 1910, and during the war tried to impose the Twenty-One Demands on China and laid claim to former German rights in Shantung; it was increasingly perceived as having embarked on an 'imperialist' path, as likely to be a threat as a source of support. But an alternative model, both geographically and culturally closer to Vietnam, emerged with the 1911 Revolution in China. While fragmented and unsta-ble, the new China offered both a republican ideology and the possibility of bases of operation adjacent to Vietnam itself.

Further away, the upheaval of World War I in Europe gave rise to more radical impulses. The war itself seriously challenged the notion that Western civilization was in any way inherently progressive and superior, while it brought in its wake the Russian Revolution and the emergence of communism as a world political force, rather than a European ideology. In 1911 the man who would ultimately become known as Ho Chi Minh had left Vietnam for Europe. From a Confucian, if anti-French, upbringing he moved in France to involvement in, and then disillusionment with socialist movements. Finally, like many young Asian nationalists, he was drawn to

Marxism and ultimately to the communist centre, Moscow. The appeal of Marxist-Leninist thought for anti-colonial activists was strong: it offered an explanation (through the imperialist stage of capitalism) of the fate which had befallen their countries; it offered the hope, even assurance, that the present colonial status was temporary; and perhaps most importantly, it offered a modus operandi, in terms of party organization, strategy, and the stages of revolution through which independence would be regained and a socialist society achieved. It has also been argued that certain structural similarities between Confucianism and Marxism—such as their this-worldly orientation, their claims to represent a rational, scientific doctrine of universal applicability, and their hierarchical nature and strong emphasis on political relationships and the state—facilitated moving from the former to the latter; in any case, it is largely in areas of traditional Confucian influence that popular communist revolutions have, to the present, succeeded in Asia.

These more radical strands in the anti-colonial movement gained strength in the 1920s as the age of the Confucian scholar activists drew to a close and Confucianism itself, increasingly identified with the court and collaboration, ceased to be a major force in Vietnamese nationalism. Secular groups, lacking strong ties to a traditional religion or ideology, came to the fore, in some ways differentiating Vietnam from the rest of Southeast Asia. There established religions such as Buddhism (Burma, Siam), Islam (Indonesia, Malaya), and an indigenized Christianity (the Philippines) played an important part in nationalist movements in the early decades of the century, and in a number of cases well beyond. A partial exception in Vietnam was the Cao Dai sect, which from the mid-1920s rapidly gained a large following in the south. It proclaimed a syncretic theology, and a form of conservative anti-colonialism which ultimately veered toward pro-Japanese sentiments.

The mid-1920s saw another leftward swing in the French political scene, and consequently in the colonial leadership, but the relatively mild reforms that resulted disappointed those who hoped for change within the colonial system. The failure of moderate, co-operative parties, such as the Constitutionalists, to achieve significant concessions and progress toward at least a measure of internal autonomy predictably left the field open to more radical groups. French intransigence and repression increasingly meant that there appeared to be no alternative between outright collaboration and clandestine, subversive activity.

The first of the radical groups to make a major, though brief, impact was the Viet Nam Quoc Dan Dang (Vietnamese Nationalist Party), usually known by the acronym VNQDD. The VNQDD was founded in 1927, modelled upon the then-triumphant Kuomintang in China. Based in the cities, with most of its following in the north, the VNQDD was organized along the lines of a secret society. Without attempting to build a mass base, it plotted to subvert Vietnamese garrison forces and hoped for revolutionary insurrection sparked by spectacular but isolated acts of violence. The assassination of a French official in 1929 resulted in harsh French repression, leading to a desperate, premature uprising at Yen Bai in February 1930. After brief initial success the revolt was put down, and the severe French reprisals which followed effectively put an end to the party.

The decimation of the VNQDD, coupled with French suppression of more moderate forms of political activity, left the communists well placed to compete for leadership of the anti-colonial movement. Ho Chi Minh from the mid-1920s had been operating from South China or Siam, and in 1925 had organized the Vietnamese Revolutionary Youth League. After various factional vicissitudes, in 1930 he succeeded in bringing together several left-leaning groups to form the Indochina Communist Party (a name insisted upon by the Comintern, which objected to the 'overly-nationalistic' tone of the originally proposed 'Vietnamese Communist Party').

The party's inception coincided with the onset of the Great Depression, which brought sharply lower world prices for rice, rubber, and other commodities, and in Vietnam itself increased tenancy, indebtedness, and unemployment, all seemingly favourable conditions for a revolutionary struggle. Indeed in mid-1930 large-scale rural uprisings did take place in the Nghe An and Ha Tinh provinces of north central Vietnam, and, with local officials killed or taking flight, for a time colonial authority broke down. As the rebellion progressed it took on definite communist over-tones, with the formation of 'soviets' and the adoption of various revolutionary symbols. There has been debate as to whether the communists were instigators of the uprisings or opportunistic, and possibly reluctant, late-comers whom the force of circumstances thrust into the leadership of what had started as essentially spontaneous movements.

In any case the French found it expedient to place the responsibility on 'Bolshevik' agitators, and when after protracted military operations the uprisings were put down, the expected repression and reprisals followed. In the short term the result was a serious set-back for the party, with much of the leadership inside Vietnam jailed or executed; for the longer term the uprisings did demonstrate the village revolutionary potential, suggesting a strategic orientation that the party would later adopt.

For the next few years the communists maintained a low profile, working to evolve a coherent strategy amid a number of conflicting pressures. Moscow still claimed the right to dictate worldwide communist doctrine, and Comintern policy went through unpredictable shifts be-tween 'united front from above' and 'united front from below'. Theoretical debates centred on the role of the peasantry, which Marx in his European-oriented analysis had virtually written off. Lenin had put somewhat more emphasis on the peasantry in the revolutionary scenario, but had still given a leading role to the industrial proletariat. But in Vietnam the industrial proletariat was quite small, and the 1930–1 uprisings had shown the rural revolutionary potential. There was also the example of China, where under Mao's leadership the communists were establishing them-selves in bases in the countryside. The end result was to place greater emphasis on the actual internal conditions of Vietnam, rather than foreign theoretical formulations, and by the end of the decade the party had adopted a rural strategy of revolution.

The communists were also handicapped by internal divisions. Ho's Indochina Communist Party (ICP) faced strong competition, particularly in the urban areas of south Vietnam, from 'Trotskyite' factions, reflecting a further importing of global communist schisms and polemics into the Vietnamese context.

In the late 1930s a number of developments on the world scene sharply affected and altered the prospects of the ICP. Germany and Japan emerged as aggressive, expansive nations, while in France a left-of-centre government came to power resulting, for a time, in a somewhat freer political atmosphere in Vietnam. Faced with the growing threat of the Axis powers, international communist strategy now dictated a 'united front from above', in which the peasantry and proletariat would join with the 'national' bourgeoisie and small capitalists in a broad anti-fascist coalition. This policy line came to an unexpectedly abrupt end in August 1939, with the shock announcement of the Nazi–Soviet non-aggression pact. Within days war broke out in Europe, followed some nine months later by the fall of France and the subsequent establishment of the pliant Vichy régime. The Indochina part of France's empire recognized in name, if not always in fact, Vichy's authority; it soon came under strong Japanese diplomatic pressure and the threat of military moves. The result was 'negotiations' in which the colonial authorities had little choice but to yield to demands for the stationing of Japanese military forces in northern Vietnam (September 1940) and subsequently in the south (July 1941). Meanwhile Thailand took advantage of the weakened French position, and a degree of Japanese support, to reclaim areas of western and northern Cambodia and trans-Mekong Laos that had earlier been ceded to France.

This blinding whirl of international developments radically transformed the internal situation in Vietnam, and the communists were quick to take advantage of the opportunities that seemed to have arisen. Early in 1941 Ho, who had lived abroad since sailing for Europe thirty years earlier, crossed from China into northern Vietnam, where he presided over the establishment of a new organization, the Viet Nam Doc Lap Dong Minh (League for the Independence of Vietnam), known as the Vietminh. Though it was dominated by communists, the Vietminh was a front which aimed at creating a broad coalition of anti-colonial, anti-Japanese elements; to this end it played down the more radical aspects of social revolution, stressing instead such 'national' goals as the achievement of independence.

The eve of the outbreak of the Pacific War found the communists well placed to take the leading role in the anti-colonial struggle. They had strong organization and leadership. They were beginning to develop rural base areas, especially along the northern Vietnam–China border, which included some tribal regions. These were areas in which they were strongest and their opponents—whether French colonial authority, Japanese, or rival 'nationalist' groups—were weakest. And because until the last stages of the war, the Vichy colonial administration and the Japanese were in 'alliance', the Vietminh had the unique advantage of being able to be anti-colonial and anti-Japanese at the same time. In other parts of Southeast Asia where the Japanese overthrew colonial rule, nationalists often confronted the awkward choice of supporting the new order against the West, or supporting their former colonial rulers against Japan's imperial designs. Men like Laurel, Sukarno, Aung San and others who for whatever tactical or expedient reasons chose temporary co-operation with the Japanese inevitably, with Japan's decline, faced possible charges of 'collaboration'. In Vietnam the Cao Dai and certain other would-be nationalists were also to some degree compromised, but for the Vietminh collaboration was not an issue, and their anti-colonial, anti-Japanese stance appealed to a wide spectrum of Vietnamese who wanted to see their country freed from foreign influences.

Thus the unique political configuration in Vietnam at the outbreak of the Pacific War meant great complexities but also great opportunities for the newly-formed Vietminh. Their leaders might well have echoed the Maoist dictum, 'All is chaos under the heavens; the situation is excellent.'

For Cambodia and Laos, discussion of pre-1941 nationalism is likely to emphasize the negative: why were there so few visible manifestations of nationalist activity? Certainly forerunners of postwar independence movements were not totally lacking. In Cambodia there were isolated instances of popular discontent over various colonial policies, while a Buddhist Institute established in 1930 under French and royal patronage turned, contrary to its sponsors' intentions, into something of a centre for cultural nationalism and revival. This reassertion of traditionalism was encouraged by Thailand which, particularly after the 1932 change of government, tried to expand its influence in its former vassal state, based upon a shared religion and Indic cultural heritage. From the other direction, politically-oriented south Vietnamese religious sects attracted Cambodian adherents from both sides of the Cambodian–Vietnamese border; and the Vietnamese-dominated Indochina Communist Party had from an early stage a small Khmer component, though relations between Cambodian and Vietnamese communists for much of the period since the 1930s have been more stormy than fraternal.

In Laos there was a long tradition of anti-French (and at times anti-Lao) tribal rebellions, particularly in the southern highlands, which later became an important component of the postwar communist movement. Thailand also again tried to extend its influence at French expense, aided not only by the religious and cultural affinities which applied to Cambodia, but also by the ethnic and linguistic kinship between Thai and Lao. And again the Vietnamese, through the ICP, patronized a small Lao communist movement, which would play a role in the Lao Issara group of the 1940s and ultimately find its own identity in the Pathet Lao.

Nevertheless, when contrasted with the case of Vietnam, the paucity of pre-1941 Cambodian and Lao 'nationalist' activity is striking. It is difficult to point to any organized parties, other than the Vietnamese-initiated ICP, and only a handful of individuals emerge as identifiable 'nationalists', compared to the scores of prominent figures in histories of the early Vietnamese anti-colonialist and nationalist movements.

A number of factors would seem to account for this relative colonial calm in Cambodia and Laos. In both territories the French ruled with a fairly light hand, at least when compared to the economic exploitation and political repression which characterized the colonial régime in Vietnam. Cambodia had only limited resources of interest to the French, mainly rubber and rice, while Laos had even less to offer in the way of economic potential. Indeed the colonial administration in the latter perennially ran at a deficit, requiring subsidies from other parts of Indochina.

In a sense, the French could claim to have 'saved' Cambodia, which at the height of its power had extended its rule over the Mekong delta and large areas of modern Laos and Siam. The southward and westward advance of the Vietnamese and the eastward expansion of the Thai had by the nineteenth century reduced Cambodia to a shadow of its former imperial glory, paying tribute to the courts of both Bangkok and Hué, and if the French had not appeared on the scene it is possible that Cambodia might have been completely absorbed by its stronger neighbours.

If the French can be said to have saved Cambodia, they virtually created Laos in its modern form. Pre-modern 'Laos' was composed of a number of rival principalities, often in conflict with one another and all subject to varying external pressures. From north to south, the major traditional centres included Luang Prabang, Xieng Khouang, Vientiane, and Champassak, though an unsuccessful attempt by Vientiane princes in the 1820s to throw off Bangkok's sovereignty had resulted in a harsh Thai retribution that left Vientiane devastated and depopulated. French interest in what would become modern Laos was only minimally strategic (after the early discovery that the unnavigable upper Mekong would not provide a 'river road to China') or economic. Rather it was in considerable measure the result of the initiative of enterprising individuals—romantic adventurers such as Henri Mouhot and Auguste Pavie—coupled with an almost compulsive drive to compete with the British for the grandeur of empire. The latter concern was alternately restrained or reinforced by the erratic shifts of French domestic politics but, particularly after the humiliating defeat France suffered in the Franco-Prussian War, pressures grew in some quarters to compensate for lost prestige at home by expanding possessions abroad—even in regions which might promise little in the way of tangible benefits.

Not surprisingly, many among the Cambodian and Lao élite could view the French as benevolent protectors, or at least a lesser of evils. The recent pre-colonial histories of both Cambodia and the areas which came to form Laos suggested that the realistic alternative they faced was not between French colonialism and independence, but between French colonialism and domination by one or another, or a combination, of their stronger neighbours. France at least was far away, and there was no danger of French immigration on a significant scale. French culture was also remotely alien, and while a very limited circle of the élite acquired some French education and a taste for French luxuries, the great majority of the population remained little affected by the French 'civilizing mission'; indeed, in the encounter of cultures the process was often reversed, with Frenchmen being attracted to the traditional Buddhist cultures of the Cambodians and the Lao.

This combination of a relatively benign French presence with a potential threat, should the French leave, of Thai or Vietnamese domination, obviously militated against the development of anti-colonial sentiment and contributed to the late emergence of any identifiable modern 'nationalism'.

Nevertheless, French rule inevitably did at times intrude into the lives of the people and, as noted above, there were occasional popular protests, particularly in Cambodia, and ethnically based uprisings in Laos. Amongst the élite also, not all accepted the French presence as beneficial. Factionalism and personal rivalries were common, and at times took the form of political opposition or outright rebellion. By the eve of the Pacific War even some of those who had benefited most from the colonial system were moving towards an anti-French nationalism: the soon-to-emerge Lao Issara and Pathet Lao movements were both headed by princes of a collateral line of the royal house of Luang Prabang, while in Cambodia the mercurial Prince Sihanouk, elevated to the throne in 1941 because of his youth and presumed malleability, was to prove to be much more independent-minded than his French sponsors had anticipated.

Burma

In Burma, as in Vietnam and Siam, certain unique factors specific to the country and operative throughout the period under consideration significantly affected the course of development of nationalism. Among the most important of these was the large number of ethnic groups, whether 'traditional', i.e. long present in the country, or relatively recent arrivals. The former include, among the more numerically prominent, the Burmans, the Mon, the Arakanese, the Karen, the Shan, and the Kachin, and the latter the Indians and, to a lesser degree, the Chinese. This multiplicity of ethnic groups has been a centrifugal force in Burmese history, resulting in political fragmentation and posing a constant obstacle to the establishment and maintenance of any strong, unitary authority. Similarly in the twentieth century ethnic questions were a divisive issue in the nationalist movement, especially as certain of the minority groups, fearful of the domination of an ethnic Burman majority, looked to British colonial authority for protection. In this regard, Burma has less resembled relatively more homogeneous Vietnam or Siam than parts of insular Southeast Asia, most notably the Dutch East Indies with its examples of ethnic minorities also seeking the protection of the colonial rulers. Many such groups, whether in the Dutch East Indies or Burma, were unenthusiastic about the prospect of independence within the boundaries of the colonial state and deeply concerned about the conditions under which it might be achieved. In the final postwar negotiations leading to Burmese independence, the most intractable issues were not between the Burmese and the British but between the Burmans and various other ethnic groups.

Several British actions taken immediately following the annexation of upper Burma in the Third Anglo-Burmese War (1885–6) also profoundly affected future political developments. Foremost perhaps was the abolition of the Burmese monarchy, apparently undertaken in the light of immediate circumstances with little consideration of the long-term consequences. Royal misrule had been one of the British justifications for the war, so the removal of King Thibaw was inevitable. There was no obvious candidate to succeed him, in part because Thibaw and his clique had eliminated most potential rivals when he first came to the throne. Nevertheless, many Burmese, even if critical of Thibaw personally, favoured maintaining the monarchy as an institution, and some British officials and others with experience in Burma also questioned the wisdom of abolishing what had traditionally been a central focus of Burmese politics and society, and a source of legitimacy for the state. Other colonial examples show that preserving a traditional élite, as in Vietnam, Cambodia and Laos under the French, Malaya under the British, or the Indies under the Dutch, could lend a degree of legitimacy and acceptability to colonial rule. And though it might require a Machiavelli to foresee it, the continued existence of traditional élites in a number of cases served as a divisive force within nationalist movements. Early would-be reformers often split over the question of goals, whether to seek to restore some element of the traditional élite or to establish a new order. The dilemma was particularly acute when the traditional élite actively collaborated with colonial rule, as illustrated by the differing early 'nationalist' agendas advocated by Phan Boi Chau and Phan Chu Trinh in Vietnam.

A second British action which had major consequences for the development of nationalism in Burma was the decision to link Burma administratively to India. This led to the introduction of Indian models of administration, whether or not suitable to Burmese conditions. Moreover, the Indian anti-colonial movement was chronologically far in advance of that of Burma, or of any area of Southeast Asia outside the Philippines (the Congress Party had been established in 1885); and it became an important influence on early nationalism in Burma. The Indian political experience served as a model for the Burmese, and there were also some direct contacts, with activists from Burma spending time in India, where they were exposed to new techniques of organization and strategy, and visits to Burma by Indian nationalist leaders.

The administrative tie also meant that any reforms or moves toward self-government conceded by the British in India were considered for Burma as well, potentially giving Burma the benefits of India's progress. And finally, linking the two led to virtually unrestricted Indian immigration, with the result that ethnic Indians came to play an important role in the middle and lower levels of administration and in the economy of Burma. At least in the economic sphere, the position of the Indian minority was somewhat analogous to that of the Chinese in such countries as Vietnam, Siam, and the Dutch East Indies. Census data from 1931 showed about 7 per cent of the total population of Burma to be Indian, concentrated particularly in Rangoon (which was 53 per cent Indian, and about two-thirds immigrant) and other urban centres, compared to a figure of less than 2 per cent for the Chinese; overall, ethnic Burmans totalled more than 60 per cent, and other indigenous groups about 25 per cent. As will be seen, the nationalist movement in Burma was at times to take on an 'anti-Indian' orientation, paralleling 'anti-Chinese' sentiments evident in certain other parts of Southeast Asia in the period.

The British annexation of upper Burma sparked off widespread resistance, initially in traditional guises. Members of the deposed royal house, local chieftains, and other traditional élites led an uncoordinated series of rebellions, while various ethnic groups, following long-established historical patterns, took advantage of upheaval at the centre to assert their autonomy. Despite superiority in arms and organization, it was more than five years before the British could claim to have achieved the 'pacification' of Burma, particularly the newly-annexed upper regions.

By the early years of the twentieth century these traditional forms of resistance largely gave way to new types of anti-colonial activity, conforming to what in other Southeast Asian contexts has been termed 'nationalist'. In Burma this early nationalist activity was closely linked to the Buddhist religion, which provided a powerful rallying focus against British rule but also proved in some ways a divisive issue within the nationalist movement. A number of the ethnic minorities were non-Buddhist, while in decades to come even a number of Buddhist Burmans would be attracted to Marxist-socialist thought, leading to the problem—given Marx's strictures on religion—of reconciling Buddhist traditions with secular Western ideologies.

Best-known of the early 'modernist' organizations was the Young Men's Buddhist Association (YMBA), established in 1906 (though deriving from some small, localized precursors) with obvious echoes of the West's YMCA. Initially the YMBA was largely non-political, focusing on cultural, and especially religious, revival. This programme reflected a widely perceived decline in traditional Burmese social norms and formations, in part attributed to the disappearance of the monarchy and the court, which historically had been major patrons of the arts and religion, and a concomitant deterioration in the standards and influence of the Buddhist *saṅgha* (monkhood).

The YMBA, however, became increasingly politicized in the 1910s as a result of the long-running shoe controversy, the question whether British and other foreigners should be required to conform to the traditionally unquestioned practice of removing shoes when entering the precincts of a Buddhist temple or monastery. While ostensibly religious, the issue was also political in that it challenged the right of the British overlords to determine what constituted proper behaviour in a Burmese setting; it drew the line of division clearly between the British on one side and the Buddhist communities, principally the Burmans, Mon and Shan, on the other. Despite its political overtones, the religious origins of the controversy made it a relatively safe yet formidable strategic issue on which to challenge colonial authority. The final resolution—with the British conceding to each abbot the right to determine acceptable practice for his monastery—left the power of decision in indigenous hands and was seen by nationalists as a major, if somewhat symbolic, victory.

Despite such successes, the YMBA soon succumbed to the factionalism endemic in Burmese society and politics, and a split in the movement led to the emergence in 1921 of a new umbrella organization, the General Council of Burmese Associations (GCBA). The name itself, incorporating 'General' and 'Burmese' (rather than 'Buddhist') was indicative of the intention to forge a broader anti-colonial front than had been feasible within the YMBA. One of the GCBA's first initiatives was to support a strike of students at the new University of Rangoon, beginning a long tradition of political activism among university students.

Following the end of the war in Europe, British concessions to nationalist pressures in India resulted in a dyarchy constitution allowing for a very circumscribed degree of indigenous participation in the colonial government. Burma was excluded from the arrangement, setting off a wave of nationalist protests and strikes, and the British Parliament in 1921 extended dyarchy to Burma, a change which took effect two years later. The issue raised two major questions which were to exercise Burmese nationalists throughout the 1920s and most of the 1930s. The first was whether they should continue to seek, as had hithertofore been almost unquestioned in the nationalist agenda, separation from India. This step would bring with it, *inter alia*, the prospect of restrictions on Indian immigration, but such separation now might mean that Burma would fail to share further British concessions to nationalist demands in India. Secondly, there was the question whether nationalists should participate in British schemes of limited self-government, such as partially elected councils, or adopt an uncompromising stand of electoral boycotts, non-cooperation and non-participation. Of the two questions, the latter was a more immediate and practical issue for Burmese nationalists: in the short run, only the British could define the relationship between Burma and India, but Burmese were forced to decide for themselves whether to pursue their goals within or outside the new constitutional arrangements. The debate within the nationalist movement on both questions was acrimonious, with major leaders frequently shifting position as circumstance and opportunity seemed to dictate.

These and other issues resulted in an increasingly divided nationalist movement during the 1920s. The factional rivalries that had plagued the YMBA soon surfaced in the GCBA, leading it to split over questions both of policy and personalities. Long standing urban–rural divisions also became more marked. Urban nationalists on the whole, essentially accepting the modernizing aspect of imperialism, wanted to oust the British and take over the colonial state. Many of the rural constituency wanted not only to oust the British but also to abolish the colonial institutions that had come in their wake—the bureaucratic, economic and other structures that impinged upon and interfered with traditional village life. Controversy also surrounded the increasingly open involvement of the Buddhist *saṅgha* in politics, whether in the form of ecclesiastical domination of certain factions of the GCBA, or the activities of individual monks such as the charismatic U Ottama, who after developing contacts with the Indian nationalist movement launched a campaign severely criticizing the colonial administration in Burma and calling for self-rule.

Nationalist organizations during the 1920s and 1930s sought support from all ethnic groups, yet in many respects reflected Burman interests that were not in harmony with the feelings of other groups. An emphasis on Buddhism, of little interest to non-Burman animists and a source of concern to the Christian Karen, remained a feature of Burman nationalism, and this tendency was reinforced by the political activity of Buddhist monks. Also, when Burman students during the 1920s undertook the creation of a national school system, the Burmese language was proposed as the medium of instruction, and Burmese literature and history figured prominently in the curriculum.

The Great Depression, in Burma as in Vietnam and other areas of Southeast Asia, marked a watershed in the nationalist movement. The prices of rice and other commodities collapsed, and with them much of Burma's export market, leading to severe economic hardships, particularly in areas which in the course of the vast expansion of rice cultivation since the 1850s had become dependent upon a commercialized, largely mono-crop agriculture. Economic hardship brought heightened communal tensions: violence was directed against Indians, who competed in the labour market and also figured prominently as moneylenders and, as a result of mortgage foreclosures, increasingly (if not designedly) as land-owners. To a lesser extent resentments were directed against the Chinese as well. And as in Vietnam, the economic crisis gave rise to rural rebellion, in the form of the Saya San uprising—the most spectacular, if perhaps not ultimately the most significant manifestation of anti-colonial activity between 1885 and the Pacific War.

Saya San was a former monk and a practitioner of 'native' medicine, and the traditional aspects of the revolt have attracted much attention: the reliance on amulets and magic spells, Saya San's professed goal of restoring the monarchy, complete with makeshift replicas of a palace and the royal regalia, and so forth. But Saya San also had extensive experience in more modernist anti-colonial movements, in particular in a faction of the GCBA especially concerned with peasant grievances. The main targets of the rebellion were representatives of the colonial administration, colonial taxes, land rents, and what was generally perceived as increasing bureaucratic interference in traditional life. Given that these were the targets, it has been argued (although not by the British authorities) that more fundamental social and economic causes, which had given rise to widespread village-level nationalist activity in the 1920s and were exacerbated by the depression, underlay the facade of reactionary superstition. In any case the rebellion, beginning in late 1930, spread over wide areas of lower and central Burma; while it never seriously threatened British rule, it was not completely put down until 1932.

If Saya San stood at one pole of Burmese nationalism in the 1930s, an opposite strand was developing in the form of an urban, secular, radical movement, attracting in particular young university students influenced by socialism, Marxism, and other currents of Western thought. The mid-1930s saw another major student strike at the University of Rangoon, and also young activists taking over the Dobama Asiayone (We Burmese Association), a nationalist organization originally founded in 1930 by older leaders. The student leaders appropriated to themselves the title *thakin* ('master'—the appellation usually reserved for the British rulers). They included the charismatic Aung San (whose assassination in 1947 would have severe consequences for the future of Burma, because he was virtually the only major nationalist leader who had the confidence of the non-Burman minorities), and U Nu, who later became the first prime minister of post-British (and post-Japanese) Burma and remained an active political figure down to the upheavals at the end of the 1980s.

Like the student activists of the preceding decade, the *thakin* sought to unite all ethnic groups in a Burmese nation, but as before their conception gave priority to Burman elements and envisioned the assimilation of minorities. The *thakin* adopted as their slogan: 'Burma is our country; Burmese literature is our literature; Burmese language is our language. Love our country, raise the standards of our literature, respect our language.'[27] A related issue was an initiative to unify the frontier areas with Burma proper. Burman nationalists argued that Britain, practising a policy of divide-and-rule, had disrupted a historically unified state, and rejected the British contention that the limited administrative unity introduced during the 1920s was an innovation.

As nationalist agitation increased in the late 1930s, including frequent demonstrations and strikes by both students and workers, the British responded with another round of administrative reforms. The Indian Statutory Commission (known as the Simon Commission) which reviewed dyarchy in the late 1920s had recommended the separation of Burma from India, as did the Burma Round Table Conference held in London in 1931–2. In Burma, anti-separationist sentiment had been growing in strength, fuelled by a general distrust of British motives. Action on the issue was delayed until 1937 when Burma was finally separated from India and a new constitution gave the Burmese considerably greater powers of self-government. Ba Maw, a veteran nationalist figure, became prime minister in a 'Burmese administration' responsible for such less critical matters as health and education, but the British still reserved to themselves a number of key spheres of administration—notably defence, foreign affairs, major issues of finance, and control of the 'excluded areas', the Shan states and border regions inhabited by minority ethnic groups.

The more radical, and particularly the younger members of the nationalist factions were dissatisfied with these limited British concessions, and continued to demand more fundamental changes and a commitment to full independence in a foreseeable future. Frustrated both with the British and with what they saw as the compromising, collaborationist attitude of many of the older Burmese leaders, some young activists began to think in revolutionary terms and to look abroad for possible sources of support. Initial contacts were established with Kuomintang elements in China, who by the late 1930s were not notably anti-British but could at least claim anti-imperialist credentials, but it was ultimately in Japan that a source of tangible support was found. There was a considerable element of opportunism in this: many of the young Burmese who turned to Japan were politically leftist, if still Buddhist, and not particularly sympathetic toward the right-wing militarism and emperor system dominant in Japan (the Saya San episode had marked the last pale shadow of monarchism in the

---

[27] Cited in Josef Silverstein, *Burmese Politics: The Dilemma of National Unity*, New Brunswick, 1980, 39.

Burmese context). But despite such ideological differences, radical Burmese nationalists and conservative Japanese militarists had a common
interest in overthrowing Western rule in Southeast Asia. Japan was willing
to provide arms and financial support, and the Thirty Comrades, including
Aung San, accepted the offer of aid and secretly went abroad for Japanese-
sponsored military training in Hainan. The Thirty Comrades were to
return to Burma with the invading Japanese in 1942 as leaders of a Burma
Independence Army, although as Japan's fortunes declined they ultimately switched sides, 'allying' themselves with their former British adver-
saries; from this small group would come many of the major political and
military figures of postwar Burma.

This brief sketch of anti-colonial and nationalist activities in Burma in the
decades leading up to the Pacific War suggests three general themes. One
is that the nationalist movement was disrupted by recurrent factionalism
based upon personalities, policy disagreements, and such discordant
dichotomies as the urban–rural, traditional–modernist, and religious–
secular. Compounding these causes of factionalism was the problem of
incorporating other ethnic groups, whether traditional or recent arrivals,
into Burman-dominated political movements and ultimately into a
Burman-dominated polity, a problem which remained unresolved in the
post-independence period. A second theme which emerges is the rise of a
relatively radical secularism at the expense of the more traditional, religious orientation of the early nationalist movement, although there would
be later attempts at a synthesis of the two strands (most notably under
U Nu), and an official post-independence ideology of 'Buddhist socialism'.
Finally, compared to other colonial powers such as the French, the British
in Burma were on the whole more moderate and compromising. This
encouraged at least parts of the nationalist movement to work for change
within the system, and contributed, along with historical, cultural, and
other factors, to producing a type of nationalism less politically radical
than that, for example, in Vietnam. While Burma nominally adopted a
form of socialism, communism failed to become a major force; indeed the
Burmese communist movement was split by the endemic political factionalism that affected other ideological groupings, and spent much of its
energies on internal struggles rather than providing a viable political
alternative.

ETHNIC NATIONALISM

Differences of language, social and political arrangements, and local
customs are conventionally seen as the markers of a nation, as primordial
attachments delineating a natural unit of association for political purposes,
but the experience of Southeast Asia challenges the assumption that ethnic
identity is immutable. Various peoples are known to have altered speech,
social and political arrangements, and modes of family life as personal
circumstances changed. The compilers of the 1931 census of Burma took

note of the 'extreme instability of language and racial distinctions in Burma'.[28]

The general tendency in Southeast Asia was for anti-colonial activity within territories defined by European control to provide the impetus for state formation, and 'nations' in the region accordingly tended to be communities defined by territorial and administrative systems. Ethnically-based nationalism did, however, occur, although the only state to take shape on this basis was Thailand, the sole country not subjected to direct colonial rule and the various influences which that experience entailed. Malay nationalism, although culturally based, developed within a territory where the Malay population was economically disadvantaged and barely constituted a numerical majority, and did not become a major political force until after 1945. Many culture-groups in Southeast Asia were numerically too small or lacked sufficient resources to form a viable state in their own right, and some ethnic nationalisms were directed toward securing the position of a group within a larger political entity. Other communities, such as the Karen and Shan, the Muslims in Burma and in Pattani, and the Moros, opposed the predominant nationalist political tendencies in the states where they resided. None succeeded in forming a recognized independent state, but each did form an 'imagined community' that perceived itself as a nascent nation-state.

Thai Nationalism

From the late nineteenth to the mid-twentieth century, nationalism in Southeast Asian contexts is often seen as being virtually synonymous with anti-colonialism. Siam, which retained a formal, if highly circumscribed independence throughout the period of Western imperialist expansion, could not develop a nationalism in any narrowly defined anti-colonial sense. Thai 'nationalism' was necessarily in many ways unique in the Southeast Asian region, and as such offers instructive comparisons and raises questions about definitions and models of 'nationalism'.

The beginnings of modern 'nationalism' in Siam, as opposed to traditional patriotism or national consciousness, may reasonably be dated to the mid-nineteenth century and arose, as throughout much of Asia, in response to perceived external threats. This incipient nationalism was both backward-looking and forward-looking. Backward in time it focused on the great disaster of recent Thai history, the capture and destruction of Ayutthaya by the Burmese in 1767. By the 1830s the British had effectively eliminated Burma as a threat to the Thai state, but the fall of Ayutthaya continued (and continues) to have a strong hold on the Thai historical consciousness. The moral drawn from Ayutthaya's fall was that it had been caused by a lack of *samakkhi*, an Indic-derived term meaning roughly 'to have unity' or 'harmony') among the élite. The need for *samakkhi* among royalty and the nobility, with the assumed consequent acquiescence of the rest of the population, became a recurrent theme in Thai thought as new threats emerged in the nineteenth century.

[28] *Census of Burma, 1931*, 178, cited in Silverstein, 8.

These threats came, as foreseen by Thai rulers as early as Rama III (r. 1824–51), not from Siam's long-standing major rivals, Burma and Vietnam, but from the West. For a period in the seventeenth century, European powers, and particularly the French, had played a major role in Siam's economy and politics. But an anti-foreign reaction in the 1680s had virtually eliminated Western influence, and for the next century and a half European interests and energies were largely focused on the more commercially promising islands of the region, and on rivalries in other areas of the world. Left largely to itself, Siam concentrated on traditional dynastic interests and intrigue, a foreign trade oriented particularly toward China, and wars with Burma and Vietnam.

The 'second wave' of Westerners who began to arrive in Siam with increasing frequency in the early nineteenth century differed considerably from their predecessors. In the wake of political and industrial revolutions in Europe and the Americas, they were imbued with new political and economic theories, and armed with technologies that were the product of a period of rapid advance. Mainland Southeast Asia now became a major focus of interest for its trade potential—both as a market for Western goods and a source of various commodities, for strategic reasons, and for such illusory but tenaciously pursued hopes as the discovery of new routes to the supposed riches of China.

The Thai response to the perceived Western threat has been described as a 'concessionist' policy, ceding not only economic and political privileges but increasingly giving up territory as well. Because unequal treaties were concluded with a number of states, and foreign advisers employed by the Thai government were deliberately drawn from a range of countries, the policy is often seen as a 'balancing' one, attempting to play the competing imperialist powers against one another. In practice it came closer to relying on Great Britain, which was perceived as the dominant power in the region, and as a nation whose interests were primarily economic and whose demands could thus be met without a total sacrifice of sovereignty. The French, on the other hand, were seen as having not only economic but strong religious and political motives, a quest for 'glory of empire' (especially after the European debacle of 1870–1) that could be satisfied only by territorial expansion. King Mongkut in a famous metaphor said that the choice facing Siam was whether 'to swim upriver and make friends with the crocodile [the French] or to swim out to sea and hang on to the whale [the British]'.[29] It is clear that he and his royal successors down to 1932 opted for the whale, with the result that Siam in some degree became a part of Britain's informal empire, in which British interests, particularly economic, predominated without the exercise of formal sovereignty.

Thai policy was concession and accommodation to the perceived strongest regional power (i.e. from the mid-nineteenth to the mid-twentieth century, Britain followed by Japan followed by the United States). The policy has been praised as flexible and pragmatic, and condemned as

---

[29] Quoted in M. R. Seni Pramoj and M. R. Kukrit Pramoj, *A King of Siam Speaks*, Bangkok: Siam Society, 1987, 177–8.

unprincipled. A nineteenth-century American visitor to Siam cited approvingly the opinion of a seventeenth-century French writer regarding the Thai: 'as enemies they are not dangerous, as friends they cannot be trusted'.[30] That such sentiments were not purely the product of Western prejudices is suggested by Prime Minister Phibun's alleged reply when asked, early in the Pacific War, against what potential foe Thai military planning should be directed: 'Which side is going to lose this war? That side is our enemy.'[31]

A more positive response to the Western challenge came in what, by analogy with contemporary developments in China and Japan, might be called a 'self-strengthening movement', a programme of internal reforms intended to transform Siam into a modern, stable state capable of resisting external pressures. Begun on a modest scale by Mongkut, the reform measures were considerably, albeit at an uneven pace, intensified in the long reign of his successor Chulalongkorn (1868–1910). The range of areas covered was broad, with finances, administration, and communications perhaps showing the most immediately visible results. Various Western technologies were introduced, including weaponry, as well as organizational and institutional structures. But there was also an ideological element, including a consciously promoted 'official' nationalism focusing on loyalty to the throne and introducing new terms to the Thai political vocabulary. One such was the Indic term *chat*, which began to expand from its traditional meaning of something like 'caste' or 'tribe' to 'people' or 'race' and ultimately to the Thai equivalent of 'nation' (conceived in terms of both people and territory).

This 'official nationalism', also variously referred to as 'élite nationalism' or '*sakdina* nationalism',[32] had its beginnings under Chulalongkorn; it was greatly intensified, formalized, and institutionalized by his successor Vajiravudh (r. 1910–25). The first Thai king to be educated abroad, Vajiravudh during his long stay in England and extensive travels in other parts of Europe, America and Japan had acquired many of the Western ideas and prejudices of his day, which he mixed with more traditional Thai elements into a rather eclectic national ideology. While continuing the promotion of various aspects of Western science and technology, he put a new emphasis on 'Thai-ness', a kind of cultural nationalism which stressed alleged Thai values and traditions, and a somewhat romanticized vision of the Thai past. Where Chulalongkorn and his generation had, with only

---

[30] Quoted in Howard Malcolm, *Travels in South-Eastern Asia*, 2nd edn, Boston, 1839, II. 129.

[31] Quoted in Benjamin A. Batson, 'The fall of the Phibun government, 1944', JSS, 62, 2 (July 1974) 100 n. 23.

[32] 'Official nationalism' is used in such works as Anderson, *Imagined Communities*, ch. 6. and Kullada Kesboonchoo, 'Official nationalism under King Chulalongkorn', paper presented at the International Conference on Thai Studies, Bangkok, 1984, and 'Official nationalism under King Vajiravudh', paper presented at the International Conference on Thai Studies, Canberra, 1987; 'élite nationalism' in David K. Wyatt, *Thailand: A Short History*, New Haven, 1984, ch. 8; '*sakdina* nationalism' in Chatthip Nartsupha, Suthy Prasartset, and Montri Chenvidyakarn, eds, *The Political Economy of Siam 1910–1932*, Bangkok, 1978, 31. '*Sakdina*' refers literally to the traditional elaborate hierarchical system of manpower control; as used by modern revisionist critics it has taken on such connotations as conservative, exploitative, and (somewhat loosely) 'feudal'.

occasional reservations, confidently assumed that Western techniques and methods could be assimilated without affecting the fundamental nature of Thai society, Vajiravudh now warned that with excessive and indiscriminate borrowing from Western culture the Thai might cease to be 'Thai'. Another perceived threat was the sizeable Chinese minority, rapidly growing numerically and in economic power and, particularly in the wake of the 1911 Revolution in China, the bearers of what Vajiravudh saw as alien political and cultural values.

Vajiravudh sought to counter such threats, Western or Chinese, through a promotion of martial values, intense patronage of the Buddhist religion, and, most insistently, a hierarchical élitism which above all stressed loyalty to the monarch and throne. Indeed, Vajiravudh argued that the status of the Crown was so high that Siam, in contrast to the West, had no class distinctions, only the king and 'the rest'. This ideology was summed up in the motto 'King, Nation, Religion', the officially sanctioned 'three fundamental institutions' which in subsequent decades would continually be publicized as the guiding principles of state and society. This programme was personally and vigorously promoted by Vajiravudh himself, through prolific writings, public addresses, the establishment of such organizations as the para-military Wild Tiger Corps, and numerous other channels of propaganda.

In foreign relations, Vajiravudh in 1917 led Siam into World War I on the side of the Allies. Siam's modest military involvement was motivated primarily by pragmatic diplomatic considerations, such as the desire to become a founder member of the League of Nations and the launching of a campaign, ultimately successful, to abolish extraterritoriality and other privileges that had been ceded to the Western powers under the treaty system.

Vajiravudh was and has remained a controversial figure, both in his broader role as monarch and, more narrowly, for the type of 'nationalism' he propounded. To his admirers, and in subsequent official historiography, he is the revered 'father of Thai nationalism'. Critics have pointed to the strongly élitist nature of his nationalism, in which the people are very much subjects rather than citizens, with social bonds that run vertically rather than horizontally; to the ethnically and religiously exclusive character of this nationalism, in spite of its being formulated in an existing political entity with a long history of cultural pluralism; and to Vajiravudh's lack of sympathy for other nationalist movements, which he scathingly criticized, arguing that Asians were generally unsuited for self-rule, except, perhaps, under traditional, authoritarian élites.

Following Vajiravudh's death in 1925, his rather flamboyant brand of state-sponsored nationalism took on a much more subdued tone. This was partly due to personalities: his successor, Prajadhipok (r. 1925–35), disliked pomp, ceremony, and the public eye as much as Vajiravudh had gloried in them. But it was also due to policy, for the new reign faced serious economic problems, brought on in part by Vajiravudh's excesses, and a perceived decline in the prestige of the monarchy. It responded with a deliberate dismantling of many of Vajiravudh's programmes, including the Wild Tigers and a number of other aspects of the royally-inspired nationalism. Some elements, such as the 'King, Nation, Religion' formula, were retained, but with a much lower public profile, and the more assertive 'Siam for the Siamese', heard occasionally in earlier years, was increasingly invoked. In a few areas, such as restrictions on Chinese immigration, the new reign went beyond Vajiravudh's strident but merely rhetorical condemnation, although Prajadhipok in his public pronouncements reverted to the stress on ethnic harmony and friendship which had characterized Chulalongkorn's policy. But all in all the last reign of the absolute monarchy saw a virtual abandonment of Vajiravudh's nationalist programme; it was, however, to be vigorously revived by the military leaders who rose to power in the years following the 1932 coup that ended royal absolutism.

There were in Siam, even well before 1932, those with other visions of the future, not endorsing an indefinite continuation of benevolent autocracy or a Vajiravudh-style 'nationalism from above'. As early as 1885 a group of princes and officials with experience in Europe had petitioned Chulalongkorn, calling for relatively radical changes in the system, including the introduction of a constitutional monarchy and a parliament. The king responded and showed some sympathy for their ideas, but argued that Siam was not yet ready for such innovations. The social critic Thianwan (1842–1915), with at times a certain degree of princely patronage, similarly called for wide-ranging Westernization and political modernization. On a different level, a series of rural rebellions in the 1890s and 1901–2 challenged central authority and the political ideology of the state, though now looking less to foreign models than an idealized past and a millenarian reordering of society.

In Chulalongkorn's reign such challenges were fairly easily answered, ignored, or suppressed; in the reigns of Vajiravudh and Prajadhipok they became more insistent, undermining and ultimately overthrowing the traditional order. The clearest pre-1932 manifestation of growing discontent was the 'R.S.130 [1912] conspiracy', a plot among a group of lower-ranking military officers and a few civilians to end the absolute monarchy and remove Vajiravudh from the throne. Significantly, in addition to personal grievances, the plotters cited the examples of Europe, Japan, and the recent overthrow of imperial rule in China as standards against which Siam's 'backwardness' should be measured. Revealed to the government and quickly aborted, the 'R.S.130 conspiracy' was nevertheless symptomatic of deeper stirrings among a new emerging middle class in the bureaucracy and certain trades and professions. A key group in this new class, which was to play a role disproportionate to its relatively small numbers in determining Siam's future development, consisted of students returned from abroad. Study overseas, once almost exclusively limited to the sons of royalty and the traditional nobility, had gradually become available to a broader spectrum of society. The experiences of non-élite students abroad, particularly in France, increasingly differed from those of the earlier generation of students. In Chulalongkorn's time the government had deliberately discouraged study in France, both because of traditional enmity, dating from the seventeenth and reinforced in the nineteenth century, and because of suspicion of France's liberalism and republican institutions. But World War I brought a change: Siam and France had been 'allies', and French prestige in military sciences had been much enhanced, while in Germany and Russia, traditional destinations of a number of Thai students, the monarchies had been swept away. There was also the practical consideration that the Thai legal codes were being redrafted on the basis of Napoleonic law, with the aid of French legal advisers. Thus in the 1910s and 1920s growing numbers of Thai students, particularly in law and military studies, were sent to France, most of them on government scholarships. Typically they were from the less élite elements of this privileged minority; royalty and the higher nobility, mainly private students, overwhelmingly maintained their traditional preference for study in England.

As some conservatives had feared, the students in France did come in contact with 'subversive' influences—republicanism and more radical doctrines of French socialist and Marxist thought, and a range of Asian nationalists dedicated to achieving independence for their respective colonial homelands. The result was the formation in the mid-1920s of an embryo organization committed to bringing about political change in Siam. The handful of student founders saw Siam as relatively backward socially, politically and economically; the absolute monarchy, one of the last in the world, as increasingly an anachronism; and, at a more personal level, limited career prospects in Siam's semi-feudal system, despite their high level of technical expertise.

The latter situation had in part to do with the rather convoluted course of royal politics. Chulalongkorn, in an extended power struggle with the traditional noble families who had long dominated the court and major ministries, had of necessity filled key positions with those he thought he could trust, his relatives—originally brothers and half-brothers, and in the latter part of his reign his sons. Vajiravudh, who was on bad terms with most of the senior members of the royal family, including his mother, had reversed the process, relying much more on commoners. But the basis on which many were chosen, including artistic talents and personal ties to the king, hardly produced a meritocracy, and the rapid rise of royal favourites to high official titles and positions inevitably caused resentments among disgruntled princes and veteran bureaucrats. The inexperienced Prajadhipok not unnaturally turned back to the senior relatives whom Vajiravudh had largely ignored, but the perceived result was a 'régime of the princes' in which talented commoners found their career paths blocked by the royal near-monopoly of top bureaucratic positions, particularly in such fields as the military. The students in France watched these trends with growing concern, the more so because of the strongly Anglophile sympathies of the king and most of his royal advisers.

Prajadhipok, despite his relative youth and inexperience, was generally perceptive in seeing the problems faced by the régime. Unfortunately he was less effective in taking measures that might have overcome them. In a confidential memorandum written in the first year of his reign he noted: 'The position of the King has become one of great difficulty. The movements of opinion in this country give a sure sign that the days of Autocratic

Rulership are numbered. The position of the King must be made more secure if this Dynasty is going to last.'[33] In the following year, when the political activities of Pridi Phanomyong, the chief instigator-organizer of the students in France, had brought him to the attention of the authorities, Prajadhipok, in granting a petition revoking Pridi's recall, commented that he did not believe that Pridi would become 'a serious danger to the government' as the Thai Minister in Paris had reported, but 'if the government doesn't use him in a manner commensurate with his knowledge, then things might develop in an undesirable way'.[34] And in contrast to Vajiravudh's criticisms on general principle of Asian nationalist movements, Prajadhipok's views were more ambivalent, mixing a degree of sympathy with a pragmatic assessment of Thai self-interest:

> As long as French rule continues in Vietnam it is a 'safeguard' for Siam. No matter how much we sympathize with the Vietnamese, when one thinks of the danger which might arise, one has to hope that the Vietnamese will not easily escape from the power of the French.[35]

In response to the perceived problems and discontent which the régime faced, Prajadhipok formulated a range of proposals for political change, including representative institutions at both the local and national levels and the introduction of a constitution limiting royal powers. Drafts of such measures were debated at the top levels of government, but in the face of strong opposition from the senior princes and a number of key foreign advisers the king hesitated, until the proposed reforms were overtaken by events in the form of the economic crisis brought on by the Great Depression and then the 1932 coup itself.

The last years of the absolute monarchy also saw the development of more radical political movements, both modernist and traditionalist in orientation. At one end of the spectrum, communist groups for the first time appeared in Siam, although being small in numbers and drawing their membership almost entirely from ethnic Chinese or Vietnamese, with only very limited Thai involvement, they were not seen by the authorities as a serious threat. At the other extreme were isolated outbreaks of millenarian, 'holy men' rebellions in rural areas, similar in some respects to the rural uprisings of 1901–2 and earlier periods. What is striking is how the two types of movements, so different in their underlying ideologies, should come to rather similar conclusions about the problems of Siam, i.e., the exploitation and growing impoverishment of the rural classes, and the cause of these problems—the collusion of the ruling élite, and particularly royalty, with the Western imperialists.

In June 1932, a group calling itself the People's Party, organizationally deriving from the student activists in France in the 1920s, overthrew royal absolutism. In fact 'the people' were scarcely involved, and public reaction to the coup was more indifference or incomprehension than enthusiasm. The People's Party itself had only about 100 members when it seized

[33] Quoted in Benjamin A. Batson, *The End of the Absolute Monarchy in Siam*, 1984, 288.
[34] Quoted in ibid., 79.
[35] Quoted in ibid., 177.

power (a number that then increased markedly); it was divided between a more liberal civilian faction and a generally conservative military faction, and there was considerable initial uncertainty as to the direction in which it would lead Siam. A brief radical phase saw the issuing of a six-point programme which included the promise of a comprehensive national economic plan, and a strongly worded manifesto criticizing the previous government and suggesting the possible complete abolition of the monarchy. These early pronouncements were drafted by Pridi, and alarmed not only supporters of the old régime but the more conservative elements within the People's Party. The manifesto was disavowed, with apologies, constitutional monarchy became the official policy, and within scarcely a day the radical phase of the upheaval was largely over. When some nine months later Pridi did present his draft economic plan, calling for the nationalization of large sectors of the economy and highly centralized economic planning, it set off an acrimonious debate within the government in which the conservative faction ultimately triumphed: as a result the economic plan was labelled 'communistic', the National Assembly (Pridi's power base) was dissolved, and certain provisions of the constitution were suspended. Pridi himself was sent into exile in France.

A second coup in June 1933 brought *Phraya* Phahon to the prime ministership as leader of a more moderate military faction, resulting in the recall of Pridi (but not the revival of the controversial economic plan). In October an attempted counter-coup by conservative elements, concerned in part by alleged leftist influences in the government, was unsuccessful.

In fact the régime moved not leftward but rightward, particularly with the rising influence of *Luang* Phibun Songkhram, who as a military student in France in the 1920s had been an early member of the coup group and in 1934 became Minister of Defence. Increasingly, the reluctant Phahon served as a moderating and balancing force between the rival military and civilian factions, until finally, after having been dissuaded in several previous attempts, he stepped down from office in late 1938.

Phahon's resignation resulted in the elevation to the prime ministership of the ambitious Phibun, and inaugurated a new phase in Thai nationalism. Basically, Phibun revived many elements of Vajiravudh-style nationalism, but often carried them to extremes beyond anything Vajiravudh himself had envisioned or implemented. Furthermore, advances in education and literacy meant that print-media could now reach a far larger audience than in Vajiravudh's time, while the new technology of radio, introduced in Siam in the 1920s and 1930s, made official propaganda accessible even to considerable numbers of those not functionally literate.

Philbun's programme, like Vajiravudh's, was élitist, with the difference that the focus of loyalty was no longer the monarch, now a boy-king living in Europe, but Phibun himself, as prime minister cum commander-in-chief. Indeed, the intensively promoted cult of 'The Leader' meant not only the downplaying of 'King' but also to some degree of 'Nation' and 'Religion', the other two original elements of Vajiravudh's triad, and of 'Constitution', which in the early post-1932 euphoria had often been added as a fourth 'fundamental institution'. Phibun in a statement to the cabinet early in 1942 justified his 'follow The Leader' philosophy by pointing to the contrasting frailty of the 'fundamental institutions':

> The Japanese have the Emperor as their firm guiding principle. We have nothing. What we have are Nation, Religion, Monarch, and Constitution. Nation is still a vision; Religion is not practised devoutly; the Monarch is still a child, only seen in pictures; the Constitution is just a paper document. When the country is in a critical situation we have nothing to rely upon. Thus I ask you to follow the prime minister . . .[36]

A second aspect of the ideology of the Phibun era that harked back to Vajiravudh was a form of cultural nationalism. This included a range of measures, from the promotion of 'traditional' Thai values to the forced imposition of certain Western cultural practices, particularly in the form of a series of twelve *ratthaniyom* ('state conventions') regarding various aspects of behaviour and dress.[37] At the same time there was selective discrimination against some other 'alien' cultures, including in particular a severe repression of Chinese-language media and education. The Thai language itself was 'modernized', and various other cultural traits adjusted to conform to real or imagined antecedents. This programme of cultural propaganda was in large measure co-ordinated by *Luang* Wichit Wathakan, chief ideologue of the régime, who as director-general of the Department of Fine Arts composed and sponsored the performance of a plethora of nationalistic plays and songs based predominantly upon idealized historical themes.

Cultural nationalism was accompanied by economic nationalism, militarism, and an aggressive promotion of the Buddhist religion. Economic nationalism was most particularly directed against Western and Chinese domination of the modern, commercialized sector of the economy. Under the slogan of 'nation-building', fascist-style state enterprises and monopolies were established in a number of fields, and various professions and occupations were restricted to Thai nationals. Militarism was another prominent strand of the official ideology, with large budget increases for the armed forces and a general glorification of martial values, reflecting in part contemporary trends in Germany and Japan, and the perceived waning of the influence of the Western democracies in the late 1930s. Military youth groups were also formed, again obviously patterned on foreign models. And, as in Vajiravudh's time, Buddhism received intense official patronage. While this, with rare exceptions, did not reach the point of outright repression of other religions, the message was clearly conveyed that to be Thai and to be Buddhist were virtually synonymous.

Finally, the Phibun régime was actively expansionist, in the form of a

---

[36] Thai text quoted in Thamsook Numnonda, *Fyn Adit* [Reconstructing the Past], Bangkok, 1979, 139–41.

[37] English translations of the twelve *ratthaniyom* (1939–42) are given in Thak Chaloemtiarana, ed., *Thai Politics: Extracts and Documents 1932–1957*, Bangkok, 1978, 244–54. The *ratthiniyom* and related decrees mandated such Western modes of dress as hats and gloves, and specified in detail what hours of the day should be devoted to various activities.

'pan-Thai' movement which sought to recover 'lost' territories and peoples (including some not ethnically Thai) who had once formed part of the extended Thai empire. The symbolic confirmation of the Thai irredentist drive came in 1939 with the change of name from the ethnically-neutral 'Siam' to 'Thailand', intended internally as a declaration of Thai domination vis-à-vis Chinese or Western influence, and externally to advertise Thailand as the natural home of all of the 'Thai' peoples. The first tangible steps toward fulfilling the 'greater Thailand' dream came with war against the weakened French régime in Indochina in 1940–1 and the resulting recovery of former Thai territories in western and northern Cambodia and trans-Mekong Laos, one of the rare instances when the 'official' nationalism fostered by either Vajiravudh or Phibun received any substantial mass support. Later, in 1943, Japan transferred additional Malay and Burmese territories to what proved to be temporary Thai control.

Thus on the eve of the outbreak of the Pacific War, Thailand's military-dominated régime was aggressively pursuing a type of nationalism in many ways unique in the Southeast Asian context. And with only brief interruptions, such as Pridi's return to power in 1944–7 or the 'democratic era' of 1973–6, a form of this conservative, élitist, 'official' nationalism would continue to be the dominant state ideology down through the 1980s.

Malay Nationalism

The character of nationalism in the Malay peninsula derived from economic, social and political transformations of the late nineteenth and early twentieth centuries. Before this period, Perak was a state of some importance, but the major concentrations of Malay population were in Kedah on the west coast, Pattani-Kelantan-Terengganu on the east, and Johor-Riau in the south. Selangor had come into being as a Bugis state during the eighteenth century, while the area that became the Negri Sembilan contained a collection of small Minangkabau states that were united as a single entity only under British pressure toward the end of the nineteenth century. Pahang, which the British in 1896 drew into a confederation along with Perak, Selangor and the Negri Sembilan, was a thinly populated outlying region of the Johor-Riau empire.

Within Perak, Selangor and the Negri Sembilan, the period of British rule brought enormous changes. Tin-mining, a long-established enterprise which expanded rapidly after discovery of the Larut tin fields in the 1840s and the Kinta Valley deposits in the 1880s, was the principal source of income and of government revenue until the second decade of the twentieth century when it was overtaken by the burgeoning rubber industry. Johor, too, developed a major export economy based on commercial agriculture, although there the driving force was the Malay ruling house. Labour for the export economy came from China and from India, while rice to feed the workforce was imported from Burma and Siam and Cochinchina, a situation with exact Southeast Asian parallels only in the East Coast Residency of Sumatra and in North Borneo. Export industries in British

Malaya did not draw any major inputs from the indigenous population.

Technically, Kedah, Kelantan, Terengganu and Perlis were client states of the Thai king until 1909, when Siam surrendered its rights in the area to Great Britain, although as early as 1897 a secret agreement between the two powers had given Britain a degree of influence over affairs in southern Siam. One consequence of this history was that political and economic changes came later and were much less intrusive in Kedah, Kelantan, Terengganu, and Perlis than in areas with a concentration of mines and estates, and these 'Unfederated Malay States' retained a significant degree of local administrative autonomy. The northern states tended to retain rice-based subsistence economies, and were less congenial places for non-Malay immigrants than Perak or Selangor or Johor, where tin-mining and commercial agriculture had already attracted large and growing non-Malay communities.

Malaya thus presents a picture different from most parts of Southeast Asia, where colonial administrations had to deal with large numbers of people whose lives had been substantially disrupted and whose traditional beliefs had been called into question. In making arrangements for the Malay population, the British administration saw its task as limiting dislocation rather than coping with pressures to produce increasing amounts of labour or food.

Colonial régimes lacked the status and the local knowledge of indigenous élites, and most found it necessary to seek the collaboration of some element of the local population, and to provide training in Western-style schools for junior clerical and administrative staff. In Malaya this process started somewhat later than elsewhere in the region and, with the export economy concentrated in non-Malay areas, was less pressing. A Malay College established in 1905 cultivated conservative opinion, serving the traditional élite and producing candidates for a Malay Administrative Service, subordinate to the almost exclusively British Malayan Civil Service. A second institution, the Sultan Idris Training College, founded in 1922 to conduct teacher-training programmes, drew students from village vernacular schools. By promoting the study of Malay literature, the college created an environment that encouraged political awareness and a critical evaluation of Malay society, and its graduates played a prominent role in the development of a nationalist critique of British rule in Malaya.

Modernist reform in the Malay peninsula before 1940 concentrated for the most part on religion and education, drawing on regional developments as well as ideas derived from the Arab Middle East and Turkey. The Malay press published extensive discussions of religious issues, and as in the Netherlands East Indies those involved divided into a reformist *kaum muda* (young group), seeking to purify Islam in Malaya and to set aside heterodox accretions, and a conservative *kaum tua* (elder group) seeking to maintain the status quo. One commentator on Malay nationalism has identified 1926 as a watershed in the development of Malay political attitudes.[38] In that year a group of activists formed a Malay political party

[38] Radin Soenarno, 'Malay nationalism, 1898–1941', JSEAS, 1 (1960) 9ff.

called the Kesatuan Melayu Singapura (Singapore Malay Union), providing a forum for the development of Malay thought. In that year too, Malays came into contact with Indonesian radicals, fleeing their country after the failure of the communist uprising in 1926, while Sukarno's PNI, with its demand for immediate independence, gave further impetus to this emerging strain of radical thought.

The Malay critique identified three problem areas: the Malay rulers who collaborated with the colonial government, the colonial administration itself, and the growing alien population. Criticism of the rulers was difficult to sustain among a population that traditionally gave the sultans unquestioned loyalty, and it produced a counter-movement calling for greater attention to Malay culture and identity and emphasizing the importance of the rulers. The British administration, the obvious target for nationalists, was generally sympathetic toward the Malays during the 1920s and 1930s, stressing the need to ensure adequate representation of the local population in the cohort of government employees, and taking steps to protect the interests of the Malays when they seemed threatened by an immigrant population that outnumbered them in some states of the peninsula. During the 1920s, a group of British administrators, arguing that not enough had been done for the indigenous population, began pressing the government to take stronger action to promote Malay interests. The tenor of this pro-Malay policy can be seen in comments by the High Commissioner, Sir Shenton Thomas, criticizing in 1936 proposals that Malayan-born Indians be given a greater role in the administration: 'I do not know of any country in which what I might call a foreigner—that is to say, a native not a native of the country or an Englishman—has ever been appointed to an administrative post.'[39] This left the immigrant population as a focus for Malay grievances.

When the Great Depression reduced demand for Malaya's exports, the government repatriated a number of Indians and Chinese, while an Aliens Enactment restricted new immigration and made it clear that those allowed to come were to remain only for the duration of their contracts. However, the administration soon came to doubt the wisdom of this policy. To sustain the economy, Malaya manifestly needed Indian and Chinese labour, and on-going recruitment of workers posed a number of difficulties. In India there was growing hostility within the Congress Party to the sending of unskilled labourers abroad, and it was by no means certain that this source would remain available. The continued recruitment of Chinese workers was also problematic, since conditions were unsettled in southern China, the traditional source of labour, and it was unclear whether arrangements to obtain workers would continue to function smoothly. Another negative aspect of the situation was that political agitators could easily gain entry to Malaya by coming as labourers. Accordingly the government began to explore the idea of maintaining a permanent Chinese and Indian population in the peninsula, a policy

---

[39] W.R. Roff, *The Origins of Malay Nationalism*, New Haven, 1967, 109–10, citing Federal Council Proceedings, 1936, B18.

which aroused Malay fears of being swamped in their own homeland by foreigners.

Toward the end of the 1930s the situation changed dramatically. Anti-Japanese activity among the Chinese population, as well as strikes and labour unrest, heightened Malay concerns about foreign domination. In 1937 the Singapore Malay Union formed branches in Melaka and Penang, and Malay associations took shape in other states as well. A Brotherhood of Pen Friends (Persaudaraan Sahabat Pena), which examined political affairs and particularly the position of the Malays, was formed in the same year, as was a radical group called the Kesatuan Melayu Muda or Malay Youth Union, the outgrowth of an informal student group at the Sultan Idris Training College. The Kesatuan Melayu Muda 'neither professed loyalty to the Sultans and the British nor spoke of non-cooperation, but worked to promote nationalist feelings and teachings among its members, whose strength lay in the lower classes'.[40] A Pan-Malayan Conference of Malay state associations met in Kuala Lumpur in August 1939 to attempt to draw these disparate Malay groups together in a single movement; the effort failed, but it laid the groundwork for a more successful postwar organization, the United Malays National Organization. The political initiatives of these years, both the radical tendency represented by the Kesatuan Melayu Muda and a conservative nationalism oriented toward Malay culture and traditions, survived the Japanese Occupation to inspire opposition to Britain's proposals to reconstitute the administration of the country after the war.

Moro Nationalism

The Moros, the Muslim population of the southern islands of the Philippine archipelago, strenuously opposed Spanish rule; effective Spanish control of many areas, particularly the Sulu archipelago, came about only in the mid-nineteenth century. American policy toward the Moros was set down in an 1899 agreement between General John C. Bates and the Sultan of Sulu, in which United States sovereignty was acknowledged but the Moros were assured of non-interference in matters of religion and custom. The agreement did not, however, specify the dividing line between civil and religious affairs, and the first ten years of American rule brought numerous disputes and armed rebellion.

In 1903 a Moro Province was created, and in the following year the United States abrogated the Bates Agreement, assuming direct authority over the region and imposing military rule. A number of military operations were undertaken against the Moros, culminating in the bloody battle of Bud Dajo on 6 March 1906. Following this episode the Americans adopted a more conciliatory approach, but in 1911 undertook complete disarmament of the Moros, after which a civilian administration took over.

American reforms related to education, taxes, family law and public

---

[40] ibid., 222, citing Ibrahim Yaacob, *Nusa dan Bangsa Melaju*, Jakarta, 1951, 59–60.

health measures, issues which the Americans considered strictly secular but which impinged in various ways on Islamic principles and Moro custom. During the first two decades of the twentieth century the Moros viewed the American administration as inimical to their interests, but this perception changed when American concessions to Philippine nationalism brought Christian Filipinos into positions of authority over the Moro area.

Accelerated Filipinization of the administration during Francis Burton Harrison's term as governor-general gave Christian Filipinos a majority in both houses of the Philippine Assembly and a growing proportion of civil service posts, in Mindanao as well as in Luzon and the Visayas. The avowed intention of American policy was 'the amalgamation of the Mohammedan and Christian native population into a homogeneous Filipino people',[41] and the Moros, doubtful about Christian Filipino intentions, viewed these developments with considerable apprehension. The Jones Law of 1916 removed remaining distinctions between Christian and non-Christian areas, and gave the new all-Filipino legislature full law-making powers over the entire country. It also created a Bureau of Non-Christian Tribes, responsible for Muslim and 'pagan' affairs, which the legislature placed under the Secretary of the Interior.

Filipino nationalists, accusing the Americans of pursuing a divide-and-rule policy in the south, promoted the notion that Christians and Muslims alike constituted the Filipino people, and encouraged united action against colonial rule. American officials generally accepted this argument, adopting the idea that Moros were 'substantive Filipinos', who had no 'national thought or ideals' and were likely to come into 'increasing and eventual homogeneity with the highly civilized Filipino type', producing a 'national existence' in which religious distinctions were immaterial.[42] The Americans had hoped to reduce cultural differences by appointing Christian Filipinos to administer non-Christian areas, and creating agricultural colonies for Christian Filipinos on public lands in Mindanao and Sulu (a policy initiated in 1913), but these measures only increased tension within the area. During the 1920s and 1930s American authorities received a number of appeals from Muslims for protection from Christian Filipino rule. One complained that the Philippine legislature had made no provision for the customary practices of the Moros:

> The Philippine Legislature has ... failed to recognize our religion. They have failed to pass any laws recognizing our marriages ... and according to the present laws in force in the Philippine Islands, and also the decisions of its Courts, our wives are concubines, and our children illegitimate.[43]

When preparations were under way for formation of the Philippine Commonwealth, the Moros sought to reach an accommodation with the

---

[41] Frank Carpenter, Governor of the Department of Mindanao and Sulu, quoted in Peter Gordon Gowing, *Mandate in Moroland*, Quezon City, 1983, 292.

[42] Carpenter, in ibid., 275.

[43] Quoted in Peter Gordon Gowing, *Muslim Filipinos—Heritage and Horizon*, Quezon City, 1979, 168–9.

new government, requesting that the Constitutional Convention make special provisions for the practices of the Moros and the provisions of Islamic law. The convention disregarded these suggestions, and the succeeding Commonwealth government took a number of steps which posed a grave threat to the Moros. Christian Filipinos were given strong encouragement to migrate into Muslim areas, special legal provisions contained in the Administrative Code for Mindanao and Sulu were repealed, and President Quezon declared the 'so-called Moro problem' to be 'a thing of the past'.[44] From the Moro point of view, the Americans had disarmed them, disrupted their political organizations, and then handed them over to their enemies. Armed resistance resumed in 1936, the beginning of a very long campaign to assert the claims of the 'Moro nation'.

Shan Nationalism

The leaders of the Shan states, the *sawbwa*, following British military expeditions to 'pacify' the territories during the 1880s, signed agreements establishing a political arrangement that left most administrative, judicial and revenue affairs in the hands of local chiefs. The agreements did, however, establish the subordination of the *sawbwa* to the government of Burma on the grounds that they were 'formerly subject to the King of Burma'.[45] Following the dyarchy reforms of the early 1920s, which divided Burma into two parts, central Burma (or 'Burma proper') and the 'frontier' or 'excluded' areas, the British government created an entity known as the Federated Shan States which was placed under a British Commissioner appointed by the Governor. The Shan Chiefs sat as a Federal Council, but this body served in an advisory capacity and had no executive or legislative powers, an arrangement that substantially reduced the authority of the *sawbwa*.

During the 1930s, when Britain undertook reforms in the system of limited self-government in central Burma, the *sawbwa* attempted to regain some of their lost powers, and to persuade the British administration to place individual Shan states on the same footing as the princely states of India, making them independent entities under the British Crown but separate from federal Burma. Although supporting protection of the Shan Federation from 'Burman encroachment', the British government rejected these initiatives, citing their understanding of historical relations between the Shan rulers and Burma as well as the arrangements in effect during the past forty years of British rule as precedents. British officials anticipated the eventual development of 'some form of union' between the Shan States and the government of Burma.[46]

---

[44] ibid., 176–7.
[45] 'Form of Sanad granted to Sawbwas', in Sao Saimong Mangrai, *The Shan States and the British Annexation*, Ithaca, 1965, a pp.VII, xxxi.
[46] Robert H. Taylor, 'British policy and the Shan States, 1886–1947', in Prakai Nontawasee, ed., *Changes in Northern Thailand and the Shan States 1886–1940*, Singapore: ISEAS, 1988, 36–8. The quotation is taken from Burma Office file 1506/1937.

Toward the end of the 1930s Burmese nationalists became increasingly critical of arrangements segregating the Shan States from Burma, and sought to draw the area into the nationalist movement. The Dobama Asiayone passed a resolution in May 1940 that 'powers under the Constitution should lie not only with the people of Burma proper but also with the people in excluded areas and that the interests of the *Sawbwas* should not be allowed to obstruct the way to freedom for Burma'.[47] The *sawbwa* for their part continued to press their case with Britain in 1940 and 1941, but had little success apart from obtaining approval for raising a military force. Britain continued to pursue a policy shielding the Shan States from Burmese nationalist interference, without making concessions to Shan aspirations, but during the war a scheme was devised for drawing the Shan States into a federal Burma. These plans were overtaken by events after the war, particularly the early granting of independence to Burma, but the issue of national integration and the role of the Shan remained one of the key issues with which the new Burmese government had to contend.

Karen Nationalism

The Karen established a Karen National Association (KNA) in 1880, one of the earliest nationalist groupings in Southeast Asia and anticipating Burman nationalist bodies by several decades. The unifying element behind the KNA was Christianity, fostered by missionary activity from early in the nineteenth century, and the association sought to preserve and promote the Karen identity.

Many Karen supported British rule, and the KNA gave its backing both to British pacification efforts during the 1880s and to the British cause during World War I. After the administrative realignment of the 1920s in Burma, the KNA pressed Karen claims to special consideration under the British administration, arguing that their numerical strength and loyal support entitled them to 'advance step by step along with the Burmans'.[48] The position of the Karen seemed especially precarious because they lived intermingled with other ethnic groups, and in few areas constituted a majority. In 1928 Karen leaders sought to rectify this situation by calling for formation of a Karen state, saying in a classic nationalist formulation that they wished 'to have a country of their own, where they may progress as a race and find the contentment they seek'.[49] This initiative placed the Karen squarely at odds with Burman efforts to subsume ethnic loyalties within a single Burman-dominated state. Coupled with the past loyalty of the Karen to Britain it produced a hostile response from the Burma Independence Army, which killed a number of Karen, among them a cabinet minister, in the early days of the Japanese Occupation, laying the ground for a long-running and bitter postwar conflict.

[47] ibid., 41.
[48] Silverstein, 45, quoting the Karen leader Sidney Loo-Nee.
[49] ibid, 46, quoting the Karen leader San C. Po.

Burmese Muslim Nationalism

Burmese Muslims, many descended from Indian, Persian or Arab stock and distinguished from the bulk of the Burmese population by racial characteristics as well as religion, appear in some of the earliest European accounts of Burma. They formed a distinct community, and retained strong connections with South and West Asia. After the British conquest, large numbers of Indians came to Burma, about half of them Muslim. The Muslim population of Burma followed political developments in India, forming a branch of the All-India Muslim League in 1909 and a branch of the Khilafat Movement. There were also organizations devoted to Muslim interests within Burma, notably the Burma Moslem Society, founded in December 1909, which made submissions during the discussions of constitutional reforms that led to dyarchy, and to the Simon Commission, as well as to the Legislative Council in Burma.

As the Burmese nationalist movement gained force, it adopted a distinctly Buddhist orientation, describing Burmese Muslims as *kalas*, 'foreign immigrants'; the Muslim community responded by turning to Britain for protection. In discussions of the proposed separation of Burma from India, Burmese Muslims sought an arrangement which would give a formal political role to their community. Burmese Buddhists objected to this proposal, with one leader arguing that in the context of 'Burmese-Buddhist tolerance' there was 'no reason whatsoever to entertain any anxiety on the part of the religious denominations who form the minorities in Burma'.[50] The Simon Commission recommended that special places in the Legislative Council be reserved for Muslims, but the British government did not accept this proposal and the terms of the arrangement separating Burma from India in 1937 made no special provisions for the Muslim community. A new General Council of Burma Moslem Associations was formed in 1936, and a 'Renaissance Movement' took shape in 1937 which represented the interests of Burmese Muslims, stressing the Burmese identity of this community and blaming Indian Muslims, who were excluded from membership even if they had settled permanently in the country, for sowing discord within the Burman community.

Hostility between the Burmese and the Indians, heated in any case, was particularly virulent in the case of the Muslim community. Issues relating to marriage laws and economic competition led to the outbreak of violent anti-Indian riots in July 1938, first in Rangoon and then in rural areas, leaving large numbers dead and wounded and over a hundred mosques burned, and creating enmities that remained unresolved when Burma became independent.

Pattani Nationalism

The population of Pattani, a major trading state that had been subordinated to Siam, consisted largely of Muslims of Malay stock, whose affinities lay

---

[50] 'Note of Dissent' by U Ba U, published as an appendix to the Report of the Simon Commission, cited in Moshe Yegar, *The Muslims of Burma*, Wiesbaden, 1972, 60.

with the Malay states to the south. Relations with Bangkok were often strained, and in 1817 an attempted rebellion against Thai authority led to the division of Pattani into seven provinces. Bangkok also adopted as-similationist policies for the area—Prince Damrong, the Minister of the Interior, had written to King Chulalongkorn as early as March 1896 that those entering government service, 'even though they are foreigners and uphold a different religion', should 'acquire Thai hearts and manners just as all other [of] His Majesty's servants'.[51] Administrative reforms carried out between 1902 and 1906 integrated Pattani more fully with the rest of Siam, while agreements with Britain during the same decade led to a 1909 treaty that transferred Thai rights over the neighbouring Malay states of Perlis, Kedah, Kelantan and Terengganu to Great Britain.

The 1902 reforms assigned Thai civil servants to staff the newly revamped administrative services in the area, and stripped the local nobility of their powers to levy taxes and perform other government functions. These measures provoked resistance in the Malay areas of southern Siam, and Muslim leaders sought support from Britain as well as from other Malay states. In 1901 the Malay rulers had 'bound themselves to make a united resistance to any forcible exhibition of authority on the part of the Siamese',[52] and they responded to the 1902 reforms by instituting a boycott of government activities that brought about mass resignations of local officials and led to a series of uprisings. The Raja of Legeh wrote to the Governor of the Straits Settlements complaining that Malay chiefs were forced to kneel and bow before portraits of the King of Siam and before idols. 'To worship idols is . . . strictly prohibited in Mohammadan Religion. This causes a feeling of disgust and discontent among the whole inhabit-ants of Legeh.'[53] Three rajas were removed from office by the Siamese as a result of this agitation, and a fourth, Raja Abdul Kadir Kamaroodin, ruler of the rump state of Pattani, was given a ten-year jail sentence, two years and nine months of which he served before being released and going into exile in Kelantan. Heightened Siamese nationalism under King Vajira-vudh, with its emphasis on king, nation, and [Buddhist] religion and the promotion of Thai education, led to further unrest, and Raja Abdul Kadir was behind a major uprising in 1922. After his death eleven years later, his youngest son, Tengku Mahmud Mahyideen, succeeded him as leader of the Pattani independence movement.

The uprising of 1922 brought a moderation of Thai assimilationist policies, and after the coup of 1932 replaced the absolute monarchy with representative institutions, the Pattani area cautiously began to participate in the Thai system of parliamentary government. During the 1930s the government pushed ahead with compulsory education for the region, an initiative which many Muslims associated not with political development, but with Buddhism and recruitment into the Thai army. However, Pattani

[51] Quoted in Surin Pitsuwan, *Islam and Malay Nationalism: A Case Study of the Malay-Muslims of Southern Thailand*, Bangkok, 1985, 40.

[52] ibid, 46, citing F. A. Swettenham to N. Chamberlain, 20 Nov. 1901.

[53] ibid., 54, citing Tengku Ngah Shamsooden, Rajah of Legeh, to F. A. Swettenham, 18 Jan. 1901.

nationalism was quiescent until Phibun became prime minister in December 1938 and introduced a policy of forced assimilation in the south. Phibun's emphasis on race, and his depiction of Siam as a state for the Thai race, appeared to exclude the non-integrated Malay-Muslims of the south. Traditional Malay dress was disallowed, as were Malayo-Arabic names, use of the Malay language, and Malay marriage and inheritance practices. Malay nationalism, dormant for a number of years, came alive and as before looked for assistance to Malaya, where Tengku Mahyideen attempted to enlist both Malay and British support to defend Muslim interests. During the war, the Far Eastern Committee of the British War Cabinet discussed the possibility of uniting Pattani with Malaya in a postwar settlement, but by the war's end Bangkok had adopted a more conciliatory policy, and Britain did not pursue the matter.

The Pan-Thai Movement

The pan-Thai movement, which flourished briefly in the late 1930s and early 1940s, envisioned the political and cultural unification of peoples living in at least five distinct political units. Its objective was to dissolve existing territorial demarcations, products of the colonial order, in favour of a vaguely defined greater Thai state based upon somewhat idealized historical precedents.

For nearly a century prior to the 1932 change of government, the Bangkok régime had adopted a largely defensive posture and worked to cultivate friendly relations with its British and French colonial neighbours; as late as the 1920s Thai authorities had actively discouraged any criticism of French rule in Laos and Cambodia, or displays of Thai chauvinism. The end of the absolute monarchy brought to power, within a few years, a more aggressive, military-dominated leadership; 'Siam' became 'Thailand', and with Phibun as prime minister and *Luang* Wichit Wathakan as chief ideologue of the régime, an ambitious campaign was launched to reclaim 'lost territories' and unite the various Thai peoples. The word 'Thai' was loosely construed to include all those over whom the monarchs of Ayutthaya or Bangkok had once claimed sovereignty, whether linguistically related peoples such as the Lao and Shan or the linguistically distinct Khmer and Malays.

War in Europe, and then in Asia, temporarily favoured the attainment of pan-Thai objectives, and parts of colonial Cambodia, Laos, Malaya and Burma were incorporated into a greater 'Thai' state. With few exceptions, Bangkok's irredentist campaign was not warmly received by the peoples affected, for historical memories of earlier periods of central Thai rule were often negative, and dominant identities were likely to be localized rather than 'Thai'. The more nationalistic of the Lao, for example, saw large parts of old Siam as properly not 'Thai' but 'Lao', producing a counter irredentist impulse. In any case the outcome of the war ended the dream of a greater Thailand; pan-Thai aspirations were abandoned, at least publicly, and Thailand returned to its borders as they had been defined by the colonial powers in 1909.

Pan-Islam

Political activity based on Muslim unity appeared to have the potential to become a serious threat to the administrations of the Netherlands East Indies and British Malaya, and was closely watched. Islam is a way of life, and divisions between a religious and secular sphere, or between church and state, are unacceptable, as is a situation in which non-Muslims rule Muslims. However, the potential threat went beyond the fact that substantial proportions of the populations of the two areas were Muslim. All Muslims consider themselves part of a single Islamic community, the *ummat Islam*, that transcends divisions of race or culture, and this concept gave rise to the spectre of a vast international movement mounting a holy war to displace non-Muslims, fears which were reinforced by myths and misunderstandings about Islam, particularly regarding a supposed fanaticism among its followers.

If the possibility of a united Muslim opposition was real enough, mobilizing the community to take concerted action, even in the absence of state interference, would have been extremely difficult. Within Islam there was no central figure who could speak with authority on behalf of the *ummat Islam* or command their undivided loyalty. The Caliphate, based in Istanbul and nominally the religious and temporal centre of the Islamic world, had become 'the well-nigh powerless symbol of the nonexisting unity of all Muslims',[54] an ineffectual institution even before its abolition by the Turkish government in 1924. In 1915, when the Ottoman Empire aligned itself with the Central Powers and declared war on the Western Allies, the Caliph called for a holy war against his enemies, including the colonial powers in the Netherlands East Indies and Malaya. The Dutch, neutral in the war, protested and the Netherlands East Indies was subsequently excluded from this call, but it also had little impact in Malaya where it remained in effect. Elimination of the Caliphate attracted some attention in Southeast Asia. Colonial security services kept a close watch on public opinion, but little came of the matter, although contending factions in Indonesia and Malaya used the Turkish reforms as examples of what ought or ought not to be done locally.

The elusiveness of the pan-Islamic ideal was a result of divisions within the Muslim community on religious matters, and the strength of alternative, secular concerns. Religious divisions separated those who advocated a purified Islam, those who defended Muslim practices as they had developed in Southeast Asia, and the substantial number of nominal Muslims who had little interest in such matters. Secular concerns included racial and cultural issues, and in some quarters a desire to achieve modernization and self-strengthening by means of Westernization.

Pan-Chinese Nationalism

Nationalism in China called upon the Overseas Chinese to reassess their political loyalties and, beyond that, their basic identity insofar as they

---

[54] Harry Benda, *The Crescent and the Rising Sun*, reprint edn, Dordrecht, 1983, 21, citing the views of C. Snouck Hurgronje,

might have abandoned elements of 'Chinese-ness'. Southeast Asia, with its large and prosperous Chinese communities, was a particular focus of this effort, and as various initiatives took shape, governments in the region became concerned about the development of a pan-Chinese perspective and the possible consequences of a growing sense of loyalty to China.

The size of the Chinese communities in Southeast Asia ranged from a few hundred thousand to well over a million, but with the exception of British Malaya, where the 1,700,000 Chinese constituted nearly 40 per cent of the population, the Chinese were small minorities. During the 1930s the Chinese population of the Netherlands East Indies exceeded one million people but made up only about 3 per cent of the population. The Chinese population of Vietnam was about 1 per cent of the total, of Cambodia probably around 10 per cent, and of Burma 1.3 per cent of the total, or 1.8 per cent of the ethnic Burman population.

A nationality law passed in 1909 by the imperial government of China claimed all persons born of a Chinese father or a Chinese mother as Chinese subjects. The people embraced by that definition were otherwise extremely diverse. A majority of the Chinese migrants in Southeast Asia came from southern China, but numerous dialects were represented. Most were merchants or labourers and the society in general encompassed a narrow range of social classes, although wars and rebellions in China had introduced a scattering of other social elements as losing factions fled into exile. Some Chinese in Southeast Asia lived in enclaves where the language and diet were Chinese, and where political authority was exercised by Chinese headmen. Others were isolated, routinely speaking a local language and rarely mixing with other Chinese. In most territories the Chinese communities consisted of young men, and the family life which figures prominently in Confucianism was largely absent, leading to an attenuation of Chinese customs, while some Chinese immigrants married local women and they or their offspring became integrated with the local community, learning indigenous languages and adopting local customs. The degree of assimilation achieved in succeeding generations depended to a great extent on the receptivity of the indigenous peoples. In the Philippines and Siam, children of mixed Chinese–local marriages tended to merge with the local population and in many cases became indistinguishable from them. In Muslim communities Chinese assimilation was less readily accomplished, and Baba or Peranakan communities which combined features of Chinese and indigenous culture developed in the Malay peninsula and Indonesian archipelago.

Colonial rule added yet another layer of complexity. Most colonial administrations followed the principle of *jus soli* or place of birth in determining nationality, which taken in conjunction with the policy of the Chinese government gave the Chinese in Southeast Asia dual nationality. Moreover, colonies offered education in European languages and attractive opportunities for those able to interact with the European community. G. W. Skinner has pointed out that the natural tendency was for Chinese immigrants to adapt themselves to the élite environment of the country in which they lived. Where colonial rule prevailed, they were inclined to learn Western languages and adopt Western ways. In Siam, where an indigenous aristocracy retained power, the Chinese learned Thai and adopted Thai ways.[55]

After 1900 increasing numbers of Chinese women emigrated to Southeast Asia, making it easier for male migrants to set up families which retained Chinese traditions. At the same time, however, the number of males who came for limited periods, lived in Chinese enclaves and maintained a Chinese identity also increased dramatically. In the years before 1940 three types of Chinese communities were found in Southeast Asia: China-oriented groups, Western-oriented groups, and communities which combined Chinese and Southeast Asian characteristics. It was within this context that Chinese nationalism developed in the region.

Culturally, Chinese nationalism produced a movement to reassert a Chinese identity. Politically, it stood for opposition to foreign domination and participation in the revitalization of economic and political life in China. For Chinese with a Southeast Asian orientation, or who were Westernized, these tendencies created dilemmas. Some underwent a process of re-sinification, learning Mandarin and seeing that their children secured a Chinese education. Others opted to identify with the colonial régime or to come to terms with indigenous nationalism. With regard to the latter, the anti-Western stance of the Chinese nationalists would seem to make them natural allies of local opponents of colonial rule, but nationalism in Southeast Asia was partly directed against the Chinese, who were seen as a foreign presence in the region.

In 1905 Sun Yat-sen founded the Tung Meng Hui (Common Alliance Society), and over the next six years established branches across Southeast Asia with Singapore as regional headquarters. Nationalist sentiment among the Chinese in Southeast Asia was considerably heightened by a trade boycott against the United States, a response to renewal of America's Chinese Exclusion Act in 1904. The Philippine Chinese who lived under American rule were most directly affected by the issue, but Chinese communities elsewhere in the region supported the boycott, an experience that increased political awareness and helped develop a sense of unity that transcended regional borders. Subsequent political developments in China, such as the fall of the Qing dynasty in the 1911 Revolution, the Twenty-One Demands issued by Japan in 1915, and the Sino-Japanese conflicts of the 1930s, which led to widespread anti-Japanese boycotts in Southeast Asia, further strengthened this feeling of participation in a larger Chinese community.

The deep political divisions in China—prior to the 1911 Revolution between republicans and Qing dynasty loyalists, subsequently between the Kuomintang nationalists and the Chinese Communist Party—also affected the Chinese in Southeast Asia. The Kuomintang and the communists both recruited support throughout the region, opening clubs and other organizations and establishing newspapers, and their activities met with a hostile response from colonial administrations. The Kuomintang attempted to operate as an orthodox political movement, establishing

[55] G. William Skinner, 'Change and persistence in Chinese culture overseas: a comparison of Thailand and Java', in *Journal of the South Seas Society*, 16, 1–2 (1960) 86–100.

party branches and inviting Chinese communities in Southeast Asia to elect delegates to party conferences in China. Colonial authorities considered involvement in Chinese politics on the part of the Overseas Chinese unacceptable and made protests to China over this issue, and also over a conscription law making all men of Chinese descent liable for military service in the Chinese armed forces. China did not have the power to enforce these regulations in Southeast Asia, and in fact made no effort to do so, but in the eyes of the region's administrations the involvement of Southeast Asia's Chinese population in Chinese politics raised questions of political loyalty.

Efforts to promote Chinese education with a curriculum derived from China, attempts to draw the Overseas Chinese into Chinese politics, the activities of Chinese consuls in Southeast Asia, the formation of Chinese chambers of commerce and other organizations serving Chinese interests, and a clear feeling within Chinese communities that they were participating in a national awakening aroused fears among colonial governments and the non-Chinese inhabitants of Southeast Asia alike of the possible effects of pan-Chinese political activity. The centre was China, but the sphere of activity took in the entire region of the Nanyang, the South Seas.

Governments within the region kept a close watch on Chinese political activity, and most enacted new regulations to contain the situation. In British Malaya the administration imposed controls over Chinese educational materials, took action against political and secret society activity, and introduced limits on immigration that were largely applied to the Chinese. In Siam the strident Thai nationalism prevailing after the 1932 coup had an anti-Chinese tone: Chinese schools and newspapers were suppressed to encourage assimilation, and a variety of restrictions were imposed on Chinese economic activity. The Commonwealth government in the Philippines adopted anti-Chinese policies, and the constitution as well as subsequent legislation severely limited the capacity of non-Filipinos to carry out economic activities within the country. In the Netherlands East Indies the administration considered the Chinese community largely pro-Dutch and, while restricting direct involvement in Chinese politics, imposed relatively few new restrictions on the Chinese during this period.

Baba or Peranakan Nationalism

Chinese families long resident in the Malay peninsula and Indonesian archipelago formed distinct cultural groups, known in the archipelago as Peranakan and in Malaya as the Baba or Straits Chinese. While these communities retained elements of Chinese culture, their language, dress, customs and food were an amalgam drawn both from Chinese and local traditions.

Confronted with growing Indonesian nationalist sentiment directed in part against itself, the Peranakan community in the Netherlands East Indies responded in different ways. Overtures to Indonesian nationalists offering cooperation against Dutch rule bore no fruit. The alternatives were to assert the rights of the Peranakan as a long-established community within the archipelago, using the considerable wealth of the community to support these claims, or to look to China for support. These tactics were pursued with some success, but both had serious drawbacks. The economic dominance of the Peranakan community was itself a nationalist grievance, and leverage derived on this basis had to be applied with much discretion, while the intercession of China was objectionable from the perspective of Indonesian nationalism and Dutch colonial rule alike. The Peranakan group in some respects enjoyed preferential treatment, and, facing a potentially hostile Indonesian nationalist movement, could ill afford to alienate the Dutch.

In Malaya the Babas were of less political significance than a broader category of 'Straits-born' Chinese, who retained more of Chinese culture than the Babas but shared their Southeast Asian orientation. With Malay nationalism generally unaggressive, the concerns of this group were directed toward deciding what stance should be adopted regarding China, and on this matter the community divided, some identifying with China and others with the colonial administration. However, while the distinction between China-oriented and Straits-oriented loyalties helped shape prewar political attitudes, it diminished in importance after 1945, when Singapore began the odyssey that led to independence in 1965 under a leadership in which the Straits-born Chinese played a prominent role.

Indian Nationalism

Developments in India also had important consequences for Southeast Asia nationalist movements, both in the model they provided and, more directly, in influences on reformist and nationalist activity in areas with significant immigrant Indian populations, such as Burma and British Malaya. Indian communities in Southeast Asia remained relatively unassimilated, at least compared to the Chinese in Siam and certain other areas. Indians by and large maintained their distinctive and multi-faceted identities, reflecting the great ethnic, linguistic, and religious diversity within the Indian subcontinent. They generally supported one or another faction of Indian nationalism, but remained largely apart from, and to some degree fearful of, the major Southeast Asian nationalist movements.

Outside Burma and the Malay peninsula, Indian immigration was limited and of little political significance. In Burma, Indians constituted about 7 per cent of the total population in 1931, but their predominance in Rangoon and high profile in the economy made them a target of Burmese nationalists. In Malaya 10 per cent of the 1911 population was Indian, a figure which rose to 14.3 per cent by 1931, but most lived and worked on estates and were of less concern to Malay nationalists than the more visible Chinese community. As a result of marriages between Indian Muslims and Malays, a 'Jawi Pekan' group developed in British Malaya, adopting some of the cultural characteristics of both communities.

Nationalist activity among Indians in Southeast Asia in the first decades of the twentieth century, as in the case of Chinese communities, was oriented primarily towards the home country; indeed some sections of the Indian population, particularly those classes which enjoyed relative prosperity under the colonial order, were fearful of the possible consequences of Burman or Malay nationalism, and thus tended to see British rule as a protective shield.

Nonetheless, the example of the nationalist movement in India had repercussions in Southeast Asia which extended beyond the overseas Indian communities. India offered a case of opposition to direct colonial rule, in contrast to China where 'imperialism' was more amorphous. Perhaps most significantly, Indian nationalist activity dated from an early period relative to the emergence of nationalist movements in most of Southeast Asia. The Congress Party had been founded in 1885, at a time when some parts of the Southeast Asian region, such as Annam and upper Burma, were just coming under European rule.

As in the case of Chinese nationalism, various factions competed for the loyalties, and the financial support, of the overseas communities. Though the Congress would ultimately become the main vehicle for achieving Indian independence, much early Indian political activity in Burma and in major urban centres was oriented towards more radical strands of the nationalist movement. A prominent example was the Ghadr (Mutiny) Party, based abroad, especially on the west coast of North America, which hoped to spark revolts against British rule in India and Burma. However, early militant radicalism was predominantly a north Indian phenomenon with limited appeal in Malaya, where most of the substantial Indian population derived from south India.

Radical nationalists were particularly active in times of apparent European vulnerability, for example during World War I, which seemed to offer promising opportunities to challenge British or French rule. Diplomats and agents of the Central Powers actively encouraged militant Indian nationalists, offering arms and financial support to Indian (and Vietnamese) anti-colonial movements. In Southeast Asia these German-sponsored attempts to incite insurrection in British and French colonies were directed particularly from Bangkok, where the Thai remained neutral until July 1917, and from Batavia, where the Dutch remained neutral throughout the European war. Southeast Asia became a major channel for Ghadr Party attempts to infiltrate propaganda and arms to India.

In Southeast Asia itself, the most dramatic event of this period was the February 1915 mutiny by part of an Indian regiment stationed in Singapore, resulting in a number of deaths in the uprising itself, and in the retaliatory executions which followed. The British authorities, fearful of possible repercussions in India and elsewhere, tried to play down any political motivations among the mutineers. The weight of evidence shows, however, that the regiment had been strongly affected by nationalist propaganda, by contacts with German prisoners of war (whom the mutineers were assigned to guard), and (the regiment was almost totally Muslim) by the entry of the Ottoman Empire in the European war on the side of the Central Powers.

The mutiny was quickly suppressed, with French, Japanese and Russian naval contingents coming to the assistance of the depleted British forces, but the uprising foreshadowed the situation during the Pacific War. Then, with the British again 'vulnerable', Congress dissidents and others formed the Indian National Army and fought alongside Japanese forces on the Burma front, against British and 'British Indian' troops.

More moderate strands of Indian nationalism were also influential in Southeast Asia, with growing support (as British compromises escalated) for the Congress and Gandhi's leadership; in particular, some important Burmese nationalist leaders had personal contacts and experience in the Indian nationalist movement from the 1910s to the 1930s. Such contacts also operated in the other direction, with prominent Indian leaders such as the nationalist poet Rabindranath Tagore making visits to Southeast Asia in the interwar period, and the Congress Party, on both practical political and humanitarian grounds, taking an active interest in the welfare and working conditions of emigrant Indian labourers.

The Indian example influenced some Southeast Asian nationalist movements, but for the most part Indian communities in Southeast Asia focused primarily on the evolving situation in India itself, and there was little importing of Gandhian methods of non-violent resistance. Indeed, Southeast Asian nationalism on the whole tended to become increasingly militant and revolutionary, except in cases where a colonial power such as the United States encouraged forms of collaboration which offered the prospect of a real transfer of power to indigenous groups.

THE LOYALIST OPTION

As anti-colonial and other reformist activity developed, various groups throughout the region began to perceive disadvantages to themselves inherent in independence, or in the leadership of particular opposition groups. Emerging from this tendency was what might be termed a loyalist option among people who supported or benefited from a colonial relationship.

In the Netherlands East Indies the loyalist option had a particular appeal for various groups: the Chinese, whose overtures to local nationalists met with indifference and mistrust; the Ambonese, who provided the Dutch military with much of its manpower in the archipelago; parts of the Eurasian community which inclined toward Dutch civilization and held aloof from Indonesian culture; and the aristocracy, many of whose members had participated in the Dutch administration and were accordingly a nationalist target. It was this loyalist element that the Dutch attempted to strengthen by promoting customary law (*adat*) as a basis for administration and law, and by promoting federalism after 1945.

Muslims in the southern Philippines also adopted a loyalist stance during the 1920s and 1930s as Filipinization of the administration placed Catholic Filipinos in positions of authority in the south. In British Malaya the Straits Chinese, some of whom described themselves as 'the King's Chinese', generally comprised a loyalist community. Dominant in the port cities of Singapore and Penang, this group felt threatened by the large and growing group of China-born Chinese, and potentially by nationalism in the Malay world which surrounded them. The British administration could count other potential allies among the Anglicized Indians and Malay aristocracy, and the Malay population as a whole tended to view the British as a source of support against the substantial Indian and Chinese communities in the peninsula. In Vietnam the Constitutionalist Party, the Catholic community and particularly that element of the Vietnamese population which had adopted French citizenship, formed a loyalist element. However, in contrast to the situation in Burma, where the response of the Shan and Karen to nationalist pressure from a numerically dominant group was to turn to the colonial power for protection, minority ethnic groups in Vietnam found a source of patronage in the Communist Party.

CONCLUSION

Southeast Asia before World War II produced a wide range of reformist activity, some of it directed against colonial régimes, some toward religious change, and some toward modernization and social development. The reformist strain that can be described as anti-colonial nationalism was based on a broad racial distinction between white colonizers and non-white colonial subjects. Beyond this stark division the substance of nationalism was problematic, for the people drawn together within the boundaries of colonial states were otherwise diverse in their cultures, religious practices, economic activities, social organization, and behaviour.

The period 1900 to 1940 produced three types of political movements in Southeast Asia: one based on particular social or cultural characteristics; a second based on the territories defined by the colonial powers; and a third on religious or ideological principles that transcended those boundaries. The first bore fruit in Siam, but elsewhere ethnic nationalist goals were rarely achieved. The third produced religious movements as well as socialist and communist parties. The most difficult to advance was the second, since there was little basis for unity beyond the shared experience of colonial rule, but territorially-based administrations offered a concrete political objective and became the basis of independent states after 1945.

Part of the significance of reformist organizations during this period lies in their structure, for voluntary organizations based on particular interest groups or promoting certain concepts were a departure from previous Southeast Asian practice. They provided a forum for the development of new lines of thinking, and produced the leadership that ultimately took control of the independent states that came into being after 1945. However, to some degree organizations revolved more around leaders than ideologies, and the personalities and ambitions of various individuals played a major part in determining the success or failure of the ideas they advocated and the groups they led.

The underlying racial basis of anti-colonial movements produced a heightened awareness of ethnic identities. After the war numerically predominant groups in Burma, Thailand, and Malaya would lay claim to nationalism as the vehicle for promoting their own cultural aspirations, while in the Philippines and Indonesia the governments made conscious efforts to avoid identifying national culture with any one group, as did the Communist Party in Vietnam. A paradoxical feature of both approaches was that political movements based on prototypical nationalist criteria— a shared language, culture, or set of religious beliefs and the wish to nurture and protect an identity based on these qualities—found little place within the region. They stood condemned by anti-colonial movements, and by the independent successor states after 1945, for posing a threat to 'national unity'.

In sum, modernist reform activity in Southeast Asia between the late 1800s and 1940 embraced issues that went beyond the struggle against colonial rule: more was involved than simply political independence. Changes arising from a variety of circumstances—including the Industrial Revolution, the development of a world market, responses of different elements within local societies to new opportunities, and colonial rule— had disturbed established social and political arrangements, and had set in motion a protracted debate among the peoples of the region. Colonial governments were the agents for some but by no means all of these changes, and what was at stake went beyond the question of whether outsiders or domestic élites were to hold power. The issue was to decide which of the contending visions of the future would prevail.

BIBLIOGRAPHIC ESSAY

Material on the Philippines is scattered amongst diverse sources. The study by Lewis E. Gleeck Jr, of the American period in Philippine history, *The American Half-Century (1898–1946)*, is part 5, vol. 1 of a proposed *General History of the Philippines* (Manila: Historical Conservation Society, 1984). John N. Schumacher, *The Propaganda Movement: 1880–1895 — The Creators of a Filipino Consciousness, the Makers of the Revolution*, Manila, 1973, shows how the foundations for modern nationalism were laid. The writings of Teodoro A. Agoncillo on the Philippine revolution (his 1956 *The Revolt of the Masses* and his 1960 work, *Malolos: The Crisis of the Republic*, both published in Quezon City by the University of the Philippines) describe the development of nationalism, and Cesar A. Majul, *The Political and Constitutional Ideas of the Philippine Revolution*, New York and Quezon City, 1967, sets down the philosophical and ideological underpinnings of events during this period. Reynaldo Ileto, *Pasyon and Revolution: Popular Move-ments in the Philippines, 1840–1910*, Quezon City, 1979, offers a different perspective on this period, and three essays published in the journal *Philippine Studies*, the first a review of Ileto's work, provide a contentious but extremely useful discussion of the revolution: 'Understanding Philip-pine Revolutionary Mentality' by Milagros C. Guerrero (29, 1981), Ileto's rejoinder entitled 'Critical Issues in "Understanding Philippine Revolu-tionary Mentality"' (30, 1982), and a magisterial overview, by John N. Schumacher, 'Recent Perspectives on the Revolution' (30, 1982). Maximo M. Kalaw, *The Development of Philippine Politics*, Manila, 1926, and Peter W. Stanley, *A Nation in the Making: The Philippines and the United States, 1899–*

1921, Cambridge, Mass., 1974, focus on the period up to the mid-1920s. Theodore Friend, *Between Two Empires: Philippine Ordeal and Development from the Great Depression through the Pacific War, 1929–1946*, New Haven, 1965, and his later *The Blue-Eyed Enemy: Japan against the West in Java and Luzon, 1942–1945*, Princeton, 1988, provide intriguing interpretative accounts of the 1920s and 1930s, a period also covered perceptively by Bernadita Reyes Churchill in *The Philippine Independence Missions to the United States, 1919–1934*, Manila: National Historical Institute, 1983. David R. Sturtevant, *Popular Uprisings in the Philippines, 1840–1940*, Ithaca and London,1976, deals with a variety of non-institutionalized reformist movements. Two volumes have been published specifically on the subject of Philippine nationalism: Usha Mahajani, *Philippine Nationalism: External Challenge and Filipino Response, 1565-1946*, St Lucia, 1971, and Teodoro A. Agoncillo, *Filipino Nationalism*, Quezon City, 1974; and Horacio de la Costa, *The Background of Nationalism and Other Essays* Manila, 1965, contains a thoughtful analysis of this topic. José Rizal's writings appear in numerous sources, including *Rizal: Political and Historical Writings (1840–1890)*, Manila: National Heroes Commission, 1963, reissued by the National Historical Institute as part of a comprehensive centennial edition of Rizal's works. Renato and Letizia R. Constantino's provocative accounts of Philippine history, *The Philippines: A Past Revisited*, Quezon City, 1975, and *The Philippines: The Continuing Past*, Manila: Foundation for Nationalist Studies, 1978, offer interesting if controversial interpretations. 'Quezon's Commonwealth: The Emergence of Philippine Authoritarianism', by Alfred W. McCoy, along with the other papers collected in Ruby R. Paredes, ed., *Philippine Colonial Democracy*, New Haven: Yale University Southeast Asia Studies, 1988, and Norman Owen's *Compadre Colonialism*, Ann Arbor: University of Michigan Center for South and Southeast Asian Studies, 1971, give useful details on the prewar era.

Accounts of the development of Indonesian political thinking are numerous. The classic Dutch account is J. Th. Petrus Blumberger's three-volume work, *De Communistische Beweging in Nederlandsch-Indië*, Haarlem, 1928; *De Nationalistische Beweging in Nederlandsch-Indië*, Haarlem, 1931; *De Indo-Europeesche Beweging in Nederlandsch-Indië* Haarlem, 1939. The classic account in English is *Nationalism and Revolution in Indonesia* by George McTurnan Kahin, Ithaca and London, 1952. *Politiek-Politioneele overzichten van Nederlandsch-Indië*, 1: *1927–1928*, II: *1929–1930*, III: *1931–1934*, compiled by Harry A. Poeze (The Hague, 1982; Dordrecht, 1983 and 1988) contains exhaustive detail on nationalist organizations. Other valuable overviews include Robert Van Niel, *The Emergence of the Modern Indonesian Elite*, The Hague, 1960, and Bernhard Dahm, *History of Indonesia in the Twentieth Century*, London, 1971. Van Niel's article 'From Netherlands East Indies to Republic of Indonesia, 1900–1945', in Harry Aveling, ed., *The Development of Indonesian Society*, St Lucia, 1979, provides a compact summary, as does John D. Legge, *Indonesia*, Englewood Cliffs, 1964. More specialized accounts include: Takashi Shiraishi, *An Age in Motion: Popular Radicalism in Java, 1912–1926*, Ithaca and London, 1990; Friend, *Blue-Eyed Enemy*; *Perhimpunan Indonesia and the Indonesian Nationalist Movement, 1923–1928*, Clayton: Centre of Southeast Asian Studies, Monash University,

1975, and *Road to Exile: The Indonesian Nationalist Movement, 1927–1934*, Singapore, 1979, both by John Ingleson; Akira Nagazumi, *The Dawn of Indonesian Nationalism: The Early Years of the Budi Utomo, 1908–1918*, Tokyo: Institute of Developing Economies, 1972; Harry J. Benda, *The Crescent and the Rising Sun*, The Hague and Bandung, 1958; Deliar Noer, *The Modernist Muslim Movement in Indonesia, 1900–1942*, Kuala Lumpur, 1973; Alfian, *Muhammadiyah: The Political Behavior of a Muslim Modernist Organization under Dutch Colonialism*, Yogyakarta, 1989; Mitsuo Nakamura, *The Crescent Arises Over the Banyan Tree*, Yogyakarta, 1983; Kenji Tsuchiya, *Democracy and Leadership: The Rise of the Taman Siswa Movement in Indonesia*, Honolulu, 1987; and Susan Abeyasekere, *One Hand Clapping: Indonesian Nationalists and the Dutch, 1939–1942*, Clayton: Centre of Southeast Asian Studies, Monash University, 1976. Harry J. Benda and Ruth T. McVey provide a useful introduction to events of the 1920s in *The Communist Uprisings of 1926–1927 in Indonesia: Key Documents*, Ithaca: Cornell University Southeast Asia Program, 1960, and McVey, *The Rise of Indonesian Communism*, Ithaca, 1965, is the definitive work on this subject. Extremely useful material is also found in biographies of Sukarno by J.D. Legge (*Sukarno. A Political Biography*, Sydney, London, Boston, 1972), Bernhard Dahm (*Sukarno and the Struggle for Indonesian Independence*, Ithaca, 1969), and C.L.M. Penders (*The Life and Times of Sukarno*, Kuala Lumpur, 1975). Sukarno's own views, as filtered through journalist Cindy Adams, are found in *Sukarno: An Autobiography, as Told to Cindy Adams*, Hong Kong, 1965, and an edited translation of Mohammad Hatta's memoirs has been published under the title of *Mohammad Hatta: Indonesian Patriot—Memoirs*, Singapore, 1981. *Portrait of a Patriot. Selected Writings by Mohammad Hatta*, The Hague and Paris, 1972, is also a valuable source and Mavis Rose has published *Indonesia Free: A Political Biography of Mohammad Hatta*, Ithaca: Cornell University Southeast Asia Program, 1987. Useful accounts of developments outside of Java include Taufik Abdullah, *Schools and Politics: The Kaum Muda Movement in West Sumatra (1927–1933)*, Ithaca: Cornell University Southeast Asia Program, 1971, and Anthony Reid, *The Blood of the People: Revolution and the End of Traditional Rule in Northern Sumatra*, Kuala Lumpur, 1979.

Events in Vietnam after 1945 drew attention to antecedents of the Vietnamese independence struggle, and the literature on pre-war Vietnamese reform efforts is now substantial. Among the major accounts are Joseph Buttinger, *Vietnam: A Dragon Embattled*, I, London, 1967; David G. Marr, *Vietnamese Anticolonialism, 1885–1925*, Berkeley, Los Angeles, London, 1971, and its sequel, *Vietnamese Tradition on Trial, 1920–1945*, Berkeley, Los Angeles, London, 1981; William J. Duiker, *The Rise of Nationalism in Vietnam. 1900–1941*, Ithaca and London, 1976; Daniel Hémery, *Révolutionnaires Vietnamiens et pouvoir colonial en Indochine*, Paris, 1975; and Alexander Woodside, *Community and Revolution in Modern Vietnam*, Boston, 1976, partly superseding Paul Isoart's still useful *Le phénomène national Vietnamien de l'indépendance unitaire à l'indépendance fractionnée*, Paris, 1959. Pierre-Richard Féray, *Le Viet-nam au xx siècle*, Paris, 1979, provides a general history of modern Vietnam, as do Nguyen Khac Vien, *Histoire du Vietnam*, Paris, 1974; Thomas Hodgkin, *Vietnam: The Revolutionary Path*, London,

1981; and Ken Post, *Revolution, Socialism and Nationalism in Viet Nam*, I, Aldershot, 1989, from a leftist perspective. Studies of the Communist Party include Pierre Rousset, *Le parti communist vietnamien*, Paris, 1973; and *Vietnamese Communism, 1925–1945*, Ithaca and London, 1982, by Huynh Kim Khanh. Ralph Smith, *Viet-Nam and the West*, Ithaca, 1971, and Paul Mus in an extended interpretative essay, *Viet-Nam: Sociologie d'une guerre*, Paris, 1952, examine the encounter between Vietnamese culture and the West. Helpful on specific topics are the essays in *Aspects of Vietnamese History*, Honolulu, 1973, edited by Walter F. Vella; Megan Cook, *The Constitutionalist Party in Cochinchina: The Years of Decline, 1930–1942*, Clayton: Centre of Southeast Asian Studies, Monash University, 1977; Hue-Tam Ho Tai, *Millenarianism and Peasant Politics in Vietnam*, Cambridge, Mass, 1983; and Jayne Susan Werner, *Peasant Politics and Religious Sectarianism: Peasant and Priest in the Cao Dai in Viet Nam*, New Haven: Yale University Southeast Asia Studies, 1981.

Materials on nationalist reform in Cambodia and Laos are sparse. For Cambodia, David P. Chandler, *A History of Cambodia*, Boulder, 1983, provides an accessible summary, and Alain Forest, *Le Cambodge et la colonisation française: historie d'une colonisation sans heurts*, Paris, 1980, gives thorough coverage to the period 1897–1920. For Laos, Geoffrey C. Gunn in *Political Struggles in Laos (1930–1954)*, Bangkok, 1988, covers the 1930s in some detail.

The most comprehensive recent account of political developments in Burma is Robert H. Taylor, *The State in Burma*, London, 1987, but John L. Christian's *Modern Burma*, Berkeley and Los Angeles, 1942, a thorough and well-documented account of pre-war political developments in Burma based primarily on official British sources, remains extremely useful. Four works examine nationalist activity during the 1920s and 1930s in considerable detail: U Maung Maung, *From Sangha to Laity: Nationalist Movements of Burma, 1920–1940*, Canberra: Australian National University, South Asia History Section, 1980; Surendra Prasad Singh, *Growth of Nationalism in Burma, 1900–1942*, Calcutta, 1980; Albert D. Moscotti, *British Policy and the Nationalist Movement in Burma, 1917–1937*, Honolulu, 1974; and Khin Yi, *The Dobama Movement in Burma (1930–1938)*, Ithaca: Cornell University Southeast Asia Program, 1988. Patricia Herbert, *The Hsaya San Rebellion (1930–1932) Reappraised*, Clayton: Centre of Southeast Asian Studies, Monash University, 1982, is stoutly revisionist.

The standard work on Malay nationalism is W.R. Roff, *The Origins of Malay Nationalism*, New Haven, 1967, but very useful discussions are also found in Radin Soenarno's 'Malay nationalism, 1896–1941', JSEAH, 1,1 (1960) and the articles collected in *Nasionalisme: Satu Tinjauan Sejarah*, edited by R. Suntharalingam and Abdul Rahman Haji Ismail, Petaling Jaya, 1985. Firdaus Haji Abdullah explores the relation between Islam and politics in his *Radical Malay Politics: Its Origins and Early Development*, Petaling Jaya, 1985, as does Clive S. Kessler in *Islam and Politics in a Malay State: Kelantan, 1838–1969*, Ithaca and London, 1978. The pseudonymous *Class and Communalism in Malaysia: Politics in a Dependent Capitalist State* by 'Hua Wu Yin', London, 1983, examines Malaysian history and pre-war political activity from a Marxist perspective.

With the 'reign mentality' still imposing a heavy hand on Thai historiography, a comprehensive study of pre-war Thai nationalism has yet to be written. The most substantial work specifically devoted to the subject is Walter F. Vella, *Chaiyo! King Vajiravudh and the Development of Thai Nationalism*, Honolulu, 1978, in which the richness of data contrasts with a lack of critical analysis. An earlier, more indigenous lineage for Thai nationalism is posited in Eiji Murashima's somewhat iconoclastic 'The Origin of Modern Official State Ideology in Thailand', JSEAS, 19,1 (1988). 'Official nationalism' in the Seventh Reign is discussed in Benjamin A. Batson, *The End of the Absolute Monarchy in Siam*, Singapore, 1984. Less élite strands of nationalism, culminating in the 1932 coup, have also received extensive treatment. In terms of events, perhaps the most detailed (if not always accurate) account is Thawatt Mokarapong, *History of the Thai Revolution: A Study in Political Behavior*, Bangkok, 1972; the intellectual underpinnings of the coup are well discussed in Pierre Fistié, *Sous-développement et utopie au Siam: Le programme de réforms présenté en 1933 par Pridi Phanomyong*, The Hague and Paris, 1969, and in the early sections of Yuangrat Wedel, *Modern Thai Radical Thought: The Siamization of Marxism and its Theoretical Problems*, Bangkok: Thai Khadi Research Institute, Thammasat University, 1982. General studies aside, the period between the coup and the Pacific War is poorly covered. However, useful contemporary works include M. Sivaran, *The New Siam in the Making*, Bangkok, 1936; Kenneth P. Landon, *Siam in Transition*, Chicago, 1939; Virginia Thompson, *Thailand: The New Siam*, New York: Institute of Pacific Relations, 1941; and the last historical chapters of the first edition of Phra Sarasas, *My Country Thailand*, Tokyo, 1942. An important, thoroughly revisionist critique of all English-language scholarship on Thai nationalism, and on modern Thai history in general, is Benedict Anderson, 'Studies of the Thai State: The State of Thai Studies' in E. Ayal, ed., *The Study of Thailand*, Athens, Ohio: Ohio University Center for International Studies, 1978. Various relevant documentary materials are provided in Chatthip Nartsupha et al., eds, *The Political Economy of Siam 1910–1932*, Bangkok: Social Science Association of Thailand, 1978; Benjamin A. Batson, ed., *Siam's Political Future: Documents from the End of the Absolute Monarchy*, Ithaca: Cornell University Southeast Asia Program, 1974; and the first sections of Thak Chaloemtiarana, ed., *Thai Politics: Extracts and Documents 1932–1957*, Bangkok: Social Science Association of Thailand, 1978. New directions in historical research, revealing the multifaceted perceptions of 'nation', are explored in Shigeharu Tanabe, 'Ideological Practice in Peasant Rebellions: Siam at the Turn of the Twentieth Century' and Chatthip Nartsupha, 'The Ideology of 'Holy Man' Revolts in North East Thailand', in Andrew Turton and Shigeharu Tanabe, eds, *History and Peasant Consciousness in South East Asia*, Osaka: National Museum of Ethnology, 1984.

Accounts of 'minority' groups in mainland Southeast Asia include Josef Silverstein, *Burmese Politics: The Dilemma of National Unity*, New Brunswick, 1980; Chao Tzang Yawnghwe, *The Shan of Burma: Memoirs of a Shan Exile*, Singapore: ISEAS, 1987; Sao Saimong Mangrai, *The Shan States and the British Annexation*, Ithaca: Cornell University Southeast Asia Program, 1965; Moshe Yegar, *The Muslims of Burma: A Study of a Minority Group*,

Wiesbaden, 1972; and Robert H. Taylor, 'British Policy and the Shan States, 1886–1942', in Prakai Nontawasee, ed., *Changes in Northern Thailand and the Shan States, 1886–1940*, Singapore: Southeast Asia Studies Programme, ISEAS, 1988. Pattani is dealt with by Surin Pitsuwan, *Islam and Malay Nationalism: A Case Study of the Malay-Muslims of Southern Thailand*, Bangkok: Thai Khadi Research Institute, Thammasat University, 1985, and the careful but for the twentieth century far less complete notes accompanying the edition of the *Hikayat Patani* prepared by A. Teeuw and D.K. Wyatt, The Hague, 1970. Gerald Cannon Hickey, *Sons of the Mountains: Ethnohistory of the Vietnamese Central Highlands to 1954*, New Haven, 1982, examines the modern history of Vietnam from a minority perspective. The position of the Muslims in Pattani and in the southern Philippines is compared in W. K. Che Man, *Muslim Separatism: The Moros of Southern Philippines and the Malays of Southern Thailand*, Singapore, 1990, while Peter G. Gowing provides accounts of the Moros in his *Mandate in Moroland: The American Government of Muslim Filipinos, 1899–1920*, Quezon City, 1983, and *Muslim Filipinos—Heritage and Horizon*, Quezon City, 1975. Further information is found in *The Muslim Filipinos: Their History, Society and Contemporary Problems*, edited by Peter G. Gowing and Robert D. McAmis, Manila, 1974.

The Indian community in Southeast Asia is described by Nalini Ranjan Chakravarti, *The Indian Minority in Burma*, London, 1971; Usha Mahajani, *The Role of Indian Minorities in Burma and Malaya*, Bombay, 1960; Kernial Singh Sandhu, *Indians in Malaya*, Cambridge, UK, 1969; and Sinnappah Arasaratnam, *Indians in Malaysia and Singapore*, Bombay and Kuala Lumpur, 1970.

The literature on the overseas Chinese in Southeast Asia is enormous. Victor Purcell, *The Chinese in Southeast Asia*, London, 1951, remains useful but can hardly be described as a definitive work. The effects of the 1911 revolution are considered in Yen Ching Hwang, *The Overseas Chinese and the 1911 Revolution*, Kuala Lumpur, 1976, and in a volume edited by Lee Lai To entitled *The 1911 Revolution—the Chinese in British and Dutch Southeast Asia*, Singapore, 1987. The Chinese community in Indonesia has been studied by Leo Suryadinata in a number of works, including *The Chinese Minority in Indonesia*, Singapore, 1978, *Peranakan Chinese Politics in Java*, Singapore, rev. edn, 1981, and his edited collection of documents entitled *Political Thinking of the Indonesian Chinese, 1900–1977*, Singapore, 1979. For the Philippines, Edgar Wickberg, *The Chinese in Philippine Life, 1850–1898*, New Haven and London, 1965, provides essential background information, and Antonio S. Tan, *The Chinese in the Philippines, 1898–1935*, Quezon City, 1972, brings the account forward to the beginning of the Philippine Commonwealth. For Cambodia, W.E. Willmott's two books, *The Chinese in Cambodia*, Vancouver, 1967, and *The Political Structure of the Chinese Community in Cambodia*, London, 1970, provide a thorough account, as does G. William Skinner's *Chinese Society in Thailand: An Analytical History*, Ithaca, 1957. Skinner's 'Change and persistence in Chinese culture overseas: A comparison of Thailand and Java', *Journal of the South Seas Society* 16, 1–2 (1960) is a well-known attempt to explain variable rates of assimilation among Chinese communities in Southeast Asia. Material concerning

Malaysia and Singapore for the period 1900–40 is surprisingly sparse, given the importance of the Chinese community in British Malaya, and Victor Purcell, *The Chinese in Malaya*, London, 1948, is seriously dated. Yoji Akashi, 'The Nanyang Chinese Anti-Japanese and Boycott Movement, 1908–1928—A Study of Nanyang Chinese Nationalism', *Journal of the South Seas Society* 23 (1968) deals with one aspect of Chinese nationalism. C.F. Yong, *Tan Kah-kee: The Making of an Overseas Chinese Legend*, Singapore, 1987, is a rare biographical account of a major figure, and Chui Kwei-chang's article 'Political Attitudes and Organizations c. 1900–1941' in Ernest Chew and Edwin Lee, eds, *A History of Singapore*, Singapore, 1991, provides a substantial account of political developments among the Chinese in pre-war Singapore. C.F. Yong has combined with R.B. McKenna in *The Kuomintang in British Malaya*, Singapore, 1990.

General works cited in this chapter include Benedict Anderson, *Imagined Communities: Reflections on the Origin and Spread of Nationalism*, London, 1983, Anthony D. Smith, ed., *Nationalist Movements*, London, 1976, and *Theories of Nationalism*, London, 1971, by the same author.

INDEX

abaca, 134, 147, 169–70, 180–1
Abdul Kadir Kamaroodin, 304
Abdul Karim, 220
Acapulco, 132
Aceh:
  critical historical moment, 65
  Dutch war, 8, 17–18, 50–2, 56, 72, 77,
    100–1, 195, 223–5, 233
  education, 205
  entrepôt trade, 53, 98
  Islam, 56, 100, 205, 224–5, 233, 237–8
  modernist political reforms, 271
  pepper trade, 99–100
  piracy, 54, 100
  protests and rebellions, 205, 224–5, 233,
    237–9
  Raffles and, 12, 14, 56
  social classes, 100
Achmad Chatib, 238
aeroplanes, 240
Afghanistan, 33
Africa, 176
Aglipay, Gregorio, 260
agriculture, 131, 133, 169, 174–5, 181, 183
  see also specific countries and crops
Aguinaldo, Emilio, 101, 256–7
Ahmad, Bendahara of Pahang, 66
Ahmad, Sultan of Pahang, 227
Ai Kan, 234
Alak people, 211
Alaungpaya dynasty, 30–1, 36
alcohol, 148, 206
All-India Muslim League, 303
alphabets, *see* Roman alphabet
Ahmad Daris, 205
Ambonese people, 88, 271, 312
amenorrhea, 159
Amherst, ——, 32, 43
Anawrahta, 197
Anderson, Benedict, 88, 245
Anderson, John, 26, 28–9
Andreino, ——, 35
Ang Chan, 217
Angkor, 47
Anglo-China War, 39
Anglo-Dutch treaty (1784) 10, (1824),
  12–19, 22, 25–26, 53, 55–57, 59,
  (1871), 17–18, 56
Anglo-Indians, *see* Eurasians
Anglo-Japanese Alliance, 249, 273
animals:
  draught, 129, 140
  wild, 140, 236

animism, *see* beliefs and traditions
Annam, *see* Vietnam
Antasari, 225
anti-colonial movements, *see* nationalism
anti-fascism, *see* fascism
Apolinario de la Cruz, 208–9, 228–9
Arakan, 31–2, 64, 75, 136
Arakanese, 61, 280
arson, 164
Asahan, 100
asceticism, 203, 211
Assam, 32
Association for the Restoration of
  Vietnam, 103
Association of Native Civil Servants, 270
Association of Political Organizations of
  the Indonesian People, *see* PPPKI
Auckland, Lord, 33
Aung San:
  assassinated, 284
  collaboration with Japanese, 277–8
  military training in Japan, 286
  prewar student activities, 284
  Thirty Comrades, 286
Australia, 176
Austro-Hungarian Empire, 249
automobiles, 154, 235
Ava, 128
Axis powers, 277
Ayutthaya, 31, 61, 63, 106, 305

Ba Maw, 285
Ba Phnom, 201–2
babaylan, 229–30
Bagyidaw, 33, 197, 213
Bahaman, 227
Balambangan, 23, 58
Balanini people, 53
Bali, 16, 77, 100
Balikpapan, 158
banditry, 164, 187, 199–200, 205, 207
Bandung, 165–6
Bandung Study Club, 268
Bangka, 109
Bangkok:
  administrative centre, 128, 153, 164,
    165
  cholera epidemic, 176
  ethnic minorities, 85, 106, 120, 168
  growth and size, 120, 167
  population, 165
  social classes, 128
Banjermasin royal house, 225